I$16.80 G1 2

# TAKE TWO

# TAKE TWO

EDITED BY

**SETH FELDMAN**

A Lucy-Caroll Book
in conjunction with
the Festival of Festivals

IRWIN PUBLISHING
Toronto Canada

Selection and introductory materials copyright © 1984 World Film Festival of Toronto Inc. Copyright for the individual articles retained by the respective writers.

We would like to express our sincere gratitude to the Department of Communications, Special Programme of Cultural Initiatives, and the Canada Council for their generous support in assisting the publication of this book.

**Canadian Cataloguing in Publication Data**

Take Two
Index: p. 305
ISBN 0-7725-1506-9

1. Moving-pictures — Canada — History — Addresses, essays, lectures. 2. Moving-pictures — Canada — Addresses, essays, lectures. I. Feldman, Seth, 1948–

PN1993.5.C2T3 1984 791.43'0971 C84-099029-4

No part of this publication may be reproduced or transmitted in any form or by any means, electronic or mechanical, including photocopy, recording or any information storage and retrieval system now known or to be invented, without permission in writing from the publisher, except by a reviewer who wishes to quote brief passages in connection with a review written for inclusion in a magazine, newspaper or broadcast.

Project editor: Piers Handling
Editor: Carolyn Dodds
Designer: Keith Abraham

Created and produced by:
Lucy-Caroll Limited
228 Gerrard Street East
Toronto, Ontario
M5A 2E8

Printed in Canada by Gagne Printing Ltd.
Typeset by Q Composition Inc.

1 2 3 4 5 6 7 8 91 90 89 88 87 86 85 84

Published by Irwin Publishing Inc.
180 West Beaver Creek Road
Richmond Hill, Ontario
L4B 1B4

# TABLE OF CONTENTS

# LIST OF CONTRIBUTORS

**Kay Armatage** teaches Cinema and Women's Studies at the University of Toronto and programs for the Toronto Festival of Festivals. She has written for many Canadian publications, and her recent films include *Speak Body* (1979), *Striptease* (1980), and *Storytelling* (1983).

**David Clandfield** is a Professor of French at the University of Toronto. He has contributed articles to *Ciné-Tracts* and has a special interest in the work of Pierre Perrault.

**Marshall Delaney** is the pseudonym of Robert Fulford, who edits *Saturday Night* magazine, writes a weekly column for the *Toronto Star*, and co-hosts a TVOntario program, *Realities*. He is the author of the collection *Marshall Delaney at the Movies: The Contemporary World As Seen on Film*.

**R. Bruce Elder** is an experimental filmmaker, critic and teacher whose works have been widely screened throughout Canada, the United States, and Europe; his best known films include *The Art of Worldly Wisdom* (1979), *1857 (Fool's Gold)* (1981) and *Illuminated Texts* (1983). He is the author of numerous articles on the Canadian cinema and is a Professor of Film at Ryerson Polytechnical Institute.

**Seth Feldman** is an Associate Professor of Film Studies at York University. A founder and past president of the Film Studies Association of Canada, he co-edited with Joyce Nelson *The Canadian Film Reader*, and with Eugene Walz an issue on Canadian film for the *Journal of Canadian Studies*; he also produced a program on documentary film for CBC Radio's *Ideas*.

**Sandra Gathercole** was chairperson of the Council of Canadian Filmmakers for several years. Currently she is a consultant in film and broadcasting.

**Piers Handling** is presently a freelance critic. He has taught film at Carleton University and Queen's University, and established the publications program at the Canadian Film Institute before being appointed associate director. He is the author of *The Films of Don Shebib*, and has edited, among others, *Self Portrait: Essays on the Canadian and Quebec Cinemas*, and *The Shape of Rage: The Films of David Cronenberg*.

**Peter Harcourt** studied at the University of Toronto and Cambridge University. After working for the British Film Institute, he returned to Canada in 1967 to establish a Film Studies Program at Queen's University. The author of *Six European Directors, Movies and Mythologies* and *Jean Pierre Lefebvre*, he has taught at York University and is currently a Professor of Film Studies at Carleton University.

Entertainment columnist for *Toronto Life* and theatre critic for *Saturday Night*, **Martin Knelman** has also been the movie critic for the *Toronto Star* and the *Globe and Mail*. The author of *This is Where We Came In* and *A Stratford Tempest*, he has written for major magazines in both Canada and the United States.

**James Leach** obtained his Ph.D. from Birmingham University, and now teaches film and dramatic literature at Brock University in St. Catharines, Ontario. He is the author of *A Possible Cinema: The Films of Alain Tanner*.

**Brenda Longfellow** has been a community video producer in Ottawa, and a writer, assistant editor, researcher and women's film festival organizer in Montreal. She has taught film at McGill University, Concordia University and Carleton University, and is currently producing a film on divorced mothers.

**Lianne McLarty** teaches film at Queen's University. She studied at Brock University and Carleton University and is presently completing a thesis on the films of R. Bruce Elder.

**Peter Morris** teaches film at Queen's University and has also taught at Concordia University and the University of Ottawa. He founded the Canadian Film Archives at the Canadian Film Institute in 1964 and was its curator until 1975. He is the author of *Embattled Shadows: A History of Canadian Cinema 1895-1939* and has edited and translated Georges Sadoul's *Dictionary of Films* and *Dictionary of Film Makers*.

**Al Razutis** is an experimental filmmaker, holographer, video artist and contributor to avant-garde theory and criticism. He is an Associate Professor of Film at Simon Fraser University and has also taught at Evergreen State College, Washington; Emily Carr College of Art and Design; and the Banff School of Fine Arts. He has just completed the *Amerika* project, a series of eighteen films, and *Visual Essays*, a six-film project.

**Jay Scott** is the film critic for the Toronto *Globe and Mail*. Twice winner of the National Newspaper Award for Criticism, he is the author of *Changing Woman: The Life and Art of Helen Hardin*.

# PREFACE

Nothing is as foreign to Canadians as Canadian culture. The seemingly natural places to look for first class art, entertainment and critical thought are always somewhere else. What we make here is a kind of highly subsidized folklore, work that strains to be taken at something better than face value. As a result, art in Canada is often seen as an imposition and an obligation. At best, local productions in any medium are seen as small-scale jobs well done. But the accent is on "job." Canadians seem to have trouble empathizing with the reverie of their own artists or seeing that reverie as an essential human quality.

Film, at least as it is popularly perceived, is just that essential reverie. Canada has with some success done the job of cinema; it is, after all, an admirable organizational feat just to make the thing possible. But, like the other arts, film often takes on the character of an imposed task. It is as if a giant bureaucratic Mickey Rooney were talking a somewhat reluctant Judy Garland into getting the kids together for yet one more show in the barn out back. His arguments are getting somewhat strained. The audiences seem barely larger than the cast. Worse still, the original purpose, the job behind the job, seems to have been an illusion. Cinema is not a nation-building tool—not in this barn. Its small audiences are even more divided by Canada's linguistic fissure than is the nation as a whole. Anglophone and francophone cinemas are strangers to one another. Regional cinemas are as alienated as their regions. It is, by and large, easier to see the work of important non-Canadian directors than it is to become familiar with films generated on the far side of a provincial border.

The practical response to all this is to recognize that the media are, by definition, American. We can pack up and go home. Alternatively, we can recognize that we are home. We can take stock of what has been done. We can try to redeem the promises we have made to ourselves.

The history of Canadian cinema is caught between these two options. As such, it is a history of beginnings. Promising silent features in the twenties were followed by a decade of "quota quickies." Almost totally without support, the thirties generation of Canadian filmmakers were forced to work as primitives amid the medium's international abundance. With the founding of the National Film Board in 1939, Canada moved to the centre of world documentary production. A decade later, the federal government agreed to Hollywood's demands for the Canadian Cooperation Project, a deal that quashed the possibility of a feature film industry in exchange for a token recognition of Canada's existence in their real movies. Canadians, C.D. Howe could argue, were bartering an art form they didn't have for the good will of that huge market to the south. For Canadian filmmakers, the Canadian Cooperation Project transformed the National Film Board and, later, the CBC, from jumping-off points to safe—though confining—oases. Something had been blunted. For two decades that confinement produced remarkable individual efforts. Canadians could develop their cinematic skills up to the point where they realized they would have to go elsewhere.

Two decades after the Canadian Cooperation Project, the situation once again reversed itself. The heady atmosphere of Centennial nationalism brought new support for a feature film industry in the form of the Canadian Film Development Corporation. But even more important than the CFDC, or any other government policy, was the sense that a cinema culture was growing to the point where it would be here to stay. Independent filmmakers became more than a rarity. Their experimental works and documentaries began attracting attention, and were even exported. More good minds began writing about Canadian film. New journals and festivals appeared. Universities began teaching filmmaking and film criticism.

Yet one disgruntled academic vice-president declared that "The next thing you know, they'll be teaching salmon fishing." His suspicions and (very Canadian) conservatism are useful reminders that the decision to have a national cinema is far from unanimous. The mini-booms and major busts given us by federal tax policy and the CFDC (now Telefilm Canada) have yielded many of the memorable titles discussed in this volume. Federal film policy has also produced no small degree of embarrassment to those who demand that film be something more than a cultural industries make-work project. Independent documentarians and experimental filmmakers have built and sustained a network of small businesses and co-ops. Collectively, though, independents express the frustration of people who are kept from the assurance of recognition and a future. They told the Applebaum/Hébert committee that the old institutions have been transformed from oases to cocoons that refuse to open. Meanwhile, the journals, festivals and university programs repeat the same zero-based struggles for existence.

Still, the reveries emerge. Part of the achievement of Canadian cinema is that it can produce strong work despite the uncertainties that define it. More optimistically, the cinema as a whole can grow. The adolescent nature of many of the early CFDC features has been replaced by a new maturity and vision. The independents are tougher, deeper, more professional. The same may be said of the journals, the film festivals and the various support organizations.

*Take Two* has been compiled as evidence of a cinema culture that has learned from its struggles and that may, finally, free itself from the shuttle between centre stage and oblivion. Part of what we wish to do here is to point out the individual achievements in all areas of cinema practice. We hope to make the case for the enormous potential of Canadian talent—even if circumstances have in many cases cut short that potential. We wish to look back at the history of beginnings. But we also want to give some sense of the depth that the best of our filmmakers and film critics have been able to achieve. When I co-edited the *Canadian Film Reader*, a companion to this anthology, in 1977, it was difficult to find lengthy, detailed studies of Canadian work. That has changed. This volume is meant to assert the possibility of studying Canadian film with an intensity and seriousness usually reserved for foreign cinemas. The issues of contemporary cinema studies—the nature of representation, sexual politics, language—are our issues too.

Ideally, we would like to see *Take Two* become a guide to future work. The volume is meant to provide a guide to the films of some of our major directors. We recognize and regret the omissions. A further problem is that little has been written about some of our major filmmakers; much work remains to be done. It should also be mentioned that this is an English view of our cinema. At some point the thoughts of our Quebec colleagues will have to be translated, but that task lies outside the parameters of this book. At the same time, we make no apologies for giving space to the most invisible films of our invisible cinema, the work of our universally acclaimed Canadian avant-garde.

Credit for this presentation of Canadian cinema and the work needed to put it between covers goes well beyond the name on the title page. Piers Handling is, at least, co-conspirator, and Peter Harcourt and R. Bruce Elder were always considerate with their advice. Geoff Pevere relieved us of gaps and mistakes. The input of Carolyn Dodds, our copy editor, was invaluable. Karen Cowitz was extremely patient in retyping manuscripts. We would especially like to thank the many Canadian film writers, editors and filmmakers who have served as advisers. Sincere appreciation must also go to those magazines, journals and publications where many of these articles appeared for the first time.

Seth Feldman
June 1984

# I

# *The Big Picture*

# *Artists in the Shadows: Some Notable Canadian Movies*

## BY MARSHALL DELANEY

*Feature filmmaking, big money American feature filmmaking, survives on the planned obsolescence of its endless stream of productions. America's audiences are encouraged to see the history of movies as a set of waves—a gangster film wave, a science fiction wave, a dance film wave—each replacing its predecessor with newer and more exciting stars, bigger and better production values. What there is of the past is orchestrated as nostalgia and aimed at celebrating the industry as a whole. Whether old or new, American films point to the assurance of an unbroken and unbreakable heritage, a vast quantity of work from which endless pleasures may be distilled.*

*Canadian cinema can never be viewed with that assurance of plenty. As Marshall Delaney (Robert Fulford) points out, its pleasures require more careful extraction, more deliberate documentation. Our smaller scale of production leaves us connecting the dots of achievement, hoping that there will be enough dots to begin making a picture of ourselves. The films Delaney has foregrounded in* Saturday Night *have provided an excellent beginning to that process. The viewer who has sought out (often with some difficulty) films like* Les ordres, Outrageous!, J.A. Martin photographe, Les bons débarras, Ticket to Heaven, Heartaches *and* The Grey Fox *is rewarded with the sense of an emerging national culture—a sense of self. That viewer has also actively pursued those moments of excellence that this nation's film industry can afford to provide. It is our hope in the remainder of the volume to provide more dots worth connecting, to aid in that pursuit.*

As long as it has existed, the Canadian feature film industry has been seen as a problem, an issue to be worried over rather than an accomplishment to be celebrated. In the world movie business it exists as at best a marginal element; in the consciousness of Canadian moviegoers it lives a kind of shadowy half-life, neither quite present nor altogether absent. From time to time it seems to be moving promisingly toward a more vigorous life—a government policy makes more production possible, a remarkable director emerges, a single film produces a powerful impression. But each time, the industry moves back toward oblivion. The government policy fails, the director finds he has no work, the single film is not followed by another.

In a sense the history of our film industry is a history of broken promises. But somehow, in the midst of this more or less permanent depression, the most interesting of the Canadian film artists manage occasionally to make valuable movies. Some of them are never adequately distributed (most people I know have never seen *J.A. Martin photographe*, and many have never heard of it), but in a healthier culture these films would lodge themselves in the national consciousness and become part of the public discourse. That they remain largely in the shadows—and that there are relatively so few of them—is the result not only of inadequate specific policies but of something larger—an endemic failure of nerve, a crippled self-awareness, a complacent acceptance of permanent colonial status.

The pieces that follow—all of them originally appeared in *Saturday Night*—catch the Canadian film industry on the run. Each of them deals mainly with a specific film, but most of them touch on the underlying issues that have shaped our movie industry since the sixties and will continue to shape it in the foreseeable future.

## CANADA'S TRAUMA AND MICHEL BRAULT

The marvellous thing about Michel Brault's film *Les ordres* is that it goes far beyond the War Measures Act, Quebec, Canada, and 1970: it reaches a kind of universal dimension by forcibly readjusting the audience's views not only of the Montreal political prisoners it depicts but of *all* prisoners in *all* jails. We read every week in the paper that someone was picked up by the police, kept in jail for a few days, then released. We assume that this was a trifling incident, a mistake of no significant proportions. But of course we—most of us—have no idea what it is to be in jail for even an hour, much less days. Brault tells us.

He shows us five characters: a textile worker and his wife, a social worker, a young man who is unemployed, and a radical doctor. Each has a fictional name, but each is based on one or more of the 450 innocent people who were picked up by the police after the War Measures Act was proclaimed. Their stories are composites, but the details are all drawn from Brault's sixty hours of tape-recorded interviews with fifty of the real-life victims.

For the time the film runs, the audience lives inside the experience of these people. Brault's direction is so involving, and his use of the actors so skilful, that our identification is complete. We watch them wakened in the night, we hear the screams of their children as the police pound on the doors, we are stuffed into the back seats of police cars, pushed, prodded, insulted, and humiliated. We identify with their degradation as they are stripped and examined, as their beards are cut off and their clothes taken away, as officious guards herd them like cattle.

Moreover, we grasp the extreme intellectual and spiritual deprivation a prisoner may suffer. A part of everyone's humanity is his connection with other humans and if you can control the information a prisoner receives you can reduce him to a sub-human level. These people are cut off from two vital elements of humanity: their family and friends on the one hand and the world of public events on the other. They don't know what's happened to their children or wives or husbands. No one can visit or phone them, and they can't phone out. The doctor's wife is about to give birth, so as the days in jail drag on he doesn't know whether he's become a father or not or whether she's in desperate trouble. Another man's father is dying and he knows nothing of it. Equally, the prisoners are shut off from the news: they don't know, for instance, that on the second day of their internment Pierre Laporte has been found dead; they have no idea of the hysteria now gripping the whole country, or of the chilling effects of the War Measures Act proclamation. They have thus ceased to exist as fathers, husbands, and citizens. The state has imposed on them a kind of temporary death.

The doctor, at one point, looks through the bars of his cell at another prisoner washing the floor. That man has a little more freedom than he does and has something to do, so the doctor envies him. "Your whole life," he says voice-over, "is turned upside down. All of a sudden it's a privilege to wash the floors. And you *want* that privilege." Later he looks back and says, "I think we'll all carry this scar the rest of our lives." The young unemployed man puts it even more clearly: "I felt like a part of me had been destroyed."

In his treatment of the policemen and guards, Brault provides the film with a kind of subtext. One of his themes is man's will to express his own grievances and resentments by humiliating, degrading, and ultimately destroying other men. The policemen and guards, his film suggests, are not doing all this just because (as one says) "We've got orders and we have to follow them." On the contrary, they are *glad* to do it; otherwise they couldn't perform with such passion and ingenuity. *Les ordres* makes in a fresh way the point that every society contains willing servants of totalitarianism: when the Communists or the fascists take over there is never a shortage of guards because the things guards do are the things that come naturally to many men. The War Measures Act didn't create this negative force; it released it.

This is perhaps the most profound of the film's several messages. We need to have recalled to us that dictators and hoodlums are waiting among us, eager to take over. The only barrier that stands between us and them is the carefully and sensitively applied rule of law. The War Measures Act tore this barrier away. Most Canadians don't comprehend that yet, and perhaps *Les ordres* can help move us some slight distance toward understanding.

Michel Brault, who is now forty-six, has been one of the major figures of Quebec cinema since its beginnings in the fifties. He is almost certainly the finest cinematographer Canada has produced, and in France (where he has worked with the anthropologist-filmmaker Jean Rouch) he has been classed among the world's best. He operated the camera for *Mon oncle Antoine* and *Kamouraska*, and those films demonstrate both his high craftsmanship and his versatility. In 1963 he was co-director with Pierre Perrault of *Pour la suite du monde*, the memorable feature-length documentary about some rural Québécois who revive their island's ancient skill of catching whales in the St. Lawrence. In 1967 he directed *Entre la mer et l'eau douce*, a beautiful though largely overlooked film that starred Geneviève Bujold and Claude Gauthier.

Brault uses Gauthier again in *Les ordres*, this time as the unemployed young man whose jaunty dignity is stripped away by the guards. Gauthier gives a marvellously subtle performance, understating perfectly the slow destruction of the character. Jean Lapointe is the textile worker through whose eyes we see a large part of the film: he, too, handles highly dramatic material in a calm, clear, restrained manner. As his wife, Hélène Loiselle seems to embody all the miseries of women who are placed on the receiving end of life's indignities. Toward the close of the film, when a petty official gives her back her freedom—freedom that should never have been taken away—she looks at him with pitiful gratitude. It's a moment to shame anyone who ever held power over another human being.

Brault's use of the material—he wrote the script and shared the camerawork as well as directing—is almost always on a high level. (Perhaps the one exception is his rather arbitrary use of colour film for some scenes, black and white for others.) Many of the scenes are so tactful and have such a feeling of artistic wholeness that they could be the work of, say, François Truffaut. *Les ordres* affirms Brault's permanent importance as a director and provides us with a major landmark in the history of Canadian cinema.

At the same time, it leaves questions unanswered. Part of its power, in fact, is the ability to make us want to know a great deal more about this crucial event in our history. Just as Brault omits all facts about public events of the moment (because his characters can't know them), so he ignores the specific guilt of the public officials involved. He never suggests why these 450 people were picked up rather than some other 450; who made the list? Nor does he inquire deeply into the background of his characters. He presumes their legal innocence in the FLQ activities, but he never touches on the more sensitive question of moral complicity. When we first meet these people they are free and both James Cross and Pierre Laporte have been kidnapped. What do they think of those events? Are they delighted or appalled? Brault never hints at an answer, and for good reason: to know that might complicate, perhaps unnecessarily, our emotional involvement with their ordeal.

*Les ordres* is the first major work of art inspired by the trauma of October, 1970, but I hope it won't be the last. We still need to know a great deal more about what happened to Canada and its collective life in that period. The sad fact is that we forget much too easily. *Les ordres* brought this home to me with special vividness when the Lapointe character, in a rage, says to his guards: "Someday somebody is going to pay for all this." Wrong. Quite wrong. Nobody ever paid. They all got away with it.

*Saturday Night*, June 1975

## THE DRAG QUEEN AND THE SCHIZO

The last great division in human life is gender: the widest and most fearsome social chasm of all is the terrifying and unbridgeable space between male and female. The fascination of the female impersonator lies in his eccentric ability to play with that fact. He dances nimbly up to the line separating the sexes, gingerly leaps across, then quickly jumps back to safety. In the process he shapes a richly ambiguous comedy out of the very subjects—sexuality and gender—that make all of us most nervous and apprehensive.

In the performance of a really good female impersonator there's something that's more challenging than even the most radical political statement: it reaches far deeper than our reasoned opinions and attacks us at the point where the seat of our anguish is most likely to be found. But the female impersonator does something else as well: usually he impersonates the great female show business stars, like Streisand or Dietrich, and in doing so he pricks cheerfully at those overblown graven images of our time, mocking the very concept of stardom that gives life to his art. In the ambivalence of his affection he expresses our own uneasy and resentful feelings about those we so enthusiastically elevate above us.

All this is true of Craig Russell, who plays an up-and-coming female impersonator in *Outrageous!*, the Canadian film written and directed by Richard Benner. Russell is a chubby, engaging comedian (or, when the script calls for it, comedienne) who reads his lines with great and communicable pleasure and delivers marvellously funny/grotesque versions of Channing, Garland, Pearl Bailey, Bette Midler, Joan Crawford, and a few more. Russell in his "real" life is actually a female impersonator, so perhaps it's not entirely surprising that he does this side of the film so well. But he's equally effective in his off-stage acting, playing nicely against the other performers. For contrast, Benner also gives us a few versions of female impersonation when it doesn't work so well, or when it works in outlandish ways. There's one unhappy young man who's decided to go to a drag ball as Karen Black in *Airport '75*—"Ah can't fly this plane alone!"—and *he's* funny just because he's so totally convincing. And there's another who wears a nun's habit while miming to a record of *Ave Maria* on roller skates. That's when the film actually lives up to its title and becomes outrageously funny as well as just hilarious.

What makes *Outrageous!* work, though, is that the lines are so often good, so irreverently and precisely representative of the gay world—the world of leather bars, drag queens, and hustlers—that the film in its best moments describes. When the phone rings at one point Craig Russell says: "If that's Dino De Laurentiis, tell him I'm not speaking to him and *he* knows *why*." That line, like many others in the film, speaks out of the defiantly self-satirizing comic sense that is an integral part of homosexual culture at almost every level.

Craig Russell's character, Robin, is a self-hating and mildly successful hairdresser who is tired of both himself and his boring suburban clients. He expresses himself with a kind of bitchy and defensive self-righteousness when he says of his clients: "They treat life like a can of Coke. They're afraid to drink it because then it will be gone. Life isn't a can of Coke." Luckily, he doesn't follow that up by telling us what life *is*, but instead begins to look for escape and glory in show business. We follow him through a few tryouts in Toronto to something vaguely resembling stardom in New York. At the end he's triumphant, both master and mistress of his queer art form.

At the same time we follow the life of his dear friend Liza, a schizophrenic young woman who is at almost any given moment on the edge of despair and self-destruction. At the beginning of the film—which is based on a story from Margaret Gibson's book, *The Butterfly Ward*, and therefore indirectly based on Gibson's own long-term psychic anguish—Liza has just escaped from Morningside, a mental hospital where the doctors were expecting to keep her forever. Before the end she has experienced a stillbirth, many hysterical incidents, and a few fleeting occasions of pleasure.

Benner can't altogether avoid sentimentality in the handling of the relationship between Robin and Liza. Each is perversely proud of the outcast status that society has forced on them, and in the course of expressing their pride the film verges on the corny. Robin tells Liza: "You'll never be normal, but you're special—and you can have a hell of a good time."

That's nonsense, of course. All that's special about her is that she's crazy—she sees strange creatures from another planet, sometimes speaks a language she made up, and believes that something called the Bonecrusher is leaning on her from time to time. (Benner makes her moments of paranoid anguish especially effective by focusing on the empty spaces of room or hall where she believes she sees *it* coming after her.) These creatures terrify her to the screaming point and make her life miserable; the specialness which Robin celebrates is precisely what stands in the way of her ability to have a hell of a good, or even a bearable, time. The script is clearly influenced (as Gibson's fiction is) by the tenuous theories of R.D. Laing, who sometimes sees in schizophrenia not only an understandable reaction to pressure from the world but also a kind of accidental wisdom, a visionary power. Liza, so far as we can see, is long on craziness but short on wisdom, and her visions are never less than excruciating. (She's also, incidentally, weak on metaphors—her best one, and she's clearly striving to be "literary," is something to the effect that Robin is a caterpillar unwilling to turn into a butterfly.)

In her most serious moments, Liza is not exactly a fount of wisdom. In fact, it's hard to know at times whether we are expected to find her attractive. I don't. Her wispy solemnity and her strained smiles are mainly repellent, and Hollis McLaren is unable to rescue lines like "My baby was born dead—I'm dead inside." But in the scenes where she's going to pieces McLaren gives a chillingly accurate and totally compelling account of a woman who's lost control of her mind; indeed, I don't think I've ever seen anything in a movie so close to the truth of this matter.

She's equally good when she confronts her nurse, her doctor, and her mother, all of whom want to shut her away. The doctor—an extremely plausible figure, by the way—says at one point, "They've opened the new wing at Morningside. It's bright, clean . . ." But, as Liza says to Robin, "They only make me crazier. The doctors have got keys to lock up my brain." In the end she's unlocked, at least temporarily, and sharing Robin's joy in his new-found near-stardom; and somewhere along the way we who are watching her have, willingly or not, found ourselves identifying with at least a significant part of her hysteria, her defensiveness before authority, and her total dread of "the locked ward."

When a film is made for only $167,000, and by an unknown director at that, it's traditional to describe it as "unpretentious" and (even worse) "promising." What's so nice about *Outrageous!* is that—once it gets past its rather clumsy and earnest first eight or ten minutes—it *is* pretentious. With no money and no stars it has the utter gall to be as exuberant, unpredictable, delightful, glitzy, and romantic as any rich Hollywood production, and on its own terms it succeeds magnificently. And it can't be called "promising" either. The promise, of both writer-director and star, is fulfilled with their first film.

*Saturday Night*, October 1977

## INTO THE PAIN AND INTIMACY OF MARRIAGE

Jean Lapointe, in the minor role of Adhemar in *J.A. Martin photographe*, carries the burden of personal defeat with the air of a soldier who has endured too many losing campaigns. Once, long ago, Adhemar had a romance with Rose-Aimée, who is the central and commanding figure in this film. Now, in early middle age, he encounters her again, as she and her photographer-husband visit her uncle and aunt. He blunders in the door as they are having dinner, then quickly retreats, then is persuaded back in. Rose-Aimée smiles at him, her eyes full of happy reminiscence—he's the young man she occasionally throws up at her husband (and her husband, as we know from an earlier scene, speaks dismissively of Adhemar as "the one nobody would marry"). For her this is a happy moment, the encounter with an old love. She recalls how she and Adhemar, as adolescents, would say the rosary together and kiss after each bead.

But for Adhemar, shy and isolated, the memories involve nothing but pain. Rose-Aimée chatters on, and the uncle and aunt indulgently explain what Adhemar is doing now—he seems to have some kind of part-time job cooking at a lumber camp. Adhemar shrugs, squirms, reaches for his glass of gin once, then again, gulping eagerly. When the uncle realizes the bottle is empty, Adhemar volunteers to go out for more, and we follow him to the next room where he opens a fresh bottle by himself and gulps down more of it, looking for oblivion, or at least comfort.

Jean Lapointe is a richly endowed actor—you may have seen him as the most appealing of the victims in *Les ordres* (the one whose father dies while he's unjustly held in prison) or as the French Canadian gangster in *One Man*—and he brings to this moment in the film an impressive range of associations and feelings. In his few minutes on the screen he seems to sum up all the loser-bachelors of the world, all the men who fail to make binding connections with women and whose lives—for this among other reasons—dwindle into pointlessness. As he responds to the jokes of his old girlfriend, and endures the hostile glances of her comparatively successful husband, and accepts through habit the condescension of the uncle and aunt, he gives the appearance of being ashamed to be alive. He doesn't fit in here, and probably doesn't fit in anywhere.

Lapointe's little scene is important and stays with you not only because it presses on the main theme of the film—the delicate, easily broken web of connections between men and women—but because of the way Lapointe conveys the weight of this material. The script—by the director, Jean Beaudin, and the co-star, Marcel Sabourin—is written with considerable subtlety, and nowhere more than here. But it's the physical movement on the screen that counts most, and Lapointe's handling of his part has the grace and precision of a ballet performance. His thick body and clumsy hands speak with weary eloquence of his place in life. When he vanishes from the screen we are aware of just who has been there and what he has been trying to tell us.

The style of *J.A. Martin photographe* is insistently visual, pointedly physical. It has the air of a slow, stately ritual—a ritual that at times is *too* slow. Beaudin makes his crucial points through the style of his performers, encouraging from them a deliberateness that seems oddly out of place in a film of the seventies. He emphasizes this manner by his own method of fading out each scene slowly, as if he wanted us to contemplate it for a second before moving on to the next piece of action. He's daring enough to demand patience from his audiences, but he rewards our patience with a density of feeling that is rare in recent movies.

Monique Mercure, playing Rose-Aimée, exudes a strained tension as the dissatisfied wife of a rural French Canadian photographer. Her movements, particularly in the early scenes, have a nervous power, as if she were resisting violence only by an act of will. Sabourin, as J.A. Martin, conveys a crippling Jansenist inhibition. He has only a few cards, and he plays them close to the vest. He has fathered a family of five and made himself into a moderately successful craftsman, and somewhere along the way he has gone emotionally dead. The world has taught him, apparently, that to show his feelings about anything important—to admit that he *cares*, even a little—will jeopardize what he has made of himself. So he keeps quiet, as much as possible.

Rose-Aimée has decided this is not enough, and it's her decision that fuels the story. She senses she has lost the interest of her husband, both as companion and lover. Early in the film she complains to her mother-in-law, who refuses to see the point. "He's a good worker and he doesn't drink," the mother-in-law says. Rose-Aimée isn't satisfied: "Maybe if he drank he'd talk more." She decides that the way to regain her husband's attention is to travel with him in his horse-drawn wagon on his annual five-week trip in search of portrait business.

The decision in itself is scandalous enough—this is around 1900, and rural French Canadian women do not leave five children in the hands of various relatives in order to follow a whim. What is more painful to J.A. is that she pushes herself into his life, sometimes clumsily, sometimes with loving helpfulness. He isn't prepared for either; his history has made him a loner, and anything else is disturbing. Wives should be quiet, contained, and undemanding.

Beaudin, Sabourin, and their beautifully integrated company of actors are playing here with some of the major issues of marriage, whether in 1900 or 1977, and it will be a very rare married couple who can sit through *J.A. Martin photographe* without both some discomfort and some flashes of recognition. Monique Mercure is at once so sympathetic and so emphatic in her performance that her character's life problem seems to reach out far beyond the story itself. And Sabourin's responses to her thrust toward a more meaningful life are so appropriately frightened, so typically baffled, that he seems to stand for every man in history who ever realized that he has married more than he knew. When Rose-Aimée says to her husband, "I'm fed up being alone," her words have the same terrifying echo as the sound of Nora closing the door.

There's probably no altogether satisfactory way to resolve material as emotionally complicated—and, in the seventies, as politically charged—as this. Certainly Beaudin and Sabourin didn't find one. Toward the end, Rose-Aimée, with a good deal of help from alcohol, achieves a sort of Dionysian pleasure by dancing and singing ecstatically at a country wedding as her husband watches in edgy disapproval. The next day she has a hangover as they lumber toward home, sitting together behind the horses on his wagon, and J.A. reacts with a certain sympathy. When they get home she's enormously glad to see her children—the implication is that she has seen the great world, and shared some of her husband's life, and is now reconciled to her existence. J.A. hasn't changed a great deal, so far as the movie tells us, but at the end they are making love—something we have not seen them do at any earlier point. *They* may be happy, but I doubt whether most audiences will be pleased with the last ten minutes; and my guess is that this is the part of the film that least satisfies the people who made it.

But *J.A. Martin photographe* is more than a battle over marriage: it's also a work of social history on a high level. Beaudin helps us grasp the isolation of the period—Rose-Aimée, at one point, mentions that she hasn't stayed in a hotel since her honeymoon fourteen years before, and we understand that she hasn't done much of anything else either. Now she and her husband stay at a shabby commercial hotel, go to an outdoor country wedding, encounter death in an isolated little farmhouse, visit and photograph a rich English-speaking family, and spend a few minutes among the deprived young workers who made the English family rich. What emerges is a sense of rural Quebec as it may have been seventy-five years ago, and it's an enlarging sense—there's a feeling at the end that you have been somewhere you always wanted to go but never had the chance to visit before.

In at least two important ways, incidentally, it differs from most of the art and fiction dealing with that time and place: 1) There's no snow—the whole film is photographed against an idyllic summer landscape; 2) There's next-to-no religion—at the end we see a crucifix over the Martins' bed, and we've seen grace at meals and a few references to prayers and priests, but the oppressive religiosity that plays so large a part in much of Quebec fiction is here mainly absent. Whether this is accurate, or merely a retrospective wishing-away of the church by contemporary filmmakers, is a question for more learned students of that era.

The National Film Board made *J.A. Martin photographe*, and this raises a question that requires lengthier treatment at some other time. The NFB goes in and out of the business of making features—almost, it sometimes seems, by accident. When I was invited to a screening of *One Man* a few months ago, the Film Board's publicity man left a message with my assistant to the effect that this was the last NFB feature film; it sounded as if I was being called on to catch one final glimpse of a vanishing species.

My point is that the species should not vanish. *J.A. Martin photographe* is just the kind of movie—well, one of the several kinds of movies—that the Canadian film industry should be making. If only the NFB can make them, then the NFB should go on making them. Most of our tax money is spent in much less important ways.

*Saturday Night,* December 1977

## CLOSE TO HOME

In the Laurentians a glum rural poverty exists side by side with the gleaming summer homes of the Montreal rich. Michèle, the central figure in *Les bons débarras,* never directly comments on this social anomaly. She earns part of her living by chopping wood for the rich to burn in their fireplaces, but if she resents this she never says so. The director, Francis Mankiewicz, sharply contrasts the shack in which Michèle lives with the glass-walled palace owned by one of her customers. Michèle, for her part, has other problems.

She lives with her simple-minded brother, Guy, and her dreamy and intelligent thirteen-year-old daughter, Manon, who has no father and seems never to have had one. Michèle has a boyfriend, Maurice, an affable local cop, who is a decade or so older than she is. Maurice likes to turn on his siren on the way to visit his girlfriend, just to clear other cars out of his path. He's a cheerful, middle-aged anarchist who could exist as a policeman only in a Quebec film—and this *is* a Quebec film; it's so eloquent and so rooted in current Quebec realities that it revives all those hopes we felt for Canadian movies only a few years ago, before the deluge of Hollywood imitations.

Guy seems to be Michèle's main problem. His simple-mindedness is the kind that in a child elicits our warm sympathy but in an adult can draw forth only our sense of dread. His bitter frustration has made him an ugly alcoholic, and he drives their ramshackle pick-up truck with an angry recklessness. Maurice wants Michèle to have Guy put in an institution, but her loyalty, and perhaps her love, resist that notion. She gets what work out of him she can, and she tries to keep him from robbing her purse to buy beer. She understands, or seems to, why he must drink to the point of insensibility and fight with other young men. She has made mothering him a central part of her life.

But as it turns out Guy is less dangerous to her future, emotional and otherwise, than her thirteen-year-old daughter. Manon, whose fantasies centre on the Gothic melodrama of her currently favourite book, *Wuthering Heights*, loves her mother with a neurotically pubescent ardour. Michèle's announcement that she is pregnant, by the policeman, violently distorts Manon's love. In the end it's Manon's jealousy of competitors for her mother's love—competitors born and unborn—that turns the plot, making destructive all those elements that in the beginning seemed merely threatening.

The film looks as if it didn't have an art director, which is possibly the best kind of art direction. Mankiewicz and his cinematographer, Michel Brault, place this corner of Quebec on film as if it were there, just this way, when they arrived—the family's broken-down house in the middle of nowhere, the cheap roadside tavern where Michèle goes for a drunken reunion with an old boyfriend, the worn ice-skating rink where they all go together near the climax of the film. Brault long ago proved he could make an aesthetically pleasing film—the beautiful pictures in *Kamouraska* are his, to take just one example. In this case he resists the urge to idealize and prettify; the surroundings express the alienation and the aimlessness of people who have never found out how to organize their lives and never will. These rural characters could conceivably be descendants of the turn-of-the-century artisans and farmers in Jean Beaudin's *J.A. Martin photographe*, but if so, they and their environment have both slid a long way downhill.

This gritty realism carries over to the performances, and the director's handling of the actors. For long periods we seem not to be watching actors at all; magically, it's as if the cameras had silently intruded at crucial moments in otherwise hidden lives. Marie Tifo, as Michèle, conveys through her peculiar horse-faced beauty both the nervous fatigue of her life and the flickering moments of joy it contains. Germain Houde, as Guy, makes us share his despair and fear it at the same time. The child-actress Charlotte Laurier draws us into Manon's web of schemes and fantasies, and as her innocence turns to malevolence we understand why.

Outlined at a story conference, *Les bons débarras* might sound like one of those Gothic monstrosities of evil childhood that have recently enjoyed a turn of popularity. On the screen it's the opposite: here the adolescent is shown not as an isolated demonic element but as part of social and psychological reality. Her diabolism springs not from supernatural forces but from a carefully described Freudian romance of the family. In the solidity and depth of the characters, in fact, *Les bons débarras* feels like a skilful novel. This isn't altogether surprising, since the author of the screenplay is Réjean Ducharme, possibly the most interesting writer in contemporary Quebec.

What *is* surprising is that in this script Ducharme turns away from the dominant style of his novels. Where the novels are allusive, pun-infested, and edged with irony, *Les bons débarras* is written with directness and force; the humour emerges not from authorial comment but from the characters themselves, particularly from the wryness in Michèle's view of the people around her. The film represents a shift for Ducharme: Just by writing a script of this kind he's embracing the Quebec film culture he has himself satirized. But *Les bons débarras*, while it deals with melancholy themes, has none of the fashionable despair that often afflicts contemporary filmmakers. These unconnected and haphazard lives are often lived with affection, and there's a kind of affirmation in the characters' willingness to grab whatever joy is available to them. When Michèle finds out she's accidentally pregnant, she expresses a gladness that a militant feminist might condemn as atavistic but almost anyone else will want to share. These characters may not be satisfied with their lives but they have the sense to know that only the very stupid fail to appreciate the epiphanies that a grim destiny allows them. As a character in a Ducharme novel, *L'Hiver de force (Wild to Mild)*, says: "Happiness is the time during which surprise at having ceased to suffer lasts."

For about fifteen years, through good times and bad, through boom and bust, French Canadians have been trying to show English Canadians how to make movies. The rules seem simple enough: depict the people you know best, your own people, in their own setting; deal with private and occasionally public issues that move them; use your own community's best actors, writers, and cinematographers. Following this system, you may produce memorable films. English Canada has resolutely set its face against this advice. We know better: import Hollywood actors and sometimes writers; disguise the settings so that they look like Nowhere, USA; follow the formulas used in Hollywood four years previously. The two approaches have naturally produced different results. French Canada has created some memorable movies. English Canada, in recent years, has not. Producers in English Canada could argue that the Quebec films don't attract audiences outside Canada, but then English Canada's films usually don't do that either.

*Saturday Night*, November 1980

## TICKET TO NOWHERE

The pseudo-religious cults that sprang up across North America in the seventies, turning thousands of young people into spiritual zombies, illustrate Karl Marx's remark that when history repeats itself it turns into farce. The cults—the subject of Ralph Thomas's first feature film, *Ticket to Heaven*—are a hideous joke on the counter-culture movement that died around 1971, the point at which the cults began to grow strong. The cults take each of the characteristics of the counter-culture and push it to its limit. Did the counter-culture turn children against parents? The cults go one giant step further, brutally cutting family ties and in some cases teaching their members that parents represent Satan. Did the counter-culture preach openness to experience? The cults subject their members to searching public self-examinations in which they reveal personal feelings that can be used to manipulate them. Did the counter-culture indulge (usually through drugs) in mind distortion? The cults push their new members into psychosis, carefully inducing nervous breakdowns from which new members can then be rescued only by experienced leaders. Did the counter-culture preach that you are what you eat? The cults prove it, feeding their members low-protein food that reduces their ability to deal intellectually with the bombardment of simple-minded world-saving ideologies with which they are surrounded.

Those ideologies make a further connection with the sixties. People vulnerable to indoctrination turn out, quite often, to be those who had at least a brush with the various leftist ideologies. Benji, the central figure in Josh Freed's impressive book, *Moonwebs* (1980), from which the film has been adapted, was part of a group in Montreal to which Freed himself belonged and which he describes as "a community of our own, a mix of community workers, urban activists and unemployed, all somewhat attached to our tattered neighborhood . . . we were a casual and disorganized bunch." To people like this, the cults were initially appealing because they confidently claimed to have answers to important social issues. In *Ticket to Heaven* a speaker at an indoctrination service demands of his youthful listeners: "Why is the idea of building an ideal world so crazy?" Some of them listen in skepticism, but to others his banal theorizing is as appealing as it is familiar. What his well-intentioned listeners don't know—because for various reasons no credible person or institution has been able to teach them—is that we are all most vulnerable to irrationality and evil when we self-consciously set out to do good. The idealism of many a young German went into the process that ended at Buchenwald, and mountains of communist altruism lie behind the history that now culminates in the Gulag.

In much the same way, the young recruits are unequipped to understand that the confessional style of discourse developed by the human potential movement is dangerous as well as potentially helpful. In even an innocent situation, "sharing" may turn into emotional intimidation; when someone in the group has the cynical skills of a manipulator, the results can be devastating. Every therapy group contains a seed of fascism, and it is this seed that the cults bring to fruition.

Sun Myung Moon, the owner of the Unification Church, seems to understand all this, and his understanding has made him an extremely rich man. Ten years ago he brought from Korea an indoctrination process apparently based on brainwashing techniques developed in the Korean war, but he did not apply it rigidly in North America. He allowed his system to be significantly changed by one of his collaborators, a California teacher of English who coated it with the language and attitudes of the counter-culture, thus making it palatable in its initial stages to the disaffected young and connecting it to ideas they had learned to cherish.

What is most remarkable about *Ticket to Heaven* is that Ralph Thomas (who directed and with Anne Cameron wrote the script) makes entirely believable a process that most of us would initially regard as outlandish. His central character, David, played with great imagination and energy by Nick Mancuso, falls accidentally into the hands of a cult while visiting a friend in California. He finds himself at a nightmare version of a summer camp, the place Josh Freed described as "a strange mix of boot camp, kindergarten and psychotherapy session." Very early on his first morning he's awakened by a group of initiates singing, with ghastly enthusiasm, "When the red, red robin comes bob, bob, bobbin' along." This begins a physically and psychologically gruelling series of games, lectures, folk songs (someone sings Bob Dylan), and intimate discussions, all of them leading toward

David's breakdown. He resists the whole absurd business in the beginning, but the initiates appeal to his niceness. Won't he just give it a try? They are nice, too: friendly people who know how to exercise the tyranny of earnestness.

After a couple of days David is confessing his guilt in certain past relationships, weeping over the failure of his life, and turning to the experienced members for the help they are all too eager to provide. At one point, driven nearly mad by the intimacy of the encounter sessions, he tries to run away. The others pursue him and coax him back. "You've got to be strong, David," one of the women says. What she really means is that you've got to keep getting weaker until you finally collapse. David's collapse, his life as a robot selling flowers to enrich the movement, and his eventual rescue by his friends and family, are portrayed carefully and honestly.

Thomas has made some gestures toward turning his story into fiction. The cultists are called Heavenly Children and worship an otherwise unidentified Oriental they call "Father"; Moon's name does not appear. Benji has turned into David, and the home city of the major characters has changed from Montreal to Toronto. Josh Freed (who helped rescue Benji, sat through the deprogramming sessions, and won a National Newspaper Award for his 1978 *Montreal Star* series) has been turned into Larry, an accountant who moonlights as a bad comedian at Yuk Yuks and is played with considerable charm by Saul Rubinek. At the end of the film, among the credits, there's the usual line about this story not containing any reference to "actual persons, living or dead." But since the credits also say the film is adapted from *Moonwebs*, and since *Moonwebs* is about Moonies, and since many of the speeches in the book and many of the incidents have been transferred directly to the screen, and since Benji himself came to the location and helped Thomas and his crew get it right, *Ticket to Heaven* is in a sense a documentary.

A documentary, at least, in that one can regard it as a more or less accurate account of something that happened. But it is also a documentary in another sense: It fails to rise above its material. The story is fascinating, but on film it lacks a dimension that could have been provided by narrative imagination. (The kind of narrative imagination, for example, that brings *Breaker Morant* to life.) Ralph Thomas, who started out as a newspaper reporter, has made a distinguished career at the CBC with his *For the Record* series of dramatized documentaries. *Ticket to Heaven* demonstrates that he remains tied to the form he has learned to handle so adroitly. Unfortunately, there's never a moment when the film surprises us by soaring into uncharted regions of art.

Still, it's an exceptional achievement. Josh Freed, who briefly enlisted in a Moonie camp as part of his research for *Moonwebs*, wrote an account of listening to a lecturer set forth views that in any other context would be ridiculous: "The energy in the room was so high I could feel it pulsing through me, and I found even myself wanting to believe in this crazy sheer idealism. It was all so ridiculous, but after nearly forty-eight hours in this twilight reality, our egos battered by confusion, our minds numbed by information—anything seemed possible." It's the triumph of *Ticket to Heaven* that it allows us to share, and understand, one of the most bizarre experiences of our time.

*Saturday Night*, September 1981

## NOTHING BUT HEARTACHES

In a sense Don Shebib's shaky career can stand as an emblem of moviemaking in English Canada. His life as a director progresses with the same erratic, stop-and-start motion as the industry and art of which he remains an enigmatic part. Shebib promises much and delivers only a little, but like Canadian movies as a whole he commands our hopes because we have little else to cling to. Shebib has a style of his own, and a vision, and in a period when most of our movies are directed by soulless and rootless robots, those qualities make him important. At times we may ruefully reflect that his work is a poor thing but our own. And like most of our own, it's been badly used—often denigrated, usually unsupported, and sometimes ignored even at its best.

His first feature, *Goin' Down the Road* (1969), was the first English Canadian movie of consequence made outside the walls of the National Film Board. Its account of two Nova Scotia losers adrift in heartless Toronto was appealing not only to Canadians (who saw their lives authentically reflected, a rare experience) but to audiences in several other countries who understood the universally poignant relationship between a dying rural culture and an urban culture still waiting to be born. I remember the joy of that afternoon when *Goin' Down the Road* received its first public screening at a Yonge Street theatre in Toronto, a few blocks from some of its settings. The audience applauded with grateful surprise, not only because the characters were part of the life around us but because Shebib handled them with honesty and understanding and a measure of originality. On that afternoon both Shebib's career and the movies of English Canada seemed about to blossom.

Neither did. Most of us understand now the national disgrace of the movie industry: how, under the federal government's capital cost allowance, it became a tax-shelter playground for underemployed stockbrokers and overpaid dentists. As for Shebib, he moved on from commercial success to failure to failure. *Rip-Off* (1971) described with a certain loving insight the lives of aimless, fad-prone teenagers—and no one wanted to watch. *Between Friends* (1973), possibly his best film, was a sensitive account of some young men blundering into a rather stupidly organized crime—and it was barely shown in theatres at all. *Second Wind* (1976), his slickest movie, focussed on a current craze by depicting a man obsessed with running—and if you saw it you didn't remember it the next day. *Fish Hawk* (1979) was a project not of his creation, on which he was brought in late to take over from another director.

Through all of this Shebib remained hopeful (like our industry), full of plans for the future, yet always apologetic about mistakes of the past, even the recent past. His new film, *Heartaches*, was his own idea from the beginning, but after completing it he acknowledged that it was only sixty per cent of the film it should have been. There had been trouble with the money, trouble with casting, trouble with his star. Meeting Shebib at a screening of *Heartaches*, even after you've more or less enjoyed the film itself, is not an inspiring business; you go away wondering how he manages to endure all this, what can possibly reward him for the grief he continually suffers. But he does endure, he does persist in bringing some measure of gritty honesty to his movies; and *Heartaches* is worth seeing.

If you saw *Heartaches* in Bulgaria, or even in California, you might wonder just where it took place. Torontonians, and many other Canadians, will recognize the skyline as Toronto's (it has seldom looked so glamorous as Shebib makes it look at night), but there are anomalies. A politician running for local office is described on a sign with the American term "councilman," whereas in Toronto such people are called aldermen; when someone borrows a ten-dollar bill it's American rather than Canadian. These details, which Shebib explains as concessions to the producers, are the result of Canadian moviemakers' belief that no one outside this country is interested in a Canadian story.

*Heartaches* also has two leading actors who are Americans, but it is rooted in

recent Canadian experience. The characters are Ontario Primitive, the setting (most of the time) is densely Toronto. The action includes a traumatic encounter between an immigrant Italian factory owner's handsome nephew and a Canadian girl enchanted by exotic sexuality.

At the core of *Heartaches*--as in *Goin' Down the Road* and *Between Friends*—is a friendship, this time between two women. Bonnie (Annie Potts) has through a brief indiscretion become pregnant by a friend of her husband. She has left the husband, his alcoholic friends, and his obsession with car racing in their small town and moved to Toronto to get an abortion. She meets and lives with Rita (Margot Kidder), one of those vaguely defined movie characters who touch crucial emotions because they acutely resemble so many people you've known or observed.

The problem of *Heartaches* is also its greatest blessing: It isn't clearly defined, it doesn't always tell us just what to think, and there are even moments when Terence Heffernan, the scriptwriter, apparently forgets where he's going. Sometimes he seems to be in danger of writing something boring and sententious about the solidarity of women; Rita, after describing the shiftless men in her life, says, "Oh, Bonnie, where are the real men?" and for a while it appears likely that the two women will settle down to raise the baby together and end up as a feature story in the *Toronto Star* family section.

This looseness of conception is just what Margot Kidder needed all along. Her career has been a long succession of promising disappointments. She's one of those actors who spend many years threatening to turn into movie stars. Again and again she's come across as engaging but finally lifeless. Now, as the near-tramp Rita, who keeps believing that in the middle of a disastrously squalid life something magic will happen, Kidder suddenly makes a deep impression. As Rita she's a later version of the kind of woman people used to call "kooky" in the early sixties, but there's a sadness about her that's appealing. She isn't always dazzling, but she moves this time from her standard cuteness to a style that makes us believe in her and want to know more about her. She's a woman whose kookiness no longer seems amusing, even to her; she's one of those people (Shebib seems to specialize in them) who have found a role, lived it, then outgrown it and discovered there's nowhere else to go.

The people around her aren't so interesting, but sometimes they come to life. The cuckolded husband (Robert Carradine) and his friends are the kids from *Rip-Off*, grown older and meaner but no wiser. Almost everyone in the film has that Shebib touch of shaggy reality, the unslick description of believable moments that puts Shebib as an artist in a class with some good Canadian writers like W.P. Kinsella and Carol Bolt and Marian Engel. If we had managed things better we would now have many films like *Heartaches*, and Don Shebib would be making two movies a year rather than half a dozen in a decade. He would be a lot richer, and so would we.

*Saturday Night*, March 1982

## MINER MYSTERY

It's hard to know from the evidence of *The Grey Fox* just how Bill Miner established his heroic legend in the interior of British Columbia in the nineteen hundreds—a legend some of us have been hearing about for decades. *The Grey Fox* does everything it can to make train robbing into an act of independence and courage. This is a crook's-eye view of pioneer western Canada, just as Arthur Penn's *Bonnie and Clyde* (1967) was a crook's-eye view of the American Depression. Miner is played with courtliness and controlled energy by the veteran American stuntman Richard Farnsworth; his lover, played by Jackie Burroughs, clearly regards him as a figure of nobility as well as the answer to her prayers; the force of the law is represented by a smug and repellent detective from Pinkerton's; and the only Mountie we get to know is clearly on the side of our train-robber hero, even to the point of helping Miner escape from the police. On several occasions we're forcibly reminded that the people around Kamloops, where Miner hides out from the cops, regard him with sympathy: When he and two confederates are carted off to prison they're cheered like royalty at the railroad station.

Still, his heroic quality remains elusive. What makes him special? He doesn't, after all, rob *many* trains (three, that we see) and he doesn't rob them with much efficiency—in one case his helpers enter the wrong railway car and Bill ends up getting away with nothing but $15 and a bottle of liver pills. Unlike Jesse James, who in some of the Missouri legends was running a campaign against the banks and the railroads, Bill doesn't seem to have any particular social purpose in mind, even a quirky one. He's no Robin Hood. The closest he comes to helping the poor is his gift to a child of a single orange he's stolen from a store.

The strength of Bill's reputation remains a puzzle, but there's no question that the filmmakers are resolutely on his side. Bill is treated at all times with the utmost respect. His behaviour arises, apparently, out of an innate sense of independence ("I'm just no good at work that's planned by other hands"), and he treats robbing stagecoaches in his youth and trains in his old age as a serious craft. "A professional always specializes," he says solemnly, and proudly, when another crook suggests they collaborate on a bank job. We never see Bill do anything mean or cruel—unless you happen to think it's mean or cruel to point a gun at someone's head and terrify him into handing over his employer's or the public's property. We are meant to see Bill's eventual victory over authority as a kind of vindication of the loner, the outsider who refuses to fit in. At a preview screening in Toronto the director, Phillip Borsos, remarked that the film represents "in some ways the little guy winning in the end." But we don't see even this. Bill's escape from a Canadian prison, apparently into a happy old age shared with his lady friend, doesn't appear on the screen. It's conveyed by printed words, and at the end we catch just a brief glimpse of Bill, in striped prison uniform, making his way nimbly to freedom.

In a sense, that's typical of *The Grey Fox*: The film is as notable for its evasions as for its statements. What makes this often exhilarating movie unsatisfying is that it never comes to grips with its central character or its theme. The mystery of Bill's personality is left as unresolved as the puzzle of his reputation. We know, because the introductory titles tell us, that he robbed stagecoaches around the time of the Civil War, then spent thirty-three years in San Quentin prison and emerged a grey-haired, rather tired-looking survivor. But we learn nothing about where he came from in the first place, or why he became the dignified gentleman he clearly is when we meet him (did San Quentin routinely turn out graduates like this?). More important, how was it possible for this product of a nineteenth-century, all-male world (the frontier, then prison) to fall in love so winningly with the pioneer feminist photographer played by Jackie Burroughs?

John Hunter's script, so expert in its details, is flawed in structure and shape. It starts themes that it never adequately explores. At the beginning the titles tell us that Bill was released from prison "into the Twentieth Century," which prepares us for a Rip van Winkle plot about a man out of his time. Technology, we can imagine, will baffle the old frontiersman, and there's a hint of this in the beautifully played opening when a travelling salesman on a train sells Bill the latest consumer gadget, a mechanical apple-peeler. But as it turns out Bill adapts extremely well to the new century, not only when he chooses the most interesting woman around but when he goes to a movie (it's Edwin S. Porter's 1903 *The Great Train Robbery*) and realizes that it suggests his new career. The Rip van Winkle theme quickly disappears, leaving the movie shapeless and rather pointless. Bill's exploits are set before us not because one of them leads dramatically to another but because that's more or less the way they happened, according to history or legend.

The filmmakers may have been too faithful to the myth. They haven't made the necessary leap from documentary to fully fleshed drama. They've even been praised for this—one Toronto critic said that "to their credit" Borsos and Hunter "resisted the temptation to turn it into a dream." They should have surrendered. It is just this temptation that is the first step on the long trek from elegant documentary to substantial art. To resist it, an all too common impulse of Canadian artists, is to put a brake on imaginative achievement. Our filmmakers and writers will come convincingly to grips with the Canadian past only when they realize that historical events and legends can be no more than the beginning of dramatic art, and that historical personages are available for manipulation and development at the hands of a good writer. Fidelity or distortion is not the question; what matters is that history be turned into stories with meaning and resonance.

All that said, *The Grey Fox* is a remarkable moment in Canadian filmmaking. If it fails to find a large dramatic vision, it partly redeems that lack by the marvellously convincing quality of its best individual passages. Many of them, I suspect, will stay with us in memory for a long time: the claustrophobic frontier court in which Bill and his partners are given their prison sentences; the bedroom scene in which the Burroughs character lovingly elicits Bill's explanation of his tattoos; the scene in which Bill buys a Colt revolver, turning its cylinder with the affection of a sculptor feeling a new piece of wood. These and a good many other moments demonstrate that in Phillip Borsos—whose first feature this is—we have an important new director, an artist of style and sensitive imagination. *The Grey Fox* is gravely flawed as drama, but in its handling of the intimate details of character and its visual splendour it reaches a new level of romanticism in Canadian movies.

*Saturday Night*, June 1983

# *After We Came In*

## BY MARTIN KNELMAN

*Like Marshall Delaney, Martin Knelman is a veteran of the ongoing struggle to notice and appreciate achievement in Canadian cinema. His 1977 book* This Is Where We Came In *was an attempt to put some of his front-line critical journalism into a perspective from which the future efforts of the Canadian film industry might be judged. The articles republished here represent Knelman's work from that perspective. His writing tends to balance the vision of filmmaking as an art form against the demands of a society impatient for escapist entertainment on a Saturday night. Moreover, the discussions of these films come with a sense of the newsworthiness of the fact that their production is taking place at all.*

### LE MAUDIT CBC

To prepare myself for the CBC's new television miniseries about our old friends the Plouffe family, I thought it might be amusing to have a look at the original half-hour show, which made its television debut in 1953.

Roger Lemelin's adaptation of his own popular novel about a typical French Catholic family in Quebec City had already been turned into a successful radio series, and when *The Plouffe Family* made the transition to television, Lemelin personally turned up in our living rooms to announce a startling experiment in electronic bilingualism. Professing to be surprised by all this public attention, in the manner of a bewildered parent whose child has unexpectedly become a superstar, Lemelin urged us to think of the Plouffes as close friends and neighbours—a hard-working family. "If you like the Plouffes," he purred, moving in for the emotional kill, "I will be doubly proud. It was in such a family that I grew up." What was even more remarkable than this cozy fireside chat with the author was the announcement that every week, on live national television, the French Canadian actors would repeat in English exactly what they had done the previous day in French on the Radio-Canada network. Now here was something truly unprecedented in the history of Canadian culture.

Then we were introduced to the Plouffes themselves. Mama Plouffe was in the kitchen singing a little *chanson* while rolling dough for her pies. Papa Plouffe, with his broken bike, was reminiscing about his glory days as a provincial bike champion in 1910, and complaining: "If only we had a subway like Toronto . . ." In the premiere episode, we learned that "Joe," the youngest of the three Plouffe boys, was in training, and that the oldest brother, Napoléon, had the responsibility of keeping him away from girls so he could make the NHL. We also learned that Cécile, their sister, was stalling her boyfriend, a bus driver, and was in no rush to marry him, despite the warnings of her mother that she would lose him. (What got left out of the television version, presumably because it would have shocked the 1953 television audience, was that Cécile's boyfriend happened to be a married man with several children.)

The television show wasn't exactly a sitcom, and it wasn't exactly a soap. No one will ever be able to measure its impact on the minds of English Canadians, but it had a vast captive audience (in most parts of the country people watched either the CBC or nothing), and for children in Saskatoon or Halifax, this may have been as close as they were ever going to get to the reality of knowing a French Canadian family. Yet however warmly the Plouffes were received, what this program represented was already finished. The television show, after all, seemed to be promoting exactly the stereotype that the enlightened prophets of the impending Quiet Revolution felt they had to fight against if they were ever going to bring Quebec society into the twentieth century. Long before the weekly half-hour series left the air in 1959 (the year Duplessis died), the parochial, reactionary, church-dominated mentality it cheerfully chronicled had become an embarrassment.

It's a measure of the success Quebec radicals have had in the sixties and seventies that the Plouffe family no longer seems counterrevolutionary. Now we see these characters as figures of folklore from a period that has at long last receded into the past. With Duplessis being resurrected as a folk hero and the Plouffes slipping back into the CBC schedule, it might be tempting to conclude that things have come full circle. But this isn't the same family saga as the one that became so familiar in the fifties. It is not so much the characters that have changed as the ways in which we are invited to perceive them.

This new version—which came out as a feature film last year and is now running on the CBC as a serial on Sunday evenings—was packaged in several different ways. In Quebec, the movie released to theatres ran nearly four hours. In English Canada, the subtitled version ran just under three hours. The special Cannes Festival version, which won rave reviews when it was shown in the Directors' Fortnight, was neither as long as the movie shown in Quebec nor as truncated as the one released in Toronto. The television version—six hours including commercial breaks—is a leisurely, filled-in family chronicle, with material that wasn't seen in any of the movie versions. The problem with the series on the English-language network is not its length but the insipid English dubbing. Stripped of the rich nuances they express in their own language, the Plouffes become merely the Waltons *manqués*.

The loss is ours, and it is tragic, because it robs the large anglophone audience of a chance to experience the full impact of a highly rewarding production. The director, Gilles Carle, is one of Quebec's most distinctive, most prolific directors, and he has made *Les Plouffe* into his greatest triumph in a decade. Collaborating on the screenplay with Lemelin, Carle has managed to transform what could have been tired leftovers into a series of stunning tableaux aglow with social history and emotional resonance. For Carle, *Les Plouffe* seemed at first an unlikely project, out of whack with his manic, satirical parables about the violence and boondocks comedy of Quebec society. There were suspicions that Carle had sold out, and certainly it would have been easy to recycle *Les Plouffe* as soft-headed nostalgia. Instead, Carle gives himself up to the material in a way that he never has before. For the first time, he suppresses his own personality; the tone of *Les Plouffe* doesn't announce that this is a Gilles Carle movie.

Superficially, the characters are the same ones we may remember from the old television series, but the portraits are filled in now, and we get to see all the disturbing details that had to be left out before. The Plouffes are no longer the happy-go-lucky dummies they once seemed. Théophile, the father (played by

Emile Genest, who used to play the oldest son, Napoléon, on television) sits in his chair grumbling about visits by the Royal Family and conscription, and we can see the subtext of discontent so long concealed behind the smiling-faces stereotype. When Napoléon refuses to give up his girlfriend even when she goes into a sanatorium, when Ovide (Gabriel Arcand) discovers that he's as ill-suited for the monastic world as he is for the secular world, when Guillaume (Serge Dupire) signs with the Cincinnati Reds but finds that he's destined to throw grenades in Europe instead of baseballs in America—well, these are not the elements of television sitcom blandness.

Many things are marvellous in this sprawling saga: the tumult in the streets when Guillaume Plouffe interrupts the procession of the royal limousine by throwing a baseball across the street; the comic pathos of the scene in which Ovide presents his own mini-opera, *Pagliacci*, in the Plouffe living room, and suffers a deep humiliation; the seething-with-repressed-sexuality of the monastery that Ovide tries to enter, and from which he is eventually driven; the rich ironies of a religious procession punctuated by the cry of a priest, "Sacred Heart of Jesus, save our sons from conscription."

We are drawn into the family chronicle in the same way we were drawn into the family chronicle in the *Godfather* movies. Carle is never condescending toward his characters. Those great steps dividing the Lower Town from the heights of Quebec City seem to be a historical barrier as well as a geographical one. Once we enter the terrain of the Plouffe family, we take it on its own terms. We begin to see the world through their eyes. Understanding their loyalties to the parish, family and tradition, and their fears of sexuality, modernism and the anglophone North American giant surrounding them, we come to share the anguish and the poignance of their unwilling break with their own past.

The commercial realities are such that it would take a miracle to attract even a minority audience in English Canada to even a very fine Quebec movie. The CBC, with its mandate to promote national unity, might be expected to jump at the chance to bring the finest Quebec movies to a popular audience. Yet those English Canadians who have seen *Mon oncle Antoine* on television have seen it mutilated not only by commercial interruptions but also by English dubbing which almost always destroys the nuances and the flavour to the point where the film no longer seems to have any connections at all with the culture of Quebec. The CBC could perform an invaluable service to the country by bringing the best Canadian movies to a large audience in as unadulterated a form as possible. The movies produced in Quebec in the past twenty years provide a unique window for English Canadians on that other solitude, but the CBC keeps the shutters closed. It's true that subtitles on television present special problems, but special techniques *have* been developed for dealing with them. Originally *Les Plouffe* was to have been produced simultaneously in two languages (just like the original television show) but there wasn't enough money to do it. If the CBC had the courage to show *Les Plouffe* with subtitles, some people may have been too lazy to watch it, and perhaps it would have been harder to sell the commercial spots, but then I've never thought the CBC should be in the business of selling commercials and catering to the lowest common denominator. At the very least, a dubbed version with some French accents and the voices of the original actors (which is what we got when *J.A. Martin photographe* was shown on CBC) would have been far preferable to what we're getting.

The format of the television miniseries is perfect for this material. It allows Carle and Lemelin exactly the kind of leisurely pace and intimacy that is right for this story. They're able to tell the parts of the story that had to be left out of the movie, so we're not left wondering what happened to various characters who appeared at the beginning and then vanished, such as Cécile Plouffe and the young journalist Denis Boucher. There's a satisfying sense of fullness about the long version. I suppose we should be grateful for getting *Les Plouffe* in any form whatsoever, but so much of the richness is needlessly lost. When we're forced to get Mama Plouffe through the uncredited but unmistakeable voice of Barbara Hamilton, we really do have to ask ourselves: is there *nothing* sacred left in this country?

*Toronto Life*, February 1982

## MUM'S THE WORD

The arresting combination of sly humour and buoyant generosity in *By Design* is so identifiably stamped with Claude Jutra's personality that it's like the insignia on some of the designer clothes featured in the picture. For the first time since he stopped making feature movies in Quebec seven years ago and began working in English in Toronto, Jutra's distinctive sensibility breaks through the material he is working on and embraces the audience, the way it did in his greatest French-language movies. When Jutra is on, he can make us giggly and intoxicated even while exposing the worst and saddest aspects of his characters' lives. He cherishes little secrets, and makes the audience come alive at the discovery of them. Like the clerk Fernand whom he portrayed in *Mon oncle Antoine*, Jutra has the stance of the quiet but knowing bystander, who picks up all the unstated tensions around him, but also assimilates them into his own cheerful little private reveries—humming knowingly to himself.

*By Design* is an audacious comedy about two lesbians who want to have a baby, and it represents the reemergence of Claude Jutra as Canada's finest writer-director. When the feature film industry dried up in Quebec in the mid-seventies, Jutra was one of the saddest casualties. After years of making shorts and documentaries at the National Film Board and waiting for his big chance, Jutra achieved a breakthrough in 1970 with *Mon oncle Antoine*, still the best movie ever produced in this country. *Kamouraska*, a historical epic based on the Anne Hébert novel, was filled with exquisite tableaux and marvellous bits but never achieved the popularity it deserved. *For Better or For Worse*, a low-budget domestic comedy with a cast of four principal actors, including Jutra, wasn't a success, and it turned out to be his last French-language feature.

In the mid-seventies, Jutra began working in television in Toronto. He directed two *For the Record* dramas: *Ada*, based on a Margaret Gibson story about women in a psychiatric hospital, and *Dreamspeaker*, an award-winning piece of high-minded fakery about a runaway white boy and an insufferably wise old Indian. There was also a lovely television version of Mordecai Richler's *The Street*, with Saul Rubinek. But Jutra never pretended that working in television was his first choice. A few years ago, he told a magazine interviewer: "Nowadays I don't even talk about the movie projects I dream of doing. That way it saves everyone a lot of heartbreak."

When Jutra made his first full-length film in five years, the circumstances were less than ideal, and the results were discouraging. The movie was *Surfacing*, based on Margaret Atwood's novel. Producer Beryl Fox came to Jutra days before shooting was to begin. Eric Till had backed out at the eleventh hour. The financing was endangered, and if she didn't find a name director in a hurry, the movie would have to be cancelled. Jutra and Fox made a pact: He would step in to direct

*Surfacing* if she would agree, in exchange, to produce a movie he wanted to do. That movie was *By Design*.

There wasn't much that Jutra could do to salvage *Surfacing*. It was too late to do a major rewrite on the script, which transformed Atwood's unfilmable quest allegory into a simple-minded feminist equivalent of a woodsy *Boy's Own* adventure story. Even if the script hadn't been impossible, the casting was lethal: the cow-eyed, tiresomely sincere Kathleen Beller as the searching heroine, and the loutish jock mannequin Joseph Bottoms as her boy friend. Unlike many Canadian movies, *Surfacing* at least came out of honorable intentions, yet the reputations of Jutra and Fox were seriously damaged by its deficiencies. People who weren't troubled by the idiocies of *City on Fire* or *Running* for some reason got indignant about *Surfacing*.

*By Design* is a loopy, surprising comedy with a charmingly original point of view; though the story is set in motion by a series of outrageous notions, the characters all retain their basic innocence, and when things work out happily and bizarrely for them, we don't experience this as an artificial device but as an intrinsic element in Claude Jutra's outlook. Jutra's universe is ruled by a quirky deity, perhaps a bit squirrelly and with a fondness for chaos, but still essentially benevolent.

*By Design* emerged from an original script by Joe Wiesenfeld, who shares the screenplay credit with Jutra and David Eames. The two heroines live together in Vancouver and run a fashion business. The more restless, driven one, played by veteran American actress Patty Duke Astin, yearns for a baby. The dreamy, mysterious one, played by Sara Botsford (a Canadian newcomer who was once a supporting player at Stratford), is willing to go along with the idea, but it is not that easy. In a deliciously nutty sequence featuring the gifted Clare Coulter as an eccentric social worker, we discover that society, at the official level anyway, is made very nervous by the idea of sanctioning lesbian parenthood. The alternative of artificial insemination also gets shot down in a comic vignette.

Finally, there's only one possibility: the traditional solution of finding an appropriate man. The unlikely stud selected is a sex-obsessed photographer—entertainingly well played by Saul Rubinek—who is very slow to get the picture. In the most bizarre sexual sequence of the year, poor Rubinek is driven to thumb through a pornographic magazine while trying to make love to a distracted Astin—who is brought to orgasm by the murmurings of Botsford, herself in bed elsewhere with a sensitive young Swede trying to get rid of his virginity.

Throughout the movie, Jutra keeps control of his material and never stoops to frantic sex farce. There's a basic grace and generosity in Jutra's approach. He relishes the absurdity of the situation, but he never sets up gags at the expense of his characters. You feel that he respects their obsessions. One of the most wonderful scenes in the movie is of the two women tangoing into the dawn at a disco. As a couple, they're a Mutt-and-Jeff mismatch, and many things about the relationship are funny, but there's something magical at the heart of it, and this movie knows better than to trample on it. The comedy in *By Design* induces knowing chuckles rather than rampant guffaws, and there's a delicacy that stays with you after you've forgotten the jokes. The seeming frivolity of the surface is deceptive; *By Design* has a subtext that affects the way you see the world. It's mellow and wised-up, in the manner of Louis Malle's *Murmur of the Heart* and Paul Mazursky's *Next Stop, Greenwich Village*.

For reasons I can't quite fathom, *By Design* has provoked a great deal of hostility. (The picture has been awaiting release for more than a year.) The attacks have come not only from the usual unreliable sources, such as Leonard Klady (writing in *Variety*), and Gerald Pratley, who tends to regard the Canadian film industry as a private finishing school for girls with himself as its shrill headmistress. *By Design* has also been badmouthed by journalists and industry insiders who normally know better. Is it because they're still trying to punish Jutra and Fox for the dreariness of *Surfacing*? Is it because they're made uncomfortable by the whole notion of lesbianism as a subject for comedy?

The advance word in Toronto on *By Design* has been so adverse that it may be the picture won't be given its due until it becomes a success in New York. Almost unbelievably, it was rejected by Toronto's Festival of Festivals, which in recent years has featured Canadian movies as inept as *Suzanne* and social comedies as dispiriting as *Only When I Laugh*. A film professor, astonished to hear of my favourable response to *By Design*, demanded to know what I liked about it. When I told him I found it very funny, and that I laughed a lot, he asked incredulously: "You mean you thought it was *intended* to be funny?"

Well, yes, at the risk of being out-of-step with fashionable opinion in this most fashion-conscious of cinema capitals, I'm afraid I did. *By Design* strikes me as easily the outstanding Canadian movie of 1982, and one of the most original and delightful surprises from any country—on a level with *My Dinner With André, Diner*, and *E.T.*

Yes, really. No kidding.

In fact, I have only one serious complaint. The clothes are ghastly. And in a movie about fashion designers!

*Toronto Life*, August 1982

## THE VARNISHED TRUTH

When Terry Fox got the bad news from a doctor—that the pain in his knee was caused by a malignant tumor, that his leg would be amputated, that his chances of surviving were only slightly better than fifty-fifty, and that a classmate with a similar problem had recently died—he said, "Oh fuck, I'm not ready to leave this world." According to the book about Fox by *Toronto Star* reporter Leslie Scrivener, at that moment Rolly Fox, Terry's father, went into shock. It wasn't the terrible news about his son that so startled him; it was his son's language. Terry had never talked that way in his father's presence before. In that moment, there might be the beginning of an interesting family drama, but in the new movie *The Terry Fox Story*, the script and the director, Ralph Thomas, back away from it. In the movie, Terry says angrily to the doctor, "What the hell am I supposed to do without my leg?" and Terry's father natters, "Don't swear, Terry." And some of us in the audience wonder: Can there be a family on this planet in this century in which a father would be distracted from shattering news by hearing his grownup son say "hell"? Were the moviemakers so determined to make Terry Fox into the most saintly all-Canadian boy who ever lived that they couldn't risk offending anyone in the audience?

The notion of a one-legged kid running across the country might have been dismissed as a sick joke, but the image of Terry on a deserted highway, wearing his grey running shorts and a white T-shirt emblazoned with a red maple leaf and map of Canada became an icon for the whole country. He turned into a member of that most endangered species, Canadian heroes, and his death completed the legend. Ticking off 5,342 kilometres of his 8,000-kilometre route from one coast of Canada to the other before illness knocked him off the road, Fox not only raised more than $24 million for cancer research with his Marathon of

Hope, he also touched off a bizarre media circus that not even his death could stop.

There are a number of interesting questions about Terry Fox that an intelligent movie might explore, but, of course, the temptation is to take the shameless, facile approach. Here was the ultimate human-interest story, combining all the elements that gladden the hearts of mass-circulation newspaper editors: youthful ideals, spectacular misfortune, a freakish athletic contest, a doomed hero. It's the kind of sensational story that can generate an orgy of hypocrisy of the type satirized by Ben Hecht when he wrote the 1937 movie *Nothing Sacred*, in which self-congratulating slobs enjoy weeping crocodile tears over a girl they think is dying of radium poisoning while the girl (Carole Lombard) and her mentor (Frederic March) chortle at their phoniness.

Terry Fox couldn't have better served the purposes of *The Toronto Star* if its editors had invented him. His story, with its daily guarantee of fresh incidents and locales, was the ideal circulation booster; it appealed to that huge, elusive constituency of common folk to which the *Star* addresses itself, often with a quasi-biblical sense of mission. The editors could feel they were not only getting great copy but improving the world. The decision of the country's largest-circulation newspaper to assign a reporter to follow Fox was a turning point which the movie alludes to without examining its implications. At the beginning of his run, Fox made little impact. By the time he reached Ottawa, he was important enough to rate an audience with Trudeau, but the Prime Minister didn't seem to know who he was or even which direction he was running in. Thanks to the *Star*, though, public attention reached a crescendo when he arrived in Toronto; his reception in this city was a spectacle which would have made Cecil B. DeMille blush.

Fox may not have realized it at first, but the *Star*'s interest in him cancelled his right to a private life. In her book, reporter Scrivener recalls how Terry tried out on her the idea of having a girl join his party to alleviate his loneliness. Perhaps he understood that she had him in the position that the Hearst press had Hollywood stars in the days when an actor's career could be destroyed if his personal life didn't meet Louella Parsons' moral standards. The *Star* couldn't have its front-page saint tainted by even the hint of sex. Scrivener, by her own account, advised Terry that it wouldn't be a good idea. Even if she knew and he knew that nothing improper was going on, it would be best if the public weren't given reason for doubt. In *The Terry Fox Story*, as in *Chariots of Fire*, jock heroism is dressed up in the most puritanical attitudes. The hero is required to be so clean-cut that the audience won't be allowed even to entertain the notion that a twenty-one-year-old might have sexual needs. When he gets involved with a woman, she has to be not only a therapist but a born-again Christian, and he tells her the marathon comes first—he can't be distracted by any involvement with her.

*The Terry Fox Story* isn't the kind of film that looks too closely at its hero's relationship with the media, because essentially this movie shares the *Star*'s mentality. It's inspirational and idealistic in a simple-minded way, and by not going deeply into anything, it avoids rocking boats. Ralph Thomas came to movies via CBC television's drama department, where he created the *For the Record* series. His first theatrical release, *Ticket to Heaven*, stuck with the docudrama format, but the subject had an explosiveness, and it seemed to release something in Thomas. *The Terry Fox Story* is a docudrama in the worst way; it's a bigger, more expensive *For the Record*, with that deadening air of earnestness and rectitude that makes one reach for the button on the converter, looking for a channel with some lively American trash. Still, it could well be a popular success, especially among school kids who prefer to keep their myths naive and uncomplicated. People who come to *The Terry Fox Story* determined to be moved by it probably will be moved by it, even though the style is thin.

The film is naively faithful to the superficial facts of the case. It not only doesn't answer the more interesting questions, it fails to notice them. What was it about this boy and his family that made him take on this challenge? We're given no clues. It's as if the moviemakers think *any* boy who lost a leg to cancer would run across the country. It didn't occur to them to delve into his character and background in a way that might prepare us for this startling decision. The screenplay is credited to Edward Hume, but there's no script, really; it's more like a collection of newspaper clippings laid end to end. First this happens and then that happens, but no one shows us why. The closest thing to dramatic tension is the arguing between Terry and his friend Doug, who goes along to drive the van and do the dirty work. The arguing is unpleasant but never in a witty or illuminating way, and then it's cancelled by a reconciliation scene that rings false. Robert Duvall, the American actor, brings a little vigor to the proceedings in the role of a Cancer Society official, but he can't do much; the role is too innocuous. How did the Cancer Society respond to Terry Fox, and did his unorthodox approach to fund raising create problems? The movie doesn't tell us.

Given the unshaped script, only one thing could have redeemed this film, and that was a mesmerizing performance in the title role. The only Canadian I can think of who might have brought this off is Brent Carver, who once played a one-legged athlete in a CBC drama, but Carver may be too old for the part, and the moviemakers didn't want him. Eric Fryer isn't an actor, and he doesn't have an actor's presence. He's likable and willing, but it's obvious that his main qualification is that he's a one-legged young athlete, so there was no need for a double or trick photography. He just doesn't have the personality to carry a whole movie—especially one with a weak script. The hero's main function is to receive standing ovations, like Luciano Pavarotti in *Yes, Giorgio!*, but by stressing the "ordinary," "typical" side of Terry, the movie makes him seem bland, as if he were afflicted with insipidness as well as cancer.

At a recent press conference to announce distribution plans, some of those involved in the business side of the picture could barely contain their sense of self-congratulation, as if their involvement in this project were a kind of penance for other, baser-minded movies. This time they were on the side of the angels; not only were they bringing the public an uplifting film about a folk hero, they were also getting points for sticking to a truly Canadian subject. The producers and investors give themselves credit for going ahead at a time when there was no guarantee anyone would buy the picture, and in the end their faith was justified when Home Box Office, the huge US pay television operator, became involved. But *The Terry Fox Story* is so safe and tame that it hardly seems like a daring venture. It stays within the conventions accepted by the television audience. This film won't offend anyone except those offended by calculated inoffensiveness.

*Toronto Life*, June 1983

## NOVEL APPROACHES

It's one of the curiosities of Canada's beleaguered, inglorious movie industry that until now relatively few of our major literary works have found their way to the screen. Fewer still have made that perilous voyage successfully. Now, suddenly, two celebrated Canadian books have been filmed simultaneously: *The Tin Flute*, based on the novel by Gabrielle Roy and Timothy Findley's *The Wars*.

International film history is filled with demonstrations of the point that literary classics more often than not resist well-intentioned efforts to transpose them to the screen. Great novels have their own internal logic, and when you lose Tolstoy's or Faulkner's voice and way of seeing, and the characters' thought processes, there's always the danger of stripping away everything that made the original great, so what's left seems empty and ordinary. (Dickens is an exception; his works invite dramatization, and several good movies have been made from them.) Second-rank literature, such as *The Maltese Falcon*, frequently inspires better films than those inspired by first-rank literature. There's nothing more tiresome or embarrassing than a movie that seems oppressively "literary."

Gabrielle Roy wasn't Tolstoy or Faulkner, and when you examine the ludicrous ineptness of the new film based on *The Tin Flute*, it's less than honest to pretend that the problem doesn't have something to do with the original material. Like *Uncle Tom's Cabin, The Tin Flute* falls into the special category of "Not good, but important." After all the years of being told it's a Canadian literary classic, it may be impossible for us to see it simply as an interesting first novel which, for various reasons having to do with sociology and cultural history, became historically significant. This saga of a downtrodden French Canadian family living on the edge of poverty and psychological desperation through the Depression and the Second World War has heavy doses of masochism and sentimentality, and it has a Dickensian social conscience without Dickens' ebullience and wit. But whatever one's reservations, Gabrielle Roy had her own view of the world, and one never doubts her authenticity or integrity. In effect, she insisted that attention must be paid (to borrow a phrase from the noble wife in *Death of a Salesman*). For the first time, Roy elevated the plight of those trapped in the grim realities of French Canada's lower depths to a matter of international literary importance. She made her debut just at the time when concern for the poor was an article of literary faith (Steinbeck was in; Fitzgerald was out), and by winning the most prestigious prizes in both France and Canada, she changed the way Quebec was seen by educated people in Paris and Toronto.

It's probably impossible to give a contemporary movie audience a sense of what this book meant when it was published in 1945, but there's no excuse for turning *The Tin Flute* into the crude, ludicrous soap opera that has reached the screen. Claude Fournier, who directed it, is best known for a Quebec sex comedy, *Deux femmes en or* (1970), which was one of the most profitable movies ever made in Canada, but he's way out of his league here.

No doubt at the Moscow Film Festival, at which Marilyn Lightstone won a special prize offered by the Committee of Soviet Women for her performance as Rose Anna Lacasse, the saintly matriarch, *The Tin Flute* was seen as an exposé of what capitalist society does to ordinary people. But how was it possible for the audience at the Montreal Film Festival to sit through this movie in solemn appreciation? At the screening I attended, a small group shrieked with laughter. And no wonder. Without Gabrielle Roy's point of view or narrative style, and without any historical context, the material becomes absurd. The script (credited to Fournier and producer Marie-Jose Raymond, with additional writing by B.A. Cameron) is full of thuddingly terrible lines, which have a way of becoming inadvertently hilarious.

As Florentine, the naive waitress who falls in love with a cad and then marries an unsuspecting soldier from a prosperous family to escape scandal and poverty, Mireille Deyglun is caught in a hopeless situation because the filmmakers haven't found a way to present the character's sexual innocence without turning it into a joke. As her seducer, Pierre Chagnon is villainous enough to induce giggling fits. Michel Forget as her father, an unemployed dreamer, gives the sort of performance that makes one wish the character had thought of suicide an hour earlier in the proceedings, and as her mother, Marilyn Lightstone kvetches and suffers with such relentless intensity that when her husband remarks that she has endured so much without ever complaining, you want to shake him and ask what the hell he's talking about. The best performances are given by the rats, who keep reminding us of the social conditions in which these people find themselves.

Making matters worse than they might otherwise have been is the fact that *The Tin Flute* has been cut and pasted together in so many versions. There's the five-part miniseries for television and this theatrical feature; in each category there's the French version and the English version. Maybe because it's condensed from a longer, episodic series, the movie has a deadly structural problem—the calamities arrive one after another, creating an accidental spoof of soap-opera conventions. One minute a child is dying; the next the father is losing his job and the family is being evicted; and before you've had time to react, the heroine is facing the ultimate shame. Awkward post-synching in the English version makes all this even sillier. The audience can't fail to crack up when Marilyn Lightstone, with her tummy swollen with child once again and her face squinched up in the usual agony, whimpers, "It was so much easier to find a house when there were only ten of us."

*The Tin Flute* is a very sad chapter in the history of this country's feature film industry. Almost everything that could be wrong with this movie *is* wrong with it, down to an especially irritating pop song that is totally wrong for the era, and the banal lines ("Have a nice day") that throw you right out of the period. (Given the dialogue, a more appropriate title would be *The Tin Ear*.) The picture is a veritable festival of clichés and stereotypes, down to the poor, happy French Canadian family escaping for a day from urban misery to the simpler joys of frolicking in the country during the maple syrup season. God knows the sap runs deep in *The Tin Flute*. The National Film Board and the CBC were involved as co-producers, and the Canadian Film Development Corporation also contributed to the $3.45 million budget. At least the blame can be spread around. One comes out of it feeling depressed to be a Canadian.

Next to *The Tin Flute*, the new movie based on Timothy Findley's *The Wars* may seem like a masterpiece. Though this is by no means a great film, it's civilized and polished and respectable. You get the secure feeling that the director, Robin Phillips, has control of the material and knows what he's doing, even if the movie isn't up to as much as he may think it is. And there's a particular virtue that puts you on his side and makes you root for the movie—the fact that Phillips has had the courage to cast the gifted Canadian actors he has worked with often at the Stratford Festival (and now the Grand Theatre Company in London, Ontario) without being bullied out of it by film financiers who might prefer Americans with names recognizable outside Canada.

Martha Henry looks good in Edwardian hats, though after this movie and last year's CBC television series *Empire, Inc.* she could be in danger of being permanently cast as a cold, controlling upper-set WASP matron, and, given the range of work she has been able to do on the stage, that would be a great pity. She seems to be suffering almost as much as Marilyn Lightstone in *The Tin Flute*, but in this case, we're encouraged to feel she *deserves* to suffer. After all, she's a rich WASP, with a limp husband (William Hutt), and she's always trying to control people. She, too, has a dying child, and the child's death is associated with symbolism almost as heavy-handed as that damn tin flute itself. Here it's the rabbits of the dead child that must be killed in some sort of grotesque ritual.

*The Wars* is worlds away from *The Tin Flute*. Here the background is the First

World War rather than the Second World War, and we are concerned with the prosperous WASPs of Rosedale rather than the downtrodden French Canadians of Montreal. The lavish garden parties seem to be thrown for the sole purpose of providing ironic counterpoint, and the conversation is terribly measured and literary. The story concerns the apprenticeship of the brother of the dead girl, who goes off to war against his mother's wishes ("I can't keep anyone alive," she murmurs, "not any more").

Robert Ross, played by Brent Carver, learns a little about life and observes the horrors of war. There's the usual set piece about the sensitive boy going to the brothel with his fellow-soldiers, and there's a romantic interlude in which he has a supposedly torrid affair in a frightfully British manor filled with a creepiness that will be familiar to veterans of Joseph Losey films. The bizarre climax involves his decision to release horses from a burning barn in contravention of his officer's orders, and somehow we're supposed to feel that his needless death is caused by the coldness, bitterness and general hatefulness of his family. Robert has to free the horses to make up for those damn rabbits, and he has to defy military orders to get back at his parents. Down with Rosedale!

If *The Wars* is a bit pat, the limitations are probably those inherent in Findley's 1977 novel, which has some great sequences and an impressively sustained ironic distance to make up for its lack of emotional depth and original ideas. Phillips has managed to catch the tone of the book, which is what usually gets away in a film, and he has framed the action effectively and given it the resonance of being filtered through time and memory. Jackie Burroughs, looking wrinkled and mystical, is very effective as an old servant, though her role isn't as entertainingly flamboyant as the one she had in *The Grey Fox*. The supporting cast includes many Toronto/Stratford actors—Alan Scarfe, Barbara Budd, Domini Blythe and Clare Coulter—and the handsome art direction is by Daphne Dare, one of Phillips' most loyal collaborators.

The slightness of Findley's conceit was partly camouflaged by his narrative style, but it becomes more apparent when dramatized. But many people will be impressed by this film, because it does something that hasn't often been achieved in Canadian movies; it's an elegant-looking, expertly crafted period piece. There's a conventionalism at the heart of *The Wars* which suggests something for PBS that could be treasured by people who hate television (and all pop culture), and it's not my favorite kind of movie. But unlike *The Tin Flute*, *The Wars* has been made with enough style and finesse to ensure that audiences will take it seriously. This is one of the few English Canadian movies likely to be received as a cultural event. The literary establishment can accept it. And those who've been wishing Canadian movies could be more like Australian movies will love it.

*Toronto Life*, November 1983

# *Burnout in the Great White North*

## BY JAY SCOTT

*Most of what we have chosen to include in this volume has been selected for its ability to present detailed, coherent arguments pertaining to specific areas within the broad spectrum of cinema in Canada. Our instincts mitigated against overviews that attempt to deal simultaneously with the aesthetic, cultural, political and economic nature of feature filmmaking in both official languages. This said, we could not resist sympathizing with the task taken on by Jay Scott here: an explanation to a largely American audience of Canada's systematic undermining of a filmic milieu. Scott's generalizations concerning films, filmmakers and vast areas of modern Canadian life are as accurate as they are disturbing.*

*What Scott does here is to offer us the seemingly innocent reminder that there was to have been a Canadian New Wave. The world expected more* Goin' Down the Road*'s and* Mon oncle Antoine*'s. It was a bit disappointing when they turned out to be* Final Assignment *and* Happy Birthday, Gemini. *And yet, as Scott argues, despite all obstacles, talented filmmakers do stay in Canada and work here. His recognition of Francis Mankiewicz, Zale Dalen, Jean Pierre Lefebvre and Ralph Thomas in an American publication makes a genuine contribution to the long-overdue celebration of genuine Canadian talent. And, as Scott's postscript indicates, there is still some hope for the production and distribution of Canadian features by and about Canadians.*

Prologue and Epilogue:
December 15, 1980

Prime Minister Pierre Trudeau, in black tie, a blood-red rose ever so slightly wilted on his satin jacket collar, looked pensive. A journalist had gestured toward the ballroom at Toronto's Four Seasons Hotel, the scene of Canada's most elegant and expensive movie premiere party to date. As usual, the party was better than the movie to which it paid tribute, which was *Tribute*. Taking in the furs, the diamonds, the hairdos, the journalist had commented, "Your government is in some sense responsible for all this." The prime minister smiled. "It's amazing what a few tax laws can do," he said. Then he added, with a shrug, "There are now many Canadian films. But there aren't too many good ones, are there?"

In fifteen words, Trudeau not only summed up the state of the Canadian film industry, he also implied that the Canadian Film Development Corporation, charged with creating a film industry in Canada, and the Film Festivals Bureau, charged with promoting that industry, were less than truthful. For months, they had been telling the world that Canada was the Australia of North America. And now the man whose government had made an unprecedented movie production boom possible—by allowing passage, in 1978, of a liberalized tax shelter law for film investment—was joining the critics. A year after the offhand comments at the *Tribute* party, the Trudeau government would announce substantial revisions to the tax shelter law—revisions clearly designed to control what had become a flood of con men, carpetbaggers, and some folks with real ability (such as Louis Malle) to the "Hollywood of the North." From 1979 to 1981, a staggering 130 feature films were financed in Canada (compared with fifteen a year in the mid-seventies); as 1981 drew to a close, almost half had yet to see theatrical release.

The future of the industry in Canada remains uncertain. What is beyond doubt is that the government is determined not to repeat the wildest weeks of the past few years—weeks when movies were being made from coast to coast, when second-rate American stars were being paid fabulous sums to appear in disaster films shot "entirely on location in Montreal," when inexperienced producers sent the negative and only print of a $5 million picture through the luggage system of a commercial airline, when to comply with government regulations Canadian personnel were listed in movie credits while the real jobs went to Americans, when Dennis Hopper would say, "Canada's a positive place, maybe I'll move there," and when Canadian actress Colleen Dewhurst, disgusted by it all, would recall her first day on the set of a thriller fittingly entitled *Final Assignment*. "It was supposed to be in Russia," Miss Dewhurst said in her inimitable growl. "I walked up and fingered the set. It wiggled. I was to perform in front of a *cardboard Kremlin*. Dear God, I knew then we were in trouble. It was another Canadian film that was supposed to fool the audience into thinking it was an American film. We Canadians are *people*. Surely our stories are as universal as French or German stories."

Dewhurst's complaint has been the most common criticism of the New Canadian Cinema—that there *is* no New Canadian Cinema, that there is instead a New American Cinema on Canadian soil. The Australians make movies about and usually with Australians. The Canadians make movies about and often with Americans. *Middle Age Crazy*, starring Bruce Dern, was set in a Toronto disguised as Houston, and *The Changeling*, starring George C. Scott, was set in a Vancouver disguised as Seattle. A continual, cavalier disregard of their topography, not to mention their culture, infuriates many Canadians.

Outfitting New York as Paris on a movie set might not bother Americans, but Americans, insecure about so much, are not insecure about their identity. The very definition of Canadian identity, however, is that it is too insecure to be defined. And Canadians have noticed that the quality films of other countries do not go out of their way to grossly curry favour with the Americans. The filmmakers of Italy do not seem terrified that a film with an Italian locale will be dismissed out of hand by an American audience merely for being *set* in Italy. But Canadian producers were convinced, for a time, that American audiences would bolt from the theatre should the words Winnipeg or Toronto or Ottawa fall from actors' lips, save in jest; Canadian designations were permitted only when used as representations of the names of impossible, colourful, comic places.

## ROOTS I: THE OLD NEW WAVE

Canadian cinema—what there was of it—came into the seventies carrying naught but goodwill. John Grierson had made the National Film Board the toast of the civilized cinematic world, and animator Norman McLaren was its in-house saint. It was true, as writer Robert Fulford remarked to critic Martin Knelman, that "English-speaking Canadians grew up believing they would eventually *graduate* from Canada. Real things happened elsewhere." But it was also true that Canadians were trying to understand the reasons for that phenomenon and that in so doing they would soon release a remarkable series of films. At the end of the sixties and in the early seventies, there were, for example, Don Shebib's *Goin' Down the Road*, about two hicks in the big city of Toronto, and Claude Jutra's *Mon oncle Antoine*, widely thought to be the greatest Canadian film ever made. It's a study of a mining town through the eyes of a child, and a politicized version of *The 400 Blows*.

*Goin' Down the Road* and *Mon oncle Antoine* were the strongest examples of the new wave; strength to Canadians meant that the Jutra and Shebib films opened in New York to good reviews. But there were others. William Fruet's *Wedding in White*, with the then unknown Carol Kane as a pathetic child-woman trapped in a Second World War prairie town, was one of them. Today, Fruet, who also wrote *Goin' Down the Road*, directs horror movies of execrable quality (*Death Weekend, Cries in the Night*, the forthcoming *Death Bite*). In 1972, Gilles Carle's *La vraie nature de Bernadette* contained the dazzling debut of Micheline Lanctôt. Today, after embarrassing himself with *Fantastica*, a self-indulgent ecological musical that mercifully vanished after opening the 1980 Cannes Film Festival, Carle has returned to prominence with *Les Plouffe*. It derives from a popular novel of a French Canadian family, and has been made into no fewer than three popular movie editions (and Canadians are not an extravagant people)—one for Quebec, one for English Canada, and one for an international audience.

Allan King's 1969 cinéma vérité record of *A Married Couple*, ninety-seven minutes in the bickering lives of Billy and Antoinette Edwards, anticipated *An American Family*. Today, King is the director of Ellen Burstyn's *Silence of the North*, an inept paean to a pioneer woman, and a box-office flop. Don Owen in 1964 directed *Nobody Waved Good-bye*—"Marvellous," wrote Brendan Gill in the *New Yorker*. Today, Owen has become a sadly familiar fixture in Toronto, reduced to talking about projects he may never be allowed to realize. In 1970, Paul Almond caused nationwide controversy with *The Act of the Heart*, in which Geneviève Bujold set herself aflame to protest the way we were. Today, Almond is famous as the director of *Final Assignment*, which is famous for its cardboard Kremlin.

Most of the old new wave came to grief, on the beach. The reasons are various, most traceable to money, the rest to bad timing. After the surge in the early seventies, directors were left without outlets, unless they wished to work for the National Film Board or the Canadian Broadcasting Corporation. The days of independent shoestring movies were all but over. By the end of the decade, when tax shelter productions were going strong, it had been years since many of the old guard had worked. But their services were frantically sought, and they were perplexed recipients of big stars and big budgets from producers who often had no experience with either. There were exceptions—Garth Drabinsky, producer of *The Silent Partner, The Changeling*, and *The Amateur*; Denis Héroux and John Kemeny, producers of *Atlantic City* and *Quest for Fire*—but they were of the rule-proving sort.

Worse, in conforming to the demands of "international production," directors who did work under the tax shelter laws were wrenched from subjects they knew, in order to direct ersatz American product. They were asked to move comfortably in genres and styles hopelessly alien to them. Paul Almond's cinema is personal and mystical—ergo, he is hired to helm an international thriller. Jutra's greatest achievement is the stylized celebration of a specific rural French Canadian milieu; he is therefore restricted to other people's scripts in a language not his own (English). The tax shelter laws appeared on the surface to be great equalizers: Everybody got a chance. It was the exact nature of the chance that was the problem; for some of the old new wave, being given a chance meant you never had one.

## ROOTS II: THE NEW NEW WAVE

In the mid-seventies, two Canadians were busy imitating American movies to commercial, if not aesthetic, advantage. Ivan Reitman made something called *Cannibal Girls*. David Cronenberg made *The Parasite Murders* (a.k.a. *Shivers* and *They Came From Within*), which Reitman produced. Then Reitman coproduced *National Lampoon's Animal House* and directed *Meatballs* (the most successful Canadian film of all time.) Then Cronenberg directed *Scanners*. Now Cronenberg is completing *Videodrome*, starring Deborah Harry, the ice queen of another kind of new wave.

Back in 1975, Bob Clark made an effectively nasty horror flick, *Black Christmas*—and went on to *Murder by Decree*, with Christopher Plummer as Sherlock Holmes, and to that glossy $8 million Jack Lemmon fan letter, *Tribute*. Daryl Duke made *Payday* in the early seventies and *The Silent Partner* in the late seventies.

Ted Kotcheff (*The Apprenticeship of Duddy Kravitz, North Dallas Forty*) and Norman Jewison (*In the Heat of the Night, Jesus Christ Superstar*), proud of being Canadian and prouder still, perhaps, of getting regular work in the United States, became the elder statesmen of Canadian film.

One of the upstarts unexpectedly fell short: Richard Benner, the American expatriate who directed *Outrageous!*, the $167,000 Craig Russell picture that in 1977 caused a sensation in both New York and Toronto with its robust profile of an outlandish female impersonator. Benner moved back to New York and brought a version of the Albert Innaurato play *Gemini* to the screen. The result, *Happy Birthday, Gemini!*, was greeted in most quarters as a harbinger of herpes.

## WHERE WERE THE YOUNGSTERS? WHERE WERE THEIR ELDERS?

1. Where one of the elders could be found: a demonstration of what could go wrong in Hollywood of the North.

Claude Jutra was hired by Toronto producer Beryl Fox (who did the Vietnam documentary *Mills of the Gods*) to direct *Surfacing*, based on a novel by Margaret Atwood. The book is in the we-are-the-Swedes-of-North-America tradition of Canadian literature; it is a bleak, allusive, metaphoric interior odyssey in which the unnamed heroine comes to terms (maybe) with her dead father, with the Americans she nationalistically despises, with the land that begat her (the lake country of northern Quebec), and with the land to which she has repaired, the dank terrain of her own self-destructiveness. Imagine *The Bell Jar* in the bush.

Fox hired an American screenwriter, Bernard Gordon, best known for *55 Days at Peking*, of all things, to adapt the book. She hired the American actress Kathleen Beller as the Atwood alter ego, and the American actors Timothy Bottoms and his younger brother, Joseph. Canadian actors, who in general respect Fox and the feminism she stands for, were furious—but privately. (When the elder Bottoms dropped out, though, the Canadian R. H. Thomson took over.) Jutra, when it was all over, intimated he was enamoured of neither novel nor screenplay; what he did not need to intimate was that he needed the work. When *Surfacing* finally emerged, an intransigently Canadian, intransigently anti-American novel had become an astonishing thing: a film *with* Americans, a film somewhat *by* Americans, and a film almost *for* Americans—a film in which anything that might offend an American audience was carefully excised. (Canadians have yet to recognize a law to which the British have profitably adhered for years: Yanks will queue up for highbrow insults.)

2. Where one of the youngsters could be found: a demonstration of what could go right in Hollywood of the North.

Francis Mankiewicz is a relative of Herman (*Citizen Kane*) Mankiewicz and Joseph (*All About Eve*) Mankiewicz. He is in his early thirties, he lives in Montreal, he is bilingual. He is the director of *Les bons débarras*, a film that won for Marie Tifo the best actress award at the 1980 Chicago Film Festival and that won virtually every Academy of Canadian Cinema award possible. And it did mighty fine in its New York release.

*Les bons débarras* is as Canadian as self-doubt. The film, set in a small Quebec town, was written by Réjean Ducharme in a poetic French Canadian patois impossible to adequately translate—consider a Gallic Tennessee Williams by way of Flannery O'Connor. (Mankiewicz was anxious to see John Huston's adaptation of O'Connor's *Wise Blood* and said of Huston's *Fat City*, "It's a perfect Quebec movie.") *Les bons débarras*'s conflict is between a woman (Tifo) having an affair with a cop, and her preternaturally mature thirteen-year-old daughter (Charlotte Laurier). The daughter reads *Wuthering Heights* and greets *mère*'s announcement she is pregnant with, "A baby cop? You make me sick!" The picture was made on a minuscule, $625,000 budget without taking advantage of the tax shelter laws. Thanks to the expertise and artistry of Mankiewicz and Ducharme, and thanks to the genius of cameraman Michel Brault (director of the galvanizing 1975 documentary *Les ordres*), *Les bons débarras* has become one of the most honoured Canadian movies in history.

## WHY SOME STORIES HAVE NO ENDINGS, HAPPY OR OTHERWISE

Mankiewicz was lucky: *Les bons débarras* was distributed. Zale Dalen was not so lucky. He is a Vancouver filmmaker whose first picture, *Skip Tracer*, a tough portrait of a bill collector, has been a staple on the festival circuit. His second film was *The Hounds of Notre Dame*, based on the renowned (in Canada) exploits of Père Athol Murray, who ran a school for boys on the prairies during the Second World War. As stunningly brought to larger-than-life in the film by actor Thomas Peacocke, Murray is a cross between Jean Brodie and Mayor Daley. In accepting his Genie for best actor, Peacocke thanked the cosmos and then noted ironically, "No one's seen the movie." *The Hounds of Notre Dame* opened briefly in western Canada; it has never played Vancouver, Montreal, or Toronto.

Most of those sixty-odd Canadian films that have failed to find distribution are dreck. But as Margo Raport, editor of *Filmworld*, the Canadian trade paper, observes, "They should be sold somewhere. There are all kinds of markets." The federal government's Canadian Film Development Corporation (CFDC), which invests in both commercial and arty films, with an unfortunate emphasis on the former, has been supremely successful at getting movies made. But its mandate is sadly sketchy as to what it can or cannot do once they are in the can; the CFDC refused, for example, to assist in underwriting *Les bons débarras*'s New York opening.

## WITHOUT HANDS: THE POST-TAX SHELTER FUTURE

Jean Pierre Lefebvre is Canada's most accomplished filmmaker, director of some twenty features, among them a sympathetic study of an act of high school vandalism, *Avoir 16 ans*; a look at the commercialization of human emotion by late-night phone-in shows, *L'amour blessé*; and the finest film extant on the subject of Canadian identity, *Le vieux pays où Rimbaud est mort*. Conceptually indebted to Godard, Lefebvre has refined his minimalist technique. *Avoir 16 ans*, his most recent feature, which critic Peter Harcourt has described as combining "the human feeling of Renoir with the formal austerity of Michael Snow," was shot in colour in 35mm. It cost approximately $100,000. "You can make movies for ten people," comments Lefebvre, whose visual essays are admittedly "difficult" and are rarely distributed outside art galleries. "But if you make movies for ten people, they better cost ten bucks."

There are and probably will continue to be funds for films perceived as sure things: for Ralph Thomas's drama about Moonies, *Ticket to Heaven*, which got greater critical and commercial acclaim in New York than anywhere in Canada; for Charles Jarrott's *The Amateur*, a thriller with John Savage filmed in Toronto and Vienna, to be released this spring. Nothing else is predictable. Lefebvre's economy works well for him, but the nurturance of a nascent Francis Coppola in Canada is unthinkable right now.

"We are in a third era," Margo Raport says. "The first was pre-tax-shelter, the second was tax shelter and now we have entered the post-tax-shelter era. That means that new ways of financing will have to be sought, and I think you will see co-ventures with the major studios. The French will be less affected, because they never used the law much. Ironically, they were just getting ready to, but the revisions make it worthless for them. Pay television is going to determine to a large degree the direction of feature production. With Ottawa's Canadian content regulations, at least twenty-five and up to forty new films have to be produced in this country every year for pay television. That's at minimum two a month, in a country of twenty-two million. How?"

There is no answer to Raport's question. The metaphor most often employed for Canada vis-à-vis the United States is of a mouse sleeping next to an elephant: The elephant can move with impunity, but each twitch is for the mouse a potentially life-threatening situation. Many Canadians—French and English—think that the United States' cultural colonization of their nation may be, with the advent of pay television, a fait accompli. The tax shelter law was seen as a last-ditch effort to create a film industry nearly sixty years too late; for everyone but the producers, the result was a deluge of disappointment.

Shortly before the law was set in place, Pierre Berton looked at the development of Canada's image of itself at the movies. He entitled his witty book *Hollywood's Canada* in recognition of a bizarre paradox: From the twenties on, Canadians bought at American movies an image of themselves that had nothing to do with their own reality. But given the opportunity to bring their disparate experiences to the screen, to engender their own dreams and to immortalize their own mythologies, they opted in most instances for a slavish imitation of American dreams, for a crude approximation of American mythology and its attendant iconography. The recent record of the Canadian film industry might be called Canada's Hollywood.

*American Film*, 7, No. 5 (March 1982)

Margo Raport was right. Pay television did to some extent influence the course of Canadian filmmaking, most happily vis-à-vis that bona fide Canadian success story shot for Home Box Office, *The Terry Fox Story*—and the industry otherwise calmed down and began producing a reasonable string of successes and failures.

By the summer of 1984, there was an impressive list of achievements (including but not limited to *The Grey Fox* and *The Wars*) and an equally predictable list of fiascos (including but not limited to *The Tin Flute* and *Maria Chapdelaine*). In all, the industry was neither ailing nor admirable; it was at last consonant with, and to some degree reflective of, the size, ambitions and culture(s) of the country.

1984

# *The Best Film Policy This Country Never Had*

## BY SANDRA GATHERCOLE

*The history of any aspect of Canadian life, we are often told, does not begin before the creation of an institutional structure designed to contain it. Exploration waited for the Hudson's Bay Company; westward expansion was organized by the Mounties and the* CPR. *The same interpretation of Canadian history tells us that the arts languished before the creation of the Canada Council and that our cinema was a sometime thing until the Film Act of 1939. As a corollary, the future of artistic creativity, particularly in something as complex and expensive as film, must wait for a definitive policy statement.*

*Sandra Gathercole's contribution here is a history of that statement and why we have had so much trouble making it. What is most telling about Canadian film policy, she argues, is the simplicity of the conclusions that are arrived at in study after study. Given our vulnerability to the economics of Hollywood production, one of a very small number of feasible protectionist measures must be taken. The size of the Canadian audience mandates a few, rather obvious, proven forms of support. Unfortunately, as Gathercole points out, the history of Canadian film policy is one of sustained and determined avoidance of the obvious. What is missing, she tells us, is the will to get the job done.*

*Is it a job worth doing? Is the creation of a national cinema—as art or industry—a realistic priority when so many Canadians are perfectly content with the imported product? Cinema is one of the few American products that remains unchallenged abroad. Does Canada really have the resources to make that challenge and, having done so, to sustain the wrath of our largest trading partner? In a sense, Canada is a test case for how much indigenous popular culture the American imagination machine will allow. As Gathercole sadly concludes here, it may be a test that we have programmed ourselves to fail.*

There is a story, perhaps apocryphal, of a 1965 Canada-US partnership agreement negotiated by America's Livingston Merchant and Canada's Arnold Heeney. Halfway through the numerous clauses (Heeney having conceded every one of them to the US) Livingston Merchant leaned across the table and said, "You take this one for Canada, Arnold. It will look good when you get home."

Over the years, the Canadian government's record of success in negotiations with American government and business interests has been a running joke. The Americans have come to know and love us as the country which, given an inch, will take half an inch and go away happy. Rather like the good old days when the

Indians sold Manhattan Island for trinkets. The Indians, of course, woke up long ago.

American control of Canadian cinemas has epitomized the syndrome. Canadian movie houses were built to show American movies and have remained a territorial monopoly for American distributors. Canada is Hollywood's number one foreign market, paying ninety-three per cent of all theatrical film rentals to the likes of Paramount and Warner Bros. Approximately one and a half per cent of the massive $240 million annual Canadian box office goes to Canadian film production which is thus limited, and chronically under-financed.

For fifty years, the Canadian government has been bemoaning the situation:

> For years I have been convinced that the film situation is one of very great danger to this Dominion . . .
>
> Prime Minister R.B. Bennett
> September 16, 1931

For thirty years, the government has been threatening to do something about it. In 1948 there was the Canadian Cooperation Project: Hollywood's response to pressure from Mackenzie King, C.D. Howe and Louis St. Laurent (later a member of the board of Famous Players) to leave behind some of the millions they were extracting from the Canadian box office. This was the first "voluntary agreement" and Pierre Berton enshrined it in *Hollywood's Canada* as "what the Americans had always wanted it and intended it to be: a public relations operation and nothing more."

Since the formation of the Canadian Film Development Corporation in 1968, successive secretaries of state have publicly scolded Hollywood's representatives, and threatened drastic action (some form of quota protection and tax on box-office earnings) if the Americans didn't clean up their act.

> Secretary of State Judy LaMarsh, yesterday served notice on Canadian cinema chains . . . that the Government expects them to show more Canadian-made feature films in the future. If this is not forthcoming, she indicated the Government may have to impose quotas on foreign films.
>
> *Globe and Mail*, June 21, 1968

> . . . we are looking into quota systems . . . and the problem of foreign ownership of our distribution companies and film theatres.
>
> Secretary of State Gerard Pelletier
> Film Policy Speech, July 1972

By 1973, moral suasion of this sort having failed, a new secretary of state, Hugh Faulkner, set up a new "voluntary agreement" for the showing of Canadian films, to be replaced by a legislated quota if it did not succeed within one year. After a year it was clear that this "voluntary agreement" was not performing. The newly formed Council of Canadian Filmmakers demanded legislative action, and CFDC executive director Michael Spencer told the *Toronto Star*, "We want a levy (box office tax). We want a quota." His Advisory Group passed a resolution backing him up. In May 1975 secretary of state Hugh Faulkner stated in a speech to the Commons Committee:

> In July, 1973, I negotiated a voluntary quota with Famous Players and Odeon . . . I am not satisfied with the results of this agreement . . . It has been evident for some time now that a more effective system must be found.

On August 5, the "more effective system" was announced. It amounted to a more effective voluntary agreement, and Faulkner said:

> I am gratified that Famous Players and Odeon have seized the initiative and responded positively to this increased quota plan. This new agreement, much broader in every way than the earlier one, has the potential to be really effective.

The potential was not realized. Famous Players met thirty-seven per cent of its commitment; Odeon lagged behind. The 1976–77 Annual Report of the CFDC stated:

> Tabulations for the first year's performance of Famous Players under the Quota Program show that, if the Program is to be literally interpreted, this company has not met its commitment . . . As for Odeon . . . the program was not a success . . . .

In 1976 John Roberts burst into the secretary of state's office like a heavy-weight Man From Glad. Roberts was informed, sympathetic, and he talked tough to the Americans, making it clear whose interests it was his job to protect. If the Hollywood companies were aghast, the Canadian film industry was buoyant. It had found a champion.

Last November, Roberts presented Cabinet with a Memorandum on Film Policy which confronted foreign control head-on. The document proposed a ten per cent tax on distribution revenues, with a rebate which would have functioned as a quota for Canadian films. Such measures would have doubled the funds available to the CFDC while virtually eliminating the need for the $4 million annual tax subsidy it receives. Roberts justified his fiscal proposals this way:

> Canada is the largest foreign market in the world for American films. Despite this fact, distributors have never really contributed to the development of the Canadian industry, either by investment or by assuring effective distribution of Canadian films in Canada or abroad. . . . Almost all other countries have already adopted equivalent measures (if not more radical ones) than those which we are recommending here. . . . By imposing such a tax, we would not be inventing anything new but would only be adopting a practical measure utilized by other countries. . . . They [fiscal measures] must constitute the essence of an important policy which I propose to announce in the next six weeks.

Because the measures had teeth, Roberts took the precaution of checking with a top financial house to ensure that they didn't contravene provincial, national or international tax obligations. He also warned the cabinet that:

> Foreign distributors will violently oppose these fiscal measures and will use their influence in Washington. The American Government will likely threaten to take counter measures, for example, excluding Canadian films from the American market.

On January 30 of this year, Roberts made it clear, in the following exchange in the House with the Conservative culture critic, that he was still planning a strong policy:

> David MacDonald: Mr. Speaker, can he [Mr. Roberts] say . . . that it will be more than just a continuation of the present voluntary agreements which are obviously hopelessly inadequate?
>
> Hon. John Roberts: Yes, Mr. Speaker . . . it will be much more extensive than a continuation of the voluntary agreements. . . .

Last month Roberts stood before the Commons Committee on Broadcasting, Film, and Assistance to the Arts (now called the Committee on Culture and Communications) and announced a lame excuse for a film policy—a pale shadow of his original design. It was precisely what he had assured Mr. MacDonald it would not be: a continuation of the hopelessly inadequate voluntary agreements.

Somewhere along the line—in Cabinet or, more likely, in Jean Chrétien's office—the film policy we were supposed to have had been sabotaged. The bold statements about the cultural *raison d'être* and the necessity of fiscal measures were gone. Roberts was now taking a "pragmatic" approach: "jigging" the present system rather than "renovating" it.

And jigging it was. The only substantive moves—a marginal increase in National Film Board contracting to the private sector; a $1 million increase to the CFDC earmarked for made-for-television movies; and a secondary distribution network—were an attempt to make the public and private sectors compatible and reroute Canadian films away from the main arenas into church halls and television. Other measures, such as improvement of an element of the capital cost allowance for film investors, were helpful but minor.

When it came to the central problem of foreign control of the educational and theatrical markets, the policy was a dead loss. The core of fiscal measures had been stripped out and the problem had been thrown back on the provinces (with whom the federal government has been playing political football on this issue for years), and onto gentlemen's agreements. Roberts repeated the diagnosis of the ailment offered in his November policy; it was the remedy which had changed:

> It is not acceptable that the present system works so overwhelmingly to present foreign films and so little to develop a market for Canadian material. . . . I expect them [distributors] to find methods . . . to provide a better distribution of Canadian films. . . . I intend to renegotiate an improved *voluntary quota* to ensure that Canadian films have better access to our cinemas. [emphasis added]

Noting that only one and a half per cent of the Canadian box office was going to Canadian filmmakers, Roberts said he was "hopeful" that the distributors would "take steps quickly to ensure greater investment." The people who brought us the problem were, once again, assigned to its solution. The most that distinguishes this new attempt from previous voluntary agreements is that the companies involved are, this time, under investigation by the federal governments in both the US and Canada for monopoly practices. Two of those companies have been charged under the Canadian Combines Investigation Act.

But the difference between the two policies was the difference between a sovereign nation and a colony, and it made clear who's in charge here. The first policy told the Americans what the rules of the game were and what the cost of doing business in their richest and softest market was going to be. The second policy was a supplicant, begging concessions from the landlord, and leaving the Canadian industry to operate on sufferance in its own country.

That difference was reflected in the disparate reaction the policies drew from Canadian and American sectors. The Canadians may have liked the original policy, but their response to the final version was incredulity and sarcasm. Coming after years of concerted lobbying (briefs, telegrams, meetings, and a 1,000 signature petition to Parliament signed by people like Norman Jewison and Norman McLaren) in support of a levy, the policy was a bitter disappointment.

ACTRA—whose position on voluntary agreements has always been that they are about as effective as voluntary income tax—called the policy a failure and said they would continue to work for a real policy.

The Canadian Film and Television Association's president, Fin Quinn, termed it "the proverbial elephant giving birth to a mouse," and asked what, given the past record of voluntary agreements, made the minister "think there will be an improvement now?"

Director Peter Pearson observed that the minister "went into Cabinet with a lion of a film policy and came out with kitty litter."

Kirwan Cox, chairman of the 14,000 member Council of Canadian Filmmakers, told the *Toronto Star*:

> The Government is under the delusion that you can support Canadian culture without interfering with American control of the marketplace. . . . Without some form of levy, the film policy is irrelevant.

The CFDC's Michael Spencer was quoted in the *Star* as saying:

> I thought there should have been a box-office levy, five cents on every ticket price, and that would have made the difference between profit and loss.

The Canadian public, according to a February CROP poll, agrees. That survey reported that a majority of Canadians would require all movie theatres to show Canadian films at least ten per cent of the time, and almost half would agree to pay an extra thirty-five cents on every ticket to support Canadian movies.

But the Liberal Cabinet wasn't listening to Canadians—the public, the industry, the CFDC, or even the secretary of state—when they nixed the original film policy. They were responding instead to the American threats, real or perceived, which Roberts had predicted. The Americans acknowledge their intervention but disclaim anything more than a gentle nudge in the right direction. An official of the US state department was quoted in the April 17 issue of *Maclean's* magazine as saying that his office had assumed the ten per cent tax wouldn't be approved "so we only had a junior officer call the (Canadian) embassy to tell them we wouldn't much like it." To add insult to injury, finance minister Jean Chrétien cavalierly told the same magazine that the tax had been chucked out because no one in the Canadian film community had made a case for it.

The Americans were as pleased with the final result as the Canadians were outraged. The ironically named Canadian Motion Picture Distributors Association (which is as Canadian as its members, among which are Paramount, Columbia, Universal, United Artists, Warner Bros., and 20th Century Fox), gave it rave reviews. Executive director Millard Roth said the film policy was "rather consistent with a lot of the views which we presented." George Heiber, CMPDA president, and Canadian general manager for United Artists, said:

> I'm pleased at this moment with the film policy statement. I think it is very fair. There were no limitations put on it. We're not putting any on the Government and they're not putting any on us.

Perhaps the most pernicious aspect of the policy was its capacity for extending the branch plant control of Heiber's member companies from distribution and exhibition into production. For example, a voluntary investment program, as opposed to a levy, leaves the control of the funds, and therefore control of what films are made, in their hands. The American companies have also made an agreement with Mr. Roberts to read and assess Canadian scripts, but the exploitative proviso is that the writer sign an unconditional waiver releasing those companies from any claim in the off chance that they produce a film which is "identical or similar" to the script submitted.

It may, therefore, not be a great loss if this latest incarnation goes the way of its predecessors and becomes merely another postponement of what everyone knows must eventually be done. Certainly Roberts himself has no real expectation that his agreement will amount to anything more. In response to press scepticism of the policy, he said:

> I don't think I ever said that I had faith that they would respond. I said that I was hopeful. . . . If we are going to take another approach . . . we must provide no excuse whatsoever for the argument that . . . they haven't been given a chance to show what they can do.

Short of a sign from God, the evidence of what they can do would seem to be in. Roberts came closer to the real reason for not proceeding with legislation in the following press comment:

> The chief factor hampering my policy formation was the economic reality. . . . We can't support an industry without access to the international market. And it's very difficult to get the co-operation we need from foreign distributors if we're clobbering them here. That's the key conundrum.

Last November—before he was spooked by the Americans or the cabinet or both—Roberts didn't see it as a conundrum. Then he was prepared to call the Americans' bluff. When he warned the cabinet of American threats of reprisal, he also advised them that "it is unlikely that the Motion Picture Association of America, or the American government, would want to risk the loss of the extremely profitable Canadian market." Precisely. If it comes down to a game of brinksmanship, Canada is holding all the cards. Our market is worth $60 million to the Americans, but it's doubtful we earn one per cent of that in theirs. The $6 million gain from the proposed levy would, at any rate, more than compensate us for the losses in the American market, were it ever totally withdrawn.

What Roberts appears to have forgotten, in the interim, is that his original levy proposal is a universal remedy which most countries have applied against the Americans. Because the Americans' commercial success is achieved at the expense of everyone else's (there is no commercially viable film industry, in an unprotected market, outside the US), levy has become the norm, rather than the exception, for the world's film industries. To it we owe Bergman, Truffaut, Fellini, Buñuel and most of our non-American film experience.

The countries applying this sanction have no less access to the American market than Canada. Our fear is based on a myth which other countries have discarded: the myth that somehow, if we are a good branch plant and forfeit control of our own market, the Americans will allow us into theirs where we will have a shot at the pot of gold at the end of the rainbow. The fact of the matter is that there is no entry to the American market—on a large scale—and there is little hope of realizing profits from films which do gain entry.

America is a media imperialist. It invented the concept of the free flow of information to justify its own unilateral penetration of foreign markets. The country which controls the world's film markets has not neglected to control its own. In fact, America is the world's most xenophobic and protectionist media market. It shares with Red China the distinction of having less (two per cent) of its television time devoted to foreign programming than any other nation (Russia imports five per cent). The last time UNESCO checked, the US stood alone as the world's most protected movie market: ninety-five per cent of all movies are domestic.

As for the pot of gold beyond the magic door . . . it doesn't exist for independent producers, be they Canadian, Timbuktuian, or even American. The list of independents who made a million in the American market fits on a postage stamp. The list of those who were ripped off is long and international. CFDC director, Michael Spencer, commented in the April issue of *Trade News North*:

> We've been in bed with the major companies from the very beginning. . . . There was *Fortune and Men's Eyes*; we never got any money back on that. You know, *Act of the Heart, Fan's Notes* . . . We never got any money back on any of these pictures. . . . We gave up on the US major companies sometime around about *Duddy Kravitz*.

Peter Guber, producer of *The Deep*, which made over $100 million at the box office, told the Los Angeles Filmex symposium that he had not seen a penny of profit. Al Ruddy, producer of *The Longest Yard*, made a similar charge at a Canadian seminar in January.

Just as the world will get solar energy, in a serious way, when and if Exxon figures out how to claim ownership of the sun, Canada will get their features into the American market if and when the American majors (which are themselves owned by massive multinationals like Gulf & Western and Trans-America), gain financial and creative control over our production. That is a possibility which suits too many of our pseudo-producers too well. Being agents for the Americans is personally profitable for them and many have made a life's work of compradorship. It also interests Hollywood: Universal Studios has already set up a Canadian production arm.

But personal profits for the American majors and a handful of Canadian businessmen is a very different thing from the potential social and cultural benefits for Canada in having a production industry of our own. A film industry designed to serve limited commercial imperatives will be a branch plant, and branch plants have no potential to serve a nation's larger goals in any industry, particularly not in the communications industry.

Despite the recent bonanza of truly excellent, and truly Canadian, features like *Why Shoot the Teacher, Outrageous!, Who Has Seen the Wind, One Man*, and *J.A. Martin photographe*, the Canadian industry is hovering on the edge of becoming such a branch plant. The majority of funds invested—and movies made—have nothing to do with this country. They are films which disguise their Canadian location by replacing Canadian flags and license plates with American; films which defy the fundamental truth of all great art—that it is uncompromisingly set in its own specific physical and social milieu. Such films amount to international nonsense and receive neither the critical nor the commercial success of the best of our indigenous products. Britain, having suffered this bitter lesson of concessions to internationalism, is now attempting to recover and is dedicated to making unashamedly British films.

If the Canadian industry is permitted to further drift in the American-controlled market system it was born into, its purpose will be perverted beyond redemption. Commercial logic will have triumphed over social logic once again in this country and the government will be hard pressed to explain what its multimillion dollar investment has been all about.

Unfortunately, the final film policy has encouraged, rather than retarded, that drift. If we are not going to be America's number one communications colony forever, the government is going to have to accept the world's wisdom and intervene in its own market, as John Roberts originally proposed. That's going to require making the essential distinction between good neighbourliness and selling out.

In the meantime, policies such as the Liberals have just delivered for film are compromising the country's needs. They mean the export of talent, jobs, and millions of dollars, which Canada has been doing since the days of Mary Pickford.

They put another generation of talent on hold. They postpone our development and blunt our sense of self. Ultimately, they are going to cost us our political and economic independence. They simply don't make sense.

*Cinema Canada*, 47, June 1978

It is 1984. Six years, and many millions in tax allowance subsidies to private production have gone under the bridge since John Roberts' aborted attempt to deal with theatrical distribution.

Open skies policies are turning Canadian television screens into the kind of extension of the American market that Canadian theatre screens have always been. Two per cent of the $360 million Canadian box office now goes to domestic films, up one half of one percentage point in the decade since Hugh Faulkner negotiated his notorious "voluntary agreement."

Pay television and the one hundred per cent Capital Cost Allowance have come and gone as the great white hopes for financing Canadian production. The Canadian Film Development Corporation, armed with a $35 million Broadcast Fund, has shifted focus to made-for-television production—tacit acknowledgment of the theatrical distribution blockade, and the surging expansion of television markets.

Despite the CFDC funds, production is stalled in the "bust" end of the boom-and-bust cycle, private Canadian investment having evaporated with the collapse of the CCA boom. Bankrolls that do exist tend to be American, and most production being financed owes its socks and soul south of the border.

These mirages of pay television, voluntary agreements and the Capital Cost Allowance have taught painful lessons:

- Without a secure distribution base at home, Canadian production will perpetually prostitute itself to the American market.
- There is no point in pouring public funds into production without corresponding measures to open domestic distribution.
- Moral suasion is not as effective as legislation when dealing with Hollywood, cable companies, or pay television licensees.

Now in its dying days, the Trudeau government delivers the National Film and Video Policy. It arrives almost as an afterthought, delayed by years of re-drafting (evident in an opening page phrase, "as we *enter* the 1980's"), just as the minister and the government are on their way out the door. It is riddled with unrealistic rhetoric: It refers to the CCA and pay television as "foundations" on which to build; it fears the "possibility" that Canada may be culturally swamped by the United States.

Even the policy's title is a form of Newspeak, since there is nothing "national" about its focus on exportable English-language feature films to the exclusion of French-language and regional filmmaking. Similarly, the "video" revolution it describes is not addressed in any practical terms within the document. The only indication that the authors recognize a problem with the performance of the CCA is unintentional: In a list of critically successful Canadian films, the hundreds of productions financed under the CCA are conspicuous by their absence. But bravado dissolves into parody when the document turns to theatrical distribution. Declaring itself ready to "Fight US Film Control," as *The Globe and Mail* put it, the policy proposes—you guessed it—a new round of voluntary agreements with the Americans.

This time negotiations will be with the Canadian Motion Picture Distributors Association rather than with theatre chains, and, as the minister is at pains to point out, these negotiations will be conducted on behalf of the government, not merely the minister. Failure to cooperate within six months will result in legislative measures which, it is stressed, remain available to the federal government. No reference is made to provincial jurisdiction over theatres, nor to the history of American intimidation of the federal government in this area.

Assistant deputy minister David Silcox tells the press that the CMPDA is likely to comply because "we have a lot of arrows in our quiver," which raises questions. How many arrows can a government in the process of dissolution have? Where will Francis Fox be in six months? These threats, and their impotence, remain the same; only the ministers change.

In rationalizing this return to a tried-and-failed approach, the policy echoes the 1982 Report of the Applebaum-Hébert Committee: Legislative market mechanisms are "protectionist" measures which would restrict the choice available to the Canadian audience. The document does not explain why voluntary arrangements designed to achieve the same purpose would not similarly limit choice.

For all its sabre-rattling, what this policy amounts to is an "if you can't beat 'em, join 'em" capitulation to the overriding commercial strength of Hollywood. Evidently the minister believes that entry into the American market is more essential to Canadian films than is repossession of their own market. To this end, he is going to attempt to negotiate the distribution of films into both markets via the CMPDA rather than legislate their distribution in Canada.

If the first thrust of the policy is acceptance of the Americanization of distribution, the second thrust is the privatization of production. Here again the policy reflects the export-oriented industrial strategy of the Applebaum-Hébert Report. As that report recommended, subsidy is to be further shifted from the publicly mandated National Film Board to the private sector.

While this policy stops short of the Applebaum-Hébert proposal to take the Film Board out of production entirely, it does transfer the NFB's traditional role as chosen instrument of government policy to the CFDC, herein renamed Telefilm Canada. The Board's international marketing function also goes to Telefilm Canada, while the private sector assumes all government-sponsored production. Freelance filmmakers are to be engaged for the bulk of the Board's remaining inhouse production. Several other NFB operations are transferred to government departments, or to oblivion, while the NFB is to concentrate on research and training.

No provision is made for improved distribution of the NFB's award-winning films either in theatres or, as the Board has requested, on a dedicated cable channel. It would appear that the NFB, which the policy terms "a synonym for excellence" of production is being penalized for ineffectual distribution, while the private industry, purveyor of assembly-line facsimiles which are deliberately unrecognizable as being Canadian and also poorly distributed, is being rewarded with increased subsidy.

This paring away of public production, begun with last year's Broadcast Policy that directed that fifty per cent of CBC television's non-news production be contracted out to the private sector, rests on the assumption that a heavily subsidized private sector can fill the uneconomic mandates of public production while remaining dependent on export markets for cost recovery. To this end, the film policy provides marketing subsidies to compensate producers for the continuing hostility of their domestic market.

But there is a fallacy. Production naturally takes on the cultural assumptions of its primary market. As long as the private sector is left stranded without assured access to its own market, and with its present over-reliance on the American market, it will produce those numbingly anonymous films with American flags and Home Box Office formulas to the exclusion of more economically marginal French-language, regional, or even Canadian productions.

Public subsidy schemes which require matching private funds actually exacerbate this branch plant syndrome by making producers dependent on investment which is increasingly available only from American sources. Consequently companies such as HBO are able to lever a disproportionate degree of control over publicly subsidized Canadian films. Any traces of Canadian origin left in by a Canadian producer may be removed by fiat from New York.

The fact that this policy cuts the core out of the National Film Board, while instituting measures which force private producers into export strategies, identifies it as industrial rather than cultural in nature. What cultural purpose can possibly be served by taking responsibility for Canada's international film image out of the hands of people (the NFB) who have brought home forty-six Academy Award nominations in forty-five years, and entrusting it to people (Telefilm Canada) whose job it is to sell *Porky's* and *Meatballs*?

The quid pro quo, of course, is job creation. So long as filmmakers are working, does it matter what they are making? But this is myopic. Branch plants are notoriously poor long-term employers. Even while they are in operation, the best talent is drawn away to the decision-making centre, leaving the less ambitious to toil as hewers and carriers—not the route to Academy Awards.

An ironic footnote to this production-for-export policy is the simultaneous expansion of a Bronfman-financed film conglomerate. The small Cineplex theatre chain has purchased the large Odeon chain, reportedly with Bronfman financing. This acquisition puts the largest block of Canadian theatres, as well as First Choice pay television and the Astral-Bellevue-Pathé laboratory and distribution companies all under the direct or indirect management of Harold Greenberg, producer of that quintessential branch-plant production, *Porky's*.

However these fine points were glossed over by press and producers alike. In the Liberals' best electioneering tradition, national interest was forfeited to vested interests, thereby muting criticism. Virtually no protest came from those most directly concerned, private producers. Canadian Film and Television Association president Stephen Ellis stated that, "This is a landmark in Canadian film history. Fox has taken our cause to heart." One had to wonder how much Canadian film history Ellis can know.

Far more disappointing was the fact that filmmakers like Allan King and Norman Jewison, who do know Canadian film history and are on the record in support of legislated rather than voluntary market intervention, reversed themselves to support the policy's voluntary approach. Said King, "This is a major step." The optimistic interpretation by François Macerola, newly appointed government film commissioner, surprised many: "It's a good policy which reaffirms the role of the National Film Board as a national distributor of socially and culturally relevant films." Ironically, it was Telefilm Canada's executive director André Lamy who rained on the Fantasy Island parade. CBC Radio reported his observation that, without market intervention, what we would be stepping toward would be a branch plant.

When the CFDC was being established, Liberal cabinet minister Jack Pickersgill warned that Canadians had to be careful that they didn't wind up making Hollywood's movies for it, and paying for the privilege. After sixteen years of pump-priming, the jury is still out on Pickersgill's prognosis. Can we indeed, in Hollywood's lengthening shadow, maintain a production industry which is anything more than a branch plant?

The odds are against it. Natural barriers of distance and language aren't there (with the exception of Quebec), and it is increasingly clear that legislative barriers are not going to stand in their stead. The government's ideological commitment to an unprotected market means that policy is perpetually being built in economic quicksand. The belief that Canada can play ball with the Americans and win has been maintained in the face of consistent evidence and advice to the contrary.

When he was president of the American Screen Actors' Guild, Ronald Reagan claimed that 107 countries of the world discriminated against American films. Canada was not among them.

On November 28, 1972, Famous Players' president George Destounis told a public forum at Toronto's St. Lawrence Centre, "My personal opinion, in case somebody is scared to ask the question, and not representing the opinion of the industry or my corporation, is that I favour quotas."

Quebec's Bill 109 requires distributors to invest a percentage of their gross annual revenue in Quebec films. The 1983 Federal Task Force On Distribution and Exhibition (Cohen Report) recommended federal intervention in the theatrical market.

But Ottawa is a town that trades in information while paying no attention to facts. It remains a true believer in the myth of the free market. Hollywood, in turn, goes on exploiting Ottawa's ingenuousness. That, after all, is Hollywood's business.

1984

# II

# *The English Screen*

# *The Silent Subject in English Canadian Film*

## BY SETH FELDMAN

*Given its common language, geographic proximity, and nearly complete economic dependence upon the United States, it is no surprise that English Canada has traditionally had some difficulty in establishing a truly independent form of self-expression. This is particularly true of our mass media. The history of the English Canadian feature film begins with decades of stillborn attempts at establishing Hollywoods of the North, and ends with the officially sanctioned (and subsidized) use of Canadian locales and Canadian talent to depict virtually anything American. Canadian radio and television were structured on the inspiring heritage of British public broadcasting. Both have since been remodelled by people who make no secret of the fact that they think of themselves as* de facto *American network affiliates.*

*This cultural domination has a prominent place in twentieth-century English Canadian folklore; the consideration of its effects is perhaps the beginning of a way out. What is suggested here is that the enforced silence of the culture in its most economically vulnerable medium, cinema, has become a tradition that is incorporated into the works themselves. The question of locating and maintaining a voice is inherent in characterizations, plots, voice-over narration and the lack of it. Silence, in a good many English Canadian films, takes on a certain majesty. It has a connotation of asserting the identity of a place and the people who inhabit it. Silence unites a pioneer people against the linguistic cultural dominance dictated from the Imperial centre.*

*Silence, then, becomes a voice for English Canadian cinema. It is not perhaps terribly different in its nature and intent from the feminist voice discussed elsewhere in this volume by Kay Armatage (see "About to Speak: The Woman's Voice in Patricia Gruben's* Sifted Evidence*"). It is the silence that accompanies a contemplation of photographic reality identified by R. Bruce Elder as central to Canadian cinematic pursuit ("Image: Representation and Object—The Photographic Image in Canadian Avant-Garde Film"). And, if in the context of Peter Harcourt and David Clandfield's articles on Pierre Perrault, it posits cinema without a "living" voice, then perhaps the theory of a silent English Canadian cinema may offer a point of comparison between the central realities of Canada's two distinct cinematic endeavours.*

A language is, among other things, a society's manifestation of its political realities. Canada's two official languages, protected tongues (native speech) and unassimilated ethnic languages are defined by the nation's history as political manifestations existing primarily in relation to one another. This definition goes beyond the legal bartering of language rights between the various constituencies. It is fought out daily on a personal conversational level. Within the flux of Canadian multilingualism, the language of any conversation is understood to be nothing more than a *lingua franca*, a temporary agreement entirely dependent upon the immediate situation and the good will of the speakers. The historical meta-linguistic context becomes painfully evident to an Anglophone stopped for speeding in rural Quebec. But it is no less present when two recent British immigrants sit down to tea in Victoria. Their language too is a bargain struck in defence of ethnic and individual integrity. Like all bargains, it works toward the exclusion of those not taking part. Taken together with the millions of daily bargains that constitute language in Canada, it helps to define that language as the reflection of all the happy and not so happy compromises that shape the nation itself.

Added to their meta-linguistic function is the self-contradictory nature of the two official languages in fulfilling the political and cultural objectives of the cultures that speak them. First French and, much later, English Canadians used the old Imperial languages as a means of declaring a certain distinction from those around them. Part of the affinity between the francophone intellectual and his anglophone counterpart comes from an appreciation by the latter that the British usages with which he differentiates himself from the Buffalo weatherman are a pale and late imitation of the manner in which the French language has protected culture in Quebec. But the flaw in this strategy—for both cultures—has been the need to enforce a linguistic conservatism in the face of what appears to be perfectly natural linguistic evolution. The American-style consumerism practised in English Canada tends to be preached in a half-hearted translation of "color" into "colour" and "zee" into "zed." Quebec—confronted by both the American plastic language and its Canadian Anglophone bastardization—has reacted with a more-academie-than-vous legislation of archaic, irrational but correct French usage.

The linguistic siege mentalities in both English and French Canada have been central in the shaping of their respective cinemas. In Quebec, the equation between language and cinema is self-evident to the point of being clichéd. The importance of language to that cinema is well described by Peter Ohlin as he paraphrases the intentions of Pierre Perrault:

> . . . when the filmmaker reproduces the images and sound of a person speaking, this is a way of reliving or reviving an experienced event; and just as the spoken language is a kind of memory, consisting of a lexicon of words and phrases with different associations grappling with an experience of the past, so the language of film is a similar memory. And that action which consists of photographing a speaking person can be experienced by both the filmmaker and the spectator as an attempt to rediscover the language—maybe just those words or that aspect of language which rationally or emotionally defines your relation to history or society, for instance, through the linguistic tradition. To rediscover language this way is to unite the past with the present, linguistically and historically. This union can be made concrete in different ways, but above all it belongs to the basic situation of the filmmaker and his work, that is the reorganization of the material which occurs when he cuts into the celluloid strip and decides what to include and what to exclude. This is not a matter of objectivity, but rather of that creative mystery which makes it possible for one human being simply to respond in language to another human being.[1]

What Ohlin asserts, first with regard to the manner in which both the subject and spectators locate themselves within language, and second with regard to filmic codes as mediators in the process, is especially valid in discussing Perrault's work and the observational genesis of contemporary cinema in Quebec. To study cinema in that culture is to listen for achievement. As a founder of a distinct Quebec cinema, Perrault set as a priority for that cinema a realization of form through the search for linguistic nuance and dysfunction. David Clandfield points out that Perrault shapes his film around the finding of language.[2] And, although Perrault is far from universally admired in Quebec, his colleagues and successors have generally perpetuated filmic constructs that owe much to Perrault's anthropological ear. Jacques Leduc, in films like *Tendresse ordinaire* and the *Chronique de la vie quotidienne* series has, if anything, extended Perrault's aural patience. Jean Pierre Lefebvre has dramatized it, Mireille Dansereau has feminized it and Andre Blanchard has explored its regional connotations. Even the directors of what are to be bilingual productions—for example, Gilles Carle's *Les Plouffe*—must work by balancing the integrity of their characters' *joual* against the possibility of a meaningful translation.

However when we attempt to characterize English Canadian cinema, we cannot attribute to it the innovative, open narrative structures and the highly loquacious sound-tracks generally associated with film in Quebec. The simple explanation is that English Canada has not yet had its Perrault; there has yet to be an English Canadian filmmaker who is willing to distinguish the nature of his or her culture on the basis of language. There are, to be sure, films in which deprived groups are recognized by and suffer for their use of foreign tongues or heavily accented Canadian English. On the other end of the social scale, those affecting inappropriate British or Scots accents may be singled out as aristocratic villains. But seldom, in either documentary or feature films, are local usages allowed to stand as themselves when a more universal British or American English may be substituted.

This too has its history. Embodied in English Canadian usage is the lost struggle with the two Imperial anglophone entities that have dominated and continue to dominate the nation. More specifically, local usages tend to be associated with narrower utilitarian functions while the Imperial centre (London or New York) generates the language of thought. The language of English Canada, in this context, has the function of naming the kinds of wood to be hewn and water to be drawn. Canadian English could be the basis for speech in anthropological films. But it would serve to make those films solely anthropological, portraits of native workers made by those who, having conquered, may study them.

But there is another, more positive aspect to colonial language. All the peoples of the New World have shared the difficulty in naming an inherently unknowable other, an environment whose characteristics do not lend themselves to the syntax of a "mother tongue." As a result, they have embedded in the history of their language a certain doubt as to the efficacy of language itself; the grammar of the New World is always undermined by the grammar of change. There is the possibility that the naming process, the assimilation of a new environment into the restrictions of an older civilization, will not work. Margaret Atwood's poem, "Progressive Insanities of a Pioneer," offers a succinct vision of the dilemma when she writes:

> Things
> refused to name themselves; refused
> to let him name them . . .

And a few lines later:

> the green
> vision, the unnamed
> whale invaded.[3]

Civilization, as Atwood defines it here, is the product of a linguistic, and thus conceptual, conquest of that which is found by the pioneer. The implication of the poem is that the colonial naming process will never be satisfactory and that the namer will be forever limited to the chaos of inadequate conceptualization.

The distinction between Atwood's characterization of English Canadian culture and Pierre Perrault's interaction with the "found" poetry of Quebec is as straightforward as the distinction between English and French traditions of colonization in North America. The English "cleared" the land, destroying what they could not assimilate. The French proclivity for "going native," that is, assimilating themselves into the demands of the environment and practices of native cultures, was perhaps the product of necessity (small populations, the relative disinterest of the mother country). But, for a variety of cultural, political and psychological reasons, the Québécois' tendency to unite with the found Other has been rejected by anglophone Imperialism in Canada as an affront to its entire historical context. The *coureurs de bois*, Métis and the FLQ's armed *habitant* are the bogeymen of the English Canadian imagination, just as Kurtz's "the horror" in Joseph Conrad's *Heart of Darkness* is the unnamable nightmare of anglophone Imperialism as a whole.

Nowhere is English Canada's fear of the unnamable more evident than in the products of the first years of the National Film Board. By bringing with him the language of the Imperial centre—in this case, the international lexicon of geopolitics—John Grierson arrived in Canada with the confidence of a linguistic pioneer. "The green vision," to use Atwood's term, would become the Greene version. Lorne Greene, the voice of the Board's prestige documentaries and newsreel series, could not only define the images (usually "found" footage) of the vast landscape of the Second World War, but he could do so with a speed and efficiency that defied nuance and contradiction. More than simply naming images, voice-overs in the wartime films twisted them into preconceived ideas. The image of a wall (one wall, a specific wall, somewhere) was made by the voice-over to signify (only) the idea of a facade. Clouds parting became a new era. And, with the careful editing of sound, image and music, these conceptual impositions upon specific images could be layered one atop the other to form increasingly complex and didactic arguments.

Given the wartime priorities, this practice of making films by locating images within named concepts was as necessary as it was foreign to the Canadian context. The aesthetic itself was a microcosm of British civilization as the decoder of a hostile world; it was an amelioration of the barbaric images produced (found) by the newsreel cameramen covering the war. Grierson never denied that his was a conscious ordering of perception. The Board's own film on war propaganda, *The War for Men's Minds*, told its audiences quite bluntly that "truth is not enough." The NFB's aim was not only to redeem images from Nazi distortions, but to restructure them as more effective weapons. A finely honed unified understanding was the raw material out of which the war machine was finally to be fashioned.

Significantly, the voice-over aesthetic that worked so well in the war documentaries and newsreels seemed less amenable to the domestically oriented films made at the wartime Board. The very first of these, Stuart Legg's *The Case of Charlie Gordon* stakes its credibility on synched recordings of its subjects, unemployed young people undergoing a retraining program. *Listen to the Prairies, Coal Face, Canada* and even *The Proudest Girl in the World*, all in very different ways, sold themselves on the (usually faked) spontaneity of synchronized recording. Even in a film like James Beveridge's *Northwest Frontier*, an otherwise model adaptation of Griersonian voice-over to a domestic subject (the coming of white society to the Northwest Territories), highlights a particularly significant instant with the suggestion of an on-screen voice. When a telephone hookup is successfully completed between a mining town and Ottawa, the on-screen subjects, for one small moment, burst out of their puppet-like obedience to the narrator and talk, unimpeded, *to each other*.

It would be tempting to say that from the beginning modern English Canadian cinematic practice forged itself in rebellion against the imposition of the Imperial Voice, that it looked toward the French model of assimilation with a found landscape—the recording of local voices and images as themselves. The actual history of English Canadian cinema is far more complex. If, for instance, there was a widespread sympathy with a Québécois sensibility, that sympathy is far from evident in the work of the Film Board's first generation. Until the mid-fifties, French production at the NFB was sporadic at best. The film that would for years introduce English Canadians to their francophone countrymen, Jane Marsh and Judith Crawley's *Alexis Tremblay, Habitant* (1943) made use of an orthodox Griersonian voice-over to further mould impossibly idyllic images of unchanging life along the St. Lawrence. It would be more than a decade before anyone recorded in synch the real language and anger of contemporary Quebec.

As Peter Morris notes,[4] the postwar NFB saw a variety of attempts made to continue the break away from the Griersonian voice-over. But that aesthetic continued to dominate the majority of documentaries produced around the world. Even in the Board's proto-features—films like *The Feeling of Rejection* and *File 1365: The Conners Case*—the narrator, to a greater or lesser extent interdicts the freedom of zombie-like on-screen characters. To audiences conscious of experiments in cinema narrative, the narrated dramas may take on a certain Brechtian flavour. But to the vast majority of those watching them, the voice-over continued to represent an imposition of order both in the films' stylistics and, more often than not, in their diegeses. The disembodied voice shaped the lives of the largely mute characters who suffered beneath it and who learned (the hard way) to heed its suggestions.

When rebellion against this Griersonian voice finally did come to the English Canadian NFB it was, in a sense, a more complete rebellion than that undertaken by the Québécois. Put simply, the Québécois *cinéma direct* filmmakers who emerged in the mid- to late fifties liked what they found in front of their cameras. English Canadian filmmakers used the same equipment, the same rebellion against voice-over, to make anti-documentaries, films that questioned the entire nature and worth of what they purported to represent. Roman Kroitor's Paul Tomkowicz grabs the microphone from the previously anonymous narrator (or so the film tells us) to declare that nothing is certain about who he is or what he does. Pierre Berton, in *City of Gold*, takes us all the way to the Klondike to say that the old time prospectors' motivations would always be a mystery. The music track that replaces voice-over in Colin Low's *Corral* creates a similar mystery: are we looking at a man at work or simply an idealized myth?

It is perhaps no coincidence that the filmmakers cited above were Westerners or, in the case of Wolf Koenig, a first-generation Canadian. Unit B and its descendants in the Film Board's tradition of experimental documentary were characterized by a pioneers' uncertainty at capturing the landscape before them. The task facing Englishmen like Terence Macartney-Filgate and Derek May, or Australian Michael Rubbo, was as impossible as that of Atwood's pioneer. And the films they produced questioned the very idea of naming the unnamable, of finding easy definitions of their subjects. Whether we see this self-reflexive despair as true innovation[5] or whether we question it as audacious misrepresentation,[6] it is difficult to disregard the intensity with which the anglophone documentarians moved in the sixties and seventies toward the institutionalization of open-ended forms, the failure of judgement and silence.

Ultimately, what the Board has institutionalized is not the original rebellion or its resulting style, but rather the signification of veracity through the withholding of both voice-over and the structuring that voice-over can impose. It is a strategy that is likely to backfire. We may believe that the formless *Challenge for Change* films are free from manipulation (though, of course, there is no reason we should). But we have come to associate this withdrawal from form with the withdrawal from social context that the voice-over once provided. Like Berton's prospectors or the protagonists of Rubbo's *Waiting for Fidel*, these are people whose social context is indefinable or ludicrous. The most attractive subjects—for example, Billy Crane in *Billy Crane Moves Away*—seemed to be those least able to articulate the realities of their situation.

Contemporary Film Board work still suffers from the paradoxical silence of a foregrounded subject. *Ted Baryluk's Grocery*—which combines *City of Gold*'s use of stills with the *Paul Tomkowicz* protagonist voice-over—provides the usual sense of indefinable despair. At the same time, the film's structure masks its actual content. What we are hearing on the sound-track is not Baryluk's voice (he died during production) but that of one of the filmmakers, his foster son. That the entire film revolves around Baryluk's daughter's refusal to take over her father's store would seem to demand some acknowledgement of the generational interaction that went into its very production. Yet again, what is known and can be examined is silenced in order to equate veracity with a fatalistic ennui.

More insidious than the unannounced usurpation of Ted Baryluk's voice is the manipulation of what we are told is to be taken as testimony. Jennifer Hodge's *Home Feeling: Struggle for a Community* uses the clichés of *Challenge for Change*—long takes of meetings, confrontations and interviews—to hide the structuring of a case that may or may not be sustained by the evidence. The film tells us that police in Toronto's Jane-Finch area are harassing black residents. The various incidents we see are, at best, undefined and, at worst, severely influenced by the camera's presence. In any event, what we see and what is said about it in meetings and interviews cannot be proven. We are continually thrown back to the narrator for an evaluation of what we have not, in reality, seen or heard. Despite the veracity lent to the film through the use of cinéma vérité techniques, the Jane-Finch residents need not have spoken. As for the police, the testimony of the most sympathetic officer, a young black man, is prefaced by the narrator's declaration that, "the neighbourhood kids call him The Bounty Hunter." The man is effectively silenced.

As might be expected, the move toward a silent subject in National Film Board documentary is reflected in the realist features that have grown out of the Griersonian tradition. Don Owen's *Nobody Waved Good-bye*, which began as a documentary, features as its protagonist a kind of anti-prophet whose every word turns false. When Peter declares that there are no patrol cars on Toronto's outer boulevards, he is immediately arrested. If he declares that he will have no trouble with his exams, he fails. His arguments for any kind of self-definition or support from those around him are easily brushed aside.

The undermining of Peter's language in *Nobody Waved Good-bye* is overseen by the same Imperial Voice that controlled the fate of his predecessors in the Board's proto-features. The only difference here is that the Voice has now been internalized in our perception of the film; it need no longer be articulated on the sound-track. Sympathize as we may with Peter's adolescent awkwardness, we have been told—by our entire heritage of socially responsible documentary cinema—what must happen to him. We watch Peter from the perspective of the Imperial Voice, confident that what he can't articulate (his various social dilemmas) can be named. But he won't name them and, in the long run, the words that we use to name them are not our own.

What is true of Peter in *Nobody Waved Good-bye* is true of the entire line of losers in English Canadian features. One can cite Gordon Pinsent as Will Cole in Peter Carter's *The Rowdyman*, or the protagonist of Peter Pearson's *The Best Damned Fiddler From Calabogie to Kaladar* for an exuberance of language equal to their erratic behaviour. The more they speak, the more certain we become that their words are divorcing them from their actual circumstances. Even Duddy Kravitz, the most interesting loser of the bunch, can only talk himself into self-defeating achievements. The better he manipulates the complex linguistic challenges of Jewish Montreal, the more crushing his defeat.

A recognition of this counterproductive nature of speech has led in the English Canadian feature film to the use of silence as a privileged entity. As Peter Harcourt has written of one major English Canadian feature film director:

> This feeling of emptiness, of restlessness, often of irrelevance pervades the films of Don Shebib—not only his features but much of his other work as well. And this feeling is often conveyed without the help of words.[7]

Shebib's characters are linguistically battered into silence. Roger, in *Second Wind*, as Harcourt asserts, must suspend speech in the film when he realizes that neither he nor it have the vocabulary to describe what is going on. Pete, in *Goin' Down the Road*, falls into a similar reverie when the conceptual world of his Maritime sureties falls apart in the face of what must seem to him to be the Imperial Voice of downtown Toronto. The teenagers in *Rip-Off* are stripped of their platitudes. And, in one of his most telling subversions of language, Shebib dutifully presents the nuances of legal arguments surrounding the insanity plea. Then, in the rolling titles that conclude *By Reason of Insanity*, we are told that all these fine words have served to ensure the eventual release of an untreated psychopathic killer. We, like Roger, Pete and the *Rip-Off* kids, are left suspended in silence beyond the limits of our tongue.

There are, of course, other responses to the failure of language. One is to associate successful articulation with the villains and outcasts of English Canadian society as if their powers of speech automatically signify social deviance. The Peter Welsh character in *Empire, Inc.*, the debt collectors in *Skip Tracer*, and Martha Henry in *The Wars* see clearly through every problem. But the perceptual and linguistic trumps they hold are held precisely because of their alienation from more sympathetic characters. Conversely, insanity—to the degree that it distorts articulation—centralizes a character. The child in Jutra's *Dreamspeaker* is our key to a world beyond language, a world made whole. Craig Russell and Hollis McLaren in *Outrageous!* survive the nagging Griersonian voice (and English Canada) with the proclamation that they are both "alive and sick in New York." Even Louis Del Grande, in the television series *Seeing Things*, must use his second sight to escape the corners into which he paints himself with endlessly excessive verbiage. And, if passion may be regarded as a kind of insanity, it too reduces language to scorn. The best example is the love scene in Owen's *Partners* in which consummation is preceded by a mutual disavowal of sexual terminology on the part of the Rosedale princess and her Yankee lover.

Over and above any of these works is a small body of English Canadian films which seem to celebrate the conscious renunciation of language as central to their protagonists' triumph. The earliest of these is the first masterpiece of English Canadian cinema, David Hartford's 1919 production, *Back to God's Country*. Nell Shipman, who starred in and shaped that film, is characterized as a nature child whose instinctive understanding of human and beast seems to distinguish her from the two-dimensional pulp utterances of the film's other characters. As the plot develops, Shipman is unable to settle any of her melodramatic crises through human discourse. Her redemption comes only from her ability to communicate with the film's professed hero, a dog, and perhaps as well from the congruence between her silence and the vast frozen landscape in which she performs her most heroic acts.

Equally to the point in elucidating the value of this pantheistic silence are the films of Jack Darcus. Darcus' array of bickering Bergmanesque people speak merely to undercut each other's articulation. *Deserters,* for instance, chronicles a spoken diatribe in which the most articulate participant, the American Sergeant, is also the person least able to define his own position. He can only talk himself into one about-face after another. The silent and silenced characters around him—an American deserter and a rather vacuous Canadian couple—swing around in tandem to the Sergeant's overpowering monologues. In his other work—for example, *Proxyhawks* and *Wolfpen Principle*—Darcus implies that these interchanges are finally of less worth than the howls and screeches of the various animals with whom his characters are obsessed.

On his part, Phillip Borsos silences the characters in *The Grey Fox* not through the pointlessness of their talk, but rather through a combination of the landscape in which they operate and the mythology of cinema itself. An identification of the protagonist with nature begins in the title. It extends through a magnificent visual metaphor of the entire plot, a scene in which Bill Miner, rustling a small herd of horses, is accidently pursued along a narrow stretch of track by an unrelenting locomotive. That Miner's actions speak louder than anyone's words is established in incident after incident within the plot. And what remains of the dialogue is further distanced by Borsos' insistence upon associating his film with Edwin S. Porter's silent classic, *The Great Train Robbery*. The final pursuit of Miner and his gang departs from the film's diegesis to be intercut with the climax of Porter's film. More subtly, the appearance of the Mounties at the end of the chase defies modern cinematic reading; as was the case with *The Great Train Robbery*, the "good guys" simply appear before quarry unable to discern their approach through off-screen space.

Borsos' chase scene in *The Grey Fox* is reminiscent of what is probably the English Canadian feature's most innovative use of silence, Joyce Wieland's *The Far Shore*. From the beginning, that film sets out to question the integrity of language as dictated by the Imperial Voice. Eulalie, a transplanted Québécoise, invites us to ridicule the pompous Remembrance Day address delivered by her husband to the servants in their Rosedale home. A Toronto art dealer can find no terminology with which to fit the Tom Thomson character's work into the aesthetics of his culture; the subject of that work is the wilderness that transcends the utilitarian understanding of art. Later, in the climactic chase set in the painter's wilderness, Eulalie's husband and his far more villainous companion find their words undermined as they pursue the fleeing couple through a silent landscape. Presaging Borsos' chase, Wieland suspends normal rules of continuity, confusing the direction of the action and subverting what should be the characters' realization of one another's presence. Temporal signifiers are made subjective when the physical consummation of Eulalie's affair is depicted in a manner that would ordinarily indicate an impossibly lengthy coupling.

Wieland's strategies in subverting both spoken and cinematic language result in a work that locates characters and action firmly within the silence of an unnamable landscape. *The Far Shore*, in this regard, is an expansion of some of the ideas worked out in her experimental films. The most obvious example of this is *Reason Over Passion*. In that film, Trudeau's call for an objective acceptance of logic is shattered as the very letters of the slogan are permutated into meaninglessness against the backdrop of a photographed Canadian landscape. True understanding of the land is equated not only with a destruction of its description, but with a call for the undermining of description itself. The same may be said of *Sailboat, 1933,* and *Rat Life and Diet in North America,* as well as Wieland's politically oriented experiments.[8]

Other Canadian experimental filmmakers have interested themselves in the use (or uselessness) of the word. R. Bruce Elder's work—*The Art of Worldly Wisdom, 1857: Fool's Gold* and *Illuminated Texts*—speak to the arbitrary nature of representation in general. Yet in these films, the word is reduced perhaps even beyond the reduction of the duplicity of imagery. The voice reading what purports to be Elder's autobiographical text in *The Art of Worldly Wisdom* is not his voice. The multiple texts of *1857* prove as useless against the magnitude of that film's landscape as Trudeau's words did against the landscape of *Reason Over Passion.* The language of *Illuminated Texts* simply illuminates its own complicity in the folly of all human dependence on codified mediation.

Finally, the silenced subjects of the Griersonian voice-over, the false liberation of the anti-Griersonian rebellion, the puppets of an internalized voice found in the realist features, and the most innovative exploitation of the silent landscape are best exemplified in Michael Snow's *So Is This.* The vast silence of the soundtrack leaves the word itself as landscape. Snow's playful bantering of this landscape hints at a kind of synthesis between what is here and how we, as English Canadians, may perceive it. The landscape has finally done its work on the language. What is left is, again, best described in Atwood's poetic rendering of the pioneer confronting his environment:

> This is not order
> but the absence
> of order.
>
> He was wrong, the unanswering
> forest implied:
>
> It was
> an ordered absence.

This is based on an article published in *Canadian Film Studies*, 1, No. 1 (June 1984).

---

1 Peter Ohlin, "The Film as Word (Perrault)", *Ciné-Tracts* No. 4 (Spring-Summer, 1978), p. 65.
2 David Clandfield, "Ritual and Recital: The Perrault Project," reprinted in this volume.
3 Margaret Atwood, *Selected Poems* (Toronto: Oxford University Press, 1976), p. 63.
4 Peter Morris, "After Grierson: The National Film Board, 1945–1953," reprinted in this volume.

5 See Peter Harcourt, "The Innocent Eye: An Aspect of the Work of the National Film Board of Canada" in *Canadian Film Reader*, ed. Seth Feldman and Joyce Nelson (Toronto: Peter Martin Associates, 1977), pp. 67–77.
6 R. Bruce Elder's critique of the "observational structures" of National Film Board documentaries is applied in his "Two Journeys: A Review of *Not a Love Story*," reprinted in this volume.
7 Peter Harcourt, "Men of Vision: Some Comments on the Work of Don Shebib" in *Canadian Film Reader*, op. cit., pp. 199–208.
8 See Lianne M. McLarty, "The Experimental Films of Joyce Wieland," *Ciné-Tracts*, 17, (Summer-Fall 1982).
9 Atwood, op. cit., pp. 61–62.

# *Paul Almond's Fantastic Trilogy*

## BY JAMES LEACH

*Paul Almond was to have been the prototype of the English Canadian auteur. His work as a* CBC *director, beginning in 1954, took full advantage of the "golden age" of Canadian television. Almond's video dramas brought him the ultimate compliment, an invitation to direct series episodes for American and British networks. Then, like his contemporary, Robert Altman, Almond turned his attention away from television to the possibilities of intensely personal feature filmmaking. Calling upon all his skills as a writer and a producer, Almond completed the three films discussed here by James Leach between 1968 and 1972. As director of the trilogy, Almond's moulding of Geneviève Bujold in all three works is reminiscent of Sternberg's shaping of Dietrich or, to use an example closer to home, the interplay between Gilles Carle and Carole Laure that Leach alludes to elsewhere in this volume (see "The Sins of Gilles Carle").*

*As Leach recounts, the critical reception to Almond's trilogy—certainly his most important work to date—was not encouraging. The films were not what Canadian critics and the public had expected from the newly created Canadian Film Development Corporation. Disturbing and idiosyncratic works,* Isabel, The Act of the Heart *and* Journey *seemed to presuppose the kind of creative freedom that far older and more confident national cinemas allow their most esteemed auteurs. But Canada was not quite ready to tolerate a native Bergman, Kurosawa or Renoir—a director who could engage in the kind of anti-generic manipulation of the medium that Leach describes. As a result, films that should have served to herald the maturing of a major talent became impediments to the further development of Almond's career. Fortunately, that career has survived and is enjoying something of a revival with the release of his new film,* Ups & Downs *(1983).*

"If a commercial film isn't illusion, what's the point?" asked Robert Fulford, complaining that he had not been convinced that Geneviève Bujold was actually burning herself alive at the end of Paul Almond's *The Act of the Heart* (1970).[1] The question was, of course, intended to be rhetorical, but it does point to the issues at stake in assessing the critical and commercial failure of Almond's films. Part of the problem is the general resistance of Canadian reviewers, distributors, and audiences to Canadian cinema. Fulford makes clear that this resistance can be attributed to the dominance of the "Hollywood" model which equates reality with illusion and which was challenged by many Canadian films during the sixties and early seventies. But in Almond's case, the challenge to this model is also bound up with the genre to which his films belong.

According to Tzvetan Todorov, the genre of the fantastic is based on "that hesitation experienced by a person who knows only the laws of nature confronting an apparently supernatural event."[2] Although Todorov himself limits the genre to certain literary works of the eighteenth and nineteenth centuries, the idea of "hesitation" has been effectively applied to a number of films which call into question the comfortable spectator/screen relationship of commercial cinema.[3] The fantastic also undermines the notion of secure genre boundaries, since it is itself hardly a self-sufficient genre, constantly merging as it does with the "uncanny" (the apparently supernatural event is given a natural explanation) or with the "marvellous" (the presence of the supernatural is confirmed) (41).

The tensions and uncertainties generated by the fantastic "hesitation" figure prominently in the trilogy of which *The Act of the Heart* forms the second part, and they are associated in each case with the consciousness of the central character (played by Bujold in all three films). In *Isabel* (1968), the death of her mother forces her to return from Montreal to the family farm in the Gaspé peninsula, and she begins to see the ghosts that local superstition connects with the family's violent and incestuous past. When the film was released, Hollis Alpert complained that it fails to make clear whether these ghosts are actual or imagined, and insisted that "movies that deal with the supernatural had best be clear whether we are to believe in the damned things or whether it's all in the character's imagination."[4] The film will not fit comfortably into the horror genre (or, in Todorov's terms, the "marvellous"), or into that of the psychological thriller (Todorov's "uncanny"), and so it remains in the precarious domain of the fantastic, much to the discomfort of critics who insist that genre conventions be respected.

In *The Act of the Heart*, Martha has come to Montreal from the country with the intention of becoming a professional singer, but is troubled by religious doubts and sexual fears. These are intensified when she falls in love with a Catholic priest, and she finally burns herself alive to provide an example for a world which has forgotten Christ. The "hesitation" here stems not from doubts about the status of the images, but from the problem of interpreting Martha's actions. As Janet Edsforth points out, the film leaves unanswered the question of "whether Martha was in fact a saint or a psychotic."[5] If she is a saint, her self-immolation takes on a mythic resonance (and the film moves into the genre of the "marvellous"); if she is a psychotic, her death simply confirms her fear that life is meaningless (and the film becomes "uncanny"). The film does not allow us the comfort of either resolution, and even the difficulty of representing her final act (which so disappointed Fulford) adds to the central concern with the struggle to give physical expression to spiritual desires.

In *Journey* (1972), an unnamed woman arrives mysteriously at an isolated commune on the banks of the Saguenay. The "hesitation" experienced by the heroine (whom the leader of the commune names after the river in which he found her) is based on her inability to decide what the commune represents; the clothes and way of life of its members suggest that they are early settlers, but is this because Saguenay has been transported back in time (a "marvellous" explanation), or because the commune is founded on a rejection of the modern world (an "uncanny" explanation), or because it is a product of Saguenay's imagination? This last explanation runs counter to the film's emphasis on the physical reality of the life of the commune and its natural surroundings, but it gains some support from the oblique way in which the narrative is presented. Robert Fothergill was driven to object that the film is constructed "with an elusive indirectness, with the result that for much of the time the spectator is not quite sure what is going on, or what the characters are talking about."[6]

Almond himself has described *Journey* as a "visionary allegory," and it is tempting to try to explain away its obscurities by an allegorical interpretation.[7] Similar suggestions have been made with regard to the difficulties raised by the two earlier films, but attempts to pin down the meaning of the allegory usually lead to frustration. Thus Guy Morris felt that *Isabel* is "a simple story that can be made complex if you want to play the game of looking for hidden messages," and Jean-René Ethier complained that "the allegory in *Journey* continually hides its keys."[8] As Michel Euvrard argues in his article on *Journey*, allegory presupposes that "the public has the key to the system of signs used by the author"; he suggests that the necessary communal myths do not exist "in an urban, individualist, pluralist society in which only the memory remains, unequally preserved, of the different religions and mythologies to which the population has subscribed in the course of history."[9]

Despite the problems involved with modern allegory, however, Euvrard suggests that the "allegorical elements" in *Isabel* and *The Act of the Heart* allow Almond to dispense with "traditional psychological analyses and motivations" and that "the (partial) allegory makes it possible to move directly from the concrete—from existence and physical presence—to the *typical*." He goes on to argue that the "(complete) allegory" of *Journey* makes possible a further leap over "historical and sociological determinations" to create a direct movement "from the concrete to the *abstract*":

> The way of life of Undersky is meant to establish directly the bond between physical and material realities and that spiritual reality which socio-historical obstacles prevent from being attained in Montreal (or any other large city of the consumer society).[10]

Martha's experiences in Montreal in *The Act of the Heart* confirm the difficulty of attaining "spiritual reality" in a modern urban setting, but the fact remains that *Journey*'s spectators are also products of the consumer society. Its allegory is complete only in the sense that the images consistently resist literal interpretation and not in the sense that they refer to communally accessible keys. Indeed the Undersky commune is an attempt to create a community that its members could not find in the outside world, and the spectator's difficulty in resolving the film's enigmas parallels the problems of the commune in coping with the tensions introduced by Saguenay's arrival.

The presence of communal "keys" in allegory leads Todorov to banish it from the realm of the fantastic; the availability of an allegorical interpretation would eliminate all possibility of "hesitation" (32). Although *Journey* goes much farther than either *Isabel* or *The Act of the Heart* in demanding a more-than-literal reading, its basic strategy is to evoke and then frustrate the need for keys. In so doing, it reinstates "hesitation" and relates it to the problems of communal experience in the modern world with which the trilogy is centrally concerned. If the films are seen as fantastic rather than allegorical, their tensions can be linked to the difficulty of creating the kind of direct relationship between the material and the abstract which allegory requires. As might be expected, these tensions stem largely from the unstable relationship set up between camera viewpoint and the central consciousness of the heroine, and the effect of such a strategy can be well illustrated by examining the opening sequences of each film.

The opening sequence of *Isabel* introduces the everyday, "normal" world which Isabel is leaving. A train moves rapidly through a snow-covered landscape, telegraph wires speed by outside the windows, a young woman reads a telegram informing her of her mother's illness; this is the familiar, modern world of rapid communications and technological domination over nature. The "official" bilingualism of the ticket inspector suggests a comfortable accommodation to the linguistic differences that will be seen to have deeply affected Isabel's family. But already the spectator has to cope with a number of unexpected images which disrupt the linear development of the sequence. Close-ups of Isabel's inexpressive face relate these images to her consciousness, but *how* they relate remains unclear. Some are images of nature of the kind that will punctuate her later experiences and link them to the slow coming of spring to the Gaspé countryside; others show the dark interiors of what will later be identified as her family home and anticipate the terror that she will undergo there. Although most of these images are flash-forwards, they cannot at this point be distinguished from flashbacks, and their effect, as they interrupt the "present" action, is to suggest that memory and anticipation are fused together in Isabel's consciousness.

In the first sequence of *The Act of the Heart*, the camera moves slowly past the pews in a deserted church and Martha is only glimpsed as a still figure almost obscured by the shadows. But we are quickly plunged into her consciousness: A close-up of her face is accompanied by the sounds of fire, and then the camera rushes toward a coffin which bursts into flame. The fusion of death and fire in Martha's consciousness will lead to the physical horror of her self-immolation, but is first related to the cantata, "The Flame Within," which is being rehearsed in the next sequence. The contrast between the dark, disturbing images of the opening sequence and the mundane reality of the rehearsal is jarring, but this second sequence does show that Martha's fears have their roots in "normal" experience. Michael is introduced as a Catholic priest looking for a soprano to sing in a performance of the cantata. His presence creates an uneasiness which is given sexual overtones when he makes a joke about Catholic choirs having no girls, and when the boys snigger at a line in the cantata text, "A body descends by its own weight to the place that is fitting for it." The sexual innuendo underlines the fusion of sexual and mystical connotations in the flame imagery and anticipates the tensions created by Martha's love for a priest.

The alienation of the heroine from everyday reality in both *Isabel* and *The Act of the Heart* is reinforced by the way in which these opening sequences challenge our "normal" perceptions of time. The flashes in *Isabel* are only later seen to be premonitions rather than memories; Martha's experience in the church makes her late for choir practice, but seems to exist apart from the time-scale of the rest of the film. In addition, in both films, there are important "absences" that contrast with the physical presence of the environment which the heroine finds oppressive. Although Isabel writes and receives letters, none of the flashes refer to the city where she claims to have found a new identity; her psychic life is confined to the landscape which gives her roots, but also threatens to imprison her.[11] Conversely, in *The Act of the Heart*, Martha's life before she came to the city is not shown, although she does receive a letter and a telephone call from her father. These temporal disruptions and "absences" become the basic structural principle of *Journey*, in which we remain unsure whether the distance between Undersky and Saguenay's unseen "past" is a matter of space, time or imagination.

The opening image of *Journey* is an extreme close-up of a woman's face. We hear indistinctly the sounds of a car braking, footsteps, and a door opening (or perhaps a rifle being loaded); the woman speaks the name "Damien," and says, "you've come back." As she calls his name again, the camera pulls back to reveal that she is adrift on a log in the middle of a river. She is rescued and carried to a cabin by a man who will later be identified as Boulder, the leader of the commune. A succession of brief sequences, separated by fades, involve us in her gradual recovery of consciousness as she catches fragmented glimpses of the commune. But we also share the point of view of the members of the commune as they examine this nameless woman who has mysteriously appeared in their midst.

This double perspective—Saguenay's look at the commune, their look at her—involves the spectator's look in the tension between self and other which is central both to the trilogy and to Todorov's theory of the fantastic. The "themes of the self" deal with "the fragility of the limit between matter and mind," while the "themes of the other" form a chain which leads from desire through cruelty to death (120, 135). Each of the heroines in Almond's trilogy undergoes an experience which exposes "the fragility of the limit between matter and mind," and which is bound up with her association of sexual desire with male aggression and with death. It is the crisis caused by this experience that generates the fantastic "hesitation" and disrupts the heroine's relationship to her social and natural environment as well as the spectator's relationship to the film. The interaction of themes of the self (the problem of consciousness) with themes of the other (desire, cruelty, death) creates the structuring tensions of the films. A brief analysis of how each of the films deals with these tensions will make clear the importance of the themes and techniques of the fantastic in the total effect of the trilogy.

The narrative structure of *Isabel* is built around the questions of Isabel's social and sexual identity and her fear of death. After she returns to her family home and finds that her mother is dead, there is a sudden cut from the face of the mother in an open coffin to Isabel jerking awake in her bed in the morning. Later, she contemplates her body in a mirror and raises her arm so that she can smell it. This confrontation with her own sexuality and mortality is intensified by the pressures on her to take over her mother's role. She discovers that her mother had once been housekeeper and mistress to Cedric, Isabel's grandfather. Her mother then married Isabel's father, but when he went away to war she became the mistress of his brother Matthew. After her husband died at sea, the mother stayed on as Matthew's housekeeper, and it is suggested that she died from the effort of looking after the farm alone after Matthew suffered a stroke. This history of incest, promiscuity and exploitation may be exaggerated by its retelling in local gossip, but it reinforces the pressures which prevent Isabel from accepting her own sexuality.

Despite this lurid (and repressed) family history, the mother was extremely strict toward Isabel and forbade her to attend the local dances. Isabel, however, discovers that this apparent paragon of virtue was "human like the rest of us." These are the words of Herb, who had proposed to Isabel before she left the village, but Herb is one of the men who attempt to rape Isabel when she finally does go to a dance. The mother's strictness is thus apparently justified, just as the community's suspicion of the outside world seems to be endorsed by the news that Isabel's friend in the city has found another roommate and that she has lost her job. The mother's puritanism and the community's chauvinism, however, only intensify the violence and desires which they attempt to repress. Isabel has to overcome the fear of nature generated by the sexual, linguistic and religious divisions within her family.

The males of the Garnet family have taken possession of the land, but have often met violent deaths. Nature takes its revenge: Isabel's father and brother died together in a storm at sea, and her uncle Jacob is said to have bitten the heads off chickens and to have been killed by the pigs. Although the patriarchal family gives authority to the men, they are themselves victims of a society that requires them for its wars. Cedric was driven mad in the First World War, and the house is filled with images and relics of war. Isabel sees herself reflected in a framed picture of a battle and the sounds of shells and gunfire accompany her own gradual breakdown. The family structure is itself breaking down, and Matthew tells Isabel that her father would turn in his grave if he knew that the Garnets were no longer farming their own land. As he makes this remark in the cemetery, he looks down at the site of his own grave and shows Isabel the one that has been set aside for her. The family's ties to the land offer Isabel nothing but a grave site.

The divisions within the family are most fully exposed in the figure of Estelle, Isabel's older sister, who also returns for the funeral. She left the village to become a nun only a week after Isabel was born, and the two sisters have never met. Estelle speaks only French (Matthew speaks English, Isabel is bilingual), and is shocked to find that her mother, who was a French-speaking Catholic, has chosen to be buried in the Protestant cemetery beside her husband. There are a number of allusions to the sexual desires aroused by Estelle before she became a nun, but she has escaped the sexual and domestic role imposed on her mother by renouncing her sexuality. Yet she becomes part of the social forces trying to impose such a role on Isabel when, at the funeral, she thanks God that Matthew has Isabel to look after him. As she says this, the image dissolves so that we see Isabel cleaning her uncle's house as if she is emerging from the head of the nun. Like the mother, Estelle has internalized the values of the society which oppresses her, but her spiritual authority as a nun loses its force with the revelation that Cedric was probably her father.

Isabel is able to break out of the impasse created by inner fears and external pressures through her relationship with Jason, who buys the farm from her uncle. She first sees him climbing on to the jetty from his boat, loaded down with tackle, looking like a monster emerging from the sea, but she comes to learn that he is "human." His masculinity is neither dominant nor aggressive: He sings gentle folk ballads, can laugh at himself when he falls into the water on a fishing trip, and can rescue Isabel from rape only by diverting the attack to himself. As an outsider, he can overcome the sexual fears caused by her incestuous family background. After the attempted rape, the drunken Matthew tries to seduce Isabel, and she races off on her bicycle to find Jason. When she finds him on the jetty, her hysterical condition makes her run away from him, but he catches her and the film ends with their primal coupling. As they make love, she sees him as Cedric, Matthew, and Arnold (her brother), before he finally becomes himself again.

The nightmare is over, but the fantastic "hesitation" is not completely negated. There are several suggestions that the "apparently supernatural" elements are not entirely generated by Isabel's imagination. Although the brief glimpses of "ghosts" would seem to be projections of her consciousness, some doubts are raised when she finds a chicken flapping about with its head bitten off. Jason later suggests that she must have disturbed a fox, but even Jason's down-to-earth presence has some mysterious qualities. Although he is an outsider, he is also the "spitting image" of Arnold, whose photograph we see on several occasions. Isabel claims that she has never seen him before, but he has some memories of her. When she asks him where he comes from, he replies "back there," and gestures vaguely beyond the farm. The reality seems to be that he comes from a lower-class family looked down on by the Garnets ("Me a Garnet!" he cries when Isabel says she feels that they are related), but the workings of Isabel's consciousness prevent us from being quite certain how to evaluate him for most of the film.

The problem is to decide how much of what we see is filtered through Isabel's consciousness. There are several long shots of her in the farmyard which seem to suggest an unidentified observing presence, but there are also many shots which are clearly identified with her point of view. In most cases, however, the relationship of the images to her consciousness is more difficult to establish. Thus the frequent brief inserts of melting snow and waves breaking against the jetty relate Isabel's psychological struggle to ongoing natural processes. But *how* they relate to her consciousness remains unclear; they represent an "objective" external world not seen through her eyes, but they often seem to be generated by the psychic pressures that she undergoes. "Objective" and "subjective" interpenetrate to the point that it becomes difficult to separate them. When Isabel receives a letter informing her that she has lost her job, she reads it in a neighbour's truck during a rainstorm while he is visiting a sawmill, and the buzzing of the saws and the rain on the windows become an expression of her inner feelings.

The tension between inner and outer vision reaches its most extreme point when Isabel is left alone in the house after Matthew goes to town for some medical tests. She is terrorized by the empty house and decides to spend the night with some neighbours. After someone claims to have seen a ghostly light in the house during the night, Isabel returns in the morning and is disturbed to find that the clock has stopped. As she explores the house, a strange noise seems to confirm her fears, but she is relieved to find that it was made by Jason. He provides a prosaic explanation for the stopped clock (it needs winding) and suggests that they go fishing. She is reassured by this return to "reality," but when she comes back from fetching her rods, she finds that Jason has disappeared and the clock is ticking. Suddenly the spectator is confronted with the possibility that Isabel has imagined his presence and that her hallucinations can no longer be distinguished from the "real" world. Although Jason does reappear to explain that he wound the clock, the tensions generated in this sequence (like the experience of "hesitation" throughout the film) provide a warning against a definition of reality that would exclude the role of perception and imagination.

*The Act of the Heart* also deals with problems of perception and imagination, since we share Martha's uncertainty as to whether or not physical and visible reality expresses a hidden spiritual or symbolic reality. As in *Isabel*, the "hesitation" is tied to Martha's sexuality and to the question of what it means to be "human." She refuses a "normal" relationship with a young man called Dietrich and will not visit him when he is in hospital. Her indifference may indicate a fear of hospitals or a reluctance to commit herself to Dietrich, and this ambiguity (like the confrontation with the mother's body in *Isabel*) links her sexual unease to an underlying fear of death. When Dietrich tells her that "some day you'll have to be like other girls," she replies, "I'm not other girls. . . . I'm different." This outburst comes immediately after the introduction of Ti-Joe, the hockey coach, whose "difference" leads to his being treated as an outcast; later, when she goes skating with Michael, Martha remarks that "for a priest, you are different." His response is to remind her that he is "human," but she is unable to treat him as a human being because he is a priest (compare the unease created by Estelle's presence in *Isabel*).

Martha refuses a "normal" sexual identity because she thinks there must be "something beyond living with a man." She wants to be "different," and relates social conformity to religious indifference. Although we learn little about her family life, she seeks human relationships to compensate for the silence of God and the absence of her family. She is living with Johane and her son, Russell. She tries to become a mother to Russell (who is having problems adjusting to the death of his father), but the relationship takes on sexual overtones when he climbs into her bed after Ti-Joe is arrested. Johane is a substitute for Martha's dead mother, but this relationship also becomes sexually charged when Russell is in hospital as the result of a hockey accident. Martha goes to Johane's bed, and later their embrace in front of the fire is interrupted by the telephone call which brings the news of Russell's death. Martha rushes from the house and ends up grappling with Michael in a sexual embrace on the church floor. Michael has been a substitute for her absent father (as a priest, he is formally addressed as "father"); Martha has moved from a boy, to a woman, to a priest whose cassock connotes forbidden maleness, and with whom the sexual act becomes both incestuous and sacrilegious.

The distortions which mark Martha's sexual and religious experience suggest the impossibility in her society of the kind of mystical experience with which the cantata deals. Mysticism fuses the spiritual and erotic connotations of the flame imagery, and Martha and Michael are briefly able to fulfil their love in the performance of music dedicated to the glory of God. But music, like religion and sexuality, is stifled by the materialism of the consumer society. Johane was once a violinist but gave up music to manage her husband's business after his death; Michael has been posted to Montreal because of his musical talents but feels that his concerts are an inadequate response to the human suffering he has witnessed in Africa. Martha finds that she must wait two months for an audition at the CBC, but the receptionist tells her that she could make money and gain experience by performing topless in a nightclub. The commercial exploitation of music and sexuality is raised again when a male guest at Johane's party suggests that Martha could earn money as a stripper, and such pressures account for her humiliation when she does eventually sing in a nightclub to support Michael after their marriage.

In the nightclub, Martha performs in a flaming red dress, which suggests a debasement of the flame/passion imagery of the cantata, but she is able to express through her song her sense of waiting for something outside herself. She sings in French, which was (presumably) the language of her mother who died when she was born, and it is Michael's clumsy (English) words after the performance that give her the idea for her final sacrificial act. His verbal clumsiness is part of his anxiety to give meaning to the suffering and indifference he sees around him. All of the characters seem to be struggling to avoid slipping into clichés, and this creates the sense of a submerged spiritual life which words conceal rather than express. The tension between English and French only adds to the problems of communication. Martha is teaching Russell French, but both she and Johane have repressed their French heritage under the influence, respectively, of father and husband. French occasionally breaks through into the predominantly English-speaking environment (the bureaucrat who tells Ti-Joe that his team can practise only at the prescribed times; Johane's business friends who glibly discuss separatism over cocktails), but offers no real alternative to the sterility of bourgeois culture.

Whether the spiritual dimension for which Martha yearns actually exists remains ambiguous, in keeping with the requirements of the fantastic "hesitation," but some enigmatic clues are provided visually by the emphasis on the stained-glass windows in the church. When images "burn out" into the colours of the glass, the effect may be related to Martha's consciousness, as the burning coffin clearly is, but it also hints at a supernatural reality which would give resonance to the religious artefacts with which she surrounds herself. The images seem to go beyond her consciousness, however, when the colours of the glass are picked up in everyday objects like the seats in the hospital waiting room. Just as Martha can experience her nightclub performance only as a humiliation, so her alienation from reality prevents her from seeing a possible continuity between her spiritual needs and the material and physical world.

Yves Lever has suggested that *The Act of the Heart* contains a "symbolic dialectic" made up of a series of tensions: "fire/snow, warmth/cold, sympathy/coldness, light/darkness, life/death, fire as inner life and outer death, human/divine, bilingualism . . . solitude/life in society."[12] The tension between inner and outer pervades all the others and governs our response to Martha's final act. After Martha and Michael make love on the church floor, there is a sudden cut to ice in the river beside which Martha is hanging out washing. The bright blue and white of the St. Lawrence in winter jars the eye after the reds and darkness of the previous sequences. Michael is working at his typewriter in their mobile home, his act of rebellion having transformed him into a controversial but poorly paid media personality. After her nightclub performance, she accompanies him to the CBC building where he has an audition, and then suddenly we see her lugging a can of gasoline along a deserted street. She pours it over herself in a bleak, snow-covered patch of urban park, and her burning body goes unnoticed as cars pass by a few yards away. Her act hardly has the force of example that Michael was looking for, but her voice is still heard in all its purity on the sound-track.

Since we share Martha's "hesitation," we can understand the frustrations which motivate her, but the coldly detached camera in the final sequences forces us to evaluate her act of the heart for ourselves. The fantastic elements prevent us from dismissing this act simply as the product of hysteria, while also preventing us from comfortably placing it within the framework of conventional Christian hagiography. Whereas the fantastic in *Isabel* derives from the tensions of the psychological thriller, it stems in *The Act of the Heart* from the crisis within Christianity itself as its vision and imagery become increasingly irrelevant in a society which lacks the communal basis to give meaning to religious, sexual and artistic experience. The religious divisions in *Isabel* and the ecumenical reconciliation within a context of indifference in *The Act of the Heart* thus provide the basis for the more mythic treatment of the tensions between body and spirit in *Journey*. It is the absence of a genuine community that torments Martha and prevents us from reading *Journey* simply as an allegory of a spiritual experience.

The central problem in *Journey* is the nature of the relationship between Saguenay's consciousness and the Undersky commune. Boulder tells her that it is "almost impossible to get here," and when she asks if this is because the commune is "too far away," he replies mysteriously, "you could say that." Added to this basic uncertainty is Saguenay's growing fear that Undersky is a product of her own imagination. She wonders if she is "still out there in the river in the dream" or if perhaps she is experiencing the last minute before her death. Boulder suggests that she may already be dead and struggling back to life. She asks if she could "have created all this," and he replies that sometimes "what we create has a habit of taking over." Yet the possibility that the commune exists only within her consciousness is balanced by the possibility that she is a projection of the fears and anxieties which haunt the commune. What we learn about the commune is that it was formed when Boulder led his followers away from the "madness" of the outside world, and that they arrived on Midsummer's Eve seven years ago. What we learn about Saguenay is that her relationship with Damien ended on Midsummer's Eve, when she followed him to the top of a cliff and tried to commit suicide after seeing him dance with evil spirits. Since she arrives at Undersky in spring, there is no logical time-sequence, but she leaves after disrupting the Midsummer's Eve celebration, claiming that it repeats what she saw on the cliff—with Boulder taking the place of Damien.

The links between Boulder and Damien are also suggested in a sequence in which Saguenay's look cues a shot of the burnt-out house which is associated with Damien, and then a shot of the Undersky farmhouse. Undersky seems to grow out of the charred ruins, but (as in the opening of *Isabel*) we do not know whether to read the shot of the burnt-out building as flashback or flashforward (is Undersky a new beginning or is it doomed to destruction?). Saguenay looks up and sees a man on a cliff looking down. Presumably this is Boulder, but we cannot be sure, and his posture anticipates that of the male figure (who may or may not be Damien) who looks down on Saguenay when she crawls from the river at the end of the film. The fusion of Boulder with Damien is, however, incomplete, and several unmotivated long shots suggest that our point of view has become that of the lurking Damien. For example, just before Boulder and Saguenay make love by the river, she looks down at the rapids; there is then a cut to a long shot of the river, apparently from her point of view, but the camera pans up to show the couple in the distance on the riverbank. This disconcerting effect temporarily identifies us with the threat from the outside, and implicates us in the tensions at work in the film.

Boulder is gradually infected by Saguenay's "hesitation." She calls into question his authority as undisputed leader of the commune, his position as dominant male, and his sanity as defined against social madness. He is brought to ask "Where am I finally?" and seems to be as startled as Saguenay when they discover the burnt-out building from her visions. He tells her that he has been thinking about "what we first came for," and that he has the feeling that he has "been here before . . . but that's impossible." His decision to cast her adrift on a raft can be seen as an attempt to avoid dealing with the doubts that her presence in the commune has aroused. From the beginning, the commune members have blamed her for the "natural" disasters that threaten their survival. Just after her arrival, "something" attacks the sheep at night; then the bull falls sick and the vegetables are threatened by a late frost. Although the night prowler turns out to be a bear, the bull recovers, and the vegetables are saved, suspicion still falls on Saguenay as an intruder from the outside world. She herself fears that Damien is lurking in the forest around the commune, but Boulder's remark that her "nightmare" will always follow her is double-edged, since it could equally well be applied to the commune's withdrawal from society.

Saguenay shares Isabel's fear of animals and is shocked by what she sees as the "natural" brutality of the daily life of the farm. She is both fascinated and repelled by the copulation of the bull and a cow, and is horrified by the killing of a pig. Although she begins to make contact with nature when she assists in the birth of a calf, her alienation from nature is bound up with the problems of sexuality and what it means to be "human." One of the women, observing the bull's effort to penetrate the cow, comments that "he's only human." For Saguenay (as for Isabel and Martha), the issue cannot be treated casually, because her consciousness (and thus her human-ness) is terrorized by the fusion of sexuality and mortality. The (possible) presence of Damien is thus both a sexual threat and a threat of death. When Boulder makes love to Saguenay by the river, he takes her brutally with her back against a rock, and the final low-angle image of Damien/Boulder suggests the continued dominance and aggression of the male.

As this final image implies, *Journey* (and thus the trilogy) does not resolve the themes of the self or of the other. As Saguenay yells at the dancers at the Midsummer's Eve celebration, one of them tells her that "you can't get out of here until you know who you are." The impasse that she faces is reinforced by Boulder's remark that "out there" was as unreal to him as Undersky is to her, but as she climbs on to the raft, she speaks of a new view of reality:

> You can't find everything . . . not all at once. It's more important sometimes to move on and move out even if you're afraid you can't get back. You need both worlds. . . . At least I'm here, now. That's where I'll start.

Ironically, her verbal affirmation of the "here and now" distracts her from the immediate reality of Boulder's casting her adrift. But her desire to live in "both worlds" involves an acceptance of the fantastic "hesitation" which has tormented the heroines throughout the trilogy. The final sequence of *Journey*, in which Saguenay pulls herself from the river to confront not only the standing male but also the signs of industrial civilisation, suggests that it will not be easy for her to live in "both worlds." Almond's trilogy of the fantastic has, however, demonstrated the possibilities of such a double perspective through the "hesitation" built into the spectator's experience of the films.

1984

1 Robert Fulford, *Marshall Delaney at the Movies* (Toronto: Peter Martin, 1974), p. 24.
2 Tzvetan Todorov, *The Fantastic: A Structural Approach to a Literary Genre* (Cleveland: Press of Case Western Reserve University, 1973), p. 25. All further references to this work will be included in the text.
3 For applications of Todorov's theory to film, see Mark Nash, "*Vampyr* and the Fantastic," *Screen*, Autumn 1976, pp. 29–67; and Steve Seidman, "*The Innocents*: Point of View as an Aspect of the Cinefantastic System," *Film Reader*, 4, pp. 201–213.
4 Hollis Alpert, *Saturday Review*, 17 August 1968, quoted in Janet Edsforth, *Paul Almond: The Flame Within* (Ottawa: Canadian Film Institute, 1972), p. 22.
5 Edsforth, op. cit., p. 26.
6 Robert Fothergill, "*Journey*," *Take One*, 3, No. 7, p. 35.
7 Almond, quoted by Fothergill, loc. cit.
8 Guy Morris, "Focus," *Cinema Canada*, September 1968, p. 18; Jean-René Ethier, "*Journey*," *Séquences*, No. 71 (January 1973), p. 27.
9 Michel Euvrard, "*Journey*: Eurydice deux fois perdue," *Cinéma Québec*, 2, No. 4, (décembre 1972), p. 11.
10 Ibid., p. 12.
11 Guy Morris reported that scenes dealing with the possibly lesbian relationship between Isabel and her roommate were dropped during the final editing, loc. cit., p. 18.
12 Yves Lever, *Cinéma et société québécoise* (Montreal: Editions du jour, 1972), p. 155.

# *Allan King: Filmmaker*

## BY PETER HARCOURT

*Like certain kinds of minimalist sculpture, Allan King's documentaries are alarming in the daring and simplicity of their intrusions.* Skid Row, *King's first major work, made in 1954, brought portable synch-sound equipment to Vancouver's Bowery with what seems to have been a determination to raise the moral issues of cinéma vérité: Was the filmmaker affecting what was happening before his lens? If not, did he have a responsibility to do so? Should he have helped the outcasts who were his subjects? Was he injecting melodrama into what should have been a more dispassionate social critique? What would happen to his subjects when their plight was publicly revealed?*

*As Peter Harcourt points out here, the films that followed* Skid Row—Running Away Backwards, Warrendale, A Married Couple, *and* Come on Children—*straddled these moral dilemmas to the point of questioning their importance. As a result, King's relationship to his subject is something unique in the genre. His loyalty to his on-screen people transcends a commitment to their privacy, their dignity or their ability to survive the flawed utopias in which they find themselves. Rather, King's commitment is to the ideal of his subject's free will. As often as not, it is a commitment far deeper than that of the subjects themselves.*

*What Allan King does has most recently come to a head in the 1983 television documentary,* Who's In Charge? *That excruciating two-hour exposition condenses the proceedings of a week-long conference arranged by the filmmaker at which a carefully selected cross-section of unemployed Canadians are subjected to the often humiliating challenges of professional, small-group animators. The outcry that followed the airing of* Who's In Charge? *had much to do with King's life-long assertion that paradise—in this case the womb-like comforts of a secluded symposium—has its price. For King's critics, the stress suffered by the conference's already distraught participants was yet more evidence of a callous media manipulator squeezing a good show out of the powerless (q.v.,* Cinema Canada *No. 102, December 1983, and* Cinema Canada *No. 107, May 1984). For his defenders, King had found a way to depict with new depth the dilemma of the unemployed caught between unforgiving economic and bureaucratic systems (reproduced by the conference animators) and their own dejection. If it provides any satisfaction to his critics, King's own defence of* Who's In Charge? (Cinema Canada, *No. 104, February 1984), is no less anguished than the protests of that documentary's subjects.*

*In his examination of King's documentaries, Harcourt traces the evolution of the questions raised by the rules that the filmmaker sets for himself. Although written before* Who's In Charge? *the article nevertheless suggests a potential for the kind of exchange that surfaced around that work. Even more ambitious is Harcourt's attempt to relate King's considerable achievement as a feature filmmaker to the documentaries.*

*I suppose that the stream that runs through most of the things I respond to is a sense of feeling, of warmth about people, a celebration of people, a sense of humanity.*

—Allan King in an interview with Bruce Martin.

W.O. Mitchell's *Who Has Seen the Wind*, published in 1947, is a loving evocation of the growth of a young boy's consciousness, of his awareness of the cycle of nature and his gradual recognition of the mystical meaning of life and death. In an oblique way, a pantheistic way, the novel is deeply religious. It is concerned with the forces that animate things, both nature and people. It is aware of the invisible. It acknowledges the wind.

In 1977, *Who Has Seen the Wind* became a film, adapted by Patricia Watson and directed by Allan King. One of the remarkable achievements of the adaptation is that in this most visual of media Watson and King have managed to convey Mitchell's sense of the invisible by moments of speechlessness. The film is full of wide-eyed glances, of silent interrogations—as if trying to come to grips with the significance of things. Largely, of course, these glances belong to the child, Brian; but they also are received by both his mother and his father, and they are shared by Digby, the schoolmaster, in the open-eyed trust with which he greets the world.

In this way, the film implies more than it can say. Even the sullen resentment of the Young Ben is conveyed through his body and his eyes. He has almost no lines at all in the film. Admirers of the novel may, in fact, be amazed at how little dialogue has been added. For all of Mitchell's imagery, for all the interpretative function of his prose, Patricia Watson and Allan King have found visual equivalents.

*Who Has Seen the Wind* is set in the thirties—a world of hard times, of depression and drought. In the last ten years, this has become a fashionable decade for the movies. There have been a number of films that depict that time—but with a difference. In Hollywood films like *Bound for Glory, Thieves Like Us* and *Bonnie and Clyde*, while the decor is authentic, the thinking is modern. Especially in *Bonnie and Clyde* which, with its New Deal posters and sense of dusty streets, is the most meticulous of them all, the gestures are totally contemporary. Warren Beatty and Faye Dunaway, while playing characters from the thirties, speak directly to our own times. They appeal to our growing suspicion about the processes of the law and to the value we now place on individual freedom.

In *Who Has Seen the Wind*, there is none of this. With his short hair and clear blue eyes, Thomas Hauff as Digby radiates the idealism that seems so characteristically Canadian—particularly in the past. King used eyes in a similar way in his adaptation for television a couple of years ago of Barry Broadfoot's *Six War Years*. In that play, it was the same idealistic innocence that projected the Hauff character so willingly into the war. In both *Six War Years* and *Who Has Seen the Wind*, Thomas Hauff seems the incarnation of those past times. So it is with everyone in *Who Has Seen the Wind*. There is nothing that seems out-of-period in their gestures or attitudes.

This is both a distinction and, possibly, a limitation. Audiences might find the film too idealistic, too trusting in the natural processes of life to be able to believe that that was how it was in those days. Whether consciously or not, audiences might also be disquieted by its comparative lack of protest. Mitchell's pantheism blurs somewhat the social and political implications of the town's persecution of the Chinese family and of both the Bens. Like the kitten that dies in the litter or the runt pig that ought to be destroyed (as both the novel and the film might seem to be saying), Nature has its rejects as part of its wholeness. While certain characters do protest—principally Digby and Miss Thomson—the whole approach is more philosophical than political, urging us toward mysticism and toward an acceptance of "God's ways."

This idealism in the film, this self-effacing acceptance, is not just fidelity to the original story. There is something of this quality in nearly all of King's work. But in *Who Has Seen the Wind*, Mitchell's prairie world of the thirties is presented to us with an admirable accuracy. The reconstruction of Arcola, where the film was shot (a reconstruction the townspeople were pleased to accept)—the circus posters, auction-sale announcements, period gas-pumps, and Bee Hive Corn Syrup cans—combine with those trusting faces, with the expressive speechlessness of their eyes, to create within the film a warmly affirmative experience—an experience rare for our times.

The trust and love within the film is largely carried by Brian Painchaud as Brian. It is his consciousness of the world around him that becomes our consciousness of the film. But by a miracle of casting, there is often a sense of tiredness about his eyes—as if in advance of knowing it, he understands that all the questions he asks about life will have no satisfactory answer, as if, finally, the thoughts that most affect him lie too deep for words.

*Who Has Seen the Wind* is a meditative film. Like the novel it dramatizes, it asks us to contemplate the meaning of human life and the formation of human values. Eldon Rathburn's musical score assists this contemplation. For those of us who know his work, largely for the National Film Board, many of his devices will sound reassuringly familiar. But they are effective nevertheless. Plucked strings and a Jew's harp help to create the boys' excitement as they prepare for their gopher hunt; and at one point in the film, when Brian walks off into the prairie to spend the night alone under the stars, a solo horn and widely-spaced strings beautifully evoke the landscape's infinite vastness and awesomeness.

Allan King's *Who Has Seen the Wind* goes farther than the book in centring this prairie world within Brian's consciousness. In this way, the film becomes a distinguished example of what is really a Canadian genre: films that create the world through the eyes of a young child. Claude Jutra's *Mon oncle Antoine* and Francis Mankiewicz's *Le temps d'une chasse* immediately spring to mind; but *Lies My Father Told Me* and *Lions for Breakfast* work in much the same way. If we extend the age to take in all the young, then the list of films is enormous—in terms of richness and productivity, virtually the Canadian equivalent of the American Western!

If *Who Has Seen the Wind* is characterized by directness and simplicity, these qualities—which are in the novel and can be found in different ways in other films by Allan King—are finally focused through Brian. Most of the world created for us is presented through his eyes—questioning the values of the life and death around him, trying to make sense of it all but drawing no conclusions. Conclusions (if there are any) would belong to another world, a more urban and sophisticated world—a world closer to our own times.

> *Certainly, in the past at any rate, it's been very much part of my character to be unsure, to be very careful; it's difficult for me to be very forthright emotionally and even forthright in talking in a general way. I'm not sure how much of it is a desire to be covert or how much of it is a simple confusion in my own head about what I feel or what I think.*
>
> —Allan King (Martin interview).

*Who Has Seen the Wind* marks a new stage in Allan King's career, for until very recently, King has not been known as a director of dramatic features. Like other Canadian filmmakers, he began in documentary. Working out on the west coast in the late fifties and early sixties, King produced a number of shorts for the CBC that earned him his initial reputation. *Skid Row* (1956), *Rickshaw* (1960), *A Matter of Pride* (1961) and *Bjorn's Inferno* (1964) established the credentials that allowed King to do a variety of items for the CBC, as well as to set up production offices in London, England. It was at about this time, however, that King began to conceive for himself more challenging projects, moving slowly but surely toward a form which he, more than anybody else, is responsible for developing—the actuality drama.

The actuality drama is a mixture of documentary and fiction. Bypassing the conventional ingredients of script and actors, it uses actual people in actual situations, but then shapes the material so that it becomes both something more and something less than that—a film by Allan King. The purest example of this way of working is *A Married Couple*, made in 1969. But before that there was an interesting predecessor—virtually an invisible predecessor because it has been seen by so few people. It was a film made for the CBC in 1964 called *Running Away Backwards* or *Coming of Age in Ibiza*. In some ways, it is one of the most interesting films that King has ever made.

It is interesting because it is so naive and embarrassing—so uncertain about what its values really are. In this way, it takes risks. *Running Away Backwards* tells the story of a group of Canadians "living it up" in Ibiza—trying to "find themselves" away from the insipidities of day-to-day Canadian life. This ambition in itself is more than a little naive; yet it is an experience that more than a handful of Canadians have felt obliged to go through.

*Running Away Backwards* offers a dilemma for the spectator. Is it a naive and embarrassing film about a bunch of Canadians sensitive to the uncertainties of their own identities? Or is it a sensitive and uncertain film about a bunch of naive and embarrassing Canadians who are escaping the demands of maturity by running away to Ibiza? To pose this riddle is to comment on the way Allan King works as a director. The directors we know most about, whom we talk about *as directors*, are generally those that impose a particular vision of the world upon whatever material they handle. Hitchcock, Bergman, Hawks, Antonioni—even Don Shebib—all have a view of life that is developed in one way or another from film to film. They often have as well a recognizable style—or at least a repertoire of stylistic effects that we learn to associate with the work of each director.

With Allan King, however, these matters are most elusive. There have been, to be sure, some thematic preoccupations. From *Skid Row* through *Warrendale* (1967) to *Come on Children* (1973), King has repeatedly concerned himself with social outcasts, with characters who cannot adjust to the conventions that our society lays down as normal. This theme is also present in *Running Away Backwards,* even though these pampered, middle-class people have melodramatically chosen their outcast state.

But more important than theme, perhaps, is King's attitude as a filmmaker, which I would characterize as one of self-effacement. Rather than impose himself on his material, Allan King tries as far as possible to let his material speak for itself. Whether it is the immense formality with which he interviews his winos at the time of *Skid Row* or his scrupulous fidelity to the original text in *Who Has Seen the Wind*, as a director King tends to make himself invisible, as if absent from his own films.

One of Allan King's closest affinities could be said to be with André Bazin, who believed that it was the cinema's chief privilege to be able to record directly a pre-existing reality. Thus he preferred the extended takes of William Wyler to the subjective camera tricks of Alfred Hitchcock; and he valued the grainy, newsreel quality of the early films of Rossellini over the conceptual editing that has been so much talked about in Eisenstein. I believe, had he lived to see them, Bazin would have also valued the films of Allan King.

Of course, King is not *actually* absent from his own films. But he does stand back in a way, whether through respect or timidity. This is what makes *Running Away Backwards* such a challenging film to deal with. Essentially, it is about discontent—the discontent of over a thousand expatriots who are seeking a "cure" in Ibiza. They are trying to draw strength from a civilization where there is still some harmony between people and their landscape, where there is still a human pace and scale to life. Yet as the old Spaniard explains toward the end of the film, these Canadians are all spectators, unable to understand. "Words which have disappeared from your dictionaries are still meaningful here," he explains.

Throughout the film, the search is presented as both futile and necessary—as a stage one must go through. There is Jake, who leaves at the end because he has seen the limitations of the histrionic self-assertions that this new world has allowed him. Meanwhile, Hank, who has resisted the idleness and sexual freedom that characterizes this expatriot community, is left behind—supposedly to do some "grad work" on himself with the young blonde woman who seems both to attract and frighten him, offering a challenge which, at least in those days, Canadians found hard to deal with on their own soil!

Looked at today, the film contains a lot of nonsense. Yet I know it is a kind of nonsense that felt real to many of us of that fifties generation. On a personal, existential level, the film registers a rejection. Yet unlike characters in the works of our existential leaders to the south—Norman Mailer, Ernest Hemingway and Henry Miller—the characters in *Running Away Backwards* make no commitment. There is no sense of politics and no concern at all with cultural analysis. They simply spend their time away, "like children playing in a Roman church," as that old Spaniard put it, and then go home again, no doubt to "earn a buck," having dabbled in sex and art.

The film, then, also registers an immaturity—an immaturity which is part of the sense of embarrassment that the film can cause, but is also part of its quality. It is as if Allan King and his associates had the initiative to make explicit some of the adolescent overassertions that certainly were felt by many Canadians of that generation, but which few of us would have had the courage to express so openly. In this way, the film documents a certain class of Canadian self-evaders, seeking escape from the monied rat-race but finally so dependent upon it that inevitably they are drawn back—running away backwards, as the film is called: people aware of an absence, of something their life has denied them, yet only able to affirm it in the most juvenile of ways.

> *If you have a sensitive, intelligent, quiet, responsive, unobtrusive and unjudging, impersonally critical cameraman or camera crew, then not only is the camera not inhibitive, but it stimulates the [people] to talk, in the same way an analyst or therapist does. You can talk if you want to; you don't have to talk if you don't want to; you do what you want.*
>
> —Allan King in *The New Documentary: a Casebook in Film-Making.*

The same attitudes and problems as those seen in *Running Away Backwards* are present in the next three major films that Allan King directed (in between doing bread-and-butter items, largely from London, for the CBC): *Warrendale* (1967), *A Married Couple* (1969) and *Come on Children* (1973). Each film represents a distinguished example of King's early way of working. They are not "just" documentaries, but they are not quite dramatic fiction either; and like *Running Away Backwards*, all three films leave us feeling a bit uneasy at the end.

Both *Warrendale* and *Come on Children* concern themselves directly with adolescents, with young people who have come to feel that they live outside society. *Warrendale* explores the "holding" therapy devised by John Brown for the treatment of emotionally disturbed children—a treatment which (in the film) involves a mixture of extreme caring and something that looks like violence—while *Come on Children* takes a group of "disaffected young people from the suburbs of Toronto" (as the opening title explains it) and sets them up on a farm where they are allowed, perhaps encouraged, to "do their own thing."

Of the two films, *Warrendale* is the more disturbing—as much because of the therapy as the filmmaking. And so, as with other films by Allan King, the experience of watching it leads us away from the film *as a film* and out into a discussion of the material it contains.

Yet the film is not neutral. Nor is the fact of filming in such an environment without its effect upon the kids. Young Tony, especially, who throughout the film is constantly telling everybody to "Fuck off!"—a touch of realism that kept the film off the grandmotherly CBC—at one point looks directly at the camera and asks, "Why do I swear all the time?" I don't think it is hard to find an answer. Like other people in the film (though to a lesser degree), he is aware of his "performance."

But the film is remarkable for the environment it creates—both topographical and psychological. The Warrendale clinic looks indeed like a warren of dwellings placed in a mud-and-rubble wasteland—a suburban nightmare which, in itself, couldn't help but increase the sense of isolation that all the children feel. In a way, then, not unlike the attitudinizing adults in *Running Away Backwards*, the kids are cut off from what might be their real culture—from their actual homes in some sort of city dwelling, hopefully more humane than this setting we see them in. While I have neither the space nor the competence to discuss fully the implications of this therapy, it is disturbing to say the least.

I can see its virtues—the virtues of confrontation. The kids are not allowed to retreat into themselves. When they shout or get violent, they are shouted back at in return and held firmly by caring arms. But sometimes this holding involves as many as three adults at a time for just one child. And the kids are expected to verbalize everything. Tony must explain why he resents Terry's bad breath, and Carol must rationalize her resentment of Walter—the fact that she misses him because he is rarely there. Now is this loving force or emotional rape? This is the question that the film leaves unanswered.

The film finds its centre in the death of Dorothy, the cook—one of those "happy accidents" in filmmaking that allow filmmakers to shape their material toward a climax. But even this, considering the nature of the event and the public way it is announced, with all the kids gathered together and the camera ready to roll, is somewhat disturbing.

But as a film, *Warrendale* is important largely because it leaves us with all these problems. It confronts us directly both with the validity of the therapy and with the ethics of filmmaking. Once again Allan King has taken on a project that many more cautious people would have shied away from.

*Come on Children* is organized in much the same way, except that there is no "happy accident." One of the girls has a baby, but this isn't dwelt upon; one of the guys shoots up speed. Another lad, John Hamilton, really becomes the "star" of the film. Through his songwriting, he is also a kind of choric commentator. He is constantly playing the guitar and entertaining us with his stories and with all his unfocused charm. A small confrontation occurs in this film when all the parents come up for a day. But even this is low-key—a sad but not basically an angry presentation of the generation gap of which these kids are so aware.

There were a number of films made at the end of the sixties, before the Youth generation gave way to what Tom Wolfe has called the Me generation: Mort Ransen's *Christopher's Movie Matinee* and Jacques Godbout's *Kid sentiment*, both made in 1968; and Claude Jutra's *Wow* made the following year. In the context of these films, *Come on Children* is admirable both because of the respect it brings to these kids and because of the quiet rhythm that gradually establishes itself as they sit around and talk and sing and do not much at all. And if the sense of intrusion seems less here than in *Warrendale*, it is nevertheless made explicit at a couple of points in the film.

During an early sequence while two of the boys are eating breakfast, one of them becomes increasingly impatient with the fact that he is being filmed, an impatience that becomes anger before our eyes. "You're fucking the shit outa me, man," he finally screams, putting his hand up before the camera. And toward the end of the film, as the kids are getting ready to leave, one of them is directly interviewed by King himself—a rare disruption for an Allan King film. "What are you going back to?" we hear King ask from behind the camera; and then a whole series of questions concerning what he is going to do, what he would like to do; if he went away, what he would do there, and so on. To each of these questions, in a pleasantly smiling but ultimately hopeless way, the young lad replies "Nothing,"—nothing in the world as he has known it. "Maybe get with whatever's happening elsewhere," as he finally puts it.

Like so many of King's films, *Come on Children* presents people without a future, without a culture to sustain them, with no clear idea of what they exist in the world to do. The film starts off with John singing the well-known Dylan song which seems to sum up the feeling of them all:

> . . . I'm walkin' down that lonesome road, Babe,
> Where I'm bound I cannot tell. . . .

Miraculously, however, King's discreet direction combines with the editing skills of Arla Saare to give this film in which nothing happens a gently reflective rhythm and distinct shape of its own. It becomes a quiet kind of drama—a drama of nice kids who have a real respect for one another but who feel there is nothing to do and nowhere to go. It's no wonder the film hasn't been seen. It would be too much like an accusation.

> *Some of the critics . . . felt that* A Married Couple *had no imagination or that it was somehow dull. I'm a little puzzled by the expectations for fantasy in film, for myth-making; it seems that if you can give people a comfortable fantasy or myth, it is easier for them to accept. If you say what you feel directly or show them the world as you experience it, this seems to cause difficulties.*
>
> —Allan King (Martin interview).

Of all the films of this period, *A Married Couple* represents King's most dramatic achievement. However, like most other distinguished Canadian films within this system of ours controlled by American exhibition outlets, it hasn't been a great commercial success. Yet its influence has been considerable, most obviously on the American television series *An American Family* but also on the parliamentary documentation done in Britain by Roger Graef—one of the old team of Allan King Associates when they were based in London.

It is not exactly an *agreeable* film—unless you like to listen to people shouting at one another for the better part of an hour and a half. It is not a film that makes you wish you were married! But what is so extraordinary is that the couple King found to consent to such a project, Billy and Antoinette Edwards, are both natural performers. They bring an energy to everything they do that makes for interesting material on the screen.

Seen nowadays, several years after it was made, the film seems like a study of oppression—largely of the man over the woman, but also of all the members of the family by the structure of family life itself. As a family, the Edwards quantify everything. Nearly all their squabbles concern money and the acquisition of material goods—a pair of $40 shoes, a new shag rug, a gas stove for their remodelled kitchen, a washer and dryer, a new hi-fi. Billy, in characteristic fashion, offers the classic male argument: since he makes most of the money, he has most of the rights—an argument that Antoinette strives constantly to counter.

As the Edwards depict it for us, in the edited version of their lives which we have on this film, married life is a struggle for dominance with all the cards stacked in favour of the male. Even their sex life becomes part of this battle. Antoinette tries desperately to defend her right, when she feels like it, to sleep in her own bed. Talk between the Edwards seems like thrust and counter-thrust, with Antoinette's suggestions becoming more and more preposterous the more aggressively they are resisted by Billy. Like their opening argument about the harpsichord, for example, a scene that reads so tersely in transcript that it seems hard to believe that it never was written:

> ANTOINETTE: Where do you think we should put the harpsichord? Over there?
> BILLY: The harpsichord. I don't know. The same place we're gonna put the rock band. What harpsichord?
> A: That I'm gonna buy.
> B: You're not gonna buy a harpsichord.
> A: Oh yes I am with part of my money.
> B: Oh no, you're not gonna buy a harpsichord.
> A: Yes, I'm gonna buy a musical instrument.
> B (*shouting*): You're not gonna buy a harpsichord. And the reason you're not buying a harpsichord is because the harpsichord is a selfish instrument just for you. The money is gonna go to buying the things we absolutely need. What do we need a goddam harpsichord for?
> A: How can I study voice again if I don't have a musical instrument?
> B: You don't need a harpsichord. I'll get you a harmonica.

If there is rarely the sense of a genuine conversation between them, rarely the sense of speech as gentle exchange, the film is not without its moments of tenderness. Billy is often presented playing with their son, Bogart, or fondling their dog, Merton. There is a lovely moment in the film when all four of them are sitting on the floor together, testing out their new hi-fi and exchanging kisses with one another (even with Merton) and listening to an old Beatles song. Right after this scene, Billy and Antoinette are alone together, dancing to "I'd love to turn you on . . .," Antoinette all wrapped around Billy as they move together, the image somewhat fractured by the bevelled glass of the French doors that the cameraman, Richard Leiterman, is shooting through. It is a most effective moment, I would argue, both because the distance suggests reticence on the part of the crew concerning this intimacy and because, through the splitting up of the image, the scene also creates a pleasant visual effect.

A sadder, more tender moment occurs after a party sequence toward the end of the film. Antoinette has been flirting with some guy in a red shirt which (as the film is fictionalized in the editing) seems to have led to a sort of squabble between the Edwards once they got home. In any case, after the party the film picks them up in close-up, cuddling on the sofa. Antoinette is crying and talking quietly to Billy—possibly the most tender talk in the film. But we can't hear what they are saying. A record they are listening to (one of Sarastro's arias from *The Magic Flute*) erases their speech from the sound-track. Although the scene actually happened this way when they were shooting it, this effect again suggests reticence on the part of the filmmakers. It also forces us to deal purely visually with the significance of the scene.

It is not an encouraging moment. Antoinette seems really disturbed, as if trying to reach Billy. But his face is largely turned away from her—as if, as elsewhere in the film, he is rejecting whatever she has to offer him. The scene ends with a dissolve to Antoinette alone in her own bed, cuddling her pillow. Then we cut to Billy, still downstairs, finishing off a drink and patting the dog.

*A Married Couple* is a highly distinctive film. There is nothing quite like it anywhere in the world. It is a frightening experience. Like the other films of this "documentary" period, *A Married Couple* is also a film about exiles, about people cut off from a culture that might meaningfully sustain them. While there is no political analysis in any of King's films, they all add up to a statement that cries out for political interpretation. They are all about alienation. They present the separation of the individual from culture. Unless we are deeply pessimistic about life and accept all these problems as an unalterable aspect of "human nature," King's films all suggest the need for social change.

Whether King himself is aware of this, I do not know. His characters certainly aren't. Antoinette and Billy see nothing wrong with the institution of marriage as it exists, with their pursuit of the perfect home. The problems are all internalized. Both Billy's dominance and Antoinette's resentment are ritualized in the routines of marriage. At one point during one of their fights, Billy is explicit about this. "The framework isn't the problem," he cries out at her. "The laws of society are not the problem in this marriage. The problem is you and me. . . . What we don't know is whether we really hate one another or not."

Like both *Warrendale* and *Come on Children*, like most of the early work of Allan King, *A Married Couple* is a film that in spite of the fine shape that King and Arla Saare finally evolved for it, leads us away from the film as a film, out to talk about the problem it contains—the problem of marriage. And the statement of Billy's could provide a central point from which discussion might begin.

Although the film ends tenderly, it also ends with non-achievement—with Antoinette and Billy seeking the creature comforts of touching one another, of holding one another, but with nothing really resolved. We know that the next day, fresh squabbles will begin. The Edwards are trapped within their own image of themselves: middle-class consumers whose life values are as empty and non-sustaining as the silly Heinz commercials it is Billy's job to supervise. As the film presents them to us, the Edwards' lives are as barren of human sustenance as the wasteland setting of *Warrendale* and as hopeless of a future as the end of *Come on Children*. It is not a comforting picture of our middle-class world.

> *I'd done most of what I wanted to do in documentary simply as a technical form. I didn't see it shifting very much from there. Also, I had always used documentary essentially as a dramatic form. I've done essay films, but I've always been interested in stories about people. It was never practical in Vancouver where I started to do dramatic work. We didn't have the budgets. We didn't think we had the experience to work in that manner. So one made films about real people and told a story about them.*
>
> *In essence, the form of* Warrendale *is a dramatic structure; and with* A Married Couple, *it is directly a dramatic structure with two central characters. The fact that they're documentaries, for me, has always been coincidental. That was economically where I could work.*
>
> *Using actors and scripts has more control in many respects and also allows for a range of experience that is beyond the scope of individuals who are playing them-*

*selves. Also, I began to feel that I wanted that kind of control. I wanted to be able to work more directly in a dramatic form, with actors.*

—Allan King in conversation with Peter Harcourt.

Since the dissolution of his offices in London and of his Toronto company after *Come on Children*, Allan King has been working more than ever with television—but now with a difference. Since 1974, he has increasingly involved himself with drama, involving real scripts and real actors. In some ways this is more conventional work than he has done in the past.

There are several reasons for his switch to drama, both financial and practical. In spite of their distinction, King's actuality dramas didn't make much money; and through John Hirsch and the revitalization of television drama at the CBC, work in filmed drama suddenly became more of a possibility. There are other factors that also may have influenced him: his increased association with Patricia Watson, now both his colleague and his wife, and his admiration for Toronto's little theatre—for directors like Paul Thompson and Martin Kinch and for playwrights like Carol Bolt, two of whose plays he has filmed.

In fact, his version of *Red Emma* (1976) has much of the old King quality about it. Helped by the constantly steady camera work of Edmund Long, King made what at some times looks like a documentary of Kinch's stage production, but at other times seems like a film version of the play itself, with Kinch directing the actors and King his film crew. Kinch worked with King again for Rick Salutin's *Maria* (1976), a film about a young woman in a clothing factory who tries to organize a union. This time, however, Kinch is simply the dialogue coach and King is the director. It is as if, by these means, King has been training himself for the different sort of challenges that dealing with actors entails.

The most innovative of these television programs is *Six War Years* (1975), a video adaptation by Norman Klenman of Barry Broadfoot's oral history of the Second World War. Working directly on tape, King was able to superimpose close-ups in colour of the faces speaking directly to us over black-and-white newsreel footage of the war; he also had a handful of actors play out a variety of roles. Apparently influenced by Paul Thompson's work with the Theatre Passe Muraille, *Six War Years* might really be described as a piece of "epic" television—a Brechtian combination of direct statement and dramatic recreation that simultaneously moved and informed us. Its achievement still represents one of the most *original* hours of television that I have seen anywhere in the world.

Less satisfactory, to my mind, is King's direction of *Baptizing* (1975), drawn from the story by Alice Munro. My own misgivings about this film centre basically on the music. While the story does connect young Del's dreams of romantic love with listening to opera, the decision to run operatic music over her later scenes of lovemaking has disquieting results. First of all, it gives to all these sequences a clichéd, Elvira Madiganish sort of lyricism. Secondly, the continued use of this music might imply that the *reality* of making love is still wrapped up with Del's dreams. It might suggest that she isn't learning anything, that she isn't growing up. But it is the point of the original story to illustrate the reverse.

Nevertheless, whatever my reservations, *Baptizing* too provided a fine experience for its viewers within the opiate world of television. It certainly offered an excellent training ground for the greater challenges of *Who Has Seen the Wind.*

It is difficult at this stage to see where Allan King is going. Since *Who Has Seen the Wind*, King has already made a film version of Carol Bolt's *One Night Stand*, and I assume that he will go on working for the CBC. But he wants to make theatrical features, and even if this means that he will be working in a more conventional mode, Allan King's artistic presence will still very much be there.

The exact nature of this presence is still hard to characterize. It has to do with innocence and also with naiveté—initially about the expected characteristics of the medium he was working in and, throughout his life, about the complexities of existence, especially when seen from a socio-political point of view. But these twin characteristics are, arguably, what make his films so unmistakeably Canadian, speaking from and to an Anglo-Saxon, middle-class culture which was at one time too dominant but which has become increasingly uncertain of itself since the Second World War. Possibly related to this too is King's lack of self-assertion: in his documentary days, his respect for the reality he was filming; now, in drama, his respect for the original text.

Thinking about King's achievement, I keep remembering Keats' notion of "negative capability"—an openness to experience that Keats believed essential to the receptivity of the artist. This Allan King has in abundance—almost to a fault. Until *Who Has Seen the Wind*, King's major films had all been about rejects, about misfits within the society that contains them. But this subject matter is never analyzed as such. The situations are simply presented to us, always with King's sensitivity and respect, but with little that might betray King's personal attitude.

Perhaps King's work on *Red Emma* and *Maria* might lead to a more direct awareness of the political issues that form a submerged dimension in all his work. But if his films present characters with no culture to sustain them—culture in the anthropological sense of shared values and conventions—then this might well explain both King's attraction to and the achievement of *Who Has Seen the Wind.*

*Who Has Seen the Wind* is a re-creation of our past, a past where society was not vitiated by generation gaps and battles between the sexes, a world where—as Helen sings at the beginning of *Red Emma*—"all their lies were true." People believed in things: in the process of Nature, in the continuity of human life, in the necessity of self-sacrifice—as they also did, more grimly, in *Six War Years.* The male-centred world of middle-class, Anglo-Saxon dominance had not yet been challenged or made aware of its increasing inability to nurture its own children.

Furthermore, the formal tidiness of fiction must be attractive to King at this stage of his career, for fiction provides a stronger sense of order than is possible when working with the raw material of actuality footage, struggling after the event to find an order in the editing. Finally, the extraordinary feeling both of sincerity and wholeness that characterizes every frame of *Who Has Seen the Wind* is all the more impressive because these qualities are the characteristics of a past that still had a strong sense of active community values, values that have virtually vanished from the suburban sprawl of our increasingly urbanized world—the setting of so many of King's previous films.

In this way, *Who Has Seen the Wind* seems to complement Allan King's previous work, as if rounding it off and bringing it to an end. But in its scope, in its newly achieved confidence in working with actors, and in the many extraordinary beauties throughout its fictionalized form, *Who Has Seen the Wind* is also a beginning.

From *The Human Elements* (Ottawa: Oberon, 1978).

# *A Canadian Cronenberg*

## BY PIERS HANDLING

*David Cronenberg is English Canadian cinema's local boy made good—and as such he can never be forgiven. With a long and growing string of independent features behind him, Cronenberg has attracted the kind of international reputation and financing that make him as alien to his colleagues as any of the creatures in his horror films. Cronenberg's success has freed him from the institutional restraints of Canada's film bureaucracy. Some would also contend that this has released him from the moral and aesthetic obligations necessitated by that bureaucracy, be they the social imperatives of National Film Board work or the self-effacing aestheticism of Arts Council filmmaking. His films are, paradoxically, criticized as either too self-indulgent or too highly dependent on the international pursuit of gothic motifs—the good old-fashioned Hollywood scream epic.*

*Perhaps it is typical of a culturally insecure society like that of English Canada that the supposed lack of nationalist impulses on the part of an internationally recognized talent threatens his critical acceptance. Elsewhere it would simply be enough to discuss Cronenberg as a filmmaker. Critics might even suggest that the master of a popular medium could have something to do with shaping the notion of a national identity. Would Americanism be the same without John Ford? Is it too much to suggest that Jean Renoir helped shape the consciousness of twentieth-century France? Did Ingmar Bergman help to make a Swede a Swede?*

*In this study of Cronenberg's work in the context of Canadian cinema, Piers Handling is not going so far as to suggest that those films in some way make us what we are. But he does maintain that the works have some connection to other Canadian films. Moreover, the gothic impulse upon which Cronenberg draws is not entirely foreign to English Canadian culture. The shapes of his films, Handling asserts, "speak to an indigenous aesthetic." In his conclusion, Handling does not quite argue for Cronenberg as a typical Canadian filmmaker. But what he does say, throughout the article, perhaps deemphasizes the desirability of the "typical" and points us instead toward the search for creative contribution.*

David Cronenberg's films are looked upon as aberrations in the cinematic landscape of this country; stylistically and imaginatively the films apparently do not belong. Formally, Cronenberg finds himself working within genres—horror and science fiction—that are totally alien to our artistic tradition. Beneath the obvious excesses inherent in these genres, it has been difficult to discern Cronenberg's thematic concerns; most critical reaction has been so obsessed with the blood and gore of parasites or exploding heads as to be heedless of what the films are saying to us. This has been unfortunate; the tone of critical response has been set by Marshall Delaney's (alias Robert Fulford) vituperative review of *The Parasite*

*Murders* in *Saturday Night*. Critically, Cronenberg has never really recovered from this article in Canada. His reputation in Europe, England and the United States is established, and a devoted coterie of admirers write about his work with great admiration. This article does not pretend to be an apology for the films. Instead, it will attempt to situate Cronenberg as a Canadian filmmaker, touching on a number of points to try to clarify some of the imaginative bases of his cinema.

The overwhelming artistic tradition within which the Canadian artist functions is realist. Realism has informed our literature, our painting, our theatre, our television and our filmmaking. Cinema in this country is virtually synonymous in many people's minds with the documentary film. Even our fictive creations are born out of this soil. It is a heritage that has an extensive history, and it stretches back through most of our filmmaking endeavours, from Richard Benner's *Outrageous!* to Michel Brault's *Les ordres*, Don Shebib's *Goin' Down the Road*, Don Owen's *Nobody Waved Good-bye* and further back into the early part of the century—*Back to God's Country, The Viking* and *The Silent Enemy*. With their particular form of narrative construction, rejection of studio shooting and use of actual events (historic and personal), they are thinly veiled documentaries, portraits of real people living in a recognizable world, as remote from the celluloid fantasies of Hollywood's Luke Skywalkers and Supermans as can be imagined. We have become highly adept at making docudramas, fictional works based on real events. Peter Pearson's CBC film *The Tar Sands* was so successful in its representation that Alberta Premier Lougheed sued the corporation for damages and won his case! The realist or documentary tradition is central to our imagination, as Bruce Elder notes:

> According to one of the most widespread convictions concerning Canadian art, the quintessential feature of our cultural tradition is the activity of documenting the landscape. Canadians, it is said, have found themselves in an alien—indeed a hostile and somewhat frightening—landscape; consequently Canadian artists have assumed the task of presenting us with an image of the landscape so that its otherness might, if not be overcome, at least be understood. For this reason, the documentary image—an undistorted image that is faithful to the object it represents—has a place of great importance in Canadian art.[1]

The documentary tradition in Canadian film was not totally due to John Grierson's influence and his creation, the National Film Board, but it was certainly consolidated by him. Robert Fulford in a recent article[2] traced the tradition back to the nineteenth century, to Methodism and Egerton Ryerson, the great preacher, by way of the educational system, the United Church, and the CCF and NDP parties, who carried this thinking into the political arena. Grierson's philosophy was essentially educative and informative in nature. It proposed that the cinema could be used as a teaching device in the broadest sense, giving people an enlarged understanding of the world that they inhabited. All this was of course totally antithetical to the escapist, entertainment cinema emanating from Hollywood, especially in the thirties, the time that Grierson was writing.

The realist tradition deserves a great deal of attention when one approaches Canadian cinema. It provides both the basis for the documentary film and the inspiration for our fictional cinema. While the tradition has been predominant, it could be argued that it has also been stifling. Fulford quotes a sentence from Robertson Davies that helps situate Cronenberg in all this:

> We live in a country where the depths of the spirit are too often sealed wells, and where the human psyche which is the womb and matrix of all great art, including poetry and great fable, is regarded with mistrust.

While the realist heritage allows work to be rooted in an identifiable social context, it also has its disadvantages. In its faithful adherence to reality it can lapse into positions that verge on determinism. In other words it depicts social and political relationships as they are, not as they can be, and there is often something immutable about this reality. Change, or the possibility of change, is significantly not felt within the majority of these films. Reality seems fixed within patterns that are beyond the power of the individual to influence. Powerlessness is often the feeling that we take away from these films.

Few have challenged the realist tradition. Who even remembers films like René Bonnière's *Amanita pestilens* or Morley Markson's *The Tragic Diary of Zero, the Fool* and *Monkeys in the Attic*. Those who have worked against the dominant practice have suffered the ignominy of total rejection. It seems that fantasy and dream, often with a strong desire for change attached to these visions, has no place in our films. Most recently, women's cinema has gravitated in this direction, perhaps in reaction to the essentially patriarchal nature of the realist tradition. Dream and fantasy, which implicitly challenge the underlying ideology of realism, can allow for the potential of change and rebellion. Mireille Dansereau explores this tension brilliantly in *La vie rêvée*, while other filmmakers like Patricia Gruben (*Sifted Evidence* and *The Central Character*), Joyce Wieland (*The Far Shore*) and Anne Claire Poirier (*Les Filles du Roy* and *Mourir à tue-tête*) have also incorporated this dialectic into their films.

Cronenberg would seem to stand outside the realist tradition. His interest in thc subconscious and its hidden depths has led him away from a strict observation of, and adherence to, surface reality. When the unconscious is given a form, it is as a grisly parasite in *Shivers*, a proboscis growing out of a woman's armpit in *Rabid*, a family of genderless, angry children in *The Brood*, telepathic power that can explode heads in *Scanners*, or the subjective hallucinations in which a gun merges into the hand that holds it in *Videodrome*. Reality for Cronenberg is immediately divisible into two perceptions of it—subjective and objective, or internal and external. While this schism is evident in almost all his work, it forms the central questions of his first two features, *Stereo* and *Crimes of the Future*. *Stereo* in particular posits a world where the gap between objective and subjective reality, what we see and what we hear, image-track and sound-track, is irreconcilable. Knowledge is completely undermined. The world remains unknowable and mysterious. When Antoine Rouge reincarnates himself as a little girl at the end of *Crimes of the Future*, his disciple Adrian Tripod can only marvel at this magical moment. It cannot be accounted for. Almost all of *Videodrome* is structured around this principle of epistemological uncertainty. Reality and illusion become indistinguishable from each other.

But if Cronenberg stands apart from this pervasive tradition of realism because of his fascination with the subconscious, has he also managed to break away from the central concerns and characteristics that have developed out of this tradition? If he has resisted the dominant aesthetic (partially through his interest in excess and release), has he also broken away from the imaginative continuum that one can trace in Canadian cinema?

Much of Cronenberg's work reveals a consciousness alienated from the world. In many of the films, architecture becomes the landscape that in so much Canadian art is seen as hostile and threatening. *Stereo* and *Crimes of the Future* use the sterile concrete constructions of modern architecture to suggest a world that has lost touch with itself. The same can be said of the Starliner Towers in *Shivers*, the Keloid Clinic in *Rabid*, the Somafree Institute of Psychoplasmics in *The Brood*, the Consec complex in *Scanners*, and even the concept of Spectacular Optical in *Videodrome*. All of these environments are dehumanizing and alienating. They do not bring people together. They also presume order and control, yet nothing could be further from the truth. Beneath the appearance of order, repressed forces of sexuality, passion and desire are lurking, waiting to be released on an unsuspecting society. It is at this moment that Cronenberg moves furthest away from the realist tradition. When the forces of the unconscious, the Freudian id, are unleashed, it is to ravage the world of apparent order. This impulse ranges from the telepathic experiments in *Stereo*, which end in suicide, physical violence and self-mutilation, through the infected multitudes of *Shivers* and *Rabid*, who wreak havoc upon the world, Nola's brood who also kill and destroy, and Darryl Revok in *Scanners*, who engages in a form of telepathic warfare, until we arrive at the destructive hallucinatory world of Max Renn's fantasies in *Videodrome*.

Cronenberg's world is full of this continual dialectic tension, incorporating the dualities of good and evil, the mind and body, the rational and the irrational, the id and the superego, liberation and repression. This tension is translated structurally into themes that are commonplace in a great deal of Canadian cinema. In some, the dialectic translates into the struggle between the individual and the community (Luther Stringfellow versus the telepathic patients who form themselves into a community to exclude him in *Stereo*; Max Renn wandering between the conflicting powers of Spectacular Optical and Brian O'Blivion's Cathode Ray Mission in *Videodrome*; or Frank Carveth taking on society in his struggle to wrest control of his daughter away from his wife in *The Brood*). In *Scanners, Rabid* and *Shivers* we are shown couples who confront communities (Cameron Vale and Kim Obrist versus Consec and Revok's gang, Hart and Rose wandering through a society gone mad, and finally the two couples of *Shivers*—Nick and Janine, and Dr. Roger St. Luc and Nurse Forsythe confronting the infected apartment dwellers). Our cinema is full of these imaginative structures. Claude and Barbara of *Le chat dans le sac* and Peter and Julie of *Nobody Waved Good-bye* sired a generation of similar characters whose struggle with their society provided the thematic groundwork for the expression of a number of Canadian concerns. More often than not the independence of the individual is destroyed (*Paperback Hero, Réjeanne Padovani, Red*), or the fusion that the couple represents, often between contradictory forces, is not allowed to take place or is ruptured (*The Apprenticeship of Duddy Kravitz, Goin' Down the Road, A Married Couple, The Act of the Heart*). Cronenberg's couples find themselves in a similar predicament. Holism is denied. Fragmentation and disintegration predominate. Whether we see Stringfellow, Max Renn or the aforementioned couples, the exterior world denies them access to each other or to the community.

*The Brood* is the most pessimistic of them all, being predicated on the abolition of the couple before a form of normality and health can be restored. *Rabid* is scarcely less bleak; the struggle that Rose and Hart undergo to preserve their relationship is as deeply felt as that of Joey and Betts in *Goin' Down the Road*. The most optimistic vision is the potential coupling of Cameron Vale and Kim Obrist in *Scanners*, but the ambiguity of the final shot, with Vale's voice coming from the evil Revok's body after the scanning battle, points toward an uncertain future.

Over all these painful struggles stands the Cronenberg father figure, more often than not a benign but misguided scientist, who wants to better the world but ends up releasing nightmarish forces that he cannot control. Luther Stringfellow (*Stereo*), Antoine Rouge (*Crimes of the Future*), Dr. Emil Hobbes (*Shivers*), Dr. Dan Keloid (*Rabid*), Dr. Hal Raglan (*The Brood*), Dr. Paul Ruth (*Scanners*), and Brian O'Blivion (*Videodrome*) preside over a variety of experiments that at some point go completely awry. None of them are immorally fiendish. When they realize their mistakes, they invariably recoil in horror from what they have done. Often there is the implication that they represent the patriarchal order. Most of them experiment on women, with horrifying results. Antoine Rouge started a clinic for skin conditions induced by contemporary cosmetics in *Crimes of the Future*, and the disease that bears his name has resulted in the deaths of hundreds of thousands of women. Hobbes invents an aphrodisiac with a venereal disease component in *Shivers* and experiments with it on a female student; and her subsequent licentiousness assures the spread of the disease. Keloid operates on Rose after a serious motorcycle accident, and the skin grafts produce an appetite that can only be satiated by human blood. Raglan's experiments in externalizing rage end in Nola's brood, the purest form of that process, killing everyone who stands in her way. Dr. Ruth, who has invented the drug that creates scanners, presides over an all-male family where no mother is apparent. He, like O'Blivion in *Videodrome*, is linked to a preponderantly male corporate world that perverts his invention.

If "society" destroys either the individual or the couple, then it is unwittingly abetted by these mad scientists. This sense of an external force beyond our control is another recurring pattern in our cinema. It suggests a power that manipulates us all, and we find ourselves helpless when we confront it. Throughout Cronenberg's films there is the implication that the various contaminations can affect or infect any of us. The parasite (*Shivers*) and the rabies (*Rabid*) are epidemic. A new generation of unborn scanners is envisioned beyond the end of that film, and we feel helpless to alter this fact. The universal implications in *Videodrome* for anyone who owns a television set are inescapable. We have lost control and, more insidiously, don't even know where control lies anymore. For if the scientists display a certain kind of control, they are also ineffective and ultimately weak. Rouge has been exterminated, Hobbes commits suicide, Keloid is infected by the rabies he has unleashed, Raglan is killed by the brood, Ruth is shot during a moment of intense self-questioning and O'Blivion, also dead, only exists through the videocassettes that his daughter assembles.

Father figures in Canadian cinema are similarly inconsequential when visible. Some are callous and remote (Peter's father in *Nobody Waved Good-bye*), others spiritually dead (*Don't Let the Angels Fall*) or crippled and consequently impotent (*Paperback Hero*). Often they are drunken louts (*Le vieux pays où Rimbaud est mort*) or born losers (*Between Friends*). *Le temps d'une chasse* gives us a portrait of three fathers on a weekend hunting trip: one is a drunk, another a sexual lout, and the third is killed. The assassination of the father is plotted in *Kill*. In *Les beaux souvenirs*, he is mad. Quebec cinema is littered with absent fathers: In *Il ne faut pas mourir pour ça* he lives in Brazil, in *La mort d'un bûcheron* he is presumed dead, and in *Mon oncle Antoine* he leaves home for the bush.

If the older generation is bankrupt, its sins are certainly passed on to its children. Yet Cronenberg's attitude to his scientist/father figures is not quite this neat. All of them are visionaries, and some are philosophers. Within a sterile world they are trying to recreate human contact. Hobbes in *Shivers* feels that the human race has lost touch with its body and its instincts. Stringfellow in *Stereo* experiments with aphrodisiacs in an attempt to prove that the sexual norm is omni- or bisexuality. Raglan's psychiatric experiments are an attempt to release repressed anger, and O'Blivion envisions a new form of person in *Videodrome*. Ironically, within many of the father figures the tension between good and evil and the rational and the irrational is held in a fine balance.

At the same time, Cronenberg's male protagonists fall into a time-honoured tradition of Canadian men. Most are uninteresting, particularly when contrasted with the scientists, have a certain flatness as characters and find themselves consigned to the periphery of much of the action. Stringfellow (*Stereo*) and Tripod (*Crimes of the Future*) drift through life without energy or force. They are laconic and ironic in their distance from reality. Tripod takes pride in the anonymity that he has achieved, and at one point decides against a dangerous course of events for fear that "my hard-won equilibrium may become a morbid stasis." At first serenely confident, Roger St. Luc in *Shivers* can do nothing to staunch the spread of the parasite. Throughout *Rabid*, Hart is continually shown on the margins of the action. In his attempt to find Rose he is always in the wrong place at the wrong time. When he finally joins her, he is powerless to prevent the outcome of the film. He falls down some stairs and knocks himself out while Rose escapes to her death. The robotlike Cameron Vale pales beside the malicious energy of his brother, Darryl Revok, although he gradually asserts more control over his life. The husband in *The Brood* is apparently the most dynamic male in all of Cronenberg's cinema, but he is as colourless and characterless as Vale (neither of these characters are helped by the performances of Stephen Lack and Art Hindle). Like Vale, he supposedly eventually triumphs, but the ambiguity of the endings of both these films suggest Pyrrhic victories. Max Renn in *Videodrome* has a real energy that so many of his counterparts lack, but he soon becomes embroiled in a web of intrigue that results in his death/suicide. Finally he, too, is as powerless as the others.

The emasculated Canadian male has been noted by many of our critics. John Hofsess has asked the question why our cinema does not deal with "stronger egos and more confident people, people who can because they think they can."[3] Robert Fothergill devoted an entire article[4] to the question. He concluded that the Canadian condition reflected "the depiction, through many different scenarios, of the radical inadequacy of the male protagonist—his moral failure, especially, and most visibly in his relationships with women." Fothergill goes a step further. The American male fought the Oedipal battle in 1776 to assert his autonomy, while his Canadian brother refused the combat and stayed dutifully at his father's side. Could this also account for the ambivalence directed toward the scientists in Cronenberg's cinema?

For someone as interested in the repressed consciousness as Cronenberg is, there is a surprising lack, or failure, of rebellion in his work. If the order of society is sterile and controlled, the forces of chaos, when they are released, never result in apocalypse or the complete destruction that we find in a *Texas Chainsaw Massacre*. He has yet to take this step. Both *Stereo* and *Crimes of the Future* view their subjects from a perspective of extreme detachment; and any hint at rebellion (the man drilling a hole in his head in the first film and the group of conspirators in the second) is either not seen or is held at such a distance that resistance is the last response we take away from these moments. *Shivers* and *Fast Company* are the closest that Cronenberg has come to endorsing a revolutionary position. In the latter work, Lonnie Johnson openly rebels against his corporate sponsor and its representative, a man who manages the racing team and coldly manipulates the people who work for him. When the parasite is released in *Shivers* there is a relief that the sanitized order of the apartment complex has been disturbed. The final shot of all the infected inhabitants serenely driving out of the building, apparently to infect the rest of the world, seems to indicate that Cronenberg approves of the release of this sexual energy. It is certainly preferable to the stifling deadness of the "normal" people who live in the tower, and it is the furthest Cronenberg has gone in sympathizing with the id. But even *Shivers* is coloured by a sense of loss. The humanism of a Janine Tudor has been destroyed, and there is implicit in the last shot a feeling of a new conformity that will replace the old.

In *Rabid, The Brood, Scanners* and even *Videodrome*, the unconscious forces of the irrational must all be destroyed. The plague in *Rabid* is not seen as the joyous liberation of *Shivers*. Nola and her brood share a similar fate. Darryl Revok in *Scanners*, with his plans to rule the world, has to be confronted and fought. Max Renn's sado-masochistic hallucinations finally lead him toward his suicide.

Yet the films are more ambiguous than this, and this has led to a great deal of confusion, a confusion that may lie at the heart of what Cronenberg is saying. The ambiguity is present *within* each film, and *from* film to film as well. *Shivers* will serve as a paradigm, although much of what I will find here is applicable to the other films. Cronenberg establishes two conflicting realities in *Shivers*: the "normal" life led by average people in the Starliner Towers, and the libidinous, frenetic delirium of those infected by the parasites. The stifling decorum of the first has to be undermined because it is so repressive and antihuman. Yet the "liberation" of these people also carries with it a sense of horror and loss. This dialectic extends most importantly to the two central relationships in the film—Nick and Janine Tudor, and Dr. Roger St. Luc and Nurse Forsythe—relationships that are mirror images of each other, although at times reverse images. Janine and St. Luc are both rational, normal, considerate people who have learned to keep their emotions in check. On the other hand, their mates, Nick and Forsythe, are more sexual, disturbing and threatening. We are also given variations on what constitutes normality and what constitutes the libido. St. Luc is a plastic, cardboard hero, while Janine is loving and caring. Forsythe is viewed as sexual but controlled, whereas her mirror image in the other relationship, Nick, is almost "out of control." These two couples embody in an extremely sophisticated fashion all the warring forces in the film. Even our response to the infection of St. Luc and of Janine is very different. When Janine eventually succumbs to the lesbian kiss, we feel a sense of loss; her care of and love for Nick has ended in defeat. When St. Luc, however, is finally trapped in the swimming pool, the response is different; at last he has been "humanized." Even one's sense of what constitutes humanness continually shifts throughout. The parasite itself incorporates many of these opposites. It is both aphrodisiac and venereal disease, shaped like a phallus yet with excremental overtones, and is the object of horror and humour.

Similar examples could be drawn from all the films—the notion of Rose in *Rabid* as both evil (she carries the plague) and human (her struggle with the knowledge that she is tainted, "out of control"). Rose's embrace is similarly equivocal, for it signifies both attack and affection in a tension that Cronenberg consciously explores. *The Brood* poses the question of exactly who has won the fight for the child. Frank drives off with her after having killed Nola, but the welts that rise up on Candy's arm are an ominous omen. Will she turn out to be just like her mother? The morality of *The Brood* seems more clear-cut; Nola is evil and Frank is good, but Nola's childhood background—she had been beaten as a child—and Frank's blandness, combined with the fact that he has turned into a murderer, muddy these distinctions. *Scanners* seems similar to *The Brood*: Vale is the hero and Revok the villain. But reality is not that simple. Revok's energy is contrasted to the colourless Vale, and, once we learn he had a confused childhood, he becomes more sympathetic. By the end of the film we still don't have a clear indication of who has won the moral struggle. *Videodrome* is perhaps the most complex of all, yet initially the distinction between right and wrong appears to be fairly clear-cut. Brian O'Blivion and his daughter, Bianca, are contrasted to the ruthless Barry Convex and his sidekick, Harlan. But by the end of the film even these distinctions become blurred. Bianca seemingly is responsible for Max's death, and there is the implication that he may have become just a tool in her revenge on Convex, the man who killed her father. Nicki Brand, the temptress, remains an enigma. Has she led Max to his death, or is she a saviour in disguise?

While the moral dilemmas are contained within each film, they are also visible from film to film. *Shivers* and *Rabid* take radically different looks at the notion of the epidemic. In the former, the release of sexuality is seen as a liberation from sterility. In the latter, the release of the disease is only viewed with horror. It must be exterminated because it serves no social function. The couple is central to *The Brood* and *Scanners*; in one it must be destroyed, in the other recreated. *Scanners* and *Videodrome* both entertain questions concerning the manipulation of the mind. In *Scanners* this allows for the potential of a harmonious scanning community, whereas in *Videodrome* we only confront the confused individual isolated from society.

The ambiguity of the films has been noted by many critics. Cronenberg has been accused of being incoherent and confused. But the films trace the path of human struggle to find within life a reason and a self-justification for all actions. This attitude has echoes in Hamlet's "there is nothing either good or bad but thinking makes it so."[5] Wagner's titanic *Der Ring des Nibelungen* poses a similar question. Where do good and evil lie and what motivates people to do either? This is not to imply that Cronenberg is a Shakespeare or Wagner of the cinema; it is only to suggest that he is traversing similar terrain. (The analogy to Wagner is not lightly made; the ambiguity of motivation and the continual blurring of moral evaluation that mark the *Ring* are shared by many of Cronenberg's films, and *Tristan and Isolde*, with its lovers yearning for the rapturous night and a common death that will unite them, has eerie echoes in Max and Nicki's rendezvous with extinction in *Videodrome*. Wagner, too, has been prone to misinterpretation at every level, a fate that has also been Cronenberg's.)

What seems to be incontrovertible, though, is the fact that everyone is a victim of one sort or another in the Cronenberg world. Vicious circles of victimization recur. Rose in *Rabid* succumbs to an experimental skin graft, and the doctor who invented the process is stricken by his own creation. This model is uniform throughout, from Hobbes and the apartment dwellers in *Shivers* to literally every major character in all the films. Finally no one is in control, no one is master or mistress of individual destiny. *Videodrome* is perhaps the most convoluted of all, with everyone manipulating everyone else. It is impossible to identify who is in control, and the film explores this ambivalence in a fashion reminiscent of the complexity of Wagner's *Ring*.

As Margaret Atwood has pointed out in *Survival*, her study of our literature, all this is archetypically Canadian. I have already noted the absence or failure of rebellion within the films, and the feeling of powerlessness that is so pervasive. A paragraph in Atwood's book carries a number of connotations for Cronenberg's films:

> A preoccupation with one's survival is necessarily also a preoccupation with the obstacles to that survival. In earlier writers these obstacles are external—the land, the climate, and so forth. In later writers the obstacles tend to become both harder to identify and more internal; they are no longer obstacles to physical survival but obstacles to what we may call spiritual survival, to life as anything more than a minimally human being. Sometimes fear of these obstacles becomes itself the obstacle, and a character is paralyzed by terror (either of what he thinks is threatening him from outside, or of elements in his own nature that threaten him from within). It may even be life itself that he fears; and when life becomes a threat to life, you have a moderately vicious circle.[6]

Atwood's thinking here is particularly applicable, for the external fear of the first films has been replaced by an internal fear in all the films subsequent to *The Brood*. The internalization of this dread achieves its apotheosis in *Videodrome*.

This sense of victimization is pervasive in our cinema. Some have argued that it expresses a colonized mentality. The land has been exploited, but not for the profit of the people who live there. In other words we see ourselves as the exploited—historically and culturally. A feeling of entrapment contributes to this idea of victimization. This is a recurring feature in Cronenberg's cinema, whether it is Roger St. Luc surrounded in the swimming pool at the end of *Shivers*, Rose alone in a room with an infected man at the end of *Rabid*, or Max Renn stumbling onto an abandoned tugboat, a "condemned vessel," at the end of *Videodrome* to live out his last moments in confusion. One of Cronenberg's television dramas deals even more precisely with this imagery. Even its title, *The Victim*, embraces this notion, and it deals with an obscene phonecaller who strikes up a friendship with a woman he calls one day. He is in apparent control throughout, until he breaks into her apartment, only to hallucinate that he has become trapped in a cage while the woman whips him as a form of punishment. Again, control has proven to be illusory.

What also becomes fascinating is the way Cronenberg examines sexual entrapment by reversing the sex roles in *Rabid* and *Videodrome*. Rose is given a penislike proboscis, and Max a vaginal slit in his stomach. Rose metaphorically "rapes" her victims, while Max is continually violated—the pushing of a videocassette into his gaping slit is a graphic image of penetration. No freedom or "liberation" is achieved through these transsexual mutations. They are both tormented by their newfound organs, victims of them in the true sense of the word.

In the final analysis the individual is powerless to change anything. All fail to a greater or lesser extent. If the films are not determinist, there is nevertheless a grim overtone of fatalism that is difficult to ignore. Society, in all its guises, conspires against the individual or the couple. Nowhere is this more tragically stated than in the final shot of *Rabid*, where Rose, now dead, is picked up and tossed into a garbage truck, a shot that communicates such tragedy and waste, and synthesizes individual and collective loss. As Wagner and Brünnhilde discover in *Götterdammerung*, love is not always enough.

Perhaps the next question then becomes, to what extent is a subversion of society depicted in the films? If the individual cannot really change the course of events, does Cronenberg imply that society needs to be changed? Some critics have noted a political subtext in Cronenberg's work; European writers in particular pointed this out in their reviews of *Shivers* and *Rabid*. Certainly in both works the bourgeois world is completely undermined. Incest, lesbianism and homosexuality all appear in *Shivers*, and "normalcy" in all its forms is almost universally ridiculed. The apparent, assuring calm of the opening sequence, a promotional slide show for the Starliner Towers, with its promise that "the noise and traffic disappear here" is gleefully ridiculed by what transpires. Traditional bourgeois patriarchal morality is consistently subverted in *Rabid*: a Santa Claus is machinegunned in a shopping plaza, a woman goes berserk in a subway and attacks a man, policemen have to shoot other policemen, and a group of workers take their jackhammers to a government minister's car. Even the traditional bastion of the family is swept away when a man returns home to find that his wife has killed their child. He then becomes her next victim.[7] In a nice parody of the imposition of the War Measures Act of 1970 (and *Rabid* was shot in Montreal!), martial law is proclaimed as society moves to restore "law and order." Rose's attacks can also be read as being directed against the traditional male predator—the truck driver, the doctor. But this point is given real resonance when the drunken farmer who tries to rape her is stabbed in the eye—a symbolic attack on the male "look" or "gaze"; and a man on the make in a pornographic cinema is stung on the hand as he tries to reach into Rose's blouse—an equivalent metaphor for the unsolicited male "touch."

This undermining of traditional morality is visible in all the other films. The nuclear family of *The Brood* (in fact there are two in the film: Frank, Nola and their child, Candy; and Nola and her mother and father) is systematically destroyed. It is seen as the root of all evil. In *Scanners, Fast Company* and *Videodrome* the collective villain has a corporate face: Consec, Fastco and Spectacular Optical. Consec, an international security organization, deals in weaponry and private armies. Fastco manufactures gasoline additives for cars, but more pertinently treats its racing drivers as mere commodities. The ideological inconsistency and immorality of Spectacular Optical are made clear when we discover that it makes inexpensive glasses for the Third World and missile-guidance systems for NATO. All of these organizations are dangerously out of control and have to be stopped. Everywhere bourgeois society is shown to be bankrupt and in retreat, using the army, the police, or its technology in attempts to restore order when it can within the hypocrisy and sterility of this society. Is it any wonder that the couple, an image of fusion and completion, cannot survive?

Not only is society morally bankrupt, but its technology is dangerous and antihuman. A cosmetics disease has killed every woman in *Crimes of the Future*. The apartment tower in *Shivers* is viewed with disdain. In *Rabid*, Hart and Rose are seen continually trying to make contact with each other by telephone. Hart is on the phone to Rose when she is attacked, and his hysteria ends in his brutally smashing the receiver. Communication in *The Victim* is done almost entirely by telephone. Cars and machines are often more important than the people who drive them in *Fast Company*. In *Scanners*, the computer is finally seen as the enemy. When Vale destroys it in the famous scanning battle, the scene ends with a telephone receiver melting in his hands. *Videodrome* is constructed to an enormous degree around fear of the machine. Here guns, videocassettes, even television sets come alive before our eyes. They seem to have their own autonomy. The power of television is awesome, apparently infinite and capable of great destruction. More insidiously, there is also a fear of the world as we know it in *Videodrome*. Technology becomes an extension of a treacherous and mendacious universe.

Finally, there is one more point I would like to make about Cronenberg's films. Most commercial cinema, and in particular the American entertainment film, is based on the concept of narrative closure. These films follow the traditional patterns of storytelling. Problems are stated, dramatic conflict is asserted, and a resolution is achieved. The concept of narrative closure has come under scrutiny recently because it is suggestive of a number of unspoken ideological implications: that the world can be reduced to identifiable problems that are resolvable; that the resolution of these problems reassures the audience and reaffirms its belief in societal standards; that good always wins out over bad, and so on. Yet a great deal of Canadian cinema has resisted this notion. By the end of many of our films little has been resolved, and often we are left with more questions than answers. What does Peter's future hold for him at the end of *Nobody Waved Good-bye*; what is the meaning of the skater gliding in circles at the conclusion of *Le chat dans le sac?* There is certainly a sense that life has not come to an end when the credits come up.

Endings without resolution—the open text—are obviously diametrically opposed to the strategy of narrative closure. The open text suggests that the world cannot be reduced to simple schematic equations. This is particularly relevant to Cronenberg. He finds himself functioning within the entertainment mainstream, and in genres (horror and science-fiction) that essentially demand narrative closure, yet every one of his films denies this principle, with the possible exceptions of *Rabid* and *Fast Company*. The final shots of *Stereo* and *Crimes of the Future* are enigmatic and diffuse. All the other films end on questions. Is the plague going to conquer the world (*Shivers*)? Will Candy turn out to be like her mother (*The Brood*)? Has good or evil triumphed (*Scanners*)? Is death the end or the beginning of a new life (*Videodrome*)? This adherence to the open text is a radical structuring principle for a commercial director, but not for a Canadian filmmaker.

Where does all this leave us with Cronenberg? I began by situating him outside the dominant aesthetic tradition in Canadian art, only to recuperate him thematically into an imaginative continuum that marks much of our best cinema. Formally, he has resisted the Canadian mainstream at two points in his career. Both *Stereo* and *Crimes of the Future* fall well within the experimental tradition of filmmaking in Canada. They are innovative, personal and minimalist, which leaves them largely inaccessible to the average audience. Nevertheless, they speak to an indigenous aesthetic. The break, when it came, was absolute. With *Shivers* he moved into the mainstream of the commercial cinema. He also moved into forms of genre filmmaking that came with their own set of codes and conventions. The absence of Canadian genres would need another article in itself, but with this lack Cronenberg found creative domicile in a cinematic form totally alien to this country. That he did so without compromising his national roots attests to his integrity.

From *The Shape of Rage: The Films of David Cronenberg*. Reprinted by permission of the Academy of Canadian Cinema and General Publishing Co. Limited.

*The Dead Zone* is a departure of sorts for Cronenberg. Apart from *Fast Company* it is the first film of his that he has not scripted, and this may account for its uniqueness. Based on a Stephen King novel, the film nevertheless bears the unmistakable Cronenberg trademark, and indeed makes an interesting companion piece to *Videodrome*. Johnny Smith may begin the film as a more conventional archetype than Max Renn, but he is soon bestowed with similar visionary powers. But while Max's hallucinations are primarily sexual and intensely personal and private, Johnny's visions are social, impersonal and often benevolent. He can see not only into the past but also into the future, and it is the latter power that becomes paramount for Johnny as the film progresses. In effect it represents a conscious choice on his part. While Max becomes mired in his erotic fantasies, Johnny uses his powers to save a child from fire or to uncover the identity of a gruesome sex murderer. If *Videodrome* traces Max's increasing withdrawal from the world and from reality, *The Dead Zone* depicts Johnny's initial withdrawal, but also his subsequent attempts to save the world, to in fact reintegrate himself into it as a social and political being. Max evades responsibility, while Johnny gradually searches it out. As Johnny becomes increasingly obsessed with the visions he has of Senator Greg Stillson destroying the world in a nuclear holocaust when he becomes the next president, he is singleminded in his determination to avert this possibility. He may be a victim, like all Cronenberg's protagonists, but he is determined to control his fate and that of others. Max and Johnny are both destroyed by their powers, but in completely different ways.

Johnny has the potential to become another Max Renn. He retreats from the world like a hermit and temporarily loses himself in an obsession for a woman (the Brooke Adams love interest), but unlike Max he escapes from this paralysis; his subsequent decisions are all situated within a larger social context, and are also determined by him (unlike Max who is controlled throughout). He does not kill Stillson to protect Sarah (Adams) but to save the world. His vision has broadened from the personal to the collective. In the last analysis *The Dead Zone* is as tragic as *Rabid*, *The Brood* and *Videodrome*, but Johnny's gesture is not futile (although it might well be, as we never know if his visions have any substance to them), because it depicts someone attempting to assume responsibility. That this results in his death only adds to the ambiguity that lies at the heart of the Cronenberg project.

1984

---

1 Bruce Elder, "The Canadian Avant-Garde," *Canadian Images Programme Book* (Peterborough, 1983), p. 27.
2 Robert Fulford, "We need to liberate ourselves from chains of puritan conscience," *Toronto Star*, 2 April 1983, p. C5.
3 John Hofsess, *Inner Views* (Toronto: McGraw-Hill Ryerson Ltd., 1975), p. 79.
4 Robert Fothergill, "Coward, Bully, or Clown: The Dream-Life of a Younger Brother," *Take One*, 4, No. 3 (September 1973). Also reprinted in *Canadian Film Reader*, eds. Seth Feldman and Joyce Nelson (Toronto: Peter Martin Associates, 1977), pp. 234–250.
5 *Hamlet*, Act II, Scene 2.
6 Margaret Atwood, *Survival* (Toronto: Anansi, 1972), p. 33.
7 See Robin Wood's chapters in *The American Nightmare* (Toronto: Festival of Festivals, 1979) for the significance of cannibalism and the family in the horror film.

# *On Television Docudrama:* The Tar Sands

BY SETH FELDMAN

*Since the publication of the following piece, the* CBC *has conceded the legal battle over docudrama. Although the case was settled on a technicality, the* CBC *was forced to pay damages to Peter Lougheed and to agree never to rebroadcast* The Tar Sands. *While no formal commitment was undertaken, it is unlikely that the Corporation will in the foreseeable future broadcast a drama in which actors appear as living public figures involved in any sort of questionable activity. "For the Record" continues to present the kind of work that was its mainstay even before* The Tar Sands, *a subgenre that its producers refer to as "topical" or "journalistic" drama. In filmmaking and film criticism as a whole, the term "docudrama" seems to have lost whatever credibility it may have once enjoyed.*

*It remains to be seen whether anything substantial has been lost with the disappearance of docudrama from both theory and practice. Certainly the issues raised by Peter Pearson and his producer Ralph Thomas in making* The Tar Sands *provided some illumination of the primacy given conventional Griersonian documentary, and of the real fear that the credibility of documentary itself could be challenged. Conversely, the issues raised by the program reaffirm the lack of credibility that English Canadian dramatic film suffers from when it attempts to present factual information. Finally, it might be suggested that docudrama be seen in the context of the larger movement that has come to be known as "neo-narrative" films (a term that is at least equally awkward). Like other neo-narrative films, we might appreciate* The Tar Sands *as an attempt at subverting narrative closure by its attack on the generic conventions that make that closure possible.*

*Good evening. I'm Barbara Frum. What you are about to see is a work of fiction constructed around certain known events. The film,* The Tar Sands, *is an imagined recreation of negotiations leading up to an agreement reached on February 3, 1975—an agreement which launched the Syncrude project in Alberta's Athabasca tar sands. It involved three governments: the governments of Canada, Alberta and Ontario; and three international oil companies: Imperial, Gulf and City Service. Most of the negotiations for this agreement took place behind closed doors. Some details were made public at the time by those involved. Others came to light through a series of leaks during and after the negotiations. To the best of our knowledge, specific facts presented in the film,* The Tar Sands, *are accurate. However, since most of the agreement was worked out behind closed doors, much of the film's dialogue and many of its scenes and characters are, of necessity, fictional. We repeat, many of the people who are actually involved in the Syncrude agreement are not portrayed as themselves in this film. What you will see is the writer's imagined version in which various roles, statements and attitudes are portrayed at least in part through fictional composite characters. The character Willard Alexander is not a real person. He is a composite, the product of the writers' imaginations, a character who represents the Alberta civil servants who argued against proceeding with the Athabasca tar sands development in the manner finally chosen. As far as we know, there is no real David Bromley, the oil company representative in the film. He too is a composite of the many oil men involved in the real Syncrude negotiations. There is, however, a real Frank Spragins, then President of Syncrude Canada. And there is a real Donald MacDonald, then federal minister of energy and now minister of finance. And there is a real Peter Lougheed, then and now Premier of Alberta. But though these are real people, they are portrayed by actors in what, we remind you again, is a work of fiction based on certain known events.* The Tar Sands.

Barbara Frum reading CBC disclaimer

*We're boxed.*

Kenneth Welsh as Peter Lougheed

Peter Pearson's *The Tar Sands* is a fifty-odd minute made-for-television film about a man with a well known name. This man, Peter Lougheed, may be identical to the current premier of Alberta. Pearson makes this contention, the CBC in its disclaimer weakly denies it, and the Premier himself continues to press a lawsuit challenging the veracity of this identification. Alternatively, the Peter Lougheed presented by Pearson may be seen as a fictional creation very much in keeping with the conventional filmic depiction of the English Canadian male. Or Peter Lougheed may be an outgrowth of the clichés that have always been part of the popular media images of leadership. Finally, the Lougheed character may be seen as the product of a rare and intelligent use of television to comment upon television's own nature.

At the beginning of *The Tar Sands*, we are introduced to Lougheed not by Pearson, but rather by the lengthy CBC disclaimer quoted above. In issuing this and a shorter disclaimer at the end of the program, the CBC, besides making a futile attempt to avoid legal repercussions, engages in the ordinary television practice of sponsors and networks commenting on the program being presented. The use of commercials to define the nature of programs will be discussed below. On its part, network commentary on programming goes far beyond warnings about violence, offensive language and the denial that characters shown belong to any particular ethnic group. Statements simply claiming responsibility for the content of programs are a subtle way of implying that the contents of these programs are controversial—potentially offensive. These programs are not, in other words, to be taken at face value.

The net effect of such network commentary on a particular program is to distance both audience and sponsor from the program and, in that way, to undermine the program's integrity. In the case of *The Tar Sands* disclaimers, what we are being told is that, despite any credibility the program might engender, its contents are not to be accepted as anything more than allegory. The words "fiction" and "fictional" are used no less than seven times in the disclaimers to remind us that no matter what the basis in fact of *The Tar Sands* may be, the final product is closer to, say, *The King of Kensington* than to the nightly news. The "proof" of this allegation of fictionality is that the program makes use of "writers' imaginations," composite characters, and a recreation of events through less than complete documentation.

The CBC disclaimer undermines not only the authenticity of *The Tar Sands*, but also the validity of the documentary technique that has come to be known as "docudrama." In doing so, the disclaimer asks the audience to maintain an unprecedented awareness of what can and cannot be proven about the veracity of the products of a particular documentary convention. In one sense, it is to be applauded for doing so. One wishes the same sort of audience scepticism had been encouraged during the early years of another documentary convention, cinéma vérité. What is insidious about the disclaimer is that it implies that it is only in the case of docudrama that the viewer need beware. Although docudrama is far from universally accepted as documentary technique, it can at least be argued at this point that there is nothing more intrinsically fictional about it than there is about conventional documentary and news. Looking, for instance, at CBC's own *Days Before Yesterday* and *Tenth Decade* programs, it is hard to see how these shows' use of narration over stock footage is any less of a performance than that of Welsh as Lougheed. Certainly, the "writers' imagination" is being used to create a very different impression than would otherwise be made by the innocuous shots of Canadian leaders captured by newsreel cameras. In daily news programs, the effect is more or less the same. Living news personalities get, at best, a very few seconds to explain themselves. Even these snippets of primary source information come only after the content of the subject's remarks is predigested and discussed by the anchorperson and the reporter sent to interview the subject. In most cases, there is no interview at all. The viewer of a news program will see only a photo or silent footage, while a ventriloquist anchorperson or reporter supplies the character's dialogue by reading a script prepared by sifting known facts through a journalistic interpretation—a "writers' imagination."

No presentation can, by itself, prove its own veracity. As a consequence, film and television makers prove the authenticity of their material by establishing and adhering to certain documentary conventions. Documentary itself is nothing more or less than the practice of whichever documentary convention or set of conventions is currently accepted. These conventions go in and out of fashion or evolve as tastes and technology change. But one documentary convention that seems to have been strictly adhered to (at least in theory) from the days of Dziga Vertov's first writings to the present is that one must never present reality by scripting scenes and hiring actors to speak these scripted lines.

*The Tar Sands* is an indication that this convention may well have outlived its usefulness. The program asserts that, in many ways, the Lougheed depicted is every bit as "real" as the Peter Lougheed who appeared the next evening on *The National* to announce his lawsuit. This is not to say that Welsh and Lougheed would be indistinguishable, should we meet either of them on the street. Rather, it is to say that the images that result from both *The Tar Sands* and *The National* are simply two interpretations of the same role, a role that may be loosely described as "the public image of Peter Lougheed." Naturally, the performer on *The National* has a larger stake in the creation and continuation of the role. Welsh's performance is, in comparison, only a one night stand. Nevertheless, Lougheed's performance as a public persona is intrinsically no more valid than Welsh's. In both cases, the basis for the performance is an incomplete set of facts (those that Lougheed is willing to make public and those that Pearson has been able to ascertain). In both cases, dialogue and action are stylized and are known to us only through the conventions of the media to which both performers play.

The legal implications of Lougheed's law suit would seem to bear this out. In the United States, it has been effectively argued that public images are, in essence, in the public domain. They may be used by interested parties with the same freedom that these parties might use official photographic images of public figures. Would a legal victory by Lougheed imply that public images can in some way be copyrighted and that the next actor desiring to play Lougheed would have to write to the Premier for his consent? This, it would seem, would be of some embarrassment to public figures, since it would be a testimonial to the synthetic nature of their public images. It would also cause some embarrassment to the news media, because they would be seen as doing nothing but reporting on the approved image. (Of course, the news media might compensate by demanding their own payment as coauthors of these images.)

Another implication of any legal victory by Lougheed would be that docudrama in general is essentially fiction and that negative documentations of given personalities through these means constitute libel. Pearson and the other writers of *The Tar Sands* (Peter Rowe, Ralph Thomas) seem to have gone to some trouble to avoid this. Their Peter Lougheed is largely created out of the public image (if not the public record), with the instances of necessary speculation growing fairly logically out of this image and out of general expectations about human personality. We learn, for instance, that the deprivations suffered by the character and his family during the Depression are one motivation for avoiding any action that might jeopardize Alberta's continued prosperity. We learn that Lougheed can become as outraged as any sane human being when confronted by the machinations of the Syncrude group, or that he can be excited when his home team scores a touchdown.

In all, this "filling in" of non-public manifestations not only plays a minor role in the depiction of Lougheed, but is also—at least to someone who is not a Lougheed scholar—entirely sympathetic. It is worth noting, though, that *The Tar Sands* does use broad theatrical characterization in drawing the composite characters. The civil servant, Willard Alexander, is shown as a hard-drinking, chain-smoking muckraker, a manifestation of the stereotype of the honest loner in a corrupt world. As such, he is as out of place in the film's staid sets and conference room tête à têtes as Humphrey Bogart would be at a Tory caucus. Alexander's composite counterpart, the oil companies' moustachioed villain, David Bromley, seems, like Alexander, to have been written into the script largely to orchestrate and intensify positive and negative audience responses.

Looking at the Alexander and Bromley characterizations, the question that naturally arises is why Pearson did not simply provide Lougheed with a fictional name and avoid the entire issue of a possible libel suit? The answer that comes most easily to the program's detractors is that the use of real names was a cheap device to give the show a notoriety that an allegorical work (such as Pearson's own *The Insurance Man From Ingersoll*) would not enjoy. Perhaps. But not knowing either Pearson or his intentions, would it not also be possible to see the show not only as a statement about the validity of docudrama, but also as a redefinition of the documentarian's responsibility when dealing with this sort of subject? If we are to be informed about the decisions leading up to the Syncrude agreement, is it not pertinent for us to have some idea of what sorts of human beings made these decisions? In conventional documentary, these "human factors" are sketched out with four types of material: interviews with the personalities involved (biased, self-serving); interviews with confidants (usually favourable—how else would they come to be confidants?); staged or semi-staged shots in which the subject acts in an informal manner (jogs, plays with his or her children, jokes with his or her secretary, *ad nauseam*); and anecdotal material provided by the narrator. On rare occasions, a bit of accidental footage (such as a Mackenzie King's "takes" as seen in the NFB's *Has Anyone Here Seen Canada?*) will give some credible insight. But in almost all cases, it is up to the viewer to draw his or her own composite personalities from the standard material.

Pearson's work would imply that the creation of this composite personality is the responsibility of the filmmaker who, presumably, knows more about the character than he or she can ever hope to transmit to the viewer through conventional means in the time allowed. The documentarian is as responsible for providing a statement on the personality of his human subjects as he is for providing photographic images and audiotapes of them. In this, he must, as he does with his audio-visual material, use some editorial judgement based on his own research and his own skill. But ultimately he must make the assertion that the personality he is presenting is as valid as the photographic and aural evidence. The means of making that assertion is to label the personality with the name of the human subject under discussion.

One counterargument to the above evolves out of the factors of cultural preconditioning and personal style that would be an inevitable part of any use of scripting to depict a living human being. Stated plainly, how much of Pearson's Lougheed is Lougheed, and how much is Pearson's cultural baggage? Certainly, much can be said about the Lougheed character as a Canadian fictional stereotype. Chief among these characteristics are his confused cultural identity and his victimization by the land. The oil executives see Lougheed as a Canadian, referring to him as the "next Prime Minister." Lougheed characterizes himself as an Albertan, though not nearly so staunch an Albertan as his cabinet ministers, who don't "give a damn about Canada." By the end of the program, Lougheed is something of an involuntary federalist, joining the previously despised governments of Ontario and Canada in a mutual victimization (brought about, in part, by their internal rivalries).

Lougheed as victim adds an ironic twist to Margaret Atwood's critical categories. He is, in a sense, the winner as loser. Alexander's final critique of Lougheed is that he is a man who with all his "guile, brains and personality could not make the system work." "The system" here might be seen not only as the political and economic system, but also as a kind of ecology gone wrong. Again, the situation is ironic because it is the wealth, not the harshness of the land that victimizes Lougheed. It is the seemingly endless supply of oil in an already rich province that makes it so easy for Lougheed to lose not only public funds, but also his freedom to exert any real control over Alberta's economic future.

What Lougheed loses over the course of *The Tar Sands* is the correlation between his image and the reality of his environment. In this, he is not terribly different from the majority of Pearson's protagonists. The Best Damned Fiddler From Calabogie to Kaladar drinks himself to death to escape the fact that he is no longer the freewheeling backwoodsman he thought himself to be. In *The Dowry*, a determined maritimer succeeds in blowing himself up in order to prove that no one can tell him how to rig his fishing boat. Most convincingly, in *Paperback Hero* Rick Dillon spurns love, money and life itself to equate the image of a small town hockey star with that of an American television gunfighter. Lougheed, convinced he is the Imperial Premier, refuses to acknowledge that his image has become little more than a front for a gang of corporate swindlers.

As Robert Fothergill, Peter Harcourt and others have pointed out, this tragic clinging to an obsolete image goes well beyond Pearson's work and is, in fact, something of a hallmark in English Canadian film. Pearson's protagonists, including Lougheed, are akin to the protagonists of *The Rowdyman*, *The Hard Part Begins*, *Wedding in White* and perhaps half a dozen other specimens of English Canadian "loser" films. Moreover, Pearson's Lougheed is not terribly different from the protagonists of the other *For the Record* CBC films. While Lougheed is a chief of state being systematically screwed by an entity larger than government itself, the other *For the Record* protagonists are engaged in the same frustrating, humiliating procedure at various lower levels. Maria, Hank, the farmers of *Someday Soon*, the workers in *Dying Hard* all discover, through their confrontations with government, that their images of themselves as free citizens have been made obsolete by political and economic systems that they can only begin to understand.

In addition to these debts owed Canadian literature and media, Pearson's Peter Lougheed seems to be a sophisticated extension of a long filmic tradition of the depiction of political leaders. Unfortunately, no one has yet written a history of the screen images of this particular minority group. However, it is possible to say that the political leaders we have seen on film and television screens have been shown to us in three general ways. The leader may be depicted with an awe bordering on reverence. In its extreme, this is manifested by clichés such as the shot of the nameless, faceless great man, his back to the camera, his shadow presiding over the frame and any lesser being within it. This sort of device has provoked suitable satirical response in which the leader is seen as a fool, corrupt, or both. At the same time, running through both these views of political leadership—as well as being manifested in its own right—has been the depiction of the political leader as an imperfect human whose personal limitations are magnified by the pressures of office. By the last scene, he may have been crushed by his office, inspired by it or he may have shaped the office around his own personality. In any case, this third approach to leadership acknowledges a complexity in both person and office that is usually lacking in the other two.

Pearson's Lougheed seems a manifestation of the third option of this third approach. A human being interacting with a high office, he is not crushed by that office, nor is he any wiser for having served. Rather, Lougheed is the agent by which the office itself and the government surrounding it face the decline in their importance. Geopolitical circumstance forces him to pioneer a new image of the chief of state: a man in a middle management position whose sole function is to facilitate the transfer of public wealth to a few private hands. That this new, lesser chief of state must be a bland figure makes Pearson's low-key depiction of Lougheed that much more damning.

That Pearson's Lougheed has antecedents in Canadian fiction, film and television and in other screen manifestations of leadership does not of itself invalidate the veracity of the character. All of these fictional modes are, after all, sustained by some correlation with reality. "The victim" in Canadian fiction and film is, after all, a response to real conditions within this country. The depiction of public leaders says much about the manner in which particular individuals and leadership as a whole have worked to change the lives of audiences who accept these depictions. Moreover, there is no format, whether it is labelled fiction or nonfiction, that is immune to this cultural baggage. Newscasters and documentarians are not only affected by the culture in which they live—they are encouraged to develop personal styles that are every bit as noticeable as the styles of feature film auteurs. More importantly, the means of production that result in nonfiction are all but identical to those that produce what are labelled as fictional products. As a result, the constraints, inducements and processes of selection become a far more important determinant of the veracity of works than do the labels of fiction and nonfiction affixed to the presentations screened.

It is in terms of its critique of these media processes that *The Tar Sands* makes its most important contribution. In its original context, the program was an attempt to provoke an audience, watching prime-time network television, into a consideration of how that television is shaping their own images of themselves and the world in which they live. That *The Tar Sands* was, as a television show, an extremely self-conscious use of the medium, is an enormously important aspect of the presentation that has been generally ignored. Contemporary trends in film policy seem to indicate that television in Canada, as it already does in Germany, will play a major role in the development of Canadian film talent. While it is often assumed that it is film which will benefit from television's sponsorship of "B-movies," Pearson's work indicates that the more popular medium will not itself remain unaffected. Put another way, as the recent spurt of Canadian films deal less and less with Canada, the directors using the medium may well come to make television the more likely forum for addressing pertinent issues.

*The Tar Sands* is an introduction to the redesigning of television for this purpose. Its discussion of the medium is more sophisticated than the references that seem to have been routinely included in the other *For the Record* productions. Its protagonist, along with all his other attributes, is enormously conscious of the power of the medium. When all is said and done, Lougheed is powerless in the face of the oil companies because he realizes that his commercials cannot hope to compete with theirs. He may, throughout the program, scoff at the "Esso-loves-you" ads. But he must, like us, eventually ante up to their sponsors.

In addition to the commercials, Pearson's Lougheed is pursued by another televised set of images, those of Richard Nixon delivering his series of Watergate speeches. Nixon's televised face is to Lougheed a kind of splitscreen image, a video conscience beamed directly onto the narrative's visuals. When we first meet Lougheed, his office is being illuminated by Nixon firing Erlichman and Haldeman on television in April, 1973. Significantly, Lougheed has turned down the sound so that he may rehearse his own speech to the Syncrude executives. Alexander enters and turns up the sound. The warning, though, is not heeded, and midway through the film Lougheed himself is forced to go on television to argue his own flimsy case. Allusions to Watergate persist throughout *The Tar Sands*, until Alexander must, in the last scene, differentiate Lougheed from the figure whose television image opened the film. He is not convincing.

Pearson's Lougheed, then, is a man who is trying not to fall into his television set. We are invited to try not to fall along with him. A program without ordinary advertisements, *The Tar Sands* provides three commercials of its own as a way of both deprogramming its audience in regard to the credibility of commercials, and of making that audience share Lougheed's fate. The advertisements—Syncrude's public relations film, Lougheed's address to Alberta, and an oil company commercial—are shown to us only after we have been given the information that proves them fraudulent. We are also shown the cynical and negative reactions of on-screen viewers of the advertisements. Lougheed and Alexander dismiss the public relations film, Alexander betrays Lougheed as a result of his television address, and the oil executives clearly label their commercial as part of a campaign of public coercion.

We learn to discredit commercials; we are told we must live as if we believed them. Donald Brittain, the film's occasional narrator, keeps track of the declining fortunes of both Nixon and Lougheed; he finally tells us that the Canadian taxpayer is committed to seventy-five per cent of the cost of Syncrude in return for thirty per cent ownership. Our last image of Alberta is that of a few bucolic and irrelevant jackpines framed like a memory in a landscape hung on Lougheed's office wall. In the months since the broadcast of *The Tar Sands*, we have watched innumerable oil company commercials while the taxes paid by those companies have been halved and halved again. We learn that commercials are not meant to convince; they are meant to define. They link a program's fantasy world to the viewer's world. And what they say comes true.

In looking for the nature of Peter Lougheed then, it is impossible to keep from coming back to his literal definition as an image making its way from the screen to the viewer's previously established notions of what that image should be. These notions might include the conventional film and documentary formats—formats that encourage us to perceive public figures as silent beings with noisy interpreters. Or, believing CBC's disclaimers, these notions might come primarily from our fictional associations. I hope, though, that these notions will come from an awareness that what we are watching is, in a sense, watching us, waiting for our feedback and constantly learning how best (from the broadcasters' point of view) to make us look at them.

> *We should like to repeat that what you have just seen is a work of fiction created by the writers and incorporating available factual information. Some of the characters in the film you've seen were based on real living people. Others were fictional composites of the many real people who played key roles in the real story. But the play remains a work of fiction.*
>
> Barbara Frum reading CBC disclaimer

*Ciné-Tracts*, 4 (Spring-Summer 1978)

# *Second Images: Reflections on the Canadian Cinema(s) in the Seventies*

## BY JAMES LEACH

*There is probably no statement concerning cinema in Canada so safe from contradiction as the assertion that the cinemas of English Canada and Quebec exist in profound and unshakable isolation from one another. History has taught the Québécois to demand a separate production arm at the National Film Board and an entirely independent counterpoint to the* CBC*—Radio Canada. The Film Board's efforts at providing versions in both languages are spotty at best, even in light of the minimal demand that each culture has for the other's product. Very few television programs survive a crossing of the Quebec border in either direction. Even within the private feature film industry where, presumably, both audiences are accustomed to "foreign" films, there are huge gaps in the catalogues of subtitled work. Perhaps the exception, Claude Jutra (the one director who has done major work in both languages), best expresses this sentiment when he declares that working outside his native Quebec is equivalent to taking a job abroad.*

*In the following article, James Leach does not set out to deny or disprove this obvious dichotomy. Rather, he attempts to document the points of contact and opposition between the two cinemas. The period he selects, the relatively prosperous decade of the seventies, provides a panorama of interesting work which elicited some of the first critical overviews of this subject. Leach also draws upon the broader critical parameters of Canadian studies and suggests that the seventies provided a body of films that might be considered not just in comparison to one another, but within the framework of our culture. Finally, Leach notes the initiatives of the federal government which, throughout the seventies, was fervent in its desire to speak equally to both language groups.*

At the end of his survey of *Le Cinéma Canadien*, published in 1968, Gilles Marsolais writes that the Canadian cinema, "will always be composed in fact of *two* cinemas: the 'Canadian' and the Québécois, of which the interests are divergent." He concludes that future critics will no longer be able to study the two cinemas together because the achievement of the Quebec cinema is intimately involved with an emerging collective awareness that can lead only to independence. Given the current political situation, it would be foolhardy to reject Marsolais' position out of hand, but the relationship of Quebec to English Canada remains a crucial factor in any account of the culture that we have known as "Canadian." The nature and extent of this relationship have been widely discussed, but assessments of what the two cultures have in common have varied greatly. As might be expected, Québécois commentators, like playwright Jean-Claude Germain, have played down cultural similarities, suggesting that they stem merely from the indebtedness of both cultures to the same "Cultural Finance Company." English Canadian critics, sympathetic to Quebec and anxious to find a basis for a Canadian identity separate from that of the United States, have argued that it is the differences rather than the similarities that are superficial. Ronald Sutherland, for example, finds that "aside from language, it is quite probable that there are at the moment no fundamental cultural differences between the two major ethnic groups of Canada."[1]

Admittedly Sutherland's exception is a large one, but many recent critical studies in English Canada (often inspired by Northrop Frye's theories) have confirmed his vision of a "mythic" dimension which underlies and binds together the two cultures. Critics in Quebec, however, influenced more by the concern of recent French criticism with the political implications of art, have tended to stress the present differences in outlook rather than the similarities of experience on which both cultures are based. While the question of identity has not usually been (openly) developed in political terms in English Canada, the urgent need to preserve language and culture has clarified the issues in Quebec and fostered the emergence of a political consciousness. In this context, the economic pressures to which Germain refers are particularly frustrating and the achievement of control over cultural institutions becomes a major political goal. Similar feelings have been expressed, more sporadically, in English Canada, but the specific measures needed to gain cultural self-determination are much more difficult to identify than in Quebec. English Canadians do control Canada's cultural institutions, as Quebec complains, but this control is often undermined by the enormous economic and cultural influence of the United States.

In the context of the cinema, the problem of cultural institutions is exacerbated by the economic demands of a medium which is both an art and an industry. The bureaucratic structure of the National Film Board and the cultural insensitivity of the Canadian Film Development Corporation have caused widespread dissatisfaction, but in Quebec these deficiencies are seen as an attempt to smother the new social and cultural awareness. These problems, however, stem from an uncertainty about the nature of Canada and the nature of film that has profound implications for the future of both cultures and both cinemas. The mandate of the NFB is "to interpret Canada to Canadians and the rest of the world," and it has built on the ability of John Grierson to use documentary techniques to project an "image" grounded in details selected from everyday reality. This approach has come under increasing pressure with growing uncertainty over the "image" that Canada should try to project and over the way it should be projected (notably a questioning of the NFB's doctrine of objectivity). But the problem also lies in the almost complete separation of the NFB from the commercial film industry, a problem that was not helped by the creation of the CFDC. The mandate of the CFDC is to create a film industry in Canada and, noting the commercial failure of the "regional" films emerging from the NFB tradition, it has tended to encourage "international" films that can compete in a distribution system which is largely American controlled. Despite investment by the CFDC in many important films, its influence can be seen in Quebec as yet another example of Anglo-American imperialism, encouraging "odourless, colourless, and flavourless films" which, like "the sale of our resources to ITT rather than the development of them by ourselves on a more modest scale," will bring about "the depersonalisation of Quebec in exchange for short-term profits."[2]

Nowhere can the contradiction involved in Canada's attitude to its cinema and its culture be seen more clearly than in the failure to sustain the impetus set up in the early sixties, both in Quebec and English Canada, by the appearance of a number of major films and filmmakers. The hopes aroused then were more impressively fulfilled in Quebec where filmmakers were able to work frequently, critics tried to come to terms with their films, and the public showed a good deal of interest. In English Canada few filmmakers have enjoyed the continuity of production necessary for the full development of a consistent and confident artistic personality, few critics have bothered to treat their films as anything other than imitation American films, and the public has not responded to what little of the output they have been allowed to see. Both cinemas have been cinemas of questioning and search rather than of reassurance and affirmation, and the most painful of searches has perhaps been the search for an audience. Québécois critics like Marsolais suggest that an audience exists in Quebec if only it can be freed from external cultural influences but that the English Canadian cinema is unlikely to escape from the lethargy and apathy encouraged by the established structures of a consumer society.

In responding to questions from *Cahiers du Cinéma* in 1966, Jean Pierre Lefebvre wrote that "French Canada puts itself the question of its existence and of its survival, while English Canada puts itself no question." The questioning nature of the new Quebec cinema was established from the very beginning in the quest for cultural roots of Pierre Perrault and Michel Brault's *Pour la suite du monde* (1963), the autobiographical self-examination in Claude Jutra's *À tout prendre* (1963), and the calculated confusions of Gilles Groulx' *Le chat dans le sac* (1964). Of this latter film, Groulx said that it "takes on all the vagueness of the French Canadians" whose "commitment has not yet been pushed to the limit."[3] Claude, the central character who cannot find a way of translating his growing social awareness into action, says, "I am Québécois, therefore I am searching." Yet this sense of rejecting old certainties and struggling to find new values has been equally important in the English Canadian cinema that also emerged in the sixties. The confusions and questioning are perhaps even more frustrating than in Quebec because there is little sense of collective struggle and hardly any hope of a political solution. In Don Owen's *Nobody Waved Good-bye* (1964) Peter, like Groulx' Claude, is an adolescent struggling to define himself in an indifferent society. His uncertainty is heightened by a sequence in which a young French Canadian accuses him of accepting an American way of life and Peter finds himself unable to express his own values except through negatives. He is unwilling to sacrifice his own individuality by identifying himself with a social movement, and thus is unable to define his own needs.

Owen uses the French Canadian as a means of focussing attention on issues of which Peter is not consciously aware but which nonetheless affect him. These issues are reflected in both English Canadian and Québécois cinema in the many characters striving desperately to free themselves from conventional values and in the search for a cinematic style that is not based on the discarded values. Lefebvre's attitude to English Canada is thus an exaggeration, but it does reflect the greater resistance to change within the English Canadian cinema, especially since the NFB existed specifically to support the establishment and the CFDC to create a commercial industry. Yet the English Canadian cinema has not developed simply as a pale reflection of Hollywood and is not wholly taken up with the issues of economics and organization that have inevitably dominated much discussion of it. As *Nobody Waved Good-bye* and many subsequent films show, one of the basic themes of English Canadian cinema is the quest for freedom from the materialistic prison that has become so closely identified with "the American way of life." There is a strong parallel between this struggle and the concerns of Québécois cinema, which reflects a society that has shifted rapidly from a state of religious claustrophobia to that of a materialistic cul-de-sac. The double struggle to escape from traditional moral values and new materialistic ones (which have become hopelessly entangled with each other) can be seen as the basis of the search for identity, whether that identity is thought of as Canadian or Québécois.

As Owen suggests, the experience of Quebec can provide a useful insight into the complexities of the forces at work in Canada as a whole. There is no need to ignore the important differences between the two cultures to see the intensity of Quebec's recent history as creating new clarity on issues which have pervaded (consciously or unconsciously) this country of contradictions. The pace with which Quebec has emerged into the modern age has concentrated the process of modernization (industrialization, "Americanization") into a relatively short period of time and has thus created more clear-cut battle lines than where the process has been somewhat more gradual. Until the late fifties, Quebec society was deeply split along class, religious, and language lines but the majority of people (the French Canadians) "lived a relatively sheltered life in a rural society in which a great measure of uniformity reigned, and in which poverty set its limits on change and aspiration alike."[4] The influence of the Church also worked toward creating a strong sense of community based on traditional values and opposition to progress. Quebec had opted out of the twentieth century and out of North America, and the Québécois were forced to accept a situation in which most of the wealth of the province devolved on the English minority or was siphoned off south of the border.

The activity generated by the war, however, accelerated the forces of change, and the emergence of Quebec into the modern world was confirmed by the Quiet Revolution. A sense of community and security based on isolation disappeared and was replaced by the fragmentation of urban and industrial life. The experience of the city and the factory gave many Québécois the feeling of being foreigners on their own soil, a feeling that contrasted with the strong ties to the land that had been stressed in the past. An atmosphere of frustration developed into an atmosphere of terrorism: the literature, theatre, and cinema of Quebec in the sixties is dominated by studies of adolescents struggling to shake off the power of the Church and of a corrupt establishment in the midst of a general apathy and numbness. The adolescent's need to find an identity and the struggle against the "hibernation" of the people during the long winter become basic images of the painful birth of a new consciousness.

The forces at work are complex and often contradictory. The new spirit, for example, rejects the reactionary influence of the Church and holds it largely responsible for the failure of Quebec to assert itself against its colonizers. One of the first of the new wave of Quebec films, Pierre Patry's *Trouble-fête* (1964), presents the impasse reached by uncertain adolescents who find all their options blocked by the clerical education system. Yet the rebellion is also against the forces of progress which the Church fought in the past: Pierre Gravel's novel *À Perte de temps* (1969), for example, relates terrorism to the sense of rootlessness created by the feeling that Montreal (which is never named in the novel, in keeping with its new anonymity) is becoming just another North American city, with its huge new buildings dedicated to commerce and profiteering. The attitude to the Church thus remains deeply ambiguous, as is that to the pioneering nationalistic efforts of Abbé Proulx. Clément Perron's *Partis pour la gloire* (1976) illustrates this ambiguity; the Cardinal of Quebec is shown giving his blessing to the invocation of the War Measures Act, while the parish priests actively or passively support the young men who resist conscription.

The basic problem is thus the need for a strategy that can revive the sense of identity that existed in the past, but that will avoid both its attendant reactionary spirit and the temptations of North American materialism. For the Parti Québécois such a strategy requires independence not only because the Anglo-Saxon establishment has exploited Quebec since the conquest of 1759, but also because English Canada has shown itself so ready to embrace the forces of Americanization and to accept its own cultural extinction. The concern for the survival of their language gives the Québécois at least a basis for a vital community, but any concerned English Canadian can understand the feeling of impotence expressed by René Lévesque in 1968:

> In a world where, in so many fields, the only stable law seems to have become that of perpetual change, where our old certainties are crumbling one after the other, we find ourselves swept along hopelessly by irresistible currents.

The new consciousness in Quebec fights these feelings of alienation and attempts to revitalize a society that Lévesque described as having reached "the point of being unacceptable even to itself." This spirit of renewal in Quebec can be defined as a shift from the perspective of the "French Canadian" who "feels in the minority in his own home," to the "dazzling, overflowing, ribald" feeling of being a "Québécois."[5]

The movement from an attitude of self-effacement to one of self-affirmation is reflected in the sudden upsurge in all the arts in Quebec during the sixties and it has led some critics to draw a distinction between the political concerns of Québécois artists, and the psychological introspection of their English Canadian counterparts. John Hofsess, for example, distinguishes between the two cinemas in these terms:

> After seeing *L'Acadie l'Acadie* by Michel Brault and Pierre Perrault, or *Québec: Duplessis et après* . . . by Denys Arcand, the requisite response is to demand, on an emotional wave of outrage, urgent social change. After seeing *Goin' Down the Road, The Rowdyman* or *Wedding in White*, one has an understanding which precludes hoping that there is a political solution for every human failing.

A similar distinction is made, from a slightly different perspective, by Ronald Sutherland who writes that "in Quebec, conveniently, there are all the ingredients for the illusion of a specific cause and a specific solution."[6] But this approach does tend to obscure the complexity of the forces at work in both cultures and it can lead to distortions, as happens in Hofsess' choice of political documentaries to represent the Quebec cinema and fiction films to represent the English Canadian. Even so his choice of films is hardly convincing: Admittedly there is little hope of specific political solutions at the end of the English Canadian films, but *L'Acadie l'Acadie* (1971) ends with the collapse of the political aspirations of the young Acadians, and *Québec: Duplessis et après* . . . (1972) illustrates the failure of Quebec politicians to translate political rhetoric into action.

There is a tremendous psychological interest in these documentaries which allow us to witness human responses to political issues. The breakdown of "old certainties" has led to the questioning of the nineteenth-century concept of psychological realism and to a new consciousness of the political dimension of works of art, but the separation of these two dimensions can lead only to a partial view of reality. The problem, of course, is that "reality" has itself become a questionable concept, but a major concern of both the English Canadian and Québécois cinemas has been to achieve a balance between the "closeness" demanded by a psychological approach and the "detachment" that is the foundation of most approaches to political cinema. This concern has been pursued consciously in Quebec in the development of a new approach to documentary, building on the example of cinéma vérité and in the application of this approach to the fiction film. The liberation from old dramatic structures and documentary conventions parallels the social changes in Quebec, but the result (for better or worse) has not been a cinema that expresses confidence in the possibility of political solutions. Rather (as in English Canada) it is a cinema of uncertainty and contradiction.

The alleged euphoria of the new Québécois spirit is not reflected in its cinema, which reflects rather the contradicting pulls and tensions to which the nationalist movement has been subjected. Michel Brault's *Les ordres* (1974) viewed the October Crisis from the perspective of some of its innocent victims and has been criticized by militants for failing to show any of its characters coming to a real political awareness of the events. The closed worlds of André Forcier's *Bar salon* (1974) and *L'eau chaude, l'eau frette* (1976) do embody a strong sense of communal values, but the perverse vitality of his characters is accompanied by an equally strong feeling of communal impotence. Jean-Guy Noel's *Ti-cul Tougas* (1975) depicts an escape to the rural isolation of the Iles de la Madeleine but the Quebec landscape is merely a transitional backdrop to the characters' continuing dreams of California.

These films imply that independence is the only way to fulfill the potential offered by the new sense of a Québécois identity, since it would allow the creation of social structures that could combat economic and cultural alienation. But they also assert the need for inner change, for the working out of the contradictions that Quebec has historically acquired. The cross-currents of thought and emotion that complicate the question of identity are extremely complex, but they can be elucidated by reference to the three basic approaches to nationalism: the inward-looking, rural-based, conservative nationalism associated with Abbé Proulx, Maurice Duplessis, and the Union Nationale; the "progressive", technological nationalism of the Quiet Revolution, associated especially with the Liberals; and the radical nationalism of a large part of the Parti Québécois, which stresses independence as a means of bringing about social justice. Even this three-way division is schematic and incomplete, and it should be emphasized that, while each of these approaches can be related to political parties or groups, they can be seen more suggestively as creating psychic tensions within most individuals in Quebec.

Similar divisions and tensions could no doubt be diagnosed in English Canada, though their expression is usually less impassioned and obscured by regional distinctions. The general tendency seems to be toward a theoretical nationalism coupled with a fear of losing the economic and cultural "benefits" derived from the United States. Recent English Canadian cinema stresses both dissatisfaction with old values and fear of new ones; by expressing Canadian identity as a feeling of emptiness created by a loss of confidence in English and/or American values, as in Don Shebib's *Between Friends* (1973) and Don Owen's *Partners* (1976); by examining the past to expose the way in which the rigid imposition of WASP principles on Canadian society created the present identity crisis, as in William Fruet's *Wedding in White* (1972) and Joyce Wieland's *The Far Shore* (1976); or by adopting the conventions of American genres to depict the pervasive anxiety underlying the apparent security of the consumer society, as in David Cronenberg's *Shivers* (1975) and Fruet's *Death Weekend* (1976). The political dimension in most of these films remains implicit, but there is a strong sense of frustration and emptiness that resembles the depiction of an oppressed society in Québécois films.

The basic difference between the two cinemas can perhaps be seen in the relative ease with which the filmmaker and his characters in Quebec can identify the source of oppression, while their English Canadian counterparts seem to function in an environment in which psychological pressures are real but political solutions difficult to envisage. It is not that political solutions are seen as irrelevant or impossible, but that the characters are prevented from attaining a political consciousness by the illusions created by the prevailing ideology. The story of Joey and Pete in Shebib's *Goin' Down the Road* (1970) grows out of the opening images of Nova Scotia in which natural beauty is contrasted with human desolation. This sense of wasted potential is continued in Toronto with the contrast between the many glimpses of homeless derelicts and the luxury and extravagance of a thriving commercial city. These contrasts are impressed on us, but we also see that Joey and Pete are unable to understand what is happening to and around them because of the dreams and myths that their culture has fostered.

There can be no political solutions, because bourgeois culture has created the illusion of the remoteness of political thought and action from everyday life. The only time that Pete becomes aware of the social forces working against him is when his application for a job in advertising is greeted with scorn. He points to the futility of getting an education in Nova Scotia when the only jobs are on the boats or in the mines, but he is told to go home or go back to school. There is no common ground between Pete's dreams and the numbing reality of the useless, unproductive job he has to settle for. The violent collision of dream and reality culminates (appropriately enough) in a supermarket parking lot, but this violence can have no cathartic effect since its victim is only a junior employee defending property that does not belong to him. Pete and Joey can only try to escape further to the west, but the film makes clear that escape is an illusion. This illusion is the American dream, the notion that "success" is freely open to all, on which modern consumer society thrives but which is shown to be in total contradiction to Canadian reality.

If this is an impossible escape from an intolerable situation, the ability of Québécois filmmakers to identify the source of oppression does not usually generate more realistic solutions. Their characters often end in a state of impasse, and the unlikelihood of change also leads to fantasies of escape, usually outside Canada, to Florida, California, New York, Mexico, the Caribbean. The experience of feeling an outsider on one's own soil leads naturally to a preference for foreign soils which offer more freedom. These characters may be more aware of where they want to go than Joey and Pete (or Peter in *Nobody Waved Good-bye*), but it is these very fantasies, confirmed by the power of the media, that intensify their alienation from their actual environment and make it impossible for them to contemplate meaningful changes in that environment or their relationship to it. While the Quebec context gives the theme of impotence a clearly political dimension, essentially the same vision of home as misery and escape as fantasy dominates both the Québécois and English Canadian cinemas.

The absence of a strong commitment to political solutions is decried by radical critics in both cultures, and their complaint is echoed by the common lament that Canadian films offer a negative and pessimistic vision that nobody wants to see. Especially when compared with the positive outlook of much of American popular culture, the Canadian cinema seems to represent an extreme reaction to escapism and an invitation to despair. Actually, this complaint is one that extends far beyond the cinema: D. G. Jones records an increasingly common belief that "Canadians have developed a kind of cultural schizophrenia, a division between their conscious aspirations and their unconscious convictions, which undermines their lives and leads to the development of a profoundly negative outlook." As Jones acknowledges, there is much to support such a viewpoint but he sets out to suggest "a general way of looking at Canadian literature which would allow us to acknowledge the many negative characteristics and yet maintain that the literature has a basically positive character."[7] The negative elements in Canadian culture have been traced to many sources, including the insecurity caused by a lack of identity, the Puritan heritage, the harshness of the climate, and the sheer frustration of trying to make a living as an artist in Canada. Yet, in the cinema as in literature, the stress on these negative aspects represents a serious distortion which only serves to increase the public's alienation from its own culture.

The negative vision cannot be ignored. It provides the basis of Margaret Atwood's thesis that Canada is "a collective victim" and that the basic motif of Canadian culture is the struggle to survive. She argues that this situation leads to a dominant concern with failure and suggests that "when Canadian writers are writing clumsy or manipulated endings, they are much less likely to manipulate in a positive than they are in a negative direction."[8] Certainly, many English Canadian films (especially) offer a vision not just of failure, but of life as a constant succession of failures, each one worse than the one before. There is often an overwhelming sense of a malevolent power against which the characters are helpless, a power which seems inevitably to create negative endings. Even those films which adopt popular formulas have none of the faith of the American popular cinema in action as a solution to moral dilemmas. The illicit love affair of Joseph and Domino in George Bloomfield's *Child Under a Leaf* (1974) is doomed from the beginning, and the death of her child (under a blanket, actually) is only one of a series of catastrophes that are inflicted on them. The downward movement of the action is punctuated by idyllic, romantic sequences which seem to take no account of the progress of the narrative. Thus the only alternatives seem to be a glossy, unreal happiness and the despair confirmed by the final freeze-frame of Domino's face as she spots Joseph's car and prepares to meet him—unaware that instead of shooting her husband he has shot himself. Similarly Douglas Jackson's *The Heatwave Lasted Four Days* (1974) draws on the sub-genre of the American thriller in which an innocent individual finds himself hunted by both police and criminals, but the Canadian hero never fulfils audience expectations that he will take control of the situation. At the end, he is alone in prison, afraid to speak out through fear for his family and separated from his wife who knows nothing about what has happened to him.

These bleak endings are all the more prominent in that the films otherwise conform to commercial formulas. But this feeling of sliding downhill is a common one in English Canadian cinema. After a series of reverses, *Nobody Waved Good-bye* and *Goin' Down the Road* end with the main characters on the road but going nowhere; *Wedding in White* ends with Jeannie trapped in her stifling environment through her marriage to the drivelling Sandy; *Between Friends* ends with Elly and Toby in a stationary car in the wastelands of northern Ontario, alone with the bodies of her husband and her father. The usual response to this dispiriting world is an attempt to ignore it through pretence and gameplaying. Will Cole, in Peter Carter's *The Rowdyman* (1972), plays the clown and refuses to grow up. His carefree attitude is a refreshing contrast to the drab respectability asserted by his society, but it is severely tested by his confrontation with the dying old man on whom he seems to have modelled himself, by his responsibility in the death of his best friend in an industrial accident, and finally by the departure of his girl for Toronto. A visit to a dying man in hospital and the departure of his girl are also among the trials of Jim King in Paul Lynch's *The Hard Part Begins* (1973); King's dreams of success as a singer are destined to failure, and are seen as an evasion of domestic responsibility. His attempts to remain free are confronted by the reality of the decline of interest in country music, just as the "irresponsible" dreams of western heroism of Rick Dillon in Peter Pearson's *Paperback Hero* (1973) conflict with the reality of the claustrophobic small town and its dying hockey team.

All of these examples are taken from English Canadian cinema (and could be added to indefinitely), but it is equally difficult to find in Québécois cinema a character who is successfully able to assert himself against the limitations imposed by his environment. The Quiet Revolution did bring a new freedom in sexual matters which led to a number of mildly erotic films, such as Denis Héroux' *Valérie* (1968), in which the audience could experience vicariously a rejection of sexual, if not social, constraint. But if the wages of sin were no longer hell and damnation, the rebellion could be contained by a final redemption through true love. Sexual release may be an important step in a society like Canada's, which, as Ronald Sutherland has shown, is dominated by puritanical attitudes fostered by the Calvinist tradition in English Canada and the Jansenist tradition in Quebec.[9] Yet the feelings of liberation generated by Héroux' film and its successors have been undercut by the many films which deal with the oppressiveness of the new morality or with sexual sickness as a symptom of a decadent society. While Valérie was moving triumphantly from convent to brothel to marriage bed, the heroine of Paul Almond's *Isabel* (1968) was more typically wrestling with the full weight of a family and cultural tradition that closed off for her any possibility of sexual fulfilment.

The problems of impotence and frustration dominate sexual relationships in both cinemas and reflect a social structure that seems to be designed to prevent self-fulfilment—except, for the chosen few, in material terms. Jean Pierre Lefebvre's enumeration of the problems of life in Quebec could be applied also (with minor changes) to life in English Canada, and his ironic way of expressing himself points to society's attempt to suppress all awareness of a bleak reality:

> THERE ARE NO PROBLEMS IN QUEBEC. I have thus expressed . . . only personal obsessions: the immobility of a society submitted to the rigours of cold and of a colonialism simultaneously British, French, American and religious; the absolute segregation at the level of the spoken language of the Québécois and consequently of social classes; imposition of capitalist structures on the economy and culture; acute crisis of communication between the individuals and the various groups of my society for the above-mentioned reasons and also, crudely and simply, for geographic reasons.

The films that emerge from such a situation must of necessity face up to the negative aspects and express an attitude that can verge on despair. But, as Lefebvre also says, "to make a film on despair, is already a sign of hope," and he argues that the Americans are mistaken "to despise despair." Since "to despair is to become aware simultaneously of the difficulty and grandeur of life and death," it becomes "a very positive kind of attitude."[10]

For Lefebvre, then, the American cinema is one that evades despair, and his own films are opposed to "that culture . . . that way of lying—to themselves, and to others." The grip that Hollywood maintains on the collective imagination of the western world is intensified in Canada for geographic and economic reasons, and Lefebvre is one of many voices warning against the temptation to create "a cinema in the image of the dominant cinema in a dominated society." The search for identity that is central to both Canadian cinemas is complicated by the way in which the "American way of life" and the "American dream" have come to define an "international" attitude to life in the postindustrial age. John Hofsess thus complains that nowhere in Canadian cinema is there "a character with the brains, balls, will or gall to master life as it must be lived in the twentieth century."[11] American culture, by its aggressiveness and emphasis on "success," not only encourages Canadians to see themselves as inferior but also creates the terms with which the problem can be discussed and the rules by which any attempt at self-assertion must be governed. There can be no doubt that in comparison with the American popular cinema, Canadian films do depict a failure to "master" modern life, but they also attest to a difficult and painful search for a mode of living that will not depend on mastery.

The title of Robert Fothergill's article 'Being Canadian Means Always Having to Say You're Sorry' restates Hofsess' complaint, but Fothergill concludes by suggesting a way out of the oppressive situation of looking up to the United States as a successful elder brother:

> Ideally there might be imagined a transvaluation of the younger brother syndrome, whereby the qualities and characteristics derived from that experience are re-affirmed as active virtues rather than passive shortcomings. By inhibiting the development of "chauvinism," both nationally and in the individual temperament, the Canadian condition has perhaps made possible a mode of self-realization that would be socially transforming.[12]

Yet the dominant feeling in Canadian, especially English Canadian, films is of the absence of a positive Canadian identity. The claustrophobic world of *Wedding in White*, for example, stems from a rigid adherence to British traditions and an unwillingness to adapt to (or even create) a new environment. Here the impulse is to remain in the past, and in *Partners* this impulse is set against the future-oriented vision of American power and progress. Despite the fact that its characters are either American or very *English* Canadians, the film works tentatively toward a middle ground that could be called "Canadian" and could overcome the artificial divisions created by Canada's history.

Fothergill's approach would allow us to see the contradiction and uncertainties that make up the Canadian experience as not necessarily negative factors. The vision of both the English Canadian and the Québécois cinemas is one in which many contradictions exist but in which the establishment has worked to suppress any awareness of them. In exposing these contradictions and compelling audiences to experience them, Canadian filmmakers have often placed themselves in an adversary position with regard to their audience and have found that their work itself has been virtually suppressed. The enemy, according to this vision, is any force that suppresses opposition, and therefore contradiction, whether it be the British spirit of *Wedding in White*, the English Canadian spirit of *The Far Shore* and *Partis pour la gloire*, the invisible government machine of *Les ordres*, the myth of masculine virility of Mireille Dansereau's *La vie rêvée* (1972) and Francis Manckiewicz's *Le temps d'une chasse* (1972), and so on. An awareness of contradiction and a willingness to allow this awareness to shape the aesthetic experience are essential elements of modern art's rebellion against the fixed viewpoint of perspective and linearity that created a sense of order and harmony in the past. Today such artificial order has come to seem an evasion of the complexities of modern reality, to be a sign not of divine providence but of an excessive rigidity or complacency. Canadian films are often condemned for their failure to conform to the old standards which still dominate the structures of much popular culture and "high" art, whereas such standards are the product of a world-view against which these films are reacting.

All this is not to excuse carelessness, shoddiness, or incompetence, but rather to suggest that there may be something in the Canadian experience which allows its culture (or cultures) to build on the contradictions of Marshall McLuhan's electronic age and to make contact with the mythic dimension to which Northrop Frye has drawn attention. If this is the case, the virtual suppression of the Canadian cinema can be seen as an example of the power of conservative elements in our culture to encourage and exploit a fear of the unknown and a resistance to change. Such a tension runs deep into the history of Canadian culture, with its garrison mentality constantly trying to impose European values on the colonial wilderness.

The assertion of rigid social structures to suppress the dark side of human nature (associated with the savages and the wilderness that they found here) was inevitable given the puritanical backgrounds of the early settlers, but this process denied any real interaction between humans and their new environment. The opposition between the spontaneous and improvised and the prescribed and inflexible that is basic to the form and content of both Canadian cinemas can be seen as a belated attempt to break free of this heritage. It involves, among other things, a questioning of the relationship of film and audience, and the experience may be unsettling for unwary audiences. But the elimination of the possibility of this experience would have consequences that extend well beyond the confines of the Canadian film industry.

*Dalhousie Review*, 62, No. 2 (Summer 1982)

---

1 Gilles Marsolais, *Le Cinéma Canadien* (Editions du Jour: Montreal, 1968), p. 104; Jean-Claude Germain, "*Théâtre Québécois or Théâtre Protestant*," *Canadian Theatre Review*, 11, Summer 1976, p. 9; Ronald Sutherland, *Second Image* (Don Mills: New Press, 1971), p. 23.
2 Jacques Godbout, "Le Cinéma de Papa Ottawa," *Cinéma Québec*, 2, No. 9, pp. 24–5.
3 "10 Questions to 5 Canadians Film-Makers," *Cahiers du Cinéma in English*, 4, p. 49; Gilles Groulx, quoted in *Second Wave* (London: Studio Vista, 1970), p. 121.
4 René Lévesque, *An Option for Quebec* (Toronto: McClelland and Stewart, 1968), p. 14.
5 Ibid., pp. 16–17; Jean Cabot, citing Gaston Miron, in an interview in *Cinéma Québec*, 3, No. 9/10, p. 86.
6 John Hofsess, *Inner Views* (Toronto: McGraw-Hill, 1975), p. 117; Sutherland, op. cit., p. 22.
7 D. G. Jones, *Butterfly on Rock* (Toronto: University of Toronto Press, 1970), pp. 14–15.
8 Margaret Atwood, *Survival* (Toronto: Anansi, 1972), pp. 34–35.
9 Sutherland, op. cit., p. 61.
10 Jean Pierre Lefebvre, in Renald Berubé and Yvan Patry (eds.), *Jean-Pierre Lefebvre* (Montreal: Université du Québec, 1971), p. 140; "Le coup de dés: entretien avec Jean-Pierre Lefebvre," *Cahiers du Cinéma*, 186, pp. 60–61; Lefebvre, quoted in Phillip Stratford, *Marie-Claire Blais* (Toronto: Coles, 1971), p. 44.
11 Lefebvre, quoted in Graham Fraser, "The Gentle Revolutionary," *Take One*, 1, No. 7, p. 13; Lefebvre, "Les signifiants et les insignifiants québécois," *Cinéma Québec*, 4, No. 8, p. 39; John Hofsess, op. cit., p. 69.
12 Robert Fothergill, "Being Canadian Means Always Having to Say You're Sorry," *Take One*, 4, No. 3, p. 30.

# III

# *Les Québécois*

# *From the Picturesque to the Familiar: Films of the French Unit at the NFB (1958-1964)*

BY DAVID CLANDFIELD

*While contemporary cinema consciousness in English Canada began with John Grierson's founding of the National Film Board in 1939, the birth of a similar consciousness in Quebec would have to wait for another two decades. Québécois had been employed at the Film Board from its inception, and there had even been a minor boom in the private sector that saw seventeen feature films produced in Quebec in the immediate postwar period. Seen from a contemporary perspective, the Québécois who worked at the Film Board in its early years, and the very different filmmakers who worked on the features, appear to have had little influence upon the tightly knit group of highly committed, technically proficient young cinéastes that emerged within the* NFB *in the mid- to late fifties. That their emergence coincided with and embraced the coming of* cinéma direct *served to distinguish them from the Board's previous work as well as from the ponderous features of Quebec Productions and Renaissance Films. More important, though, was the fact that these filmmakers matured during the Quiet Revolution. They were members of the first generation in centuries to see the isolation and idiosyncracies of francophone North America as something other than stigmas of repression and underdevelopment. Instead, they looked to their cultural identity as the foundation of a modern, independent nation.*

*It comes then as no surprise that these filmmakers honed their observational abilities on the dividing line between the old and the new.* Les raquetteurs *(1958), the film that brought them international recognition, could be dismissed by the unwary as nothing more than home movies of a snowshoe meet in rural Quebec. Yet it is just this illusory innocence that allowed Michel Brault and Gilles Groulx to find and satirize the nuances of a colonial mentality as it gives way to the liberation of self-awareness.* Les raquetteurs *and the films like it (*La lutte, À Saint-Henri*) brought forth in their straightforward iconography perceptions emblematic of the new national identity. Within world cinema culture, the films that Clandfield discusses here created a distinctive voice for Quebec. In societal terms, they yielded snapshots of the historical dialectic itself.*

*Our films have, above all, been an impassioned appropriation of the social environment. The picturesque (the outsider's view) has yielded to the familiar; the myth has yielded in the face of reality.*

Gilles Carle, *parti pris*, 7 (avril 1964)[1]

Gilles Carle was a member of the French Unit at the National Film Board engaged in the making of documentary films in the late fifties and early sixties. This branch of documentary film production at the NFB is now normally referred to as the *cinéma direct* movement. Carle made the above remark when the movement as such was ending—that is, when the tightly knit group of francophone filmmakers at the NFB was dispersing. It illustrates perfectly a characteristic dynamic which distinguishes the *cinéma direct* films of the French Unit from the Candid Eye films of Unit B discussed by Bruce Elder.[2] Technically, of course, both movements had much in common: shooting without script or conscious staging, use of light-weight equipment, a search for the real which deliberately shunned the dramatic or the heroic. However, the dispassionate empiricism of the Candid Eye, which found inspiration in Cartier-Bresson's foreword to *The Decisive Moment*,[3] is held in tension in *cinéma direct* with the "impassioned" involvement of the filmmaker in his pro-filmic material, the social "milieu."

For the Candid Eye filmmakers, the subject of the film was its subject matter rooted in objective reality. The starting point was a social or human event—ephemeral, inscribed in an ephemeral world—the form and meaning of which require the mediation of the filmic process to become evident. The function of the filmic process, then, was not to mould but to reveal form, and with it meaning.

For the *cinéma direct* filmmaker, the point of departure is the filmmaking process in which the filmmaker is deeply implicated as a consciousness, individual or collective.[4] It is this process—this consciousness—which will give form and meaning to an amorphous objective reality. Instead of effacing his presence, the filmmaker will affirm it. Instead of rendering the technical process transparent (supposedly), he will emphasize its materiality. Instead of standing apart from his object of study or enquiry, he will implicate himself within it. His search for the authentic will involve not only the critical detachment of the empirical investigator in order to strip away "myth" or misconception, but also commitment to the social project under investigation in order to avoid the pitfalls of the aesthetic or the "picturesque."

The overt personal involvement of the subject-filmmaker in the object-reality of the pro-filmic event was, then, the key distinguishing factor of the Québécois *cinéma direct* from the anglophone Candid Eye.

In this paper, a number of the films made by the French Unit at the NFB will be considered. They are generally films made to fit a thirty-minute television format, although two extend to forty or fifty minutes.[5] They were nearly all made between 1958 and 1964,[6] mostly in the two years 1961 and 1962, when the French Unit operated as a tightly knit team. The filmmakers involved have all gone on to direct their own feature films. Indeed, they formed a vital nucleus for the *cinéma d'auteurs* which developed in Quebec in the mid- to late sixties. Not all of the films under scrutiny used a purely *cinéma direct* approach. The two films by Clément Perron (*Les bacheliers de la cinquième* (1961) and *Jour après jour* (1962)) were prescripted, but exhibit such a striking similarity with the *direct* films that it would be difficult not to believe in a mutual influence. The films will not be considered in sequence as separate entities, but rather examined for the structural and formal characteristics they have in common.

Although the more personal approach of the *cinéma direct* filmmakers has often been indicated in writings on the cinéma vérité phenomenon seen as a whole, its roots in an indigenous Québécois tradition of the ethnographic film have not been recognized outside that province, and even there only in the last two or three years. In this respect, an article by Yvan Lamonde in *Cinéma Québec* of December 1974 is instructive.[7] The work of two men of the Church, *abbés*, making films primarily in the thirties, forties and fifties, is here significant. Both Albert Tessier and Maurice Proulx were travelling filmmakers, concerned with creating a personal record of life in the province, shooting in 16mm with a minimum of outside technical assistance.

Between 1927 and 1960, Albert Tessier, working as an independent filmmaker with his own funds, shot and edited about seventy short films. The running time was generally ten to fifteen minutes. He avoided the use of tripod, preferring the hand-held Bolex with a triple turret. He rarely worked from a script, preferring to trust to his eye and build the film into a meaningful whole by a laborious montage of shots taken from his continually growing collection of "stock-shots," and by the construction of a poetic commentary usually inserted as silent titles. Since he was invariably present at the screenings, his own voice would add a live commentary.[8]

The works of Maurice Proulx extend from 1934 to about 1961. In this time, he completed about thirty-three films, usually from twenty to thirty minutes in length, although the first two (*En pays neufs* (1934-37); *En pays pittoresques* [1938-39]) were of feature length. He, too, shot his films alone, without preconstructed script, using a 16mm Kodak. The funds for his films came in the form of government grants at first, and later by the sponsorship of Le service de ciné-photographie, founded by the provincial government in 1940. There was little in the way of conscious editing as a structural principle, and he claims that in his earliest films he used about four-fifths of the film shot. The commentaries were written and added by Michel Vergnes in most of the films from the forties onward.[9]

The films of both Tessier and Proulx bear witness to an era in the life of the province quite different from that of the NFB French team of the late fifties and early sixties. They might best be characterized as a "*cinéma de la fidélité*," committed to the preservation of the traditional rural way of life, based on the two intertwined institutions of the Catholic church and a conservative government. They celebrate from within the preservation of language, rural crafts, family, parish community and the Catholic religion. Nevertheless, by their overtly nationalistic concern with the definition of a cultural identity and their desire to project this image of a collective to this same public, they anticipate the aims, intentions and methods of a generation of Quebec filmmakers whose eyes were turned toward a radically changing society. The most frequently mentioned heir to this tradition, though perhaps not in a deliberate sense, is Pierre Perrault. However, the short films of the *cinéma direct* team, from *Les raquetteurs* on, reflect this search for a collective identity, but this time in an urban, industrial society.

Now this desire to penetrate a growing urban-industrial culture and to render it palpable to its members as a new identity was not confined to, nor did it spring from, the filmmakers of the NFB. It grew throughout the mass-media of the fifties in Quebec, and, in particular, through the medium of television, whose arrival in 1952 had rung the death knell for the first Quebec commercial feature film industry.[10] A new intelligentsia was forming which gradually gained access to the media and revealed the cracks in the harmonious picture of social homogeneity which had been nurtured by church and state for so long. To embark upon a project to define the new cultural identity was implicitly to take sides for or against the old order; to assert one's own national identity within a federal organism (by creating a French team) was to break away from the picturesque, the view of the outsider. Such were the conditions which served as a social background for the work of the *cinéma direct* group and the other French filmmakers at the NFB.

*Les raquetteurs* (1958) was the first film to propel this group into international recognition[11] and to bring its members into contact with the international community of cinéma vérité filmmakers. This was important not so much for the contact with the Americans as for the meetings with the Europeans, and in particular the French exponents such as Jean Rouch. This contact, in particular, was the most fruitful; not because the French cinéma vérité filmmakers brought about a change of direction amongst those directors whom they met, but because they expressed considerable enthusiasm and encouragement for the technical innovations and the ideological approach they detected in films like *Les raquetteurs*. The cachet of approval from the Parisian *Cahiers du cinéma*[12] was a welcome antidote to the cold water of the NFB hierarchy.[13] The international recognition gained from selection for Festival exhibition was a useful lever in the negotiations needed to secure approval for an expanded program along the same lines.

The very subject matter of these films reveals their filmmakers' concern with the ethnography of a modern industrial and urban society; this in sharp contrast to the folkloric conversation-pieces of before 1958, made either under anglophone supervision inside the NFB or by the members of the older Quebec elite outside it.

The attention is drawn frequently to the rituals of the urban masses: its attraction to ritualized violence in body-contact sports (boxing: *Golden Gloves*; pro wrestling: *La lutte*; ice hockey: *Un jeu si simple*); its ritualized community leisure activities (see the shriner-type convention in *Les raquetteurs*); its ritualized holidays (the Montrealers in *Voir Miami*); the vestiges of a rural culture, ritualized and modernized as in the sequence of the *radio-chapelet*[14] in *À Saint-Henri le cinq septembre*; the parade (*Québec USA* and *Les raquetteurs*); children's games (*Rouli-roulant* and the counting-out rhymes incorporated into the sound-track of *Jour après jour*); and the dance (frenzied in *Les raquetteurs*, desultory and mechanical in *Jour après jour*, the "chicken-scratch" sequence in *Voir Miami*, traditional in *Les bacheliers de la cinquième*). These activities are not presented as merely features of a popular culture, but as ritual, the formal observance of customs, and it is as such that they are inscribed into the films. The camera movements, the cutting, the sound editing, frequently serve to emphasize this formalized quality. The swirling camera movements echo or counterpoint the dance sequences in the Groulx films (*Les raquetteurs* and *Voir Miami*) just as they copy the movements of the majorettes in *Les raquetteurs*. Rhythmic cutting punctuates the soldiers' movements in the parade in *Quebec USA* and those of the majorettes rehearsing in *Jour après jour*. In *Un jeu si simple*, the dramatic implications of hockey viewed as contest are submerged in the presentation of hockey as formalized ritual (see the montage sequences of slapshots, or players being taken out of the boards, or referees signalling penalties). The abstraction is made complete by the sequence of overhead shots (linked by dissolves) of goalmouth activity near the end of the film. Mention is often made in the commentary of the vestigial nature of certain customs (the early dinners of the peasant in the working-class district of Saint-Henri; the gambling in *Voir Miami*, vestige of the gold rush ideal). In *Rouli-roulant*, the lore and skills associated with skateboards are described in unnecessary detail in a pastiche didactic commentary, and a tracking-shot of the skateboards in close-up being carried into the sunset satirizes the fetishism of surfing films. In *Jour après jour*, the children's counting-out and skipping rhymes parallel the statistical, numerical litanies which characterize descriptions of the work and artifacts of the paper factory. In *Un jeu si simple*, religious organ music accompanies shots of play, and in *La lutte* a harpsichord is used to accompany a wild wrestling bout.

The ethnographic project then tends to examine social activity in terms of ritual by emphasizing its formal qualities. This formalization is harnessed to a humanist criticism of modern industrial society associated with mechanization and automation. In *Jour après jour*, formal or associative montage juxtaposes men rhythmically manipulating rods in the factory with shots of the factory hockey team in training; we see paperbag handles jigging along a moving belt intercut in rhythm with close-ups of the legs of factory majorettes in practice; jiving couples at the factory dance are intercut with other shots of factory work; and so on. We see the pervasive mechanical rhythms of the company town's inhabitants, just as in the sound-track we hear the numerical litanies of counting-games, weather forecasts, working-hours, paper-sizes, official statistics; for instance, in the weather forecast heard on the kitchen radio:

> South coast of Nova Scotia, the Annapolis Valley: Foggy to-night.
> Madawasca: a low of 35, a high of 45.
> La Baie des Chaleurs: A low of 35, a high of 48.
> A low of 38, a high of 43.
> A low of 40, a high of 60.
> A low of 18 years, a high of 60 years.
> A low of 65 cents, a high of $2.25 per hour.
> A low of 35, a high of 48 hours per week.

Or, when enumerating sizes of paper:

> 2 by 4, 4 by 8, 30 by 40, 100 by 100, Monday to Saturday, 12 to 8, 8 to 4, 4 to midnight, father to son.

The images of *homo mechanicus* are counterpointed by the sounds of *homo arithmeticus*, and the company town's population is portrayed as the victim of mechanical and statistical processes.

In *Bûcherons de la Manouane*, the only film under consideration which is situated in a remote rural community, the influence of the city and its mechanical rhythms is again inscribed into the film. Not only does the commentary remind us of the demands of the urban economy (for example, the number of trees needed for four editions of the *New York Times*), but the loggers' activities of felling, trimming, loading, stacking, trucking and unloading into the river are shown in an accelerating montage of shots in rotation while the sound track steadily increases in volume, concentrating more and more on the mechanical roar of the logs rolling into the river on their way to the urban market. An accelerated rhythm of cutting and the isolation of certain sounds used asynchronically (such as the ringing of the axes) serves to formalize the sense of mechanical routine.

If social ritual and mechanical routine seem to be recurrent motifs of the ethnographic investigation of the modern Quebec by *cinéma direct* filmmakers, it is because these filmmakers have frequently adopted a critical perspective to their documentary material and have used cinematographic devices to give form to that perspective, to foreground it in the films themselves. Such a self-conscious mediation of the object-reality implies, at first glance, a distance or detachment from the unmanipulated reality of the pro-filmic event; a willingness to intervene, to interpose the filmic process as subject. As such, this would seem to belie the fundamental principle of cinéma vérité—its power to guarantee authenticity by registering audio-visual impressions with a minimum of overt mediation. The supposedly direct or "unmediated" vision would then rely on a rhetoric of empirical objectivity as its guarantee of authenticity. On the other hand, a vision of reality which foregrounded its mediating function by emphasizing formal elements inherent in the process would have to rely on a rhetoric of sincerity to guarantee its authenticity. The filmmaker's commitment to his documentary material must be demonstrated not by his effacement before the formal imperatives of the pro-filmic event (as in the case of some Candid Eye films), but by his honesty about his own role in the filmmaking process.

In the cinéma vérité films of Jean Rouch and Chris Marker in France and elsewhere, this was a vital component of the style. The presence of the camera, far from being dissimulated, is openly revealed not only to the people being filmed, but often to the spectator. The microphone too is often shown. This was not just a reflexive device (exposing the materiality of the process) nor simply a rhetorical device to guarantee the filmmaker's awareness in the eyes of the spectator. It was founded on a belief in the catalytic function of the camera. It was held that when people are made aware of the presence of a camera and microphone, their behaviour will become more expressive, concentrated and ultimately more revealing about their true selves. The interview, then becomes a standard procedure. Just as the probing question or prolonged unpunctuated listening by the interviewer is expected to drag the truth from the insincere subject, so too will the attentive eye of the mobile camera pick up the significant gesture which reveals the posturing or role playing of the same person. The finest example is the interview with the inventor of racing-car stabilizers in Marker's *Le joli mai* (1963). As the pompous self-flattery of the man continues, the camera zooms in to pick up a spider on his person and pans with it as it crawls across his chest and over his shoulder. So full is this man of his own importance that he does not notice, but the camera does, while the interviewer allows him to talk on uninterrupted. Furthermore, interviews in this kind of film are invariably conducted in the familiar surroundings of the subject: the inventor at the racing-circuit, young stockbrokers on the steps of the Bourse, architects on a construction site, and so on.

In the French Unit at the NFB, the interview-film as a genre was rare. *Huit témoins* is a good example, and it is noticeable that in the interviews with juvenile delinquents Jacques Godbout has chosen to occupy his interviewees with familiar activities (playing cards, shooting pool) or to remove them as far as possible from a studio ambience (one boy is interviewed sitting on a car fender at night in a parking lot, lit by car headlights). Nevertheless, when interviews are included, they are shot in the same way; see for instance the interviews cut into the films of Gilles Groulx (*Golden Gloves*, in the kitchen of one subject, or in the bar where another boxer works; *Voir Miami*, in a yacht or on the beach; *Un jeu si simple*, with hockey players at rinkside or in the canteen); and of course an important one is included in *À Saint-Henri le cinq septembre*. In most of these films, the interview is shown direct with synch sound, without the intercutting of other images or a synchronic or atmospheric sound mixing. The counterpointing of interview material with other images is a feature found most frequently in the films of Pierre Perrault, which are beyond the scope of this article. In *Télesphore Légaré, garde-pêche* by Claude Fournier and Gilles Groulx (1959), the sound-track consists of the recorded impressions of the two old folk as they saw the images of the film made about them. But this kind of experiment was rare in the films under study here.

More often than not, the filmmaker hopes to capture conversation among his subjects while the camera remains an obvious recorder of the event. Examples of this may be seen in the self-conscious enunciation of the relevant municipal by-law by the police officer in *Rouli-roulant* who is confiscating the skateboards; the grievances of the loggers in the station or at dinner in *Bûcherons de la Manouane*; the barroom antics in *Golden Gloves*; the behaviour of the boys at the Seaquarium in *Voir Miami*. These are all moments at which the presence of the camera is clearly obvious to the people being filmed and which by being retained in the final print of the film guarantee the implication of the filmmaker in his diegesis. This implication helps to close the distance opened by the formalizing tendency described above.

There are also other strategies used in these films which effectively achieve the same goal.

Frequently a sequence will begin with a wide-angle shot from a hand-held camera in *medias res*, instead of the more traditional establishing-shot which would enable the spectator to orient the action in a broader spatial continuum. The opening shots of the parade in *Les raquetteurs* are a good example of this. *La lutte* opens with a shot of two bare arms locked together in a wrestling grip seen against a black background, and it is only as the camera follows their downward movement that their broader spatial context is revealed. There is a similar use of medium-close shots of youths flexing their muscles to open the initial sequence of *Huit témoins*. The frequent use of such shots both to introduce sequences and within shots where the walking camera mingles with its subjects, constitute the practical application of Brault's concept of the "wide-angle style":

> . . . one could say that there are two techniques: there is the tele-photo style and the wide-angle style. But I belong more to the wide-angle style, that is to say that the style consists simply in approaching the people and filming them, in participating in their lives and not in observing them in secret, inside a box, or from high up in a window with a tele-photo lens.[15]

This intermingling does not merely put the cameraman at the mercy of the events he is filming; he is not merely seeking to "keep up with the action." The circling movements are often identifiable as those of a questing subject, the cameraman searching for the revealing detail which will throw the shot into relief, and convey additional meaning. This particular trait is later developed to good effect in the films of Pierre Perrault.

There is an almost surrealistic tone to the juxtapositions that are forged by such questing, juxtapositions which depend upon objective chance and the receptivity of the cameraman's sensibility to the incongruous or the *merveilleux*. In the short films of the *cinéma direct* movement, examples may be found in the shots of the Jones brothers sparring and training amidst the shunting boxcars of Saint-Henri (*Golden Gloves*), and in the shot of the departing police car after the dramatic confiscation of the skateboards, which closes with a tilt to reveal a small girl skipping in total indifference to the intervention of the law (*Rouli-roulant*). Sometimes the disorienting "surreal" effect is achieved by the choice of camera angle: for example, the shot of the jogger in Quebec who leapfrogs over a series of bollards and, seen from behind in deep-focus, seems to be jumping over the same one again and again in defiance of spatial logic (*Quebéc* USA); and the shot which frames a professional wrestler performing situps in training against a Discobolos seen in the background (*La lutte*). Sometimes the disturbing contrast does not depend upon the positioning or movement of the camera, but merely upon the attentiveness of the cameraman who shoots before the moment is lost. *Quebéc* USA has many such shots, often inserted at random, like the shot of the large gentleman with an equally large double bass who disappears without trouble into a very small car. The same disorientation can be achieved by a cut; at the end of a series of gym shots of wrestlers performing physical exercises, the film cuts to another who flings himself with superhuman abandonment into a reckless somersault which, as the camera tilts downward, reveals itself as a dive into a pool (*La lutte*). In all of these examples, the filmmaker is projecting his subjectivity, sometimes inscribing the effect into the film in such a way that it contributes to the organic development of meaning, sometimes indulging in a gag which is allowed to rupture the continuity of the work.

One of the common features of the rhetoric of sincerity in the new cinema in France of this period was to show the camera or microphone, and to foreground the materiality of the structuring process in one way or another. In the *cinéma direct* films under study here, this is rarely done. It is found in the film made by

Claude Jutra for the television series *Profils et paysages* on *Félix Leclerc, troubadour* (1960), where the arrival of the camera crew at Leclerc's house with all their paraphernalia is treated ironically. Gilles Carle inserts shots of cameramen on the high diving board into his swimming films of 1963.[16] However, in the films we are studying here, the reflexive tendency is not demonstrated in this way.[17] The most obviously reflexive film of our corpus is *À Saint-Henri le cinq septembre*, and its own self-consciousness is entirely a product of the commentary and editing of Jacques Godbout,[18] whose novels share a similar reflexive tendency closely related to certain concerns of the *nouveaux romanciers* in France.[19] The commentary amounts to an apology (or defence) for *cinéma direct* and reveals a close affinity with contemporary currents in French cinema, notably, the *Cahiers du Cinéma* group and the practicians of *cinéma vérité*:

> (Opening sequence, after song by Raymond Lévesque)
>
> "It is six in the morning, on the fifth of September. We have chosen this day at random to invade Saint-Henri, a working-class district in Montreal. . . ."
>
> "I said that we chose this day at random. This is not quite true. This Tuesday, September 5, is the day when the children go back to school. . . ."
>
> "We have chosen to live 24 hours without a break in a sort of relay race in which thirty tourists armed with cameras will be passing a lens from one to the other. We are not seeking the unusual (*l'insolite*) just because we are in America.[20] We shall be content to seek out the everyday event in its greyness or its sunshine. We have chosen to live face to face because a working-class district is rather like the shop-window of a city. . . ."
>
> "The most difficult task will be to adjust the image we had of reality to the one we discover. For if some (of us) already know the district from the inside, others have never before set foot there. . . ."
>
> (In the evening)
>
> "After the meal and the dishes, in some families people get together for rosary-hour on the radio. We wanted to capture the living scene of a family at prayer, but we discovered that *cinéma vérité* is not always that easy nor on that night was their rosary-hour . . ." (*there is considerable difficulty in tuning the radio*).
>
> "Some of us have gone home to bed; for the others the marathon goes on. In the quest for a facet of the truth, the camera seeks out noise, light. The truth. We have made this film without the slightest *mise-en-scène*, apart from this particular shot which we took because the girl was pretty. We have made this film from a spirit of adventure, out of obstinacy, out of necessity, for our own pleasure and for that of the producer. We have made it with a voluptuous love of the arbitrary, in search of the friendship of the neighbourhood residents who without hesitation have offered us their faces. . . ."
>
> "We would have liked to send Chris Marker a letter from Saint-Henri,[21] to Resnais a song of sirens,[22] to Truffaut a pianist riddled with bullets,[23] but things did not turn out that way. And if we are offering to Jean Rouch this chronicle of a neighbourhood,[24] we are also offering it to Hitchcock who would certainly have uncovered, pinned down and laid bare the mystery before your puzzled eyes."

Nowhere is the phenomenology of the NFB *cinéma direct* spelt out more clearly in one of its films than here: the questing subject on the one hand (choosing, seeking, engaging in the adventure); the undramatic, raw reality on the other hand (random, everyday, arbitrary). Out of this collision comes the creation of familiarity as distinct from the picturesque (through face-to-face contact, adjustment of the image, a desire to enter the community in friendship). The tension is clearly established between the willed surrender of subjectivity to the necessity of object-reality, and the affirmation of subjectivity in the sense of quest. This tension is held in balance by the affirmation of solidarity by the questing group with its social object, a solidarity generated by the participatory project. The prevailing tone is of positive paternalism, in which the commentator recognizes the social distance separating the filmmakers from the community, but refuses to articulate it in material or economic terms, except in the most general way. The "adjustment of the image" here means that the commentary emphasizes social harmony (lack of racial segregation, the happy faces of children), material comfort when compared with Europe (running water and electricity in all homes), and the benefits of increased education. The commentator resists the urge to emphasize pauperism:

> ". . . we have not brought back pictures of courtyards (*fonds-de-cour*), flies, filth. It is there. That is all you need to know. It should not be there. That is all we want you to know."

This passage is the clearest admission that a formative ideology (liberal humanism) has intervened to screen off a certain face of reality.

While the other *cinéma direct* films under scrutiny here do not discuss the process of their making so overtly, the filmmaker often imposes the sense of a beginning and ending to his material which echoes his own experience (as investigator) of penetration and withdrawal. The most obvious example is in *Jour après jour*, which opens with a rapid forward tracking-shot from inside a car through the streets of Windsor (Quebec) to the paper factory, and closes with the same movement in reverse. No attempt is made in this film to code this sequence as the experience of a factory worker; rather, it stands as an invitation to the spectator to share the filmmaker's experience.

A similar tracking-shot, this time from the back of a covered truck, opens *Bûcherons de la Manouane*, but this time we know that the camera is accompanying the loggers from their camp out to the worksite. The initial penetration of the investigator into his material is coded to coincide with the experience of the men being studied. The filmmaker effectively separates himself at the end of the film from his investigation (and participation) by showing another morning departure for work (Guy Charron with his team of horses), but this time the accompanying camera movement only goes so far, and then watches the man and his two horses disappear into the whiteout.

In both these films (*Jour après jour* and *Bûcherons de la Manouane*) which deal with the conditions of work in an industry, it is worth noting that a structure based simply upon a work-cycle is rejected; that is, the structure used in such Griersonian documentaries as *Drifters* (Grierson, 1929) or *Night Mail* (Harry Watt & Basil Wright, 1936). Nor is the structure based on a dramatic crescendo of activity leading to a climax, as in Georges Rouquier's documentaries on the salt industry in the Camargue or on dam-construction in the Alps.[25] Instead the structure is one that emphasizes the form of the enquiry. In this, they resemble more closely the documentaries of Alain Resnais, except that whereas Resnais focuses on the iconography of processes and artifacts,[26] Perron and Lamothe give the collective human object, the workers, a central role.

In other French unit films of this period, a common feature is still that of the opening shot showing a journey in: the arrival of American tourists in *Québec USA* or in Miami (*Voir Miami*), and the entry into Saint-Henri with the milk-delivery truck (*À Saint-Henri le cinq septembre*). The structuring of the enquiry in a closed period of time is often underscored by opening with a morning scene and closing with a night scene (*Québec* USA; *Les raquetteurs; À Saint-Henri le cinq septembre*) or closing with the "dawning of a new day" (*Voir Miami; Bûcherons de la Manouane; Les bacheliers de la cinquième*). The closing with a night scene recalls the traditional iconography of the earlier ethnographic documentaries of Proulx, for example, which frequently close with the "home-movie" sunset, but whereas these were rural sunsets invoking once again the beauties of the natural country way of life, the night or evening scenes which close the NFB French Unit films are rooted in the distinctly urban settings of Quebec, Sherbrooke or Montreal. In *Un jeu si simple*, the onset of darkness is no longer represented by an outdoor scene at all, but by a shot of the ceiling lights in the Montreal Forum gradually being extinguished. The transfer of iconography to a metropolitan environment is complete.

The opening and closing shots of *Les bacheliers de la cinquième* serve differently to foreground the experience of the subject-investigator who comes to affirm his solidarity with the human object of his study. The film opens with a traditional slow pan over the St. Lawrence, showing in sequence the river, a harbour, and then some boats pulled up on the stage. It is the familiar establishing-shot *par excellence*. The shot is repeated at the end of the film, but this time intercut with the close-up of a gazing youth who has just spent the night on the beach. The youth is one of the central characters in the film who have come to the North Shore in search of employment. The film has shown their failure to find a job for lack of education or training. The picturesque calm associated in the opening shot with the undisturbed scenery of the early morning is now re-coded as the desolate environment (a Kuleshov-effect, indeed) which greets the alienated young man who has learned that society seems to have no place for him. The naiveté of the opening shot has now yielded by its association with the unattached, marginal youth to a reappraisal of the scenic iconography. The peaceful riverside is now reseen as barren workplace. The filmmaker's gaze has been re-educated, and the experience is passed on to the spectator.

This seeking out of the gaze of the other, the identification of the camera-eye with eyes of a subject within the film, is perhaps the key to the process of participatory investigation. It most closely illustrates the link between the reflexive mode of the self-conscious filmmaker (as in the Godbout films) and the desire to express solidarity with a community (most evident in the films of Perron and Lamothe). Over and over again, shots are shown of spectators. The object of their gaze may frequently be the ritualized amusements which attract the formalized treatment of the filmmaker. The parades in *Les raquetteurs* and *Québec* USA, the sporting events in *La lutte, Golden Gloves* and *Un jeu si simple*, the Seaquarium and the rocket-launching in *Voir Miami*—all are shown extensively intercut with shots of the watching public, either as crowd or a series of individuals in the crowd. The very form of these sequences is created from this alternation of watcher and watched. Also, the form of these sequences is isomorphic with the film's avowed project, its inscription into its society; the picture of a collective engaged in watching a formalized projection of itself. Indeed, the camera often seeks out the rituals of this very watching, its mediations, through including shots of spectators taking photographs (*Voir Miami, Québec* USA); showing the varieties of photographer's poses and the mechanical winding-up of a movie camera (*Québec* USA); or by showing the presence of the technicians of the electronic media (*Voir Miami, Un jeu si simple*). In *Québec* USA, we see one shot of the parade gradually being brought into focus. We are thereby invited to participate in the mediated perception of one of the watchers. In *Un jeu si simple*, the opening television sequence commentated by René Lecavalier shows the conventional dramatic image of hockey (synthesized and mediated), including a spectacular save by Jacques Plante, and culminating in a goal by the Canadiens. This (mediated) sequence stands in contrast to the undramatic, analytical, almost abstract images of the game which close the film. In these last two examples, it might be said that the filmmakers are stating their own distance from the forms of mediation being practised by the spectators in their films, in order the better to privilege their own mediations. Nevertheless, the act of watching attracts most frequently the sympathy of the filmmaker. In *À Saint-Henri le cinq septembre*, it is with the shock of sympathetic recognition that the filmmaker finds young men occupied, like himself, in watching and waiting idly in the hot afternoon sun. It is with hope that Gilles Groulx looks upon the watchers of the skies at Cape Canaveral *(Voir Miami)*, since these watchers, the commentator implies, are the vestiges of a pioneering spirit or a spiritual aspiration which might yet transcend the unidimensionalism of a consumer society.

The formalizing tendency, the reflexive tendency and the expression of solidarity with a public about whom and for whom many of these films are made—these are dominating characteristics of the films made at the NFB by the French Unit during the period of the ascendancy of *cinéma direct*. The expression of solidarity (or sympathy) often amounted to the outermost limit of political commitment as expressed in the films. But even this was already a fairly deep commitment, since the public was now being portrayed as an urban one, its problems those of an industrial economy, its leisure activities ritualized and increasingly professionalized. The revelation of and commitment to this society meant already a commitment to the goals of the Quiet Revolution. The filmmakers themselves were often contributing writers to magazines like *Cité Libre*[27] or, later, *parti pris*.[28] They were then often committed to various forms of social democracy or socialism. Frequently, however, only a diluted form of liberal humanism pervades the commentaries of the films. Such was the impact of a federal organism which attempted to screen out more radical sentiment. The names of the companies had to be removed from the films of Perron and Lamothe on papermaking and logging. A reference to Castro and the Cuban exiles was excized from *Voir Miami*. Nevertheless, the force of the direct method and its tight editing made the inferences clear. Enough slips through in the commentary to reveal the sense of exploitation that Perron and Lamothe felt to be inherent in the industrial processes they portrayed. Groulx's films still stand as an indictment of a society in which ritualized violence, gambling or consumption offer illusory dreams of escape for the oppressed or dispossessed.

A critical eye turned upon contemporary society in Quebec, seeking to embody the new image of a changing society and politics, was tolerable within the framework of liberal democracy as long as it retained a certain rhetoric and form still linking it to the objective empiricism of the Candid Eye, end-of-ideology filmmaking of anglophone Canadians. However the formalizing tendency gradually became more pronounced as ideological commitments defined themselves. The French Unit filmmakers could not help but be aware of the constrictions of the short-film format in comparison with the feature-length documentaries of their French counterparts in Europe, or of the accession of documentarists like Resnais and Franju to the fictional feature. Although many of the filmmakers continued with *cinéma direct* shooting techniques and equipment, a certain dissatisfaction with the method grew from within. In the reflexive *À Saint-Henri le cinq septembre,* this is articulated in the commentary:

> "Midnight. The police keeps watch. It must indeed watch, for Saint-Henri has still not yielded its secret . . . The mystery remains quite complete, locked within."

The reference to Hitchcock, quoted earlier, is almost an admission, however ironic, that the truth not only remains below the surfaces open to the naive gaze, but can only be reached or exposed by the more extensive intervention or coding employed in the fictional feature.

Perhaps the most overt reservation expressed against *cinéma direct* occurs in a short film made by Gilles Carle for the television series *La femme hors du foyer: Solange dans nos campagnes* (1963). Carle has explained how he made it to satirize the methods of the *cinéma direct* as he had used and encountered them in making his own film on a marriage in the same year (*Un air de famille*).[29] The film shows a television production unit who engage in the search for an authentic country-girl to become "star for a day" on their show. Having selected an applicant from the many who replied to the invitation, they set out to engage in a *cinéma direct* reportage. In the car ride (in a convertible), the cameraman indulges in the acrobatics of a Michel Brault. At one point they stop for a series of shots of the hostess of the show in the countryside, indulging in the freeze-frames and pixillated effects as found in *Québec USA*, or the jump-cuts reminiscent of Gilles Groulx. On reaching the farm, the interviews fail to reveal the "true personality" of the girl, who persists in mythifying herself for the camera, and the naive political questions receive answers which reveal nothing about the "problems of the farmer." The team returns, and after reviewing the rushes with the producer, it is silently recognized that the experiment has been a failure.

The *cinéma direct* has not ground to a halt at this stage, but the initial élan of the French Unit as a group is henceforth lost, and many of its participants will gradually be attracted into more extensive projects, either harnessed to a more prolonged investigation in the manner of Pierre Perrault or to a progressive restructuring of the milieu in the fictionalized documentary and the dramatic feature.

*Ciné-Tracts*, 4 (Spring-Summer 1978)

The republication of this article gives me the opportunity to correct an unfortunate error at the head of the piece in which the quotation was incorrectly attributed to Gilles Groulx.

Also it gives me an opportunity to acknowledge the help and support of certain colleagues and friends: Ben Shek, who got me started in this enquiry; Bruce Elder, whose work and conversations have been an inspiration to go below surfaces; and Peter Harcourt, whose initial confidence in the article got me to write it and got *Ciné-Tracts* to publish it. In addition, I thank Ron Burnett of *Ciné-Tracts* for the catalytic effect his journal had on serious film study in Canada, and Seth Feldman and Piers Handling for their contributions to the publication of film scholarship here.

1984

---

1 Also quoted in Gilles Marsolais, *Le cinéma canadien*, (Montreal: Editions du jour, 1968).
2 See "On the Candid-Eye Movement," by Bruce Elder, *Canadian Film Reader*, ed. by Feldman & Nelson (Toronto: Peter Martin Associates, 1977).
3 See, for example, Wolf Koenig, "A note on 'Candid Eye' " in André Paquet (ed.), *How to make or not to make a Canadian film*, (Montreal: Cinémathèque canadienne, 1967), in which he quotes verbatim and at length from this foreword.

4 *Golden Gloves, La lutte* and *À Saint-Henri le cinq septembre* are "collective" films; i.e., the responsibility for the direction rests with a group of filmmakers, and not a single *auteur*.
5 *À Saint-Henri le cinq septembre* 41'36" and *Huit Témoins* 58'05". Two of the films fit a shorter fifteen-minute format: *Les raquetteurs* and *Rouli-roulant*.
6 *Un jeu si simple* is listed as 1965 in the NFB catalogue but was shot in 1963. *Rouli-roulant* is a late exception, however, dating from 1967.
7 Yvan Lamonde, "Indirectement, le cinéma direct" in *Cinéma Québec* 4, 1 (December 12, 1974), pp. 22–24.
8 See especially René Bouchard, *Filmographie d'Albert Tessier*, (Montreal: Editions du Boréal Express, 1973).
9 See especially the "dossier Proulx" in *Cinéma Québec*, 4, 6 (1975) pp. 18–33.
10 This concern to render an image of an urban society in Quebec had been anticipated in the forties by two important novelists: Roger Lemelin (*Au Pied de la Pente Douce*, 1944) and Gabrielle Roy (*Bonheur d'Occasion*, 1945).
11 It was shown at the Flaherty Symposium in UCLA Santa Barbara in 1958. Here it was that Michel Brault, who made the film jointly with Gilles Groulx, first met Jean Rouch. Brault was to be Rouch's cameraman in *Chronique d'un été* (1961) and *La punition* (1960–64).
12 See Louis Marcorelles, "La faire aux vérités" in *Cahiers du Cinéma*, 143 (May 1963) pp. 26–34; interview with Jean Rouch in *Cahiers du Cinéma*, 144 (June 1963); Michel Delehaye, "La chasse a l'I" in *Cahiers du Cinéma*, 146 (August 1963).
13 *Les raquetteurs* had initially been consigned to "stock-shots" by Grant McLean; see Gilles Marsolais, *Le cinéma canadien*, (Montreal: Editions du Jour, 1968), p. 57 and Michel Brault's interview in *Michel Brault* (Cinéastes du Québec No. 11), (Montreal: Conseil québécois pour la diffusion du cinéma, 1972), p. 7. For a discussion of the relations between the filmmakers and the executive branch at the National Film Board at this time, see R. Boissonnault, "Les cinéastes québécois. Troisième partie: la séquence du cinéma direct" in *Cinéma Québec* II, No. 4 (December, 1972) pp. 15–22.
14 Evening prayers conducted on the radio, the rosary-hour.
15 *Objectif*, 60, No. 3 (December 1960) p. 9.
16 *Natation* (Olympic Swimmers) and *Pattes Mouillées* (The Big Swim).
17 When mikes are included they are not obtrusive enough to emphasize the reflexive mode.
18 Assisted in editing by Monique Fortier.
19 In particular, *Salut, Galarneau!*, (Paris: Seuil, 1967), in which Godbout's central character is as much concerned by the process of writing as by solving his problems in life. Indeed, he coins the verb *vécrire* (p. 154) to describe his attempts to meld the two.
20 Reference to François Reichenbach's *L'Amérique insolite* (1959).
21 Reference to Marker's *Lettre de Sibérie* (Letter from Siberia) (1958).
22 Reference to Resnais' *Le chant du styrène* (The Song of Styrene) (1958).
23 Reference to Truffaut's *Tirez sur le pianiste* (Shoot the Piano-Player) (1960).
24 Reference to Rouch's *Chronique d'un été* (1960).
25 *Le sel de la terre* (1950) and *Les Galeries malgovert* (1952).
26 E.g. in La Bibliothèque Nationale in *Toute la mémoire du monde* (1956) and the plastics industry in *Le chant du styrène* (1958).
27 *Cité Libre*, throughout the fifties and sixties, a harbinger of the quiet revolution whose contributors included, along with Trudeau, Marchand, and Pelletier, filmmakers like Albert Lamothe and Jacques Godbout.
28 *Parti pris*, a more left-wing periodical of the sixties whose contributors included Gilles Carle, Clément Perron, Gilles Groulx, and Jacques Godbout.
29 In *Cinéma d'ici*, ed. by A. Lafrance and G. Marsolais. (Montréal: Leméac, 1973), pp. 112–113.

# *Pierre Perrault and* Le cinéma vécu

## BY PETER HARCOURT

*It is difficult to find in the history of national cinemas a figure whose career parallels the role undertaken by Pierre Perrault in Quebec. Perhaps, like Dziga Vertov during the golden age of the Soviet cinema, Perrault may be seen as something of a conscience or admonition to his colleagues. His contemporaries used the tools of* cinéma direct *for what, in retrospect, appears to have been research that would provide material to be fed into a commercial feature film industry. Perrault, as Peter Harcourt points out here, rejected what he saw as the feigned purity of* cinéma direct *in favour of a more vibrant and durable interactive documentary.* Le cinéma vécu*—a "lived" cinema—is Perrault's assertion that the basic research into the nuances of life in Quebec is far from complete. Nor are the tools and attitudes toward that research fully explored. The lapsed discipline of the original enquiry is perhaps best expressed by Perrault in the figure of the hapless poet-cum-hunter in his most recent work,* La bête lumineuse. *This atavistic idealist's misadventures amidst his beer-sodden buddies seems to suggest that an ill-planned orgy of self discovery can be just another party gone sour; that the land one turns to for redemption may not return the gesture; and that the seeker of truths, with or without a camera can, if he or she is really lucky, become the hunted.*

*For all the rigour of his inquiry, it may be a mistake to see Pierre Perrault as elucidating the nature of the Québécois. Like Yasujiro Ozu, whose work was once considered too Japanese to interest foreign audiences, Perrault's importance lies in his ability to present cultural nuances that are in the long run untranslatable. Even when they are adequately sub-titled (most are not), the films present a withholding of meaning from non-Québécois, and perhaps even from those who are not directly involved with the on-screen events.*

*It is to be expected that the magic inherent in giving voice to a culture would also give voice to the magician's critics. Perrault is probably the most thoroughly examined Canadian filmmaker. The* Cinémathèque québécoise *has honoured him with a book, while scholars outside Quebec have seen his films as a challenging and promising entrée into a unique culture. In this article, Peter Harcourt documents Perrault's work in the context of* le cinéma vécu. *The "shaping, selecting and provoking" that Harcourt discusses yield moments that David Clandfield, in the article that follows this one, interprets as being essentially poetic in their use of found speech.*

*Je veux faire ma chanson du peu de calcaire d'un squelette et beaucoup de géologie . . .*
Pierre Perrault, "Sève," *Portulan* (1961).

Lawyer, poet, broadcaster, filmmaker, Pierre Perrault is very much a man of words. Language has dominated his every activity. Authentic speech has been the goal of all his quests. "Speech depends upon life," he once said, "while silence is the cessation of death."[1] Concerning Alexis Tremblay, the old patriarch who appears in so many of his films, Perrault once explained that when Alexis speaks, "he bears witness. His speech is an act. He takes up a position. He makes up things while explaining his reasons. He discovers his thoughts by articulating them."[2] And speech is not just language. It is invariably accompanied by gesture, by the expressive use of hands and face. Certainly we express ourselves through language, but Perrault believes we *create* ourselves through speech.

Discouraged by the pettiness of law after two years of practice, Pierre Perrault began writing poetry and working in radio. Renouncing the codes of legal language, he began to concern himself with the creative use of speech. In 1956 he produced a series of radio documentaries on life in Quebec for Radio-Canada entitled *Au pays de Neufve-France*, after which he worked with René Bonnière to prepare a comparable series of film documentaries for television. In the course of all these series, he became acquainted with the Tremblay family and other inhabitants of the farming, boat-building and shipping community of Ile-aux-Coudres, an isolated island in the mouth of the St. Lawrence.[3] From his encounter with this community, and from his realization that he required visuals to capture the gestural aspects of speech, Perrault's real work in film began.

*Pour la suite du monde* (literally, So the World May Continue)[4] began from a hunch. Perrault knew there was a film in these people, but not a film that could be worked out in advance. Yet to raise the money, he had to have a project, and the project with which he was finally successful in interesting both Radio-Canada and the National Film Board was a film on the islanders' distinctive way of trapping the once-profitable Beluga whale. There was a problem, however: the islanders hadn't used this method for over thirty years. Perrault had to interest the islanders in reviving the tradition. But that would be his film, or at least the *pretext* for his film: while watching the islanders discuss the possibilities of reviving the tradition, and while observing them as they set about once again to construct their large traps to catch the whale, Perrault would be able to make his film. The film would not be about the whale. It would be an audio-visual record of a particular style of living, of an animated way of gesturing and of a special kind of dialect—a unique form of speech.

This audio-visual record was also to become a unique form of film. Unlike many other films, the basic thrust of which is anthropological—unlike Flaherty's *Nanook of the North* in the twenties, or the work of Arthur Lamothe on the Montagnais Indians today—*Pour la suite du monde* is a highly complex construct. With only Michel Brault on camera and Marcel Carrière on sound, shooting in 16mm and black-and-white, Perrault was working very much within the tradition of "direct cinema" or cinéma vérité developed at the Board. But he was also working with his own poet's eye, with his special relationship to these people, and with what was to emerge as an acute sense of history. Although shooting without a script and dealing with living people, he was not just observing. He was constantly shaping, selecting, provoking. This is why Perrault rejects the term "direct cinema" and speaks instead of a "lived" cinema—*un cinéma vécu*.

How is this cinema organized? What is it about its structure that makes it unique? In a way that cuts across the assumed dichotomy within film practice, *Pour la suite du monde* (1963) along with the two succeeding chapters of the Ile-aux-Coudres trilogy, *Le règne du jour* (1966) and *Les voitures d'eau* (1968), bestows upon its documentary footage the symbolic authority of fiction.

To begin with, there is the dimension of time, a dimension that is constantly related to a sense of the seasonal. *Pour la suite du monde* opens in late autumn with Captain Joachim Harvey bringing in the buoys from the St. Lawrence River. One season is ending, another is about to begin. The islanders are preparing for the freezeup of winter, the enforced isolation of which has helped to preserve their strong sense of community. Meanwhile, on the sound-track, interwoven with the synch-sound of Joachim Harvey talking to his crew and to his bosses in Quebec City, is the off-screen voice of Alexis Tremblay reading, in sixteenth-century French, from the diary of Jacques Cartier about his first voyage up the St. Lawrence in 1535.

Immediately, there are elements that invite interpretation. Two voyages are contrasted, one in a sailboat, the other in what the islanders call a *goélette*—a wooden schooner modified to run by steam. Cartier's voyage represents an opening up, Harvey's a closing down. There are also two forms of speech and three spans of time in this sequence. Alexis Tremblay is a generation older than Joachim Harvey; and Jacques Cartier, whose voice lives on through his diary, is four centuries older than either man. There is both a sense of difference and of continuity. The river has changed since Jacques Cartier's day, yet it was Cartier who gave the island its name.

Just as the schooners are brought together in the harbour to wait out the long winter months, so the islanders come together for a variety of community activities. The first one involves an auction designed to raise money to say prayers for the souls of the dead. In this sequence there is thus a fusion of the sacred and the secular. Furthermore, as in the opening, in this sequence too there is a kind of double discourse. While the auction continues, old Louis Harvey—referred to throughout as Grand Louis—is talking to Léopold Tremblay and some other men about the moon, drawing upon ancient folklore concerning its relationship to the earth. This moment not only evokes the oral traditions that still nourish this isolated community, but might also seem to equate the religious with the superstitious. Both elements are kept alive by their re-creation through speech.

The sequence ends with the inevitable group excitement of a community dance. But as the music continues, Perrault cuts outside to the snow. Night becomes day as we follow a horse-and-sleigh tearing along a snow-covered road. Then another horse-and-sleigh, and then yet another. There seem to be several horses-and-sleighs galloping through the wintry landscape as if to converge upon a single point. By this prestidigitatious piece of visual rhetoric, Perrault brings this sequence to an exhilarating close.

Couplings and contrasts abound throughout the film. If distinctions are made between the generations, distinctions are made within them as well. Alexis Tremblay and Grand Louis are of the same generation. This sameness is visually reinforced (more by nature than by art) by the fact that both men wear glasses and the same kind of cap. In fact, so similar do they appear that, on an initial viewing of the film, it is sometimes difficult to tell them apart. Yet they are very different men. If Alexis is hierarchical in his thinking and fixated by the past, Grand Louis is more adaptable. As Michel Brûlé has suggested about Grand Louis in his study of Perrault:

> He narrates important events and trivial anecdotes with the same kind of passion. His lack of any sense of hierarchy, his lack of perspective, gives him, by an obvious paradox, an immeasurable advantage over Alexis. One can see that Louis will be able to continue to live in a world in the full throes of evolution. Of course, the past has marked him; but because of this lack of perspective, the future doesn't worry him.[5]

At the same time, for all his flexibility, Grand Louis is very religious. He is constantly talking about "the souls of the dead" as the guardians of their culture. Alexis, on the other hand, is more political. "I want to vote Liberal just one more time before I die," he explains toward the end of the film. For Alexis, Jacques Cartier's diary is a kind of Bible. If, for Christians, the Bible explains the origins of the universe, for Alexis, this diary explains the origins of Quebec civilization, origins which, necessarily, are rooted in the past.[6]

When a meeting is called to discuss the revival of the whale-trapping enterprise—a meeting called together, incidentally, by a town crier—Alexis is absent. But Grand Louis is there, discussing the pros and cons with the younger men, stating that for the adventure to be successful they will have to honour the souls of the dead and yet, at the same time, wanting to be paid for any work he might do.

These discussions also play upon the contrasts that exist between the generations. The old men who took part in the custom advise the younger men about the best season for preparing the poles, the right time to plant them in the water, and the probable time that the whale might appear. The younger ones—that is, like Léopold, the forty-year-olds—remember the custom but have never taken part in it; while young O'Neil Tremblay, a twenty-year-old, has no idea of how it is done.

Throughout this film as throughout the trilogy, all these community gatherings emphasize the cohesion of the group. Unlike Allan King's *A Married Couple* (1969), a film which in its different way also transforms documentary into fiction, *Pour la suite du monde* emphasizes the structures of non-conflict, of uncontested solidarity. Yet if we look at it closely, we might get the feeling that some potential conflict is actually there.

At this meeting, for example, there are a great many people, a great many men. But not all of them speak. Nor are there many teenagers or young men in their twenties. Léopold Tremblay, Grand Louis Harvey and one or two others really dominate the meeting and move it in the direction they want it to go. If these epic conversationalists do actually create themselves through speech, they might seem to create as well their position of authority within the community. Furthermore, throughout this sequence, Brault's camera has repeatedly picked up the face of an old man. He is of the same generation as Alexis and Grand Louis. He might well have been one of the fishermen. Yet he says nothing during this meeting and it is a shot of his troubling face that brings this sequence to a close. What does his silence signify? What is his social relationship to the loquacious leaders of this community? Why, in the course of the film, is he never seen again?

Throughout the trilogy, there are very few young people. There are middle-aged people and old people and gaggles of young children, but there are almost no teenagers. The young children, in fact, are often associated with animals, running about the fields with the sheep or milling about the chickens. While a necessary part of the pantheism of this film, they seem more like fertility symbols than active participants in the island community. And of course, they are allowed no speech.

Even Marie Tremblay, wife of Alexis and mother of sixteen children, visually so prominent in the films because of her gnarled face and glistening eyes, even Marie has to wait until *Un pays sans bon sens!*—a film made after the trilogy in 1970—for her chance to tell *her* stories about the hardships of her youth. Throughout the trilogy, her voice is always secondary to those of the men. And while the dwindling economic opportunities of the island are confronted symbolically in the last film of the series, *Les voitures d'eau*, we have to wait for Michel Brault's first fiction feature in 1967 to understand in detail the absence of young people from the life of the island. The title of the film, *Entre la mer et l'eau douce,*[7] actually takes its name from something quoted in *Pour la suite du monde* from Jacques Cartier's diary; for this is the area, between the sea and fresh water, where the Beluga whales once swam in such plenitude. In this fiction film by Brault, which in turn has the authenticity of a documentary, we experience more fully the inability of these rural regions to provide a meaningful existence for young people, especially for young men. The same area that once promised such abundance can no longer sustain its young.

Within *Pour la suite du monde,* however, there are visual hints at economic changes even if there is no direct analysis. There is a sequence in which a group of young boys are rolling about in tires or riding them like broncos, as if in some kind of post-industrial rodeo. Léopold comes in to the barn and stops them because they are making so much noise. He sends them off to get some knives and cedar chips so that he can teach them how to carve a little *chaloupe,* which they can sail in the river. He is carving away when Alexis enters and complains that the boat should have two sails. Shortly afterward, when they launch their little sailboat, it soon topples over—perhaps, indeed, because it had only one sail! This tiny marine disaster not only anticipates the burning schooner that ends *Les voitures d'eau* and which symbolizes so effectively the death of a way of life, but also increases our understanding of Léopold. As with the Beluga whale venture, Léopold is old enough to want to sustain tradition but he is only partly successful. In spite of the title of the film, this world as we are experiencing it will *not* continue.

Another moment must be mentioned. On Easter morning, Grand Louis sets off before sunup to fetch water from a special stream which he believes is holy, "all part of the Great Lord's plan." Once back in the village, he offers some to the children. They seem to tolerate him, taking little sips and making strange faces, almost as if embarrassed. Meanwhile, some sheep are bleating. They want some water too, Grand Louis explains. But the tone is not simple.

As with so many moments in this film, this sequence is a loving celebration of the day-to-day details of these people's lives; yet by innuendo, it also seems to recognize the recurring contradictions that exist within this vanishing world. On the one hand there is a beautiful sense, at least for the old, of a reverence for life, of an acceptance of its mysteries, while on the other there is an equally strong sense that the young people (like the sheep?) do not understand.

This sequence is followed by a long shot of some children running through a field, while we see the sheep gambolling up a hill beside them. Then a little girl's voice is heard on the soundtrack singing a nursery song, while we cut to the children playing with some boats in a small stream—both jerrybuilt boats that one can row and little toy boats that one can sail. The scene ends with Michel Brault's camera pulling up from these children's boats and focusing through the foliage to pick up a huge steamer pushing its way up the St. Lawrence River. By this image alone is established the imminent economic death of this ancient shipbuilding community.

*Pour la suite du monde* is a remarkable film. Even its "happy ending" is not without its ironies. In the old days, the oldtimers tell us, they used to catch as many as fifty whales. This time, however, only one sad whale strays into their trap. And since they of course no longer need its meat and blubber for their way of life on the island, they end up by selling it to a marine museum in New York.

The ending of the film is simultaneously lovely and rather sad. Even the limited success of this venture can no longer be sanctified by community use, but must be justified by export abroad. Perhaps we'll catch more next year, several voices murmur. But the film ends with the ice floes coming in that will break apart the trap. This retreat into the challenges of the past will not be repeated.

If preparations for winter open this film, the fact of winter closes it. The islanders are enclosed by both climate and geography. They are also enclosed by time. Dependent on the past for their strong sense of tradition, protected from the industrialized present by the isolation of their island, this community inevitably has an uncertain relationship with the future.

It is the task of the next two films to explore this relationship. *Le règne du jour* moves further back in time while *Les voitures d'eau* attempts to move ahead. Central to both these films is the concept of the journey.

It is extraordinary how consistently Quebec artists have seized upon the natural elements of life in Canada to define their own terrain. Far more deliberately than any artist in Ontario, for instance, Quebec artists have seen the vastness of *la côte nord*, the coldness of the winter and the centrality of the St. Lawrence River as the signposts of their civilization, as the formative symbols of their imagination. From the songs of Gilles Vigneault through the novels of Anne Hébert to the films of filmmakers as diverse as Gilles Groulx, Gilles Carle, Jean Pierre Lefebvre and Pierre Perrault, this symbology occurs. Through a repetition of reference and a skill in organization, their actual country has been transformed into a landscape of the mind.

With Perrault, this transformation has involved an endless search. His voyages into the past and into unfamiliar terrain have always been made in the effort to, as he once put it, "become my own contemporary."[8] Though his situation has changed since he began working in Abitibi, at the outset Perrault journeyed less as an anthropologist in search of phylogenesis than as a poet in search of a personal symbology.

I am not sure if this inwardness, indeed, this dimension of autobiography, is very well understood about Pierre Perrault, even in Quebec. While his films have always met with a certain resistance, especially among the young, urban, politicized intellectuals—"les Canadiens de Paris," as he has called them, "les Canadiens des villes,"[9]—in the early days his work could be heralded, like the plays of Michel Tremblay, as a celebration of a particular way of speaking French and of making that way respectable.[10] Increasingly, however, resistance to his work has stiffened, especially in relation to his later films. He is now attacked for his addiction to the past, for his inability to deal with younger people and for his attachment to those elements in the culture, largely rural elements, which might be dismissed as "folkloric" or simply "picturesque."[11] These attacks may well limit the achievement of Perrault, especially from the point of view of young people in Quebec today, but they need not invalidate it. If Perrault is not really an anthropologist, neither is he a political sociologist. If he fastens on the gestures of day-to-day behaviour, it is to discover the eternal. If he examines the folkloric, it is to establish the mythopoeic. And if his films—especially the later ones—all fail to achieve this transcendence, it is through their struggle with these problems that they achieve their dialectic and their perpetual interest and vitality.

*Le règne du jour* takes the Tremblay family back to France to discover, in the cradle of their ancestors, the roots of their own values. But the France of today is no longer the France of Jacques Cartier, no longer the France that Alexis so passionately believes in. In fact, with the lace surround of her bonnet and the gentle wisdom of her face, Marie Tremblay looks more ancient than anyone that they encounter in France. And while Marie enjoys the trip, for Alexis it entails a series of disappointments and defeats. Even the grandfather clock that he brings back from France initially doesn't work. The last image of the film places this clock, now properly repaired through the initiative of Léopold, in the middle of the frame, with Alexis and Marie sitting on either side of it, looking small and insignificant beside this mighty chronicler of the hours purchased from time past. "*Ça marche,*" says Marie, as the film fades to an end.

Though the experience of the film diminishes Alexis, it achieves something positive for itself. Quebec can no longer be seen as an offshoot of the old country. It is a nation unto itself. It has its own language, customs and beliefs—characteristics only partly paralleled by those of France. If by the end of *Le règne du jour,* the personal faith of Alexis Tremblay is partly shaken, the collective faith of the Quebec nation is confirmed.

The next film, however, disturbs this vision. *Les voitures d'eau* brings the family-operated shipping enterprise on Ile-aux-Coudres into conflict with the big, industrialized companies in Montreal, companies controlled at several removes by English Canadian or American conglomerates. In this film, the attempt by the islanders to resuscitate yet another ancient tradition from the past by building a wooden dinghy directly from a model and not from a blueprint is contrasted with the final image of an old *géolette,* of no use any more, burning in the water. By signifying in this way the end of the wooden boat, except as a pleasure craft to sail about in, this final image signals as well the end of a way of life. Alexis well recognizes this when he says that the burning boat resembles the islanders. "It's old. It's finished." And indeed, a few days later Alexis himself died, suddenly, while slaughtering a pig in his barn.[12]

The journey up the river that encounters stevedores on strike at the port of Trois Rivières, thus making it impossible for the islanders to unload their cargo, is a journey toward the future which increasingly diminishes the relevance of the past. This film confronts the problem of size. The "little boats" cannot compete anymore. Even the unionized stevedores are on strike in protest against the threatened automation of the docks. The "little communities" will also soon disappear, this film seems to imply, as the young leave the regions where they have grown up to work in the cities.

But both *Le règne du jour* and *Les voitures d'eau* are more complex than the moral that might be drawn from them. While arguably not as rich in implication as *Pour la suite du monde,* they are just as subtly nuanced. They do not preach, they show; and what they show is often interpreted differently by the different protagonists. Collectively, all three films succeed in presenting us with an insight into what it is that has been unique in Quebec culture; they contrast this insight with what might be found that is similar in France; and finally, they raise doubts about the ability of this uniqueness to sustain itself into the future.

Within the history of the cinema, these three films represent a remarkable achievement. Within the history of documentary, they are without parallel. At no point is there any commentary. At no point is there a privileged voice to tell us what to think. They are all built up by a network of interweaving voices defining life values through the energy of their speech. These values are both extended and modified by a further network of images, all derived from the spaces in which these people live, yet organized so sensitively that they seem to create a national symbology. This would be a rare accomplishment for a work of fiction. It is extraordinary within the field of documentary.

To date, it would appear that the Ile-aux-Coudres trilogy represents Pierre Perrault's most distinguished contribution to the cinema, within which *Pour la suite du monde* is demonstrably his masterpiece. This trilogy was immediately followed by two films that extended the investigations implicit in the first three films. As Jeannine Bouthillier Lévesque has suggested, the next two films strive to answer the question posed by the last film of the trilogy: Will French Canadian culture manage to survive?[13]

One film casts a wide net, the other a narrow one. *Un pays sans bon sens! ou Wake Up, Mes Bons Amis!!!* deals with the French Canadian problem throughout all of Canada, while *L'Acadie l'Acadie* (1971) deals with the uncertain fate of the Acadians in New Brunswick. *Un pays sans bon sens!* is too complex—indeed, too inconclusive—to encapsulate in any way. However, within the context of this article, two or three things might helpfully be said.

To begin with, there is not the same sense in this film as there is in the trilogy of people at ease with one another within their own culture, either talking together or talking to us. Instead, Perrault employs an interviewer, Didier Dufour, by profession a biologist, who roams about the country and even goes to France in the attempt to gather data about Francophone cultures. He is trying to determine (as he keeps explaining) what images are essential for the Quebec Family Album. How does it feel to be a Francophone from Winnipeg? How do Bretons feel within the greater culture of France? How does an Indian feel within the culture of Quebec? Is national pride a matter of language, or of culture, or simply of place? How do these elements interact? Which are the most essential?

The film's controlling motif is ironic juxtaposition. A Toronto tourist sketching the "quaint" architecture of rural Quebec is followed by Marie Tremblay's account of the hardships of her childhood—a childhood passed, of course, in just such a dwelling. Marie's description of the excruciating manual labour of an old-fashioned cotton mill is accompanied by shots of the same mill, now largely automated—a scene that ends with a focus out onto the natural beauty of Montmorency Falls. Finally, toward the end of the film, Perrault recapitulates the recurring images of the pylons necessary for Quebec's industrial future in a shot that combines these pylons within a single image with a *habitant* dwelling from the Quebec of the past.[14] The industrial, which is international, is thus allied with the artisanal, which is specifically Québécois. Each seems to be necessary, yet they exist in contradiction. They imply different values, different ways of life. The film leaves us with these problems. Perhaps this is its strength.

*L'Acadie l'Acadie* unites Pierre Perrault once again with his original cinematographic collaborator, Michel Brault. In comparison with Perrault's other work, *L'Acadie l'Acadie* is, formally, a simple film. It is very much in the classic style of *cinéma direct*. It documents the protests of the students at the University of Moncton in 1968 against the unilingual policies of the then Mayor Jones. While there are many striking moments, moments that this time record some *young* people creating themselves through speech, the film ends in defeat. The students eventually leave the occupied building. The radicals leave the region they were fighting for. One is off to France, to live as a Francophone; another decides to join the Francophone cause in Quebec. "Perhaps Acadia is a mere detail," as she explains. At this time, it seems that there is little possibility that a French Canadian community can sustain itself outside Quebec.

Since 1972, Pierre Perrault has been working in Abitibi, in the James Bay region. He has apparently shot miles of footage, now working in colour, from which he has so far assembled four feature-length films: *Un royaume vous attend* (1975), *Le retour à la terre* (1976), *C'était un Québécois en Bretagne, Madame* (1977) and *Le goût de la farine* (1977).[15] None of these films has met with much approval, either in Quebec or elsewhere. While it is too soon to offer a definitive evaluation of this material, I might suggest a few reasons for its limited appeal.

First of all, as Perrault has moved further and further away from his friends on the Ile-aux-Coudres, the discovery of whom was inseparable from the discovery of himself, he has seemed increasingly distant from the material he has been filming. No Didier Dufour was needed for the trilogy. At that time there was no need for a cinematic amanuensis to bring forth for preservation the authentic speech of the Harveys or the Tremblays. Through the Abitibi tetralogy, however, Perrault has employed as his central investigating figure a man named Hauris Lalancette de Rochebeaucourt, obviously of distinguished lineage and a long-time inhabitant of this impoverished region, as well as, for a time, a local candidate for the Parti Québécois.

Hauris Lalancette is no Grand Louis. Since he is so often seen on some kind of platform, his language is less that of speech than of political harangue. Even in more private moments while talking round a table, he always seems to shout. As he is presented in the films, Hauris Lalancette does not possess an attractive personality. Whatever he is saying, no viewer could be "charmed" by his presence on the screen.

Furthermore, if Perrault began (initially with Michel Brault) by making *un cinéma de la parole*, now, increasingly, with Bernard Gosselin, he has tended toward *un cinéma de la parlotte.*[16] His cinema of speech has become a cinema of chatter and there is no longer the same dialectic tension established between what the characters say and what we are allowed, in more quiet moments, to observe. The quiet moments have virtually disappeared.

While I have found no favourable account of these films in anything I have read, I want to challenge their dismissal by suggesting that these films too have something to tell us, even if in a less poetic way, both about the country we live in and more particularly about this isolated region in Quebec.

The world of Abitibi is a world that has been ravaged. It is a world abandoned, a world in flux. The same Montagnais Indians who, in *Un pays sans bon sens!*, simply wished that they could "feel at home in the woods," are now seen with no woods left to feel at home in. The industrialization of the James Bay region—the direct presence of which has yet to appear in any of these films—has used up the woods and polluted the waters, thus killing off or driving away the life-sustaining fish and caribou.

*Le goût de la farine* opens with a shot of a derelict canoe, floating in the water—as if of no use any more. The film ends with the Indians learning to bake bread and then tasting it with laughter. If the fish have gone, these native people will have to find alternative ways to survive.

*Un royaume vous attend* and *Le retour à la terre* also depict these shifting values. *Un royaume vous attend* opens with an image of an entire house moving along a road on top of a huge truck—coming from where, going to where, I don't believe we ever know. Then we have an epigraph from Félix-Antoine Savard: "Never has God given to any people such a fine gift of clay." For all its *bavardage*, what this film depicts is the attempt of these people to make this clay work for them. And if the men do most of the talking (as in all Perrault's films), the women do most of the work. We see them peeling and planting potatoes at the opening of the film, while at the close, with the men still talking, we see two women in the distance—one incongruously dressed in a yellow bikini—driving the tractors that are ploughing the fields. But throughout this film, we keep returning to images of houses being moved along the road—houses which, in their comparative elegance, provide a contrast to the shacks in which most of these people live.

*Le retour à la terre* closes with a similar image of a house on the move. But this time, the camera follows it, as if in search of a more stable world where such a house might be a home. This film is particularly interesting, it seems to me, because it contains within itself a visual dialectic. On the one hand, we have long sequences of the inescapable Lalancette campaigning in 1973 (unsuccessfully, as it turned out) for the Parti Québécois, shouting about the state of affairs in present-day Abitibi. On the other hand, intercut throughout the film, are equally long sequences of early pastoral footage shot in the forties and early fifties by that early chronicler of *habitant* life, l'Abbé Maurice Proulx. Not only does the Proulx footage with its euphoric endorsement of the family, the church and all the sanctified values of agricultural life provide a contrast to the comparative barrenness of the Abitibi region as it appears today, but these sequences might also seem to comment on the pantheism of Perrault's first three films.

I have argued earlier about the trilogy that Perrault's interest in folklore was really part of his search for an authentic mythology. By the time he began work in Abitibi, however, he must have realized that such a mythology in a world now so unstable could only relate to the past—in Proulx's case, to what was *supposed* to have been; in Perrault's case, to what *might* have been.

If these last four films are not as sensuous and exhilarating as *Pour la suite du monde*, if they lack its symbolic authority, there is nevertheless an austerity about them, and a sense of harshness, which may be more appropriate to the world that Perrault is dealing with now. Certainly, judging both from what I have seen in the films and what I have read about them, these last four films merit a more serious analysis than they have so far received.

These comments cannot be taken as evaluations of these films. They are simply an agenda of elements to be discussed. Writing as an Anglophone, scarcely able to understand the dialogue of these logorrhoeic films, anything I say must necessarily be tentative. Nevertheless, I cannot agree with Michel Euvard and Pierre Véronneau when they complain about the "reactionary love of the past, or nostalgia, that permeates Perrault's last films."[17] On the contrary, they seem to present a barren world from which the values of the past have been increasingly eradicated. They question the value of the "progress" that has been inflicted on these people. In this way, by extension, they address the ecological problems that confront the contemporary world.

Let me end, provisionally, with a reference to the epigraph that opened this article. Pierre Perrault may no longer be making "songs" out of skeletons and geology but his films still investigate the inner structures which hold people together, and they still examine the state of the earth upon which these people live. Whatever the degree of pleasure or displeasure these last films may give us, they are still extraordinary examples of a cinema, however restricted by Perrault's present range of interests, that is still alive—*un cinéma vécu*.

From *The Human Elements*, Second Series (Ottawa: Oberon, 1981).

---

1 Jeannine Bouthillier Lévesque, "Entretien avec Pierre Perrault," *Positif*, 198, (Paris) (October 1977), p. 50.

2 In Léo Bonneville, ed., *Le Cinéma Québécois*, (Montreal: Editions Pauline, 1979), p. 675.

3 Alexis and Marie Tremblay really deserve the status of anthropological stars. While still living on the North Shore, they were the subject of an NFB documentary, *Alexis Tremblay, Habitant*, made by Jane Marsh and Judith Crawley in 1943.

4 The title bestowed upon the film by the NFB when they shortened it and imposed Stanley Jackson's voice over the speech of the Québécois is *Moontrap*. This shortened version destroys much of the formal complexity of the film.

5 Michel Brûlé, *Pierre Perrault ou un cinéma national* (Montreal: Les Presses de l'Université de Montréal, 1974), p. 22.

6 Perrault has made his own distinctions between these two men. Alexis, Perrault has said,

is in charge of anger, in charge of being against everything, while Grand Louis is the poet, the crazy man –*le fou*. See Michel Delahaye and Louis Marcorelles, "Entretien avec Pierre Perrault," *Cahiers du cinéma*, 165 (Paris) (April 1965), p. 34.

7 The subtitled print of this film is called *Drifting Upstream.*

8 In Peter Ohlin, "The Film as Word," *Ciné-Tracts 4*, Spring-Summer 1978, p. 66.

9 In Delahaye and Marcorelles, loc. cit., p. 33.

10 As Claude Jutra has suggested. In Peter Harcourt, *Movies and Mythologies* (Toronto: CBC Publications, 1977), p. 145.

11 For example, see Michel Euvard and Pierre Véronneau, "Direct Cinema," in *Self Portrait* (Ottawa: Canadian Film Institute, 1980), pp. 82–87.

12 Pierre Perrault, Bernard Gosselin and Monique Fortier, *Les voitures d'eau* (Montréal: Editions Lidec, 1969), p. 170.

13 Jeannine Bouthillier Lévesque, "Pierre Perrault, cinéaste du passé ou de l'avenir?" *Positif 182* (June 1976), pp. 25–33.

14 Perrault actually set out to find the old Tremblay home that we see in *Alexis Tremblay, Habitant*, but when he found it had been pulled down, he found one that looked similar. In *Le Cinema Québécois*, p. 707.

15 Since the time of writing (August 1980), a fifth film from this footage has appeared: *Le pays de la terre sans arbre ou le Mouchouânipi* (1980), as has (of course) *La bête lumineuse* (1982).

16 From Michel Houle and Alain Julien, *Dictionnaire du Cinéma Québécois* (Montréal: Fides, 1978) p. 239.

17 In Euvard and Véronneau, loc. cit., p. 87.

# *Ritual and Recital: The Perrault Project*

BY DAVID CLANDFIELD

*David Clandfield's detailed analysis of Pierre Perrault's writing is included here as a way of developing the concept of* le cinéma vécu *identified in Peter Harcourt's article. Just as Harcourt acknowledged the impatience with which Perrault's work is seen in Quebec, Clandfield has to his credit undertaken self-criticism of the original formulation of his thesis. The issue at hand is the ideological implication of Perrault's relationship to his subjects. The critics cited by Harcourt complained simply of Perrault's "reactionary love of the past." Clandfield, faced with more detailed objections to his classification of Perrault's use of language as "found poetry," must contend with the political context of Perrault's "finding." The author, much like Perrault himself, provides a metacommentary for his own appropriation of found language (in this case Perrault's texts). The distinction, of course, is that Clandfield has been made acutely aware of the implications of this appropriation—implications which, he concludes, must be taken into account in the consideration of language and Perrault.*

The ensuing article grows out of a study published four years ago in *Ciné-Tracts*, in which I argued that a distinctive identity could be accorded to many of the documentary films produced by the French Unit at the National Film Board in the period of the late fifties and early sixties.[1] This identity, which set them apart from other forms of "uncontrolled documentary" of the time, such as American cinéma vérité or the Candid Eye films of Unit B at the NFB, could be located in their "formalizing tendency," their "reflexive tendency" and their "expression of solidarity with a public about whom and for whom many of these films were made" (Clandfield, p. 60). I suggested that this rhetorical identity stood in continuity with the *cinéma de la fidélité* of such peripatetic, amateur filmmakers of an earlier generation as the Abbés Proulx and Tessier; but that this latter tradition was broken by the French Unit's preoccupation with the ethnography of modern urban rituals and by their apparent endorsement thereby of the goals and ideology of the Quiet Revolution. I had finally suggested that the extension of the rhetorical tradition enunciated above might be sought most profitably in the works of Pierre Perrault.

The most thought-provoking analysis of Perrault's first five feature films was written by Michel Brûlé.[2] As a sociologist of cinema, Brûlé deployed the critical apparatus developed by Lucien and Annie Goldmann in their writings on literature and cinema.[3] Genetic structuralism, as Brûlé uses it, serves to bring into focus the homology of emerging global structures in cultural constructs such as a body of novels or films on the one hand, and the encompassing socio-economic tensions of the historic moment on the other. The argument traced through Perrault's films develops into a global statement which embodies the ideology of a liberal, nationalist movement:

> The vision of Quebec which these films give us corresponds very closely to that developed by Jacques Dofny and Marcel Rioux in their concepts of "ethnic class" and "ethnic consciousness." In all of the films of Perrault, in fact, Quebec is treated as a homogeneous entity, a grouping in which all of the members share the same fundamental interests and strive to achieve the same goals. While Perrault shows us conflict between generations (i.e., attitudinal differences between the patriarch Alexis, Laurent, a young man in his prime and Michel who is still growing up), all of his characters are products of a mode of thinking which recognizes the necessity of preserving the French way of life and struggling against anything which might endanger it.
>
> There is a distinct similarity between what we are shown and the evolution of a particular group within Quebec society—that of the lower middle class which embraced the *Parti québécois* and certain elements of the *Union nationale* (Brûlé, p. 143).

The theoretical underpinning of such an analysis requires us to take the filmed œuvre of Perrault and the broader historical, social context as materially objective, developing entities. The interdependence of the two entities is taken to bring about the homologies revealed by structural analysis. An analysis drawing upon post-structuralist and hermeneutic categories engages texts in a different fashion. The processes of formation and the spectator's implication in those processes are no longer clearly distinguishable. Hermeneutic criticism directs attention to the problematic relationship between reader/spectator and text, and may seek interpretative strategies within the text itself, within what traces may subsist of authorial processes of construction or within the cultural context which controls the reader/spectator's capacity for interpretation. Post-structuralist criticism equally denies the autonomy of the text and the possibility of constructing a unitary whole from the processes of interpretation.[4]

In what follows, I attempt to rehearse the formalizing and reflexive tendencies in Perrault's early and middle works, and to show how the rhetoric of sincerity central to the *cinéma direct* movement in Quebec inevitably fails in any attempt to implicate the spectator into a *continuing* process of cultural transmission. Not only will a number of Perrault's films and written works be considered,[5] but also most importantly, as a starting point, the three filmscripts which demonstrate clearly Perrault's development of a new kind of "found poetry."[6]

In most cases, published filmscripts perform a mnemonic or referential function for scholars or any interested public. In some rare cases, the filmscript will include valuable prefatorial material to help the reader/spectator adopt an appropriate "reading" strategy or strategies.[7] Otherwise, published filmscripts either display a thesaurus of notation devices whose goal is to provide a conventional transcript, or else they are adapted to conceal or mute their derivation from a filmic artefact, representing the diegesis by means of codes usually associated with the novel. The latter two kinds of filmscript have little hermeneutic status within the filmmaker's œuvre. Perrault's filmscripts are, however, different. Not only do they provide a conventional transcript of the finished films; they also constitute the traces of a developing tendency to provide a controlled reading of each film. More and more, specific segments are highlighted or privileged in different ways, suggesting a hierarchy of responses to the text, while never allowing the derivative nature of the printed text to be forgotten.

In the *Le règne du jour* script, the traditional shooting script format is observed, with two columns. The right hand column holds the dialogues (with some description of the tone or delivery), while the left hand column carries the description of the visual image. Clear typographic conventions are observed: the visual images are described in upper-case Roman, for example. To distinguish the dialogues on the Ile-aux-Coudres from those on the trip to France (they are often intercut), the former are transcribed in lower-case Roman, the latter in lower-case Italic. The songs sung by characters (and the song composed by Perrault for the film) are privileged by being written out in verse-form in upper-case Italic. In some of the dialogues, rhythms are indicated from time to time by the use of dots to break the flow.

In the *Les voitures d'eau* script, the two-column format has been abandoned, and instead visual shot-descriptions (in upper-case script) are interspersed with dialogue from the sound-track (in lower-case script). In the latter, the choice of typeface no longer serves to distinguish the loci of action. Instead, Roman and Italic script are used to distinguish ordinary dialogue from that which is privileged as "found poetry" by the filmmaker. In this way, dialogue contained within the film is raised to poetic status by the choice of script, the layout into various shapes and stanzas, the rejection of capital letters at sentence heads, and the use of an introductory title (usually containing the words "petit poème sur . . ."). There are twenty-nine such interventions in all in the script.

With the *Un pays sans bon sens!* script, the range of typographic conventions has been further extended. In addition to the conventions used in *Les voitures d'eau*, three shades of paper are used (white for the film description, black for the page of notes accompanying and introducing the segment-title which appears in the film, and grey for Perrault's often extensive reflections about certain images either shown or spoken of in the film-sequence preceding). Different sizes of type are used, and heavy type is used for quoted key-words in the reflective notes. Privileged spoken parts of the film text are still clearly distinguished, and include not only historical extracts from Cartier's *Relations* and the words of the poet Alfred Desrochers, but also the definitive speech of the geneticist Didier Dufour on "les souris canadiennes-françaises-catholiques" [French Canadian Catholic mice], Grand-Louis' reminiscences about his schooling, and a collective (i.e. intercut) poem for five voices on "le terrible temps de la misère" [the years of grinding poverty].

As we read through these three filmscripts, we find two tendencies growing side by side: the desire to privilege certain speeches, oral interventions and anecdotes by the characters of Ile-aux-Coudres or elsewhere caught in their natural surroundings; and the desire to catch these raw poems (which Perrault calls "chouennes" or "parlêmes" in the preface to a collection of his own poetry)[8] up into a reflection upon the rich untutored cultural heritage of his *pays*. The former ambition reaches its apogee with the appearance of *Discours sur la condition sauvage et québécoise* in 1977, a collection of the "found poetry" assembled and collated by Perrault over many years of taping and filming.

Just as the filmscripts were abundantly illustrated with frame enlargements from the films, so too is this latter anthology illustrated with stills. The traces of a living oral culture are accompanied by the traces of living faces.

> J'ai dressé un inventaire de la parole, cette littérature des pauvres. . . . Mais la parole a aussi un visage. Et ce visage il est cinématographique. Il est aussi parfois photogénique. . . . C'est un simple album de famille. Le temps et la

distance changeront peut-être ces souvenirs en mémoire, ces balises en poésie.[9]

[I drew up a list of their words, the literature of the poor. . . . But words also have a face: it is cinematographic. Sometimes it is also photogenic . . . a simple family album. Time and distance will perhaps change these recollections stored in our memory, these road signs in poetry.]

The Romantic aspiration to see the simple, specific and rough-cut utterances of one place and time mellow over the years into the cultural heritage of a new collective (ces souvenirs en mémoire) [recollections stored in our memory] and acquire the privileged authority of poetic discourse (ces balises en poésie) [these road signs in poetry] is clearly articulated in this appeal to an unsophisticated, authentic past.

Having thus documented the rise to prominence of the "found poem" in Perrault's hermeneutic guides to his films, we should now examine the meanings accorded to this appropriate literature. In our readings of Perrault (in print or in film), we discover the importance accorded to popular/folk culture (v. "high" culture), the continuity of this culture across other codes (in addition to verbal ones), and the submersion of individual enactments in the commemorative culture of a people.

Perrault's earliest poems already give voice to the privilege accorded to autochthonous utterances of an untutored people:

nous avons vécu le meilleur
entre les mains de ceux-là
de ceux qui ne savaient
ni la lettre ni le chant
. . .
nous avons vécu le plus haut
entre les doigts qui ne savaient
ni lire ni écrire[10]
[We've lived to the fullest
through those
who knew neither letters
nor song
. . .
We've reached the greatest heights
through those who could
neither read nor write]

The culture which must be rejected is the imported, institutionalized one, embodied in a past colonial heritage:

ceux qui ont appris à vivre en lisant *Le Cid* de Corneille . . . refusent de se connaître.[11]
[Those who've taken their lessons in life from *The Cid* of Corneille . . . refuse to know themselves.]

Or the culture is embodied in the ossified language fixed and conserved in institutional records and dictionaries:

Je ressens parfois l'étrange désir de tuer dans l'oeuf tous les mots qui n'ont d'autre but que celui d'exprimer. Tous les mots qu'on emprunte aux lexiques et qu'on n'a jamais parcouru . . . ni fréquenté . . . ni même rencontré dans une géographie des découvrances.[12]
[I sometimes have a strange urge to suppress all those words whose only

purpose is to be descriptive . . . all those words taken from dictionaries which have never been part of anyone's life experience.]

le langage en dit plus long sur l'homme québécois que l'histoire et la littérature et les registres . . . et les annuaires . . .[13]
[language tells us more about the Quebec people than history, literature and ledgers . . . and telephone directories . . .]

et s'il advenait que toutes archives de l'âme soient le fait des mémoires négligées de littérature comme un fleuve et tout le langage à sa source vous ne me ferez pas renier le moindre mot de la bouche des misères qu'ils ont vécues sans l'assistance des dictionnaires opulents[14]
[if all records of the soul were constituted of the neglected memories of a flood of literature and all language fed its headwaters, you couldn't persuade me to repudiate a single word from the mouths of those miserable individuals who expressed everything they had experienced without recourse to sophisticated dictionaries]

In the films, Perrault focuses our attention upon those who best embody this tradition: the Tremblay family and Grand Louis in the setting of the Ile-aux-Coudres, Hauris Lalancette in the Abitibi films. But the opportunity to establish the contrast between the homegrown culture and other more sophisticated cultures is enhanced cinematographically when it occurs.

In *Le règne du jour*, the exoticism of the hunting aristocracy in France is underlined by showing us shots of the hunt while the sound-track carries Léopold's account to the folk of Ile-aux-Coudres, in which he emphasizes the distance which separates him from this aristocracy. In *Un pays sans bon sens!*, one sequence intercuts the garrulous Grand Louis in his outdoor working clothes, seen against a background of small trees and bare river, with the articulate young Franco-Albertan professor, seen in his Paris apartment, where an artful rack-focus shot draws our attention progressively from the name Vermeer on the wall-poster to the elegant tableware adorning the foreground. The subject of discussion—the relative merits of different kinds of education—is explored orally by the characters, visually by the camera, and syntagmatically by the use of intercutting. Again, in the same film, the sequence of shots of the Maillol nudes in the Tuileries, which accompanies the young professor's rapturous discourse on the sensuality of the Parisian environment, includes in the frame a Parisian streetworker apparently unimpressed in his lot with such images of ideal beauty. High culture again is juxtaposed with an image of alienated poverty, which, as the Tremblays, Grand Louis, or André Lepage demonstrate elsewhere in the film, is capable of generating its own culture.

The complexity of the oral culture which Perrault foregrounds in his work not only stands in vivid contrast to the mummified rituals, artefacts and writings of an exotic elite. It actively resists adequate representation in written codes:

Un vrai discours ne s'écrit pas. L'intonation et la tissure même de la voix, l'odeur du souffle, la dent noircie, la rondeur du palais, la conviction, tout s'évanouit: il ne reste qu'un squelette.[15]
[A true speech cannot be written. The intonation and the very timbre of the voice, the odour of the breath, the stained tooth, the roundness of the palate, the conviction, all vanishes: only the skeleton remains.]

le mot n'est pas le signe du langage parlé mais seulement son support grossier. C'est l'intonation, le ton, le débit, l'homme parlant qui donne un

> sens aux mots. Je ne réponds pas du langage. Je ne le défends pas non plus.[16]
> [words are not the signs of spoken language but merely its vulgar medium. It is intonation, timbre, delivery, in short, the speaking man who gives meaning to his words. I don't answer for language, nor do I defend it.]

But expression in a culture whose written transmission has in any event been expropriated by a distant elite is not only limited to verbal codes. Poetic celebration may be discerned in the agility of gesture or the graceful manual dexterity of the craftsman or the corporeal rhythms of the dance:

> Geste incalculable dans l'achimie du poème, réunissant les adresses du félin, la grâce du discobole et les mystères des prérogatives aux imaginations pures . . .[17]
> [Incalculable gesture in the magic of poetry, incorporating feline deftness, athletic grace and the mysterious prerogatives of sheer imagination . . .]

> un canot bien fait, en forme de poème[18]
> [a well-built canoe, in the form of a poem]

> Le tambour est récit, le tambour est acte, et sans le tambour intérieur la marche insoutenable se briserait aussi bien qu'une danse sans tambour . . . Et la danse aussi intraduisible que le langage préserve et démontre le mystère.[19]
> [The drum is narrative, the drum is action, and without our internal drum beat, the unbearable pace of the march would be broken like a dance without drums . . . And the dance, as untranslatable as language, protects and validates the mystery.]

Although Perrault clearly delineates the autonomy of cultural codes, insisting upon the futility of attempts at translation or "transcodage," at the same time he denies a hierarchy of verbal and non-verbal codes, granting equal value to gestural and verbal enactments of cultural events to the extent that the one merges into the other as communal celebration:

> La pêche aux marsouins est aussi une aventure du langage.[20]
> [Porpoise fishing is also an adventure in language.]

> Car la chasse devient exploit du langage. Et enfin le langage lui-même devient l'exploit.[21]
> [For hunting becomes an exploit of language. And, ultimately, language itself becomes the exploit.]

Returning to the film works, we are now armed with the injunction to accord equal value to both the recounting of exploits and the exploits themselves. In *Pour la suite du monde*, the most compelling visual sequence of the island fishermen planting the sapling poles into the river for the beluga-trap is accompanied by the voice of Alexis Tremblay describing the traditional stages of the hunt. The relationship between voice-off and image is not the traditional didactic, explanatory one. It shows two levels of enactment of a cultural heritage: its physical enactment and its mediated oral enactment. The same is true of the "fête du cochon" [pig-killing ceremony] sequence in *Le règne du jour*. Here, a traditional pig-killing in the Ile-aux-Coudres is intercut with a similar traditional ceremony in Bupertré, France, which the Tremblays are visiting. The sound-track carries Léopold Tremblay's voice at one point describing, but not accurately, the process to his friends on returning to Ile-aux-Coudres. The specific differences between the two communities may indeed be important in the context of Perrault's insistence on the specificity of cultures to territories. However, the importance of the differences between the enactment of the ritual and Léopold's account of it does not lie in any inference that the explanatory value of the account is undermined. What is important is that Léopold, in recounting the story in a way which mutes the differences, is responding to imperatives of his own cultural tradition, and that while the deep structural meanings of the rituals may be similar, there is a need for them to be expressed through a variety of codes (gestural, oral) and that changes inevitably emerge in the surface structure.

Nowhere is the filmmaker's desire to demonstrate this clearer than in the famous "louse story" (histoire du pou) recounted by Grand Louis in *Un pays sans bon sens!* Twice over a period of two years, Perrault had occasion to film the village raconteur, Louis Harvey, telling a story from the old days of the workcamps. He has intercut the two "performances" of the story, clearly differentiated by the age of Louis' hat and the background. Once again, the focus shifts from the events recounted in the story to the subtle changes in its telling from one enactment to another.

Again, in *Le retour à la terre*, accounts of the opening up of the Abitibi region as told to the filmmakers are juxtaposed with the films of Maurice Proulx shot at the time. If on one level there is an ironic distance opened up by the differences between the promises of the thirties (mediated through oral and filmed accounts) and the evidence of their collapse, at the same time there is a consonance between the two mediations of the collective experience in the past which are accorded equal value in the communal memory.

This reference to communal memory brings us to the consideration of the process whereby Perrault projects individual utterances (oral performances, gestural reenactments, and so on) into the collective celebration of cultural identity. The privileged individuals, such as Alexis Tremblay, Louis Harvey, Didier Dufour, Hauris Lalancette, Cyrille Labrecque, and Camille Morin, are not to be taken as artistic exemplars. They are not to be taken as individual poets celebrating the freedom of autonomous imaginations. Rather they are shown embedded within a social and historical context by the filmmaker, and thereby serve to embody the continuity of cultural experience and aspirations which define *un pays* in human terms. Perrault makes frequent reference to the collective memory of "un pays" and the commemorative value of cultural reenactments:

> Car la danse n'est qu'une façon de mettre au présent les exploits passés, les chasses à venir . . . et toutes paroles du tambour s'insinuent dans cette mémoire immense, comme l'acte même fomenté à l'avance et à jamais dans cette messe du caribou-dieu.[22]
> [For dance is merely a means of expressing in the present one's past exploits and future hunts . . . and the drum's words seep into this vast realm of memory, like the act itself fomented in advance and perpetuated in this mass to the caribou god.]

> La mémoire est une faculté vivante. Le langage est une oeuvre de mémoire. Un pays trouve aussi, dans la mémoire épargnée, son inspiration.[23]
> [Memory is a living faculty. Language is a product of memory. A nation, also, finds its inspiration in discriminate memory.]

> Il est incontestable que les pays prennent naissance dans la mémoire et que la mémoire ne manque pas d'imagination.[24]
> [It is certain that nations are born out of memories and that memory does not lack imagination.]

Such references call to mind what Eugene Vance has called "commemorative" discourse in reference to the medieval culture which bodies itself in orally recited epic poetry, and in particular the *Chanson de Roland*:

> By "commemoration" I mean any gesture, ritualized or not, whose object is to recover, in the name of a collectivity, some being or event either anterior in time or outside of time in order to fecundate, animate, or make meaningful a moment in the present.[25]

Perrault himself invokes this medieval commemorative culture on more than one occasion:

> La pêche aux marsouins est aussi une aventure du langage. À la manière de la chanson de Roland. Le poète de cette chanson de geste écrivait pour la suite du monde.[26]
> [Porpoise fishing is also an adventure in language. As in the Song of Roland. The author of this epic poem was writing for posterity.]

It is also evident in Perrault's description of the sequence of reminiscences about the years of grinding poverty ("le temps de la misère") in *Un pays sans bon sens!*:

> C'était là leur poème, leur chanson de geste, une sorte de tableau "ti-pop" de la misère des chantiers.[27]
> [That was their poem, their *chanson de geste*, a kind of popular tableau of the misery of their working conditions.]

Throughout this process of the selection and foregrounding of certain popular utterances as living poetry (distinct from the fossilized official culture), multiply-encoded (in speech and gesture), and illustrative of the processes of commemoration, we must be aware of the profound irony implicit in the project. "Found poetry" can be described as natural discourse appropriated, de-contextualized and presented as fictive discourse:

> Any verbal structure . . . can be isolated from its original context and presented in such a way (lineated, for example, or read aloud in a studied manner) as to suggest poetry and to invite our response to it as such, that is, as a verbal artwork, the representation of a natural utterance in an implicit dramatic context, designed to invite and gratify the drawing of interpretative inferences.[28]

To be sure, the distinction between natural discourse and fictive discourse is not necessarily clear when we consider the original status of the speech acts appropriated into the fictive discourse of the films. Some of the accounts (Grand Louis' "histoire du pou," for example) recorded and edited into Perrault's films have already acquired the status of fictive discourse in the community in which they are told. Again, Barbara Smith has incisively described the process:

> . . . the family anecdote becomes a tale, a fictive "telling," relished now as much for its structure, rhythms, predictable details, and bits of quaint dialogue as it was initially, perhaps, for the amusing image of a once-young parent in a sorry predicament. An episode of domestic history has acquired the status of family lore somewhat as in a nonliterate community, a fragment of presumably true national history becomes part of a natural utterance in a context of *reportage*; but, in becoming a "tale," its identity and interest become independent of that context. The factuality of the subject does not compromise the fictiveness of the tale, for it is not the events told that are fictive but the *telling* of them. That telling is set apart from reports of past events and from such allusions to them as may occur in natural discourse.[29]

The transformation of natural discourse into fictive discourse is one of the important processes in Perrault's films. It can take two forms: either a mediated demonstration of the process already complete within its community context, or a transformation accomplished by the film through the act of appropriation of discourse in its natural phase. The acknowledgement of such a transformation does not fully account for the nature of this "found poetry." To expand further upon this understanding, we can turn to hermeneutic criticism for its insights into the nature of poetic discourse as distinct from "ordinary" texts. For Gadamer, the essential difference does not lie in the sense of formal beauty or the different structure of writing characteristic of poetic utterances:

> According to the hermeneutic account . . . what is said is as important as how it is said, and the essential difference between the two sorts of texts lies in the truth-*expectations* (Wahrheitsanspruch) of the texts.[30]

The difference is one of degree, related to the greater clarity and specificity accorded by the reader to the ordinary text and the greater opacity and generality accorded by the reader to the poetic text. Poetic discourse affirms its presence to the reader by standing as tradition—tradition working itself out in the present, within the reader or audience.

Perrault's project then consists both in capturing preexisting cultural events and discourse and in converting other incidents and moments of natural discourse into poetic discourse in order to proclaim the continuation of cultural tradition through the mediations of his own films.

To complete the critical analysis of Perrault's cultural project, it is important to consider the processes of mediation as they are described by him or as they are revealed to us in his films.

There are three stages of mediation in evidence in the making of a Perrault film. There are the raw pro-filmic events, whose enactments (physical or verbal) constitute the extrinsic mediation. It is extrinsic to the filmic process as such, although the presence of the filmmakers may have served as a catalyst for the enactment. At a second stage, accompanying the enactment, is the use made of the camera, which may try to isolate the act or speaker from an environment or may look critically or ironically at that environment, using pans, zooms, or rack-focus to draw our attention to specific details at particular moments. At a third stage is the editing, whose principal interest may consist in the sequence of scenes which follows a certain logical argument transcending the internal logic of the accounts within each scene; or it may consist in careful intercutting of two scenes whose similarities and differences can best be seen by moving back and forth between them; or it may lie in the combination of one scene (reduced to soundtrack) with another (reduced to visual images); in other words, asynchronous sound-image editing.

What is uncontrolled, then, is the pro-filmic event. It constitutes the manifestation of some effort to plunge into the collective memory of a community. This may include local customs like the beluga hunt in *Pour la suite du monde*, the pig-killing in *Le règne du jour*, the boat-building in *Les voitures d'eau*, or the various activities associated with clearing the land in the Abitibi series. There may be more deliberate excursions in search of a collective past, such as the journeys to France in *Le règne du jour*, *Un pays sans bon sens!* or *C'était un Québécois en Bretagne, Madame!* The characters may be recalling an historic past as documented: Alexis Tremblay with *Le bref récit* of Jacques Cartier, or the inhabitants of the Abitibi who can refer to Maurice Proulx's films celebrating the growth of their region. But whatever the activity, physical ritual or oral account, its projection into the world of the film is clearly marked as an attempt to define the identity of a collective, whose demands, grievances and aspirations spring from a common memory.

Interestingly enough, Perrault describes the shooting of the film as a process of memory, the storage of evidence of a collective memory expressing itself: "On peut définir le tournage comme une mémoire . . ."[31] [One could define the act of filming as memory . . .]

It is not, however, passive reception. The role of the cameraman (or "caméramage" as Perrault calls him)[32] is a questing one, seeking out the visual correlatives, the visual details which will complement or throw into relief the primary subject. The finest examples of such a questing camera may be found in *Un pays sans bon sens!* The frame showing the arrival of migrating geese, which is accompanied by the reflection of the Dufours on the homing instinct and the sense of territory, also shows the looming hulk of the multinational corporation's big freighter, which is spelling the end of the local economy. Later, as Didier Dufour struggles to understand the way in which a territory can leave its imprint upon a consciousness, the camera moves around, and with selective focusing picks up two lovers on the shore some distance away for whom, presumably, this territory is now acquiring an indissoluble link with their courtship. Most spectacularly, in the scene in which Chaillot, the young Franco-Albertan, struggles to find a cultural identity, a homing-point which is neither Alberta or Paris, we see him by the banks of the Seine speaking with the Dufours. As he seems finally to light upon Quebec as a new home, a barge passes slowly behind him, and the camera shifts our attention to its name: L'Emerillon, the name of one of the three ships which brought Cartier from France to the shores of Quebec. In each of these three cases, however, the meaning we ascribe to the background detail is not articulated in the dialogue. To the extent that we accept the authenticity of the filmmaker's claim to unstaged, uncontrolled filmmaking, we may feel free to accord other meanings to these details, either by attempting to reconstruct the cameraman's motives for showing the detail, or by viewing the detail as an element of figurative discourse whose meanings are not unitary or precise, but which resonate poetically.

Once the "capture" has been made and the material has been stored in the filmic memory (the shooting is over), there begins the long period of processing, selecting and ordering (editing). This process Perrault calls a reading of the real (although this had already begun, of course, through the kind of in-camera editing mentioned above), a reading which leads directly and indissolubly into a writing:

> Editing becomes a kind of "reading for truth" as Yves Lacroix put it. But this reading becomes an act of writing from the moment I undertake to provide the viewer with the tools of perception necessary to penetrate to the core of the experience in question. . . . So, having read attentively for reality . . . I must speak, write, recount and recite my intentions.[33]

The process of expressing what had been previously captured in a rich memory, and subsequently reordered by reflection and mediated through the conventions of cinematographic constructions is, finally, offered as a replica of the processes which had led to the original pro-filmic event. This homology, then, could be the solution to the problem posed by the empirical style (distanced and detached) for the filmmaker who wishes to declare solidarity with the culture to be projected, and to implicate the film in an unbroken process of cultural communication.

This was the point reached in the first three drafts of this study. When the paper was read to the Canadian Film Studies Association in Ottawa in May 1981, a certain dissatisfaction was expressed over the apparent comfort with which a sense of closure was reached in this conclusion. This sense of dissatisfaction has led to a deconstruction of my initial reading and a radical reversal of the original thesis.

The appropriation of oral discourse into written texts as "found poetry" or into filmed and taped documentaries as "outils de réflexion" (as Perrault has called them) is essentially and inevitably a process of decontextualization. The speech acts of men and women living in their community are being uprooted from their natural surroundings, are being "disembedded," to use the vocabulary of cognitive psychology. Such a "disembedding" process may be necessary to pass from a sense of parochial identity to a sense of national identity. Indeed, this is one of the key messages of *Un pays sans bon sens!*[34] The implantation of these isolated speech acts in the new discourse of the filmmaker constitutes the passage to higher-order cognitive processes, to a sense of cultural identity which transcends the local parish and its modes of communication.

This passage ultimately undermines the meanings we accorded to "found poetry" earlier: the primacy of popular nonliterate cultural expression, the multiple coding of such expressions, and the submersion of individual acts in the commemorative culture of a collective.

With the use of print or film to transmit these moments of cultural expression, the book editor or filmmaker has rendered absolute the separation of performer and public, teller and listener, enactor and spectator. There is of course no longer a sense of living exchange: the discourse has moved from the illocutionary act to the perlocutionary act; the two-way street has become a one-way street. Moreover, having decontextualized and fragmented these moments of cultural expression, the reconstructor may freely create his/her own hierarchy of discourses, dividing them up into "petits poèmes" and recitatives as Perrault does in the script of *Les voitures d'eau*, for example. That creation of a hierarchy of discourse has passed from the autochthonous control of the local communities or individuals into the hands of the privileged individual or elite of individuals who have access to the technology of print and film. It is for this reason that, notwithstanding the bonds of solidarity that Perrault may have forged in the acquisition of the ethnographic data which informs his writings and films, the continuity of cultural transmission is radically ruptured by the recourse to modern communications technology. And yet it was the negation of codes of expression controlled by distant elites which constituted the argument for the primacy of popular nonliterate or oral cultures in the first place.

Further, deep within the Perrault project there lies the rhetorical contradiction implicit in all appropriations and metacommentaries of this kind. When, in the demonstration of cultural expression which is declared authentic and valuable, a medium is chosen which posits the relationship between speaker and listener in a radically different way (absence supersedes presence), the hierarchy of codes collapses. Perrault's work on the one hand declares the primacy of community-based oral and gestural culture, and on the other hand implicitly elevates itself (as metacommentary) above that oral culture to celebrate it. The multiply-coded "language" of that culture is now subsumed in the codes of a language-system which is foreign to it. Finally, and this is the ultimate irony, in making access to the commemorative cultures of relatively isolated communities more universal, the Perrault project has assumed the control of that collective memory. If we were to ascribe an ideological label to the project it would be that of liberal paternalism. But ultimately, the true ironies exposed by the deconstruction of the project point more to the impossibility of promoting the continuity of living, interacting cultural traditions by engraving the enactments in inert matter.[35] The *cinéma direct* is not and cannot be direct.

*Ciné-Tracts*, 16 (Winter 1982)

When I was asked if I wished to make amendments to this article prior to its republication, I was sorely tempted to rewrite the entire piece from start to finish. But then it would not have been the same article. So I have been content to make a bare minimum of typographic corrections and stylistic "improvements," and to employ what I hope is a less opaque title.

However, there are one or two possible misconceptions about this work which ought to be dispelled. The aim here is in no way to accuse the Perrault project of hypocrisy. The kinds of contradiction and discontinuity discussed here are artefacts of a critical theory which relishes the ironies of contradiction and discontinuity. The goal of such analysis and reflection is to show that the rhetorical assumptions of the *cinéma direct* are every bit as open to challenge and debate as those of the empirical, end-of-ideology Candid Eye filmmakers. It is important, then, to keep in mind that the Perrault project offers one of the richest fields for this debate in the cinema of the western world. Nor should it be felt that Perrault's later works in film (*Le pays de la terre sans arbre* and *La bête lumineuse* for the National Film Board, and *Les voiles bas et en travers*, made in 1983 for French television) and in print (some of which are published in *Caméramages*, Montreal: Hexagone, 1983) do not push this debate forward.

It is clear, I hope, that this article does not attempt to "do justice" to Perrault's films and writings by providing a definitive or exhaustive reading of them. I was trying to resituate the Perrault project within a critical debate being waged in the community of those interested in film theory and the theory of film criticism.

For those who wish to locate the Perrault project within the independence debate in Quebec, or within the larger context of the relationship between film culture and social change, this work may seem timid or coy, if not downright irrelevant. But I do hope that those whose field of interest lies beyond the perspective adopted here will understand that the debate on the forms, processes and rhetoric of the so-called *cinéma direct* is still open and problematic.

Finally, in addition to those I mentioned in the afterword to my other article included in this volume, I should like to acknowledge the contribution of Hart Cohen, whose remarks in 1981 caused me to rewrite radically the conclusion of my original paper, although not necessarily in the way he would have preferred. Also I must mention Sandra Clandfield, who has had to live through my crises of self-doubting and whose scepticism was a useful antidote to academic abstraction.

1984

---

Translations from the French by Emile Bourree.

1 David Clandfield, "From the Picturesque to the Familiar: Films of the French Unit at the NFB (1958–1964)" in *Ciné-Tracts*, 4 (Spring-Summer 1978), pp. 50–62; and reprinted in this volume.

2 Michel Brûlé, "Pierre Perrault ou un cinéma national, essai d'analyse socio-cinématographique" (Montréal: Les Presses de l'Université de Montréal, 1974).

3 See Lucien Goldmann, *Pour une sociologie du roman* (Paris: Gallimard, 1964); Annie Goldmann, *Cinéma et société moderne* (Paris: Éditions Anthropos, 1971); and also Michel Brûlé's analyses of Jean Pierre Lefebvre's early films and two film adaptations of novels by Claude-Henri Grignon in *Cahiers Sainte-Marie* 29 (1971), pp. 17–62 and *Sociologie et Sociétés* 8, No. 1 (April 1976) pp. 117–139.

4 My major sources for such criticism have been: David Cozens Hoy, *The Critical Circle: Literature and History in Contemporary Hermeneutics* (Berkeley: University of California Press, 1978); T. K. Seung, *Structuralism and Hermeneutics* (New York: Columbia University Press, 1982); Susan R. Suleiman and Inge Crosman, eds., *The Reader in the Text: Essays on Audience and Interpretation* (Princeton: Princeton University Press, 1980); Josue V. Harari, ed., *Textual Strategies: Perspectives in Post-Structuralist Criticism* (Ithaca, N.Y.: Cornell University Press, 1979).
5 Perrault's interviews may in fact properly be described as written texts, since he has always insisted on the right to amend in writing any such texts before publication.
6 Pierre Perrault, Bernard Gosselin, Yves Leduc, *Le règne du jour* (Montreal: Lidec, 1968); Pierre Perrault, Bernard Gosselin, Monique Fortier, *Les voitures d'eau* (Montreal: Lidec, 1969); Pierre Perrault, Bernard Gosselin, Yves Leduc, Serge Beauchemin, *Un pays sans bon sens!* (Montreal: Lidec, 1970).
7 E.g., Alain Robbe-Grillet, *L'année dernière à Marienbad* (Paris: Minuit, 1963).
8 Pierre Perrault, *Chouennes* (Montreal: Éditions de l'Hexagone, 1975), p. 7.
9 Pierre Perrault, *Discours sur la condition sauvage et québécoise* (Montreal: Lidec, 1977), in the preface (unnumbered).
10 Pierre Perrault, "Naguère," first published in the anthology *Portulan*, subsequently in *Chouennes* (Montreal: Éditions de l'Hexagone, 1975).
11 Perrault, et. al., *Un pays sans bon sens!*, op. cit., p. 184.
12 Pierre Perrault, "Témoignages," in *La poésie canadienne-française* (Montreal/Paris: Fides, 1969), p. 558.
13 Perrault, et. al., *Un pays sans bon sens!*, op. cit., p. 42.
14 Pierre Perrault, *Gélivures*, (Montreal: Editions de l'Hexagone, 1977), p. 191.
15 Pierre Perrault, "Discours sur la Parole," *Culture vivante*, 1 (1966), p. 19–36.
16 Perrault, et. al, *Un pays sans bon sens!*, op. cit., p. 41.
17 Pierre Perrault, *Toutes isles* (Montreal/Paris: Fides, 1963), p. 192, describing children catching eels.
18 Ibid., p. 197.
19 Ibid., p. 227.
20 Pierre Perrault, "Interview," *Cinéma Québec*, 1, No. 1 (May 1971), p. 27.
21 Perrault, et. al., *Un pays sans bon sens!*, op. cit., p. 42.
22 Perrault, *Toutes isles*, op. cit., p. 229.
23 Interview in *Pierre Perrault, Cinéastes du Québec 5*, 2nd edition (Montreal: Conseil Québécois pour la diffusion du cinéma, September 1970), p. 23.
24 Perrault, "Discours sur la Parole," op. cit., pp. 19–36.
25 Eugene Vance, "Roland and the Poetics of Memory," in Josue V. Harari, *Textual Strategies* (Ithaca, N.Y.: Cornell University Press, 1979), p. 374.
26 Perrault, "Interview," *Cinéma Québec*, op. cit., p. 27.
27 Perrault, et. al., *Un pays sans bon sens!*, op. cit., p. 184.
28 Barbara Herrnstein Smith, *On the Margins of Discourse: the Relation of Literature to Language* (Chicago/London: University of Chicago Press, 1978), pp. 54–55.
29 Ibid., pp. 127–128.
30 David Cozens Hoy, *The Critical Circle: Literature and History in Contemporary Hermeneutics* (Berkeley: University of California Press, 1978), p. 148.
31 Interview in *Pierre Perrault, Cinéastes du Québec 5*, op. cit., p. 28.
32 Interview with Pierre Perrault and Bernard Gosselin in *Cinéma Québec*, 5, No. 5 (1976), p. 13.
33 Interview in Pierre Perrault, *Cinéastes du Québec 5*, op. cit., p. 30.
34 One of the titles in *Un pays sans bon sens!* reads "Peut-on renier le village pour retrouver le pays?"
35 The reference to deconstruction refers more closely to the concept of "grammatization of rhetoric" delineated by Paul de Man in "Semiology and Rhetoric" in Josue V. Harari, ed., *Textual Strategies*, op. cit., pp. 131–140; and glossed in T. K. Seung, *Structuralism and Hermeneutics*, op. cit., pp. 269–272. See also Paul de Man, *Allegories of Reading* (New Haven: Yale University Press, 1979).

# *The Feminist Fiction Film in Quebec:* La vie rêvée *and* La cuisine rouge

BY BRENDA LONGFELLOW

*To have a growing number of committed women filmmakers within a given national cinema is, at long last, something other than an oddity. But to have a forty-year tradition of major women cinéastes is something else again. And to sustain that tradition amidst the ups and downs of filmmaking in Quebec would seem to be more or less impossible. Yet it is exactly this tradition that Brenda Longfellow insists upon here. Moreover, it is a tradition that has had a central, if neglected, place in the development of cinema in all of Canada. As with much of Canadian cinema, the nature of women's films in Quebec can be traced to their origins in the National Film Board. John Grierson began the practice of placing women in positions of responsibility at the Board, where he then overworked and underpaid them. As working conditions at the NFB improved after Grierson left, women found themselves in danger not only of slipping further behind, but also of losing the policy-making and creative positions that they had been able to secure. The success of francophone women at the NFB in their struggle against these tendencies is partially due to their central role in the overall struggle of the Québécois for a voice of their own. Beyond that alliance, though, was the unique ability of women in Quebec to articulate feminist issues in the NFB's documentaries and to be at the forefront of the move for the establishment of a feature film industry in the sixties.*

*As Longfellow points out, the growth of feminist film in Quebec came about because of demands for access to the feature industry and a freedom to shape films to fit the needs of a feminist sensibility. She addresses the nature of the feminist feature by examining in detail two highly regarded examples. Both* La cuisine rouge *and* La vie rêvée *deal with the interrelationship between subjective experience and the larger social context. An awareness of this interrelationship is also intrinsic to the struggles of Quebec culture as a whole. Daily confrontations over language and self-image are conducted simultaneously by the individual and groups within society. By understanding the nature of this discourse, women in Quebec have positioned themselves at the centre of the cinema's contribution to the forming of their society's political agenda. As Longfellow writes of women during a climactic moment in* La cuisine rouge*: "There is a freeing of language—they no longer speak in the throttled, fragmented discourse of the hysteric—and a liberation of desire." The universal desirability of this integrated being in no way weakens the uniqueness of feminist work in Quebec. But it does give us clues to the acceptance that the work has enjoyed, and to the growing strength of the women who produce it.*

## INTRODUCTION

There is no such thing as an essentially feminist film, there is no singular feminist position or critique. There is only difference and differences are articulated in differing languages. That is integral to the dilemma of attempting to build a new language of film.[1]

A survey of the work produced by women in Quebec over the last ten years clearly illustrates the difficulty of defining a feminist film aesthetic. The heterogeneity of individual styles, approaches, political strategies and concepts of feminism resists any attempt at simplistic generalization.

Given that qualification, however, one can point to two very general characteristics of the feminist cinema in Quebec that immediately distinguish it, particularly from that of English Canada, which to a great extent remains polarized between the experimental[2] and the documentary.[3] The first has to do with the degree to which fiction has been employed as a vehicle for the expression of the feminist imagination. Of the twenty-one feature films listed in the *Copie zéro*, "Des cinéastes québécoises," which covered the period up to 1980, over half, or twelve, were fiction films. In a general survey of English Canadian production over the same period, only three feature fiction films directed by women were discovered.[4]

While the majority of the features in Quebec were produced independently, many in film cooperatives, the fiction film has historically played a major role in defining French women's production at the NFB, beginning with *De mère en fille*, directed by Anne Claire Poirier in 1967. The *En tant que femmes* series, which initiated the first collective grouping of women filmmakers in Quebec, produced two realist narratives—*Le temps de l'avant*, a film about abortion, and *Souris tu m'inquiètes*, which examines the frustrations of a bourgeois wife and mother—and *Les Filles du Roy*, a fictionalized poetic documentary presenting women's historical contributions to Quebec society. The *En tant que femmes* experiment was eventually discontinued in 1975, and while a series of eight documentaries were produced by Poirier from 1976 to 1978, the focus came to be increasingly concentrated on the production of fiction features: *Mourir à tue-tête*, and the yet to be released *La quarantaine*.

The second general characteristic involves the concern, shared by a broad range of films, with investigating and expanding the formal possibilities of film language. This concern with form, moreover, is never isolated in the experimental genre, but occurs as an integral part of the project of redefining documentary and fiction to feminist purposes. One thinks of the haunting Duras-influenced *Strass Café* by Léa Pool; certain documentaries that express themselves in a mix of interview and dramatized representation—*Le grand remue-ménage*, *C'est pas le pays des merveilles*, and *Fuir*—and the self-reflexive didactic strategies of *Mourir à tue-tête*, *La cuisine rouge*, *Anastasie oh ma chérie*, and *La vie rêvée*.

What I propose to do is look at two films—*La vie rêvée* and *La cuisine rouge*—both fiction films incorporating a concern with examining the textual strategies they develop in the light of their very differing contribution toward the creation of a feminist language of film.

## THE FEMINIST FICTION FILM IN QUEBEC

Why the consistent committment to fiction, given its greater financial and production demands? While any adequate explanation would have to include institutional histories and a political economy of film production in Quebec, certain general reasons suggest themselves that have to do with the particular characteristics of Quebec cinema and the women's movement.

By the early seventies, the original enthusiasm of the *cinéma direct* movement had been nearly exhausted, its critical investigation of reality pushed to the formal limitations of the genre itself.[5] For many of the leading figures of the movement, the desire to "approfondir" their investigation of the nation was accompanied by a desire to progressively restructure that reality in a dramatic mode. Increasingly, the fiction film and the fictionalized documentary came to be appropriated as the venue for a nationalistic and class-conscious political cinema. Certainly the enthusiasm and presence of these films—their qualified success in infiltrating the Quebec market, and in creating an audience for the Quebec feature—provided an inspiration for women filmmakers.

Apart from the expanding possibilities of a national cinema, the specific orientation of the feminist movement nurtured, and indeed demanded, a very different concept of filmmaking. Mireille Dansereau commented on the making of *La vie rêvée*, the first feature to be directed by a woman in Quebec:

> They [*L'association coopérative de productions audio - visuelles (L'ACPAV)*] didn't want me to make this first film. The men thought that if I made a film on women, it should be militant. A sociological-Marxist analysis, or something like that. A very political film. But you see, that is a *man's* idea of what is revolutionary about women. They think we should get together and form a political party and fight, and give intellectual ideas about the problem of women as related to our society and to Quebec. Men thought that what would bring a change in the status of women is a clear analysis of women: sociologically, politically, and financially. They couldn't accept my intuitive, very emotional and personal approach.[6]

While the personal approach was also developed to great effect in documentaries such as *D'abord ménagères*, *Les servantes du Bon Dieu*, and *C'est pas le pays*, clearly the fiction film held a very strong attraction as a commercially accessible and powerful means of exploring feminist concerns.

Part of this attraction was born of the same forces that inspired the very strong feminist traditions in theatre (*Théâtre des cuisines*, *Théâtre expérimental des femmes*) and literature (Brossard, Cardinal, Bersianik, Theoret), which established struggles in language and representation as prominent parts of the feminist struggle in general. Many of the women film directors were drawn to fiction from backgrounds where such elements had figured, such as actresses Denyse Benoit, Micheline Lanctôt, Paule Baillargeon and Frédérique Collin, and writer Marthe Blackburn.

"It all happened at once," said Blackburn of the period, "the 'prise des paroles des femmes' . . . there was an excitement, an electricity in the air that inspired us all. Suddenly, after centuries of silence, women were speaking and writing."[7]

A large part of the attraction to fiction, however, was and is bound up with the properties of the medium itself—its tremendous emotional and psychological appeal and its particular mode of production. Fiction allows for a conscious ordering and construction of meaning through language, an imaginative freedom in the representation of reality. That, of course, had been the discovery of the "prise des paroles"—that through language reality could be challenged and reinvented, and that what had been silent and invisible through history—women's experience—could be made real.

For films such as *L'arrache coeur*, *Ça peut pas être l'hiver, On n'a même pas eu d'été*, *L'homme à tout faire*, and *Le temps de l'avant*, fiction became a vehicle for exploring the emotional and psychological depths of women's experience, a means of representing and validating the "quotidienne" or quotidian dramas that structure a woman's life: the relationships between mother and daughter, widowhood, suburban romance, pregnancy. And in giving life and words to an array of rich and complex female characters, these fiction films provided new role models, new points of identification for women spectators.

Apart from these traditional narrative strategies, a politically conscious fiction allows for an ordering of experience and representations that moves beyond the level of description to analysis, that seeks to demonstrate the interrelatedness of things. Such fiction dislocates us from reality and undermines the imaginary relations that bind us to an acceptance of a given order as natural and inevitable. Such, I believe, is the fictional impulse of *La vie rêvée* and *La cuisine rouge*.

"A woman is not born," said de Beauvoir, "she is made." This is the point of departure for both films: to investigate the process of construction of woman as feminine subject. It is to examine the traditional iconography of woman as erotic spectacle and domestic, and to displace these definitions from the realm of myth — whose operations, as Barthes revealed, naturalize oppression by posing it as eternal and inevitable. The strategy shared by the films is twofold: 1) to deconstruct patriarchal images of women; and 2) to pose alternative representations, utopic visions which suggest the possibilities of liberation.

Apart from their manifest intent, the radical innovation of the two films is inscribed in their specific modes of production. Each was produced through a cooperative effort—*La vie rêvée*, with the financial, technical and creative input of L'ACPAV, and *La cuisine rouge*, through improvisational workshops with the participating actors.

## LA VIE RÊVÉE

On one level, *La vie rêvée* is structured as an episodic narrative which concerns the developing friendship between two women—Isabelle and Virginia— and their joint fantasy for an older man. The film, however, absolutely resists being reduced to a description of its narrative, for it is above all a rich amalgam of dreams, memories, fantasies and consumer images which speak in the language of the unconscious—in symbols, lapses, and condensations of meaning.

It is a highly self-reflexive film, employing a number of devices to draw attention to the material practices which produce representations—its own and those emanating from the patriarchal definition of women. At one level, the reflexivity of the film is inscribed in the narrative, where Isabelle and Virginia are found to be working in a commercial film house, the setting furnishing the pretext for providing us with a privileged glance into the making of sexist commercials, and for the frequent visual references to consumer images of women. At another level, the language and structure of the film—the use of heterogeneous elements which comment and refer back to each other, the play with codes of slow motion and film grain, the whimsical editing and self-conscious camera—reinforce the film's consciousness of its own constructedness.

In an interview in *Cinema Canada*, Dansereau spoke of the film as realist: "I decided every frame and the atmosphere of lighting, because I wanted it to be a very realistic film . . . even if there are a lot of dream sequences—the dreams are true—and as real as reality."[8] The reality effect, however, is very different from the one we normally expect in cinema. The fantasy, dream and memory sequences, rather than reproducing, serve to undermine the status of the narrative as privileged bearer of the "real." These sequences, moreover, question the authenticity of the liberal notion of the individual as conscious centre and controller of her/his universe, and point to the role that certain unconscious forces play in structuring individual life decisions.

*La vie rêvée* is a film about female desire, about females who are subjects, actors and initiators of desire. It is a film in which the voyeuristic gaze is turned on a man as the object of female desire. But what desire? The crisis in psychoanalysis has always been the question, what does a woman want? How to speak of an authentic female desire in a patriarchal society which organizes such desire to perpetuate its own aggrandizement. The fantasy and dream sequences are concerned with investigating this structuring of female desire, showing how our primordial experiences in the family, the condensation of memory, and the subliminal fixations induced by consumer advertising, organize our desire and predetermine our object choices.

The home movie sequence, which occurs repeatedly throughout the film, shows a man carrying a little girl to the sea. Shot in slow motion on extremely grainy stock, it is like a dream, an idealized memory of a utopic past. She is laughing and clinging tightly to the man—daddy, the god-like figure of the child's first romantic fantasy, her protector, her lover. The naive memory of the first moment of desire, captured in the home movie, reveals the psychic dramas underpinning the nuclear family.

According to the classic Freudian paradigm, the resolution of the Oedipal complex for the female child occurs as she becomes conscious of sexual difference. She discovers her shame, her wound, her lack of the most desired object—the phallus. Henceforth she rejects her mother, condemning her for having produced her as an inferior being. She directs all her desire and sexual attention to the father, wants to have a baby with him, and develops her feminine characteristics to wean him away from the mother. It is this first heterosexual encounter that provides the model for all future relationships, based on an endlessly repeated pattern of paternal dominance/female submission.

Isabelle's fantasies, where she consistently represents herself as a little girl, dressed in white crinoline and headband, quite literally and vividly reiterate this pattern. The gestures and positioning of the figures in the mise en scène of the fantasy also graphically illustrate the political dynamic of the fantasy relationship. In one, Isabelle is sprawled on the rug at the feet of JJ, whom we see only from the knees down as he hands her books—the gesture of a paternalistic intellectual. In another, she is crouched in doggy position in the garden, exposing her behind—a child's gesture of polymorphous sexuality— to JJ, who again stretches above her and out of frame.

The dynamic is repeated in the fantasy where JJ and Isabelle are greeted by a flock of journalists and bombarded with banal questions on world events which elicit equally banal replies from JJ. Here we see the classic positioning of men and women within the power hierarchy of patriarchy. He is leader, authority—granted access to the world of power, politics, and ideas. She is the adored object, the planet orbiting around his sun. It is through him that she gains access to the world, living vicariously through his achievements, abnegating responsibility for her own self-definition.

"The emotion of love," says Janet Preston, in her study of Harlequin romances in a recent edition of *Fireweed*, is "inextricably bound up with the emotion of powerlessness."[9] The fantasy life and sexual identity of the individual, while explicable in terms of the Freudian analysis of the nuclear family, are also overdetermined and reproduced within the power structures of a patriarchal/capitalist society.

Romantic fantasies are not simply psychologically motivated; they are Big Business—the standard fare of domestic melodramas, pulp novels, Hollywood and pop music. Lacking any real access to positions of political or economic power, women are offered the vicarious thrill of Love and Romance—mass produced escapist fantasies feeding multi-billion dollar industries.

But it is an escape which ultimately proves to be debilitating. We remain paralyzed in positions of desire, of desire for desire, of desire for some confirmation of the fact of our existence, of desire for a rich emotional life which is refused in reality. "I'm going to write a paper on why young girls always desire unattainable men," Isabelle's childhood friend informs her.

But this hermetic circulation of desire around itself is precisely the pattern with which consumer advertising manipulates and cultivates our desire, by the constant repetition of appeals which maintain the consumer in a perpetual state of desire to consume, a desire which can never be satiated, only constantly recirculated. Isabelle's fantasy is a product of this excess of desire. Her fantasy is connected to consumer images through juxtaposition and the doubling of visual imagery—a scene of the advertisement "It's Better in the Bahamas" repeated code for code in her fantasy, including body positioning and lighting. In fact all her fantasies have the same kind of glowy, classless feel of the lifestyle ads which capitalism uses to sell Utopia. At one point, someone even mentions that JJ resembles a model in an advertisement.

By the end of the film, however, Isabelle has had enough of the frustrations of unsatisfied desire. "I'm tired of dreaming," she says. She wants to live, and to do so she must undergo a cathartic liberation from the oppressiveness of a fantasy which has paralyzed her. Urged on by Virginia, she arranges an amorous rendezvous with JJ which proves in the end to be something less than the utopic fulfillment of her dreams. But she is freed. In the last shot, an embarrassed JJ skulks away as Virginia bounces into the apartment. The two women collapse in laughter and proceed to tear down the commercial posters that adorn the apartment in a defiant gesture of their liberation from consumer fantasy and their commitment to live in the "real world."

The investigation of the construction of the female subject is also posed in certain non-narrative interruptions, which serve a kind of bracketing function. I believe these interruptions are intended to break the bond of personal identification which the narrative inspires, and to recall the ways in which the image of woman has been historically and systematically exploited by patriarchal culture: how that image has been used, as Mulvey pointed out, as the blank screen on which male fantasies are projected; and how it is transformed into a reified object, the leitmotif of erotic spectacle, connoting sex itself.[10] "She is cunt," says Andrea Dworkin, "formed by men, used by men. Her sexual organs constituting her whole being and her whole value."[11]

The first of these sequences involves two grotesquely sexist ads, one for yogurt, the other for underarm deodorant, in which we see women reduced to plastic mannequins—coiffed, made-up, mouthing the words of industrial capitalism. They are hilarious. But it is a hilarity with a keen political edge. It is the excess of the commercials, the exaggeration of the codes—the self-conscious movement and dialogue of the women, the heavy makeup, the forced smile, the banality of the text and the ludicrous association of sex and yogurt—which confronts us with the utter transparency of their ideology.

The second sequence, which we presume to be a "cattle call" for a porno flick, shows naked women, framed from waist to mid-thigh, parading in front of a fatcat: Robin Spry posing as an Anglo-Canadian porno director. This repetition of "cunt" after "cunt," and the clinical detachment with which they are presented, represses voyeuristic pleasure and brings to the fore the complex issue of our response to the naked human form. Who is looking, we are forced to ask. Reverse cutting connects the images with the director's gaze. We see them as he sees them: pubic hair up front and centre, so much soulless flesh.

Suddenly reality intrudes and the self-satisfied gaze is ruptured. The last model stands before us with a tiny visible mark of her humanity: a scar delicately etched above the right side of her genitals. This is suddenly no longer animal flesh we are viewing, but a human being who is alive, who has a history, who is vulnerable and can really be hurt and scarred in reality. It is a masterful and brilliant stroke.

The third sequence composes a mysterious dream image where a young girl of five or six, clad in a white nighty, stands in a garden and slowly lifts her gown, revealing her genitals to the camera. Dansereau herself shed some light on the image in an interview when she referred to it as one of the dream sequences she felt had succeeded. "C'est le moment où la petite fille en blanc par terre voit l'homme rêve et qu'elle essaie de le rejoindre." It is a moment of cinematic excess, where the illusory unity and plenitude of the cinema is ruptured—a freaky moment when the cinema momentarily halts the illusion to address the spectator directly; for it is he who dreams, lost in his contemplation of the young female, who, composed and coy, becomes a willing participant in his fantasy. Perhaps it is a kind of mocking gesture at a pathetic sexuality whose desire is fed through voyeurism, for she is not diminished by the gaze; on the contrary, she returns it. It is a difficult image, and the fact of her complicity remains problematic.

## LA CUISINE ROUGE

*La cuisine rouge* employs very different tactics in its endeavour to dismantle established codes of sexuality, borrowing, as it does, from Brechtian epic theatre—a natural evolution, since Baillargeon had been one of the founders of the very Brechtian-styled *Le grand cirque ordinaire.*

Perhaps it is the use of distanciation in the film, its exaggerated theatricality, that has alienated so many, for *La cuisine rouge* resolutely refuses to provide us with that fullness, that imaginary unity we are habituated to expect in film. While *La vie rêvée* engages us with its use of narrative and characters, on which we can hook our need for emotional identification, *La cuisine rouge* provides no such relief. In contrast to the rich symbolic imagery of *La vie rêvée, La cuisine rouge* employs a flat, minimalist style of representation, anti-natural acting, and long mise en scène sequences with a minimum of editing.

Strange it is indeed, but with a strangeness borne of a very conscious political strategy. Brecht has said that the central quality of epic theatre is that "perhaps it appeals less to the feelings than to the spectator's reason. Instead of sharing an experience, the spectator must come to grips with things."[12]

Given Brecht's admonition, we can see *La cuisine rouge* as a kind of moral drama whose intent is to produce knowledge of sexual role typing in patriarchal society. This knowledge is produced in typically Brechtian fashion by rendering the familiar unfamiliar, by inscribing the critical distance between spectator and representation—inscribing the "terror" that Brecht claims is necessary to all recognition.

The film presents itself as theatre enacted on a stage in an imaginary construction, taking place in an imaginary nowhere. As Carol Zucker points out, characters enter by a door and exit by the same door at the end of the film, like a curtain which falls at the end of a theatrical production.[13] The point of this theatricality is to foreground the artificiality of representation, and, by analogy, the artificiality of sexual roles themselves.

There is an absence of linear narrative or causal relation between events. Rather the film proceeds through a series of episodes, presenting a set of behaviours, gestures, and discourses which have been coded as sexual identity for clinical observation. It is ritual theatre, as in Artaud's Theatre of Cruelty, where the community comes together "to act out its destructive impulses and to express its deepest fears, . . . and through the use of satire and exaggeration . . . sting(s) society into looking at itself in new ways."[14]

In this ritual reenactment, the film alternates between two tableaux which correspond to the sexual division of labour: the women's sphere—the kitchen and the fantasy garden—and the men's—the cavernous bar, littered with the debris of some drunken debauchery.

In both spheres there is a sense of the immanent decay and dissolution of a world rigidly divided by sexual difference. The marriage which opens the film—the traditional happy ending promising rebirth and regeneration—marks the onset of degeneration. There is the oppressive heat, the disorder, the unwashed dishes. No one has cleaned for a week. There are potatoes sprouting in the cupboard and apples that spill out of the oven. The juke box and cigarette machine no longer function. The eggs refuse to be cooked.

This disorder is traced to the madness of the women inhabiting the domestic sphere—the unique site of their paranoia and hysteria, the fragmentation of language and identity. The domestic sphere, as we have come to understand through feminist analysis, is the critical site of women's oppression, where we have been systematically condemned to a life term of unpaid, unvalorized labour in the service of others, robbed of our bodily integrity and denied any authentic means of personal self-realization. Madness seems a very sane response in a world where, as Phyllis Chesler has pointed out, "characteristics such as self-sacrifice, masochism, reproductive narcissism, compassionate 'maternality', dependency, sexual timidity, unhappiness, father worship—and the overwhelming dislike and devaluation of women" are defined and institutionally enforced as the standards of sanity for women.[15]

In *La cuisine rouge*, madness is the women's defence and rebellion. They have stopped caring; the habitual cycle broken, the urgency of dishes and breakfast suspended indefinitely. The fragmentation of identity and bodily unity, however, is also connected to the very real violence and dismemberment of women in the "outside," rumours of which filter into their hermetic little universe.

The men meanwhile await a breakfast which only appears at the end of the film. They bond, coalescent in the instant solidarity of a sex that has access to power and the public domain. They argue politics and hockey. Beneath the surface of these male rituals, however, lies a tangible violence that explodes in the terrorizing antics of Thibault. As Chesler states, male bonding is "the containment of explosive and crippling male rivalries, the systematic containment of indiscriminate acts of male violence . . . the containment of the Oedipal dilemma, the containment of the urge toward male homosexuality—through glorification of obedience to male 'superiors.' "[16]

Distanciation is also created in the film by the absence of a single unifying consciousness, a subjective point of view with which the camera identifies. This absence situates the point of view in the detached observation of the camera and the feminist directors. It is they who control the field of vision, and as spectators we are positioned in the field of their ironic gaze.

The camera style serves to reinforce this sense of detachment: the extreme ironic high-angle shots which open the film; the long sequences enveloped in a single shot; and the slow camera, choreographed to the movement of the ensemble rather than a single individual. In addition, the shallow depth of field and the absence of conventional editing strategies present us with a flat perspective where actors, like cartoon figures, are set in a unidimensional world—a world we are compelled to examine, criticize and reject.[17]

Epic theatre gives life to its people whom it classifies purely according to

> function, simply using available types that occur in given situations and are able to adopt given attitudes in them. Character is never used as a source of motivation, these people's inner life is never the principal cause of the action and seldom its principal result. The individual is seen from the outside.[18]

The characters in *La cuisine rouge* function as markers of the rigid sex typing of patriarchal society. They are bearers of social definitions assigned to them: the women—erotic objects, domestic servants—and the men—artists, Marxists, businessmen, "macho." It is their very extremism as symbols that confronts us with their ideological origins and reflects back on the whole process of the construction of sexual identity in society.

I think this self-reflexiveness is what critic Claire Johnston talks about when she refers to the use of iconography as a political tactic:

> Because iconography offers in some ways a greater resistance to the realist characterizations, the mythic qualities of certain stereotypes become far more easily detachable and can be used as a shorthand for referring to an ideological tradition in order to provide a critique of it, by disengaging the icons from the myth.[19]

If patriarchal ideology attains its institutional and hegemonic force through the naturalization of given definitions of sexual identity, the subversion of *La cuisine rouge* consists in dislocating the naturalness of these associations. The connotations of terms such as female biology, erotic spectacle, nurturer, domestic, and mother are disrupted, allowing us to effect a radical separation between the individual and a role we come to identify as socially constructed and imposed on individuals through economic, social and cultural pressures. We are left with an understanding of life as a stage on which men and women enact these preconstructed roles in a language and repertoire of gestures written and directed by others—by a history of class and sexual exploitation.

One sequence which is particularly revealing of this process of "denaturalization" is the strip which occurs at the close of the film. This strip, far from being an erotic spectacle, is placed immediately in the context of work—part of the daily monotonous routine the women are compelled to undergo to earn their economic livelihood. "No, we don't want to go," they explain to Estelle, the young girl. "It's something we have to do to buy food, but we'd rather not."

The strip spectacle is completely denuded of the illusion of compliance between woman and male spectator—that she is acting out her own desire to be looked at —which in the ideological fix of patriarchy represents the projection of male desire itself. The scene, which has to be the most boring strip in the history of cinema, begins when the bride suddenly stands up, yanks her dress over her head, and sits down again in the most desultory, perfunctory fashion, obviously under duress.

All conventions associated with the strip are completely and utterly flaunted—the reassuring ritual and exoticism, the tease of the striptease, the tantalizing play of concealment and disclosure, and the building of suspense and expectation, played to the end of cultivating the desire of the other. All of these, as Barthes points out, aim at establishing the woman right from the start as "an object in disguise," "the signification of nakedness as a natural vesture of woman . . . the nakedness itself remaining unreal, smooth and enclosed, like a beautiful slippery object."[20]

In *La cuisine rouge* it is her very reluctance, her visible and willful non-compliance with her own objectification, which denies her object-status. In the moment of revelation, her nakedness is revealed not as a "beautiful slippery object" but as a mark of the real economic, social and cultural vulnerability and physical dispossession of women.

I have already said that there are two strategies in the political projects of *La vie rêvée* and *La cuisine rouge*: the deconstruction of traditional identities; and the complementary strategy of presenting us with a utopic vision of women's sensuality, friendship, and relationship to her own body and her own desire.

Adrienne Rich has spoken of the "double life" that women lead; the fact that even in the institutions of heterosexuality and the family, women have always attempted to create a community of support among other women as a means of surviving patriarchy, as a means of discovering the emotional intimacy and friendship that in the majority of cases was lacking in their heterosexual relations. This subcultural community, Rich notes, by the very fact of its existence, poses a challenge to the patriarchal order and to the hegemony of heterosexuality as the single pattern of adult intimate relations.[21]

Both films pose this community as an alternative to romantic fantasies and to the sexual and domestic servitude exacted by patriarchy. In the friendship of Isabelle and Virginia, in the garden idyll of *La cuisine rouge*, women recreate that community where, having escaped from the authoritarian regard of men, they are free to indulge their pleasures, eat, drink, sing, play tricks on others (the Wilhelm Reich fan in *La vie rêvée*), muck cake in each other's hair, dress up, and paint their faces. It is the sensual, delightful world of the child, before her entry into the public domain as sexual commodity; a world of polymorphous sexuality, fantasy and play. Like children, there is a freedom and largesse in the women's language and corporeal movements; for them it represents a reestablishment of control over their own bodies, a rediscovery of their own body sensuality.

Despite the fantasy for the older man, it is the two women who form the real couple in *La vie rêvée*. It is they who bond in a world of intimacy from which all male characters (real or imagined) are ultimately exempt. Within the threesome set up for their forest vacation, it is the two women who sleep together, both rejecting their intellectual friend as a potential sexual partner. Even the heterosexual consummation of the fantasy—which usually marks the termination of bonding between women and the formation of the *real* couple—only strengthens their solidarity.

In contrast to the emptiness of a consumer fantasy, their relationship provides for a real exchange of feelings where real human needs for intimacy are met. It is a relationship founded on equality, instant psychic communication and identification. There are numerous verbal and visual references to doubling and identification between the two women—the similarity of body type, hair style, the sharing of clothes, and the similarity of experiences they relate concerning their first lovers.

Although their relationship is not explicitly sexual, it is sensual and physical. There are numerous scenes of the two women naked together—picnicking in the graveyard, changing at the swimming pool—and there is a great deal of physical contact between the two—hugging, running and skipping together.

In *La cuisine rouge*, it is the moment when the women step into their tropical garden fantasy that the symptoms of their madness disappear. There is a freeing of language—they no longer speak in the throttled, fragmented discourse of the hysteric—and a liberation of desire. They rediscover their physical integrity and enter a kind of communion with their bodies through rituals of adornment, bathing, and eating and drinking, consuming the cake and the champagne of the wedding party. Their repressed, creative energies are released and they invent music, create art, and dance.

It is a place of sanity and a restoration of wholeness. We are all "motherless daughters" says Chesler, commenting on the sources of women's madness, "starved for maternal nurturance." Driven into adulthood, we become surrogate mothers to men and reproductive mothers to children, but for women, in the institutions of heterosexuality and the family, there is no possibility of an imaginative return to an original source of nurturing. In part, this bonding between women is an attempt to recreate the original wholeness of the relationship between mother and child. Certainly the oral and tactile sensuality of the garden and the bathing scenes, where each woman is nestled fetus-like in her own womb/tub in *La cuisine rouge*, and the nurturing relationship between the older Virginia and young Isabelle in *La vie rêvée*, would suggest the same.

*Ciné-Tracts*, 16 (Winter 1982)

---

1 Lesley Stern, "Feminism and Exchanges," *Screen*, 20, No. 34, (Winter 1979–80) p. 93.
2 Joyce Wieland, Kay Armatage, Patricia Gruben, Betty Ferguson, Lois Siegal. See B. Martineau, "Canadian Women Filmmakers," *Cinema Canada*, 71 (Feb. 1981), for complete list.
3 English Canadian documentary filmmakers include independents—Laura Sky, Holly Dale and Janis Cole, Bonnie Kreps, Dianne Corbin; Studio D directors—Bonnie Sherr Klein, Dorothy Henault, Margaret Westcott; and NFB regional directors—Norma Bailey, Ann Wheeler, Lorna Rasmussun. See Martineau, loc. cit.
4 *Madeline Is . . .*, dir. Sylvia Spring, 1970; *The Far Shore*, dir. Joyce Wieland, 1976; *I Maureen*, dir. Janine Manatis, 1978.
5 M. Robert Boissonnault, "La Séquence du Long Métrage," *Cinéma Québec*, 2, No. 5 (Jan.–Feb. 1973).
6 M. Dansereau, "La vie rêvée," Interview by A. Ibranyi-Kiss, *Cinema Canada*, 5 (Dec. - Jan. 1972–3), p. 29.
7 Marthe Blackburn, interview with author, April 6, 1982.
8 M. Dansereau, "Interview," *Cinema Canada*, 5, (Dec.–Jan. 1972–73).
9 Janet Preston, "Consuming Passion," *Fireweed*, 11 (1981), p. 20.
10 Laura Mulvey, "Visual Pleasure and Narrative Cinema," *Screen*, 16, No. 3 (Autumn 1975).
11 Andrea Dworkin, *Pornography: Men Possessing Women* (New York: Perigree Books, 1979), p. 110.
12 Bertolt Brecht, *Brecht on Theatre*, ed. and trans. John Willett (New York: Hill and Wang, 1977), p. 23.
13 Carol Zucker, "Les Œuvres Récentes d'Anne Claire Poirier et Paule Baillargeon," *Copie zéro*, 11, "Vues Sur Le Cinéma Québécois" (1982), p. 54.
14 James Roy MacBean, *Film and Revolution* (Bloomington: Indiana University Press, 1975), p. 54.
15 Phyllis Chesler, *Women and Madness*, (New York: Avon Press, 1972), p. xxi.
16 Phyllis Chesler, *About Men*, (New York: Bantam Books, 1978), p. 248.
17 See Brian Henderson's "Toward a Non Bourgeois Camera Style," in *Movies and Methods*, ed. B. Nichols, (Berkeley: University of California Press), 1976.
18 Brecht, op. cit., p. 48.
19 Claire Johnston, "Women's Cinema as Counter Cinema," in *Sexual Strategems*, ed. Patricia Erens, (New York: Horizon Press, 1979), p. 135.
20 Roland Barthes, *Mythologies*, trans. Annette Lavers (London: Granada Publishing, 1973), p. 85.
21 Adrienne Rich, "Compulsory Heterosexuality," *Signs*, Summer 1980. See Julia Lesage "Celine and Julie Go Boating," *Jumpcut* 24/25, March 1981, for extensive film analysis applying Rich's argument.

# The Sins of Gilles Carle

## BY JAMES LEACH

*Success in Canadian cinema never seems more impossible than when it is achieved. The many successes of Gilles Carle—the only Canadian director to consistently produce money-making commercial features in the course of a twenty-year career—would normally serve to make his work a central influence on his contemporaries. Indeed, the subject matter of that work, as James Leach describes it here, seldom strays from the pursuit of the mythology of contemporary Quebec. It is, if anything, a pictorialization of that mythology. Léopold Z., the much harassed* homo Québécois ordinaire, *physically occupies a prime space in his culture: a cathedral seat, front and centre, at midnight mass on Christmas Eve. And from her role as transcendental earth mother in* La tête de Normande St-Onge *to her performances as a metaphorical and literal Maria Chapdelaine, Carole Laure is used by Carle as a Jungian pin-up girl for his would-be nation's collective psyche. Even the somewhat sterilized Plouffe family, resurrected in Carle's massive production, succeed as impressions of the idealized beings that, in their original television manifestations, literally inhabited Quebec's very air.*

*Why then the difficulty in accepting Carle? Leach catalogues complaints that include "diffuseness and carelessness of structure," "the exploitation of his actors and audience," and "pessimistic endings expressive only of frustration and entrapment." These are criticisms worthy of the refutation they receive here. But they are also apt descriptions of much of cinema in Quebec, from the early postwar features to* Elvis Gratton. *The structural integrity of Québécois films are always threatened by conflict between a Hollywood influence and the equally foreign temptations of what might seem to be a more sympathetic European tradition. Much of Quebec culture (not to mention cinema culture) is about exploitation. This may lead to recurrent pessimism.*

*What finally distinguishes Carle's work from that of his colleagues in Quebec and in Canada as a whole is simply its scale. If he rejects the outright adoption of Hollywood style, he nevertheless harnesses the considerable clout of the commercial feature film industry and its television potential. This quantitative distinction makes a qualitative difference in a culture whose survival has always depended upon isolation and a certain demure articulation* entre nous. *Carole Laure as cultural manifestation is one thing. Carole Laure as international star is more problematic in a society that brings to the star system itself its own very particular cultural baggage. Is folklore still folklore in 70mm? Is the making and distribution of commercial cinema conducted in a normal businesslike manner an affront to the traditional victims of commercial exploitation? Taken out of context, Carle's films represent the considerable achievement of a world-class director. But can they be taken out of context?*

Despite their popularity in Quebec and France, the films of Gilles Carle have rarely pleased the critics. In fact, with a few notable exceptions, there has been a disturbing unanimity of response among liberal Anglo-Saxon and radical Québécois critics. There are, of course, differences of emphasis, but the "sins" of Gilles Carle can be conveniently collected under three main headings: 1) a diffuseness and a carelessness of structure that cause sudden shifts in tone and leave many loose ends; 2) exploitation of his actors and audience, especially the females among both; and 3) pessimistic endings expressive only of frustration and entrapment.

Before Carle is condemned to perdition, however, some examination of the critical assumptions on which these judgements are based might be in order. The ideal film that they imply would be based on a principle of restraint and economy of means, would be socially and politically engaged, and would avoid undue manipulation of the audience while nevertheless offering a positive (but not too obtrusive) resolution of its tensions. Many fine films have been made according to this recipe, but it rests on a limited attitude to the film experience which treats a film as a self-contained product rather than as an event. Carle's films are a direct assault on this attitude and an attempt to open up film form to cope with the contradictions that he sees around him—contradictions which are rooted in the specific reality of Quebec but which have a wide resonance.

In challenging the conventional attitudes to film form, Carle is inevitably challenging the methods of conventional film criticism. Piers Handling's analysis of Carle's "themes," for example, offers valuable insights into the iconography of his work, but does little to elucidate the originality of Carle's treatment of fairly commonplace motifs.[1] A more promising approach is suggested by Jean-Pierre Tadros in his account of *La tête de Normande St-Onge* (1975) as a "game of seduction," an idea to which I will return later.[2] In the absence of a critical theory that can take Carle fully into account, I have tried merely to outline his approach (using his own words wherever possible) and to suggest the ways in which this approach sets up a relationship with the audience that is both complex and stimulating.

Pierre Demers has described Carle's work as an attempt to escape into the past and into rural Quebec, away from the problems of modern urban reality.[3] A movement from city to country is certainly a feature of many of Carle's films, and it is often associated with an exploration of the past. Marie Chapdelaine searches for her father in *La mort d'un bûcheron* (1973) while a halfbreed tries to renounce the white side of his nature in *Red* (1969). But in both cases the return to the past is shown to be a delusion, and the characters have to come to terms with their present realities: Marie's father has died in a labour dispute that bears directly on Quebec's present state, and Red finds that the Indian way of life has become riddled with contradictions as a result of its contact with "civilization."

More successful returns to the past (both tied to a rediscovery of Indian culture) occur in two films which Carle directed for CBC television. In *A Thousand Moons* (1975), an old Indian woman is taken back to die in the country where she was born, and her spirit is passed on to the younger characters; in *Homecoming* (1978), Jenny is adopted by an Indian family and finds the stable values that she has missed in her life on the road with her father, an Indian who has become a rodeo cowboy. This concern with the past and with Quebec's cultural heritage also underlies Carle's recent adaptations of two major Quebec novels, *Les Plouffe* (1981) and *Maria Chapdelaine* (1983) (which had already supplied the name for his heroine in *La mort d'un bûcheron*).

Despite the positive outcomes of these returns to the past, an awareness of the past in Carle's films can only help to explain, but cannot resolve, the tensions of the present. His treatment of nature, too, is far from the naivety of Rousseauism; in *La vraie nature de Bernadette* (1972) the city woman finds that her ideal of a pastoral life does not take into account either the brutal side of nature or the mechanization of modern farming. Similarly, St-Pierre and St-Marie's retreat into the wilderness in *Les mâles* (1970) does not resolve the contradictions of their lives and they end up stranded in the urban desolation of Montreal. Carle has described *Bernadette* as showing "the generalised invasion" of the countryside by "the new urban society," and the invading forces are depicted in *Fantastica*, (1979) in which the bulldozers are "the tanks of the industrial world."[4] The return to the past creates an awareness that "nature doesn't exist anymore," and this is the essential difference between the world of *Bernadette* and that of *Maria Chapdelaine*.

Carle's memories of his own past in northern Quebec do provide the basis for his vision of Quebec as a locus of contradictions:

> Our radio picked up Buffalo and Montreal, always together, never separate, so that the religious broadcasts always had a pleasant background of country and western music . . . We seven children would thus recite our rosaries at a gallop, learning that in Quebec the most contradictory dreams are possible.

This recollection of childhood is not a retreat from modern reality, but part of Carle's strategy of giving that reality a mythic dimension and of linking everyday reality to the "great realities." His first feature, *La vie heureuse de Léopold Z.* (1965), originated as a documentary on snow removal, and it still contains "documentary" sequences detailing the drabness of Léopold's existence and the procedures of his job. Yet Léo is quickly drawn into a three-way conflict, present in all Carle's films, between a materialistic reality (the loan office, where even the pen is chained to the table), the myths which prevent him from rebelling against this reality (Christmas as a time for family and church), and the impotent dreams of escape from social pressures (Josita the nightclub singer; Florida or the Caribbean on credit). The audience is confronted with images which embody these tensions: as Léo is torn between hearing his son sing at midnight mass or Josita sing at the nightclub, we see his snowplow battling the storm to the accompaniment of the warm rhythms of Caribbean music.

Such unexpected juxtapositions form the basis of Carle's style and force the audience to work on its response to the film. This constant search for contradictions has led Gerald Pratley to object that Carle "doesn't give himself enough time to work out or properly motivate his screenplays, resulting in slap-dash ideas and incidents, superficiality, melodrama and ultimately confusion."[5] Nat Shuster similarly complains that in *La mort d'un bûcheron*, Carle "isn't just satisfied with telling a story," but "rides off into umpteen directions, skipping and jumping."[6] And Léo Bonneville expresses concern that *Fantastica* gives the spectator "the impression of watching two films at the same time."[7]

But these unsettling dislocations derive from Carle's rejection of "films that seem profound because they deal with only one reality," and his willingness to run the risk of "appearing superficial" by presenting his vision in "a structure necessarily complex and diffuse." The proliferation of elements exposes the poverty of the official myths and the escapist fantasies. The three brothers in *Le viol d'une jeune fille douce* (1968) are named after the archangels Joachim, Gabriel and Raphael, and they (as Carle puts it) "mythify themselves" while remaining oblivious to the contradictions between the myth and their reality as gangsters and rapists. *Bernadette* is built around the gulf between the banal and the religious in modern life, while *A Thousand Moons* contrasts the poverty of television images ("the white man's dreams") with the richness of the Indian myths which are slowly being forgotten.

Given the contradictory nature of their environment, Carle's characters cannot be the complete and fully-rounded individuals of the "psychological" cinema which he, like many others, rejects. There is no such thing as a "true nature" in Carle's films, since character embodies the contradictions of society, and personality is not fixed, but dynamic and fluid. He insists that "only impossible characters are possible today." Julie, in *Le viol,* invites our sympathy as the victim of her brothers' aggression, but we also have to watch her sit calmly by as they rape a hitchhiker. Bernadette, as Carle describes her, is "simultaneously a saint and a prostitute, a generous woman and an egoist." The spectator is confronted with characters who are "simultaneously antipathetic, sympathetic, violent, gentle, evil," and is thus prevented from achieving a secure relationship with the "world" on the screen.

The single perspective of conventional drama and film disappears, and Carle sets out to view the "drama" of life "in as many of its facets as possible." Despite the multiplicity of subjects and viewpoints, however, the element of drama is not eliminated from Carle's work: "Since I examine life and since life is dramatic, drama arises naturally from the film." The result is that Carle's films can contain strong dramatic, even melodramatic, conflicts without betraying the complexity and contradictions that he finds in life. His concern with the drama in life reaches its height in *Fantastica,* in which his aim was "to take real people and treat them as theatre people, while doing just the opposite with the theatre group."

This refusal to adopt, or to allow the audience to adopt, a single, fixed viewpoint derives from Carle's rejection of all dogma:

> I do not accept any orthodoxy, whether political, sociological or economic. Generally, man is compartmentalized, divided, reduced to a series of diverse values, and among these values some are privileged as being more noble . . . whereas what is necessary is a global vision of things and of people.

For Carle, dogma and orthodoxy represent the myths which society imposes on the individual from above in order to perpetuate the established order. This idea is most fully expressed in *Les corps célestes* (1973), which Carle describes as "a satire on ideologies." The "heavenly bodies" are both the physical attributes of the prostitutes who distract the miners from the dark reality of their subterranean existences, and the religious and political myths that come from the skies (via radio antennae). Since the film is set in 1938, the voice of Hitler dominates the airwaves, but the ending transcends time as we hear the voices of Kennedy, Nixon, and Trudeau.

Carle insists on the parallel between social and cinematic hierarchies. He tries to avoid setting up structures which impose a viewpoint on the spectator, and instead opens up the medium by treating it as "a series of elements in which all are important." Most films tend to privilege either the dialogue or the image, with the other elements merely supporting the chosen one, but Carle sabotages this approach by presenting contradictions either within the image or between the image and the sound-track. *Les corps célestes*, for example, opens with a shot of a radio antenna and a Union Jack, while the voice of Hitler is heard on the sound-track, and the film is built out of the contrast between the menacing broadcasts and the sexual escapades depicted in the images. The tension set up here can be compared to that at the end of *Normande St-Onge*, when images of Normande in a state of inertia are juxtaposed with images of her fantasies of sexual dominance, a tension that is not resolved by the final image of the old lady ungratefully stating that Normande never cared for her. In *Léopold Z.* and *Bernadette*, the cheerful music, Caribbean and country respectively, creates an uneasy lightheartedness in view of the frustration expressed in the images; the letters read on the sound-track of *La mort d'un bûcheron* provide a contemplative counterpoint to the urgency and confusion shown in the images.

These formal strategies would seem to be out of place in Carle's adaptations, which remain fairly close to the style and structure of the original works. Yet, even in Louis Hémon's *Maria Chapdelaine*, Carle found "a sort of magic 'hyper-realism' " which anticipates his own approach. He insists that Hémon's work is not a novel but a "tale" (*récit*), a genre with a long history in Quebec literature. If it were a novel, "the characters would be better defined, more developed," and the narrative would be more tightly constructed. As it is, the lack of character development and the refusal to use one scene to prepare for another suggest that Carle's strategies may have their roots in the tradition of the *récit*. His adaptation has been criticized for its emotional restraint, but he has reiterated his continuing concern to demand an active response from the spectator: "The idea was not . . . 'to deprive the spectator of all emotion' but to ask for it from him, from him as well. To make him collaborate a little. To treat him a little as if he were one of the family." Carle's films work to "destroy the patterns of what's going on," and he wants "people to feel frustrated at the end" of his films as long as they also "feel like doing something about their lives."

Just as Carle's approach to film form reflects his open approach to reality, so his objection to the compartmentalization of humanity is reflected in his treatment of the established genres which compartmentalize cinema. He sets out to mix up genres in the most startling ways, juxtaposes the comic and the serious, and claims that all his films contain elements of the love story and the crime film. Since Carle "takes reality into account," his films take on the qualities of the genre which shapes (and limits) the reality with which he is concerned. Thus *Le viol* becomes a modern version of the revenge western with the arrival of the brothers to defend their sister's honour; the entry of the police in *Les mâles* and *Normande St-Onge* turns these films briefly into crime films (comic, in the first case); *Red* intermittently becomes a gangster film, developing the genre's essential parallel between gangsterism and capitalism; while *Fantastica* juxtaposes the fantasy world of the musical with the heroine's struggle to protect the environment. *Bernadette* is a "religious western," and *La mort d'un bûcheron* begins as an erotic film (a debased modern version of *Maria Chapdelaine*), but ends as a political film as Marie moves from naive victim to an awareness of the historical forces shaping her society.

The tension between the personal and the generic in Carle's films can also be related to their concern with the individual and the collective. He sees his films as "a call to destroy big institutions and to do something as individuals," but he also stresses the need for collective action. In relation to his own filmmaking practice, Carle has spoken of his desire "to be some sort of a collective filmmaker," but adds that "I can't help having my fantasies, my ideas, my background." The search for a collective basis for his personal vision underlies the adaptations in which Carle explores Quebec's cultural myths. *Les Plouffe* is concerned with a "movement from the individual to the collective" and, whereas the popular television series loosely based on the same novel was "picturesque," Carle's film "tries to make these people familiar." The individual conflicts within the Plouffe family are gradually caught up in the tensions aroused by the war and the conscription crisis, and these tensions are seen as operating in Quebec's present situation despite all the apparent cultural changes.

The movement from being exploited to becoming aware is basic to all of Carle's films—often for the characters, but always for the audience. Yet this movement is often obscured, for those conditioned by the idea of film as mirror or as dream, by Carle's apparent playfulness. Carle himself has admitted that he has "always liked to play with names," but such games are not merely self-indulgent.

The names of his characters connect them with the contradictions and myths of their society: Léopold Z. thus has the universality and lack of specific identity of Kafka's K, but his initial also makes him, the typical Québécois, the last of men; the title of *Red* appears in the opening credits boldly printed in blue but, to suggest that the halfbreed finally achieves his identity in death, his name appears in red at the end. Red's given name is Reginald Mackenzie, an indication of society's attempt to impose its own order on the savage or unknown. Names represent a narrowing down of possibilities, and much of Carle's play with names exposes society's fear of the unnamable. Names drawn from the Bible and from Catholic mythology are, of course, abundant in Quebec, and Carle uses the idea of Christian and family names as an example of society's attempt to fit individuals into its mold. Bernadette escapes from the bourgeois identity provided by her husband's name (Brown), but can only assert her freedom by returning to the name she inherited from her father (Bonheur); she is finally crushed by the people who identify her with the saint from whom her Christian name is derived. In attempting to escape from the restrictions symbolized by names, Bernadette (like Normande St-Onge and the modern Marie Chapdelaine) is forced to face up to what Carle calls "the pagan side of the Québécois."

By exposing the inadequacy of film illusion, the inappropriateness of genres, and the loss of identity involved in naming, Carle creates a game which exposes as a game the bundle of conventions and artifice that usually passes for reality. His game grows out of the contradictions of modern Quebec and is one in which the audience is "implicated, individually and collectively." The problems of Quebec are seen as an intensification of the problems of any consumer society; frustration and violence are a result of society's attempt to suppress contradiction. The brothers in *Le viol* turn the complexities of Julie's life into a simple formula of honour violated; the gangster/businessmen of *Red* eliminate the contradiction represented by the halfbreed; the bosses in *La mort d'un bûcheron* violently suppress the stirrings of independence among the workers; and the lawyer in *Normande St-Onge* preserves his reputation by consigning his sister, and eccentric ex-stripper, to an asylum. In *L'ange et la femme* (1977), Fabienne is shot down by gangster/terrorists, is restored to life by the Archangel Gabriel, but is killed once more apparently because she refuses to remain a beautiful object and insists on finding out more about her society. In all cases, the attempt to eliminate contradiction defeats itself because of the violent means used to preserve social quiet.

The implications of a consumer society are central to *Bernadette*. The confined, bourgeois existence against which Bernadette initially rebels is imaged by the framed pictures of vegetables which decorate the walls of her suburban home. Her idealistic rebellion is translated onto a political level when the farmers dump vegetables on the highway to protest against the low prices that society is prepared to pay for them. Even this demonstration ends in frustration: The motorists, who have just stripped Bernadette's house in search of religious relics, start loading their cars with free vegetables until Bernadette opens fire on them. The mob's idolatry saves them from the responsibility of solving their own problems, and masks a desire to get something for nothing. Similarly the public outcry against the "apemen" in *Les mâles* reveals the essential voyeurism of a society that condemns rape, but which is fascinated by lurid details.

Voyeurism is the most obvious means by which an audience can become implicated in the film experience, and Carle's films often become reflections on the implications of voyeurism. He has been accused of pandering to "le milieu de 'showbiz' " by confining himself to the bourgeois conception of social revolution as a "struggle for sex."[8] Molly Haskell uses *La mort d'un bûcheron* as an example of how "a director, even with all good intentions, can hardly help turn a beautiful woman into a sex object"; she feels that "what starts as an exposé becomes exploitation."[9] But it is precisely the element of exploitation that prevents the film from becoming the kind of exposé that works up righteous indignation but leaves us essentially untouched (since the exploiters are always others). Jean-Pierre Tadros has described the "astonishing complicity between Gilles Carle and Carole Laure" (which reaches its height in the controversial lovemaking sequence in *L'ange et la femme*), and the films do dwell on the fine line between involvement and exploitation, between the erotic as a heightening of human experience and the erotic as an evasion of responsibility.[10] Almost all his films include, literally or metaphorically, the rape of a sweet young girl, and this rape is seen as a symbol of the processes of consumer society as well as of the process of film viewing.

Voyeurism and exploitation are seen as products of a desire to remain innocent, to consume without responsibility. Carle argues that "it is necessary to deflower reality so that something new and unexpected can emerge"; in *La mort d'un bûcheron* the audience "innocently" becomes part of the society which exploits Marie, but then follows her to an awareness of the contradictions of that society (and of the film experience). Julie, in *Le viol*, has been described as "a normal girl living in an abnormal society" whose mind is raped by her environment, but our response to this metaphorical rape remains as ambiguous as that to the actual rape of the hitchhiker, which we see only from the detached perspective of an extreme long shot.[11] Our response to the attempted kidnapping and rape in *Les mâles* is complicated by the girl's sexual teasing and her evident enjoyment of the experience. While the impulsiveness of St-Pierre and St-Marie offers a refreshing contrast to the hypocrisy of society, St-Marie's sculptures (which inevitably seem to take on the form of female breasts) express both the sexual frustration of the men in the wilderness and their treatment of women as objects. These absurd totempoles fit into the film's exploration of the relationships between the animal and the human and between nature and art, while the central issue becomes the balancing of the subjective and the objective both in human relationships and in the experience of film.

The world of Carle's films is one in which individuals have become so subjective, so involved with themselves, that other people have become objects. The searches which provide the basic structure of many of his films are always ultimately searches for a way out of this state of alienation and for a sense of identity. It has been objected that these searches often tend to involve a movement away from the urban centres of modern Quebec, and thus to evade an analysis of possible political solutions. Separatism and the language issue, for example, never become central to the films, although Anglo-American economic and cultural imperialism provides a background to all of them (the car show in *Red*, Brown in *Bernadette*, the cowboy outfits worn by many of his *macho* figures). Before their retreat to the backwoods in *Les mâles*, St-Pierre had been involved with union activity and St-Marie had been arrested in a student protest. But their retreat is as ineffective as that of Bernadette, who comes to realize that Thomas' political activism is more practical than her own reliance on "natural" love. *La mort d'un bûcheron* probes the realities of a society structured around paper, a society of "the lumberjack, the Scottish bosses of Canadian International Paper . . ., of the novel, of packing cases, and of electronic printing presses." *Les corps célestes* uses its basic metaphor of the brothel to equate prostitution and imperialism and "to show war as impotence, and not as a manifestation of power."

The search brings a new awareness, but rarely a sense of release. Red solves the mystery of his half-sister's murder, but is gunned down before he can expose her husband's façade of respectability; Léopold Z. goes to midnight mass with his family; the runaway lovers return to the brothel in *Les corps célestes*; and Normande

St-Onge withdraws into a world of sexual fantasy. But the key factor is that the audience's desire for an ending which resolves the issues is frustrated. An insight into Carle's purpose in this can be found in his description of Léopold Z. as a "pre-revolutionary" figure who has "many qualities, but they are unemployed."[12] The transition from pre-revolutionary to revolutionary is not made in the film, because it has not been made in reality. The audience is denied the satisfaction of a vicarious revolution.

Any resolution of these tensions is left up to the audience, Carle's chief concern being to bring them to the level of consciousness and to point to the multiple levels of reality that must be taken into account before they can be resolved satisfactorily. The issue of the family, for example, is one that dominates many of Carle's films,[13] but his attitude to it remains complex. The traditional large family of Quebec culture is examined in the two adaptations. At the end of *Maria Chapdelaine*, Maria's decision to remain in Peribonka and to marry Eutrope Gagnon is an ambiguous acceptance of both the strengths and the limitations of the values of her family. In 1945, at the end of *Les Plouffe*, the pressures undermining the traditional culture are expressed in Madame Plouffe's anguished discovery that the war has turned her son into a killer. Although Carle's earlier films reflect the postwar rejection of the myths of the *habitant* and of the large family, unsuccessful attempts to reconstruct the family unit are made by Marie (in *La mort d'un bûcheron*) and by Normande St-Onge.

But the alternatives are no more successful. The rigid family of white society might be replaced by a looser structure modelled on the Indian way of life, but Indian culture as depicted in *Red* and *A Thousand Moons* has been unable to withstand the pressures of "civilization." Even the Indians who adopt Jenny in *Homecoming* can only maintain their old ways within the reservation, and the ritual dance in which she is given their name is set against images of their children playing with an inflatable Air Canada jet. In the absence of the communal basis that gave the Indian ways their meaning, the experiments with communal living in *Les mâles*, *Bernadette*, and *Normande St-Onge* collapse because they fail to come to terms with the irrational elements in human nature.

The breakdown of the family unit is also related to Carle's concern with "cultural '*métissage*'." Characters like Red and the modern Marie Chapdelaine are literally *métis*, divided by the forces within them that link them to the opposed worlds of whites and Indians. But this condition also points to the linguistic and social divisions within Quebec, the split personalities of Carle's characters reflecting a divided and oppressed society. Thus, in *Fantastica*, Lorca's struggle against the developers is linked to her discovery of her resemblance to a certain Marie Néron who lived with Euclide and died twenty years ago. Her recognition of her other self helps her to overcome the split between her social and theatrical personalities. Even in *Les Plouffe*, Carle turns Denis Boucher into a halfbreed by giving him a French mother, and he describes the effect of the mother's death in *Maria Chapdelaine* as creating a split between "a nighttime Maria (a witch perhaps?)" and "the daytime Maria, whom we have known until then."

The attempt to heal such divisions leads to the creation of new ways of life which, however, are often undermined because their creators cannot free themselves from the dominant ideology. Carle has insisted that in *Bernadette* "the utopian ideas" belong to the heroine, and that he does not endorse them. He has also noted that in *Fantastica* Euclide (whose surname is also Brown) engages "less in a battle for the protection of nature than in a struggle to protect his own small personal paradise." The energetic pursuit of Utopia does expose the inadequacies of the social reality, but it also rests on a belief in the possibilities of "innocence" which Carle's cinema radically denies. The idea of a paradise-Utopia risks becoming complicit with the social and cinematic structures of the consumer society, and thus evading the contradictions which make up that society. Carle has called *Les corps célestes* "a fable on paradise, in a miserable country," and has said that if the action "had taken place today, I would have done it with hippies who want to create a commune, and no longer with a pimp who wants to create a paradise-brothel." The attempt to create a paradise is to impose an absolute from outside (on the model of imperialism), whereas the only possible relationship between individuals must come from within.

What is needed is a social structure that can mediate between the subjectivity of the individual and the objectivity of the world without interposing false myths or escapist dreams. Carle cannot provide the answers, even if he had them, because he would be relieving the individual spectators of their own responsibility. Ultimately Carle's concern is to create "the unexpected film"; "The first political step is to increase, not to reduce, the standard of lucidity." Carle's approach is the opposite of that of minimal cinema, but his goal is the same: the breaking down of the conventional structures of film viewing in order to encourage a more open and less conditioned response to the structures of society.

This is a revised version of an article which appeared in *Cinema Canada*, 36 (March 1977).

---

1 Piers Handling, "Themes from Gilles Carle," *Cinema Canada*, 26, March 1976, pp. 28–33; reprinted in Seth Feldman and Joyce Nelson (eds.), *Canadian Film Reader* (Toronto: Peter Martin Associates, 1977), pp. 199–207.

2 Jean-Pierre Tadros, "Le jeu de la séduction," *Cinéma Québec*, 4, No. 8, pp. 6–8.

3 Pierre Demers, "*Les corps célestes*," *Cinéma Québec*, 3, No. 3, November/December 1973, p. 11.

4 Unless otherwise stated, all quotations are taken from the following interviews with Carle: *Cinéma Québec*, 1, No. 9, May/June 1972, pp. 17–21; 2, No. 5, January/February 1973, pp. 19–26; 3, No. 1, September 1973, pp. 28–32; *Séquences*, 103, January 1981, pp. 4–16; 104, April 1981, pp. 4–5; 113, July 1983, pp. 24–28; *Cinema Canada*, 74, May–June 1981, pp. 40–44; 97, June 1983, pp. 15–19.

5 Gerald Pratley, "*La vraie nature de Bernadette*," in Peter Cowie (ed.), *International Film Guide: 1973* (London: Tantivy Press, 1972), p. 124.

6 Nat Shuster, "*La mort d'un bûcheron*," *Motion*, January/February 1974, pp. 49–50.

7 Léo Bonneville, "Entretien avec Gilles Carle," *Séquences*, 103, January 1981, p. 15.

8 Demers, loc.cit., pp. 11, 13.

9 Molly Haskell, *From Reverence to Rape* (New York: Holt, Rinehart and Winston, 1974), p. 354.

10 Tadros, loc. cit., p. 7.

11 Handling, loc. cit., p. 30.

12 Quoted in René Prédal, *Jeune Cinéma Canadien* (Paris: Premier Plan, 1967), p. 40.

13 Handling, loc. cit., p. 32.

# *The Old and the New*

## BY PETER HARCOURT

*Jean Pierre Lefebvre's career represents not only an ideal for Canadian filmmakers; it also serves in the international context as a defence of the purist conception of director as auteur. As writer-director of nineteen features since 1964 (all but two of which have been independently produced), Lefebvre has used virtually all of his work to further his personal interpretation of cinema's potential. His films range from a vaudevillian pastiche of narrative experiments (*Q-bec My Love*), through the austere, reflexive mise-en-scène of* Le vieux pays où Rimbaud est mort. *He has made a film noir in Hull (*On n'engraisse pas les cochons à l'eau claire*) and an historical farce (*Les maudits sauvages*) in which his costumed seventeenth-century Québécois bask in anachronism and generally refuse to stay dead. In even his most commercially successful works like* Les fleurs sauvages, *Lefebvre takes the time to teach his audience an idiosyncratic pacing and visual codification often described as verging on the poetic.*

*With the release of his latest work,* Le jour "S . . ." *(1984), Lefebvre found himself feted at Cannes for the tenth time in fourteen years. Yet to most English Canadians, he is still amongst the most foreign of foreign directors. Perhaps there is some justice in this. Lefebvre's experiments in all their variety point in the long run to a single unchanging question: What does it mean to be Québécois? As Peter Harcourt and David Clandfield demonstrate, Pierre Perrault asks that question through a scientist's examination of linguistic nuance and its consequence. Gilles Carle, as James Leach depicts him, strives toward a technicoloured mythology. Lefebvre seems to study the question itself before haunting his landscape in search of details that might lead to an answer. His characters, no matter how ridiculous they may appear (even to themselves), stride through the films with a dignity that belies their angst. They seem, as is appropriate within Lefebvre's acutely Brechtian constructs, to be asking not so much "Who am I?" but rather, "What part am I being called upon to play?" Totally self-alienated, these characters live in a world of objects that have become props. These props are, in turn, continually reshuffled in the hope that they may reveal themselves to be pieces of a puzzle. And the solution to that puzzle, as we see here in the examples discussed by Peter Harcourt, is not really a solution; it is a return to the original question.*

During the time of their work together, Marguerite Duparc and Jean Pierre Lefebvre had several times been invited to France for retrospectives of their films. Through the contacts they established there, in 1977 they managed to set up a coproduction with a budget and travel facilities greater than they had ever had before, though still extremely modest by "industrial" standards.[1] The film they made was *Le vieux pays où Rimbaud est mort.*

Coscripted by Mireille Amiel and Jean Pierre Lefebvre, *Le vieux pays* is demonstrably Lefebvre's most accessible film. It is full of beautiful locations and extraordinarily crafted effects. Furthermore, within its more conventional narrative, there are many interesting characters all played by actors who give splendid performances. That this film has not done well either in Quebec or in France is more a comment on the myopic policies of the two exhibition systems than on the film itself. And of course, except for an occasional festival screening, it has not been seen in English Canada at all.[2]

The film was conceived as a continuation of *Il ne faut pas mourir pour ça. Le vieux pays* picks up the story of Abel (still played by Marcel Sabourin) and sends him off to France. He wants to see, as he puts it, if his ancestors who long ago abandoned him still resemble him. Of course, they do not.[3]

In the picaresque manner that characterizes a good many films by Lefebvre, Abel drifts through the film, deliberately visiting some people, encountering others by chance. He is always withdrawn, wryly detached, as if attempting to understand. Faced with the narcissism of traditional French culture, he defines his otherness through his accent, asserting his *joual* to preserve his uncertain sense of self. People keep trying to guess where he comes from—Belgium, Switzerland, Africa, wherever. *"D'ailleurs, tabarnak!"* he one time replies. He rarely mentions Quebec.

The film is less a portrait of France than a demystification of the ancestral France that was so much a part of the schooling of every young Québécois. Like the Tremblay family in *Le règne du jour,* the second part of Pierre Perrault's "Ile-aux-Coudres" trilogy, Abel discovers that the France he has been taught to believe in no longer exists.

Like so many Lefebvre films, *Le vieux pays* is in three movements. These movements are punctuated by a guitar-playing troubadour who sings a song about the "glories" of France. These glories are chiefly defined in terms of all the military exploits that have made France what it is. Yet how can he explain to children, the song queries, the *cultural* glories of France—its *châteaux* and its parks—"glories" that are always the obverse of military aggressivity inflicted upon others? "Yet I've known Racine," the song concludes, "and if I imagine Cézanne and Rimbaud, I can smile more easily." What makes this song complex is that it directly questions the extent to which the refinements of culture are dependent upon imperialistic exploitation.

Each time he encounters it, Abel resists this song. At one time, he even shouts it away with his own song about Madeleine de Verchères. Quebec too has had her "glories." Yet it is less the sense of history that dominates Abel than a sense of landscape—the snow and forests in his head, as he says. So too it is largely the landscape that affects him in France—the three different landscapes of Paris (the centre), Charleville (the north), and Marseille (the south), which are also the three places where Rimbaud lived his life, was born, and finally died.

The Paris Abel encounters is one of insistent traffic noises, discourtesy, and tiny irritations. At an early point in the film, while in a café, we have a series of narrative disruptions in the form of little vignettes—short cutaways to typical French types that represent a variety of clichéd cultural and political attitudes. So too in a park he meets with a number of traditional French characters, all of whom note his strangeness and harrass him in little ways.

Most amusing of all is the encounter between Abel and an angry taxi driver (played by Jean-François Stevenin, who also plays two other parts in this film). He is so concerned to denounce all the abuses of a now-degenerate France that he is scarcely able to look where he is going.

For all his denunciations, however, he speaks in classical Alexandrines, a poetic discourse that Abel is able to share:

DRIVER: . . . et la TV, Monsieur, voulez-vous le savoir?
La culture française, mais c'est un dépotoir.
Au ciné: le porno. C'est le cul qui nous mène.
Et chez vous?
ABEL: Vous savez, au Québec, c'est les mêmes.

This sequence is not just playful. It implies a remnant. Like the two cardplayers in the café, whose dress and manner duplicate the famous painting by Cézanne, the verse of the taxi driver suggests the leftovers of a culture that, perhaps, was once a real source of national pride and an aid to self-definition.[4]

While in Paris, Abel visits two different sorts of people. The first, the de Cassants, are members of the *haute bourgeoisie*. Like his father in Brazil, they are French imperialists who regret the loss of their colonial investments in Africa. Throughout this sequence, Abel seems uncomfortable. He rejects their false values just as he rejects their champagne, preferring instead *une bonne p'tite bière frette!*

Abel also visits Jeanne Delpêche, someone he had met somewhere in his past. Jeanne is a single parent who works in a garment factory. After three years of marriage, her husband was killed by an accident at work. She lives alone with her daughter, Viviane; and for the moment, her brother Yves is also staying with her.

This visit provides Abel with the most humane encounter that he experiences in Paris. Abel arrives with an armful of flowers—so many, in fact, that he can scarcely get them through the door. They all have supper together, along with a pair of Portuguese neighbours—the couple who babysit Viviane when Jeanne goes off to work.

Throughout this scene, flowers are everywhere. Not only are there all the flowers that Abel has brought, but as with so many of Lefebvre's "loving" characters, Jeanne has floral patterns on her dress, and there are further floral patterns on the tiles in her kitchen.

If this film is in three movements, each movement has its particular range of colours. While browns and mauves dominate the first movement, in Jeanne's apartment there is also a subtle play with greens. After dinner, when Jeanne is sitting alone at the table, the deep green of a wine bottle is picked up by the bits of green within the floral pattern of her dress and further echoed by the slight tinge of green of the window-frame behind her. Furthermore, when we cut away to Yves sitting with Abel, this tinge of green is repeated by the colour of his trousers.[5] If the films of Jean Pierre Lefebvre have the simplicity of Rossellini, the inventiveness of Godard and at times the structural complexity of Resnais, they can also possess—more subtly, in my view, because less insisted upon—the visual delicacy of Antonioni.

The suicide of Jeanne's mother takes them all off to Charleville, the original home of Jeanne and Yves and also the birthplace of Rimbaud. This middle movement is full of sadness. If Jeanne's life has been filled with grief, however, it is a grief that has been externally inflicted. Her father is a drunken monster who tyrannizes the home; her job is tedious; her husband has been killed at work; and now her mother has hanged herself from grief. This makes her very different from Anne, whom Abel finally meets when he leaves both Charleville and Paris and goes, for a time, to Marseille and Cassis, to explore *le midi*.

The paths of Anne and Abel had crossed before when they were both in Paris, but it is not until Cassis that they actually meet—an encounter that is delightfully handled.

For this third movement of the film, blues and whites dominate the screen. When Anne and Abel first meet, sitting in the sun with their separate bottles of champagne, she is wearing a deep blue T-shirt and white slacks, while he is wearing a white shirt and pale blue trousers. Throughout this scene, the sight and sound of the Mediterranean is everywhere present on the screen. Everything seems so serene. We might even notice little boats in the distance behind them, as in some film by Yasujiro Ozu.

After a pan away from them across the blue clarity of the sea transformed by the white dazzle of the sun—"the sea swallowed by the sun," as Rimbaud puts it—we pick them up in a little alcove within the rocks, sharing bits of their life histories. The patterns of blue and white are here further emphasized by a pale blue bandana that she has wrapped about her head.

When they visit her mother in Marseille for lunch the next day, these colour patterns are reversed. Now Abel is wearing a dark blue shirt and white trousers while Anne has on a white blouse and a dark blue skirt. There is a pattern of yellow flowers on the tablecloth in the dining room, and on the wall behind the table hangs the famous Cézanne painting of a mother.

The small effect of this painting combined with the enormous vitality of Anne's mother suggests that there are still pockets in France where tradition has been continuous, where people still live in harmony with their past and within their natural surroundings. "She is the best part of me," Anne had explained when speaking of her mother.

While Anne grew up in the south, she now lives in Paris—a thoroughly bourgeois life. Married to a man who has no time for her, she no longer is at peace with her world. She is restless and discontented. If Jeanne's grief has been largely forced upon her, Anne's grief is more an existential choice. She prefers suffering to feeling she doesn't exist. She feels tired, she explains—a bit like her old country. But for Anne there exists the possibility of another kind of choice.

Her friendship with Abel becomes a short "affair," involving a love scene that Lefebvre handles most imaginatively and obliquely. Lefebvre has no need to display realistic details. He doesn't *show* us the action. He *informs* us, through his images, that the action has taken place. Furthermore, Anne's long confession about her unhappiness which, in real time, obviously *follows* the lovemaking, is so structured by Lefebvre that, in film time, it *frames* the lovemaking. This stylistic restructuring both suggests that her unhappiness was inevitable and invites us to establish a fresh relationship with what we are witnessing on the screen.

This long confession on the terrace of Anne's villa is most delicately handled. While Anne is talking to Abel, her face turned slightly to one side, she keeps glancing up and looking at the centre of the screen, which is to say at us. Her bright blue eyes are parallelled by the bright blue of the bathrobe she is wearing. Behind her, below the terrace, are the bright green leaves of the immediate foliage. Behind that are the grey-blue colours of the Mediterranean, beyond which are the misty browns and greens of the hills across the bay. In the gradation of these colours, this sequence partakes of the visual sensitivity of Cézanne.

Before I had seen *La chambre blanche*, I had never understood Anne's phonecall to her husband. I couldn't understand why she would want to confess her "affair" on the phone or why she would assert that there is no such thing as false love. Although we don't hear his voice, her husband is obviously annoyed. Once again his "work" has been interrupted. He doesn't understand what she is saying. But her contact with Abel has given her an insight. "The only true love," she explains, "is the love we decide to consider real . . . . Otherwise, everything we do would mean the same thing." To make reality real, one has to *choose* to make it real—if, unlike Jeanne, one is sufficiently privileged to be able to make that choice.

Anne's husband's name is Jean. But they are not the Jean and Anne of *La chambre blanche*. To become so, they would have to reinvent their relationship, to reexamine the grammar of their lives. Given the Jean that we have seen in this film, they are unlikely to do so. Anne will go on choosing misery in order to feel that at least she is alive.

Most central to this film is the poetry of Rimbaud, a poetry transformed by Sabourin's accent, like a gesture of appropriation. The denunciatory aspect of Rimbaud's verse provides a useful counterbalance for the celebratory values of the troubadour's song. During a reflective moment in Charleville, when Abel visits the grave of Rimbaud, a number of poems occur in voice-over—or lines from poems. Even in Rimbaud's time, he railed against the pollutions of a military industrialization. One poem ends:

> Chained to goodwill, we will have a ferocious philosophy—
> ignorant of science, ruthless for comfort, death for the world
> around. This is the real march. Let's go![6]

Frequently in this film, Abel is attempting to sketch with his chalk on a little blackboard—both of which imply a perishable record. But he can't even do this. The past can't be recorded, let alone preserved. As he lowers his slate, Abel's voice-over cites a line from another poem: "As for me, I have my saintly poetry and my modesty."[7]

The artist cannot change the world. S/he can only observe its contradictions and point out its absurdities. But s/he can do so with the authority and insight which are the prerogatives of the artist. If this was true of Rimbaud, it is equally true of Jean Pierre Lefebvre.

*Le vieux pays* establishes an ambivalent relationship between the "glories" of France and the uncertainties of Quebec. Abel has something missing—recurringly, a button from his shirt. This lends itself simultaneously to both a personal and a cultural reading. On the personal level, as much as in *Mourir*, Abel seems ineffectual, as if withdrawn from the pain of life. When Jeanne is so distressed at the death of her mother, he cannot fully comfort her. When he decides to leave Charleville, he doesn't even say goodbye. So too with Anne: while he can "hear" her confession, he cannot really help her. He seems more at ease with her mother—with someone who couldn't make emotional demands.

If Abel is a pilot (for we do not really know), he several times mentions that he flies only "little" planes. Like Jean-Baptiste before him, Abel still contains within himself the uncertainties of his culture. As we pan around his *chambre de bonne* toward the opening of the film, among the many things we see is a poster of Quebec. Framed in black like an obituary notice, this poster is a white space waiting to be filled, with the word "Kebek" printed along the bottom. This is the white space to which he must return. France has no solutions. Both Rimbaud and Cézanne are dead.

Reviewing the film at Cannes, Jan Dawson understood beautifully both Abel's dilemma and Lefebvre's achievement with *Le vieux pays*:

> By turns gay and sad, and for the most part langorously beautiful, its beauty remains as separate from its Québécois hero as the Cézanne paintings on the museum walls. The France of his ancestors, the France he has come to find, exists only in museums and in his imagination. And it is Lefebvre's genius that he has invented a visual language for describing this shadowy terrain between the public gallery and the corridors of the mind.[8]

As with most films by Lefebvre, Rimbaud ends with its beginning. Throughout this film, in a way appropriate to its painterly delicacy, there has been no camera movement. Every shot has been classically framed, each image has been securely held in place. Only at the end, when Abel has finished his farewell to Anne, does the camera move in toward them and past them out over the Mediterranean, a shot that then dissolves into an aerial shot travelling over the ice-floes of the St. Lawrence while the final tri-colour titles begin to roll.

If this ending takes us back from the balmy Mediterranean to the cold and ice of the Canadian winter, this is where the film began. *Le vieux pays* opens with a blizzard taking place in Montreal. Over images of wintry streets we hear the traditionally reassuring voice of an air hostess asking us to buckle our seatbelts and extinguish our cigarettes. She then tells us that this return flight to the old country will take only two hours, thanks to the abbreviated route made possible by the abstractions of the cinema! *Rimbaud* thus declares both its expected duration and the fictive condensations possible in film.

Since wintry landscapes are so prominent in the films of Lefebvre, we should return to the questions asked about *Le révolutionnaire:* What do they mean? What feelings might they convey? Do they suggest paralysis or acceptance? If the endings of both *L'homoman* and *Le révolutionnaire* did contain an element of paralysis, the ending of *Le vieux pays* seems more an acceptance. Abel's decision to return home does imply a conscious acceptance, perhaps even an increased ability to "change the course of events." However we will have to wait until Lefebvre makes the third part of this Oedipal trilogy that will concern itself with the father before we will really know.

Two years after *Le vieux pays où Rimbaud est mort,* Jean Pierre Lefebvre made *Avoir 16 ans.*[9] Initially he had wanted to make a documentary on school vandalism; but when every school refused him access to their buildings, Lefebvre was pleased, finally, to have the greater formal authority of fiction. Though based on an actual event, *Avoir 16 ans* is less about school vandalism than it is about the institutional repressions that stifle our lives.

As Lefebvre explained in the preface to the script of this film, working this time as co-writer with Claude Paquette:

> In this "true" story, what really struck us was the recognition that institutions of a secondary order and the people in charge of them are a direct relation of the institutions of a primary order—those of the top politicians, top civil servants, top technocrats. Briefly, this "true" story developed in the same way as the October crisis in 1970. We would even go so far as to claim that this story couldn't have taken place in the way it did without the October crisis as a model. Hence the urgency that we have felt in writing and filming *Avoir 16 ans.*[10]

*Avoir 16 ans* combines the human feeling of Renoir with the formal austerity of Michael Snow. Yet this austerity is itself part of the expressive integrity of the film, the fusion of its subject matter with its form. To quote from Paquette and Lefebvre again:

> It must be evident that the structure of the film is as rigid as the structure of the society it describes.

For this film, they wanted to oppose "the coldness of the structure to the tenderness of the observation," in this way once again creating those twin values that tug at us in all the films of Jean Pierre Lefebvre—the values that deny and the values that affirm.

After a short poetic prologue, the film consists of four basic sections within each of which there are a number of scenes. Each scene has a distinctive camera movement and an individual relationship established between the images and the sounds.

For the poetic prologue, we have a long, slow tracking-shot down an apparently endless corridor, while the voice of Louis recites a poem that rejects his "educational" incarceration, here drastically abbreviated and freely translated.

> . . . within this hypnotic neon
> I learn that I must
> learn to learn
> with no access to life
> with no access to love
> with no access to myself . . .
> My food has no taste
> My skin has no light
> I am the deodorized product
> of a stinking civilization
> I am no longer the child of my mother
> I am no longer the child of my father
> I am the child of the right
> I am the child of the left
> I am the child of unionized inflation
> At the centre of an ideological amplification system . . .
> Within this cold neon
> Without access to life
> Stuck in front of the desks
> of knowledge
> I hibernate
> in an indifference
> without a sun
> that might return to me
> my own seasons.

This prologue prepares us for the dominant feeling of the film. Like their parents, these young people possess a poetic potentiality that is imprisoned in long corridors which are not of their own choice.

The three teachers in the film—a Darwinian, Freudian, and a Marxist—are similarly trapped within the explanations of their own disciplines. Like the psychiatrist who appears later on in the film, they are victims of their own rhetoric, incapable of responding directly either to people or events. They have lost or surrendered their inner personal poetry.

After the prologue, the first section of the film is a slow zoom out from Louis on the stage of the school auditorium. We see him performing his irreverent play and then smoking a "joint," to the spontaneous delight of all his fellow students. This scene is followed by a slow zoom in over the heads of a roomful of students in the school cafeteria. This zoom gradually singles out Louis and his "gang" discussing his play. "I'm sure it expresses the thoughts of many people," we can finally hear him say. "We must take a stand," his friend Louise declares.

If the students feel imprisoned within the regimented aridity of the educational system, Lefebvre imprisons us within the perceptual restrictions of these zooms. In the cafeteria scene especially, so many faces appear to be interesting, but we are denied access to their speech. We have to wait until the end of the shot to hear intelligible words.

Other zooms occur in this first section of the film. We zoom back from the economics teacher explaining to his class the maximization of profits as dictated by "Uncle Sam." And there are a number of tracking shots, alternately moving inwards and outwards with the characters. We move in along the corridor with the principal of the school as he plucks Louis out of a line of hopeful escapees and chastises him for having smoked a joint on stage; and we move outwards with both Louis and Louise, walking homeward along their wintry country road.

Like *Patricia et Jean-Baptiste*, each section of this film is precisely dated, thus establishing a clear relationship between filmic and actual time. And if the first section of this film was characterized by zoom and tracking shots, the second section of the film begins with a series of pans. Also, if the first section of the film was shot with synch sound, the second section of the film establishes only an intermittent correspondence between the images and the sounds. For these Sunday morning scenes, as elsewhere in the film, Paul Piché's music provides both a lyrical uplift and a kind of choric comment to what we see on the screen.

Similarly, the act of vandalism is obliquely handled. Just as Louis' "poetic" sensibility has no relationship with his institutionalized education, so for this scene there are only occasional "synched" relationships between the images and the sounds. We see and hear Louis entering and rearranging the desks in a classroom. He smashes the clock and throws a crucifix into the wastepaper basket. Then he sits contentedly in the chair of the teacher upon the dais of authority and smokes another joint.

However, aggressive electronic music and off-screen sounds of breaking and entering had declared his anger and destruction. As in the lovemaking scene in *Le vieux pays*, these moments of destruction are not presented, but are simply referred to by this dislocation of the images from the sounds. This scene ends with Louis writing the letters FLEQ on the blackboard, a sign not immediately decodable. Later on, however, it is identified as the Quebec Students' Liberation Front, an identification that unites this group of student rebels with the FLQ, whose terrorist activities supposedly prompted the "overkill" of the War Measures Act in October 1970.

The next section of the film is entitled "Repression."[11] It begins with a title that recapitulates what Lefebvre and Paquette had already written in the preface of the script for this film: "Governments change but institutions remain the same." What happens in this section is a kind of overkill similar to that which took place during the October crisis.

All of Louis' gang are rounded up and interrogated—not just by school authorities, but also by the police. The absence of synch-sound for all these scenes reinforces the impersonality of terror.

Louis is pulled out of the classroom in a scene of total silence. We see the room full of students, their eyes attentive to what the teacher must be saying. Then all their eyes turn left as the impersonal backs of the principal and a police sergeant enter the room. Then their eyes look at Louis as he is summoned to the front and the eyes also follow him as he is escorted from the room. Finally—good students that they are—their eyes return their attention to the teacher.

Similarly, descriptions of police brutality are narrated over a shot of an empty interrogation room, with an ominous telephone on top of an uninhabited desk. So, too, an account of Louis' mother visiting him in prison is delivered over a shot of an empty cell.

A more structuralist account of Lefebvre's distinct use of cinema could make much of these sequences, as it could as well of similar effects in *Ultimatum*. These films insist that we "read" cinema in an entirely different way. They insist that we recognize the different degrees of signifying potential that exist within fresh combinations of images and sounds. With Lefebvre, however, whatever his structural innovations, there is always a human purpose at his centre. If his films encourage us to think, they also allow us to feel.

Like the backs of the heads that symbolize the impersonality of authority which we see throughout this film, these scenes—devoid of human characters, accompanied by sounds that evoke human grief—intensify the lack of humanity with which authority always imposes itself. They are not just magnificently structured from the point of view of cinema; they convey as well both the inhumanity of institutionalized thinking and the loneliness of individual human suffering.

These "interview" scenes move from the total impersonality of the principal, the police sergeant, and a social worker to an increasing degree of sympathy and understanding. After these three impersonal interviews, each of which is terminated by the further impersonality of a telephone call, we see Louise with her parents, their faces now in profile, thus signifying a measure of human exchange on the screen. The last scene, of course, concerns Louis. While his father is distressed at the grief that his behaviour has caused his mother, there is a strong sense of forgiveness and acceptance. "We retain our confidence in you," his father concludes. "We made you."

As punishment for his crime, Louis is sent off to a clinic. "Just looking at madness makes it real, " we hear Louis's voice explain; then we hear him screaming over a shot of a blank screen. After a slow zoom out from the "professional" rationalizations of a psychiatrist, there is a splendidly tender moment of Louis with some sort of fortune-teller. While this scene is very intimate, it is also depersonalized by Lefebvre's decision to film it from an overhead shot. As we slowly zoom down on them, we see the tops of their heads, but not their faces. They are using a deck of personalized tarot cards which Louis lays out on the table in different patterns of association which his companion attempts to explain. "It's between your father and your mother that you'll find your origins—*un pays*," she finally concludes. This statement implies far more than the actual mother and father that we see in this film. It is a recapitulation of all the antagonistic dualities that we have seen in other films—love and war, summer and winter, the country and the city, the female and the male. People do not exist in and by themselves. They exist in the spaces between themselves and other people. They exist within a kind of interpersonal circuitry that is provided by their culture. This an insight central to all the work of Jean Pierre Lefebvre.

The bulk of this section, however, consists of the cross-cutting between two different Christmases—one with Louis' family, the other with the psychiatrist who had lectured about Louis. These two Christmases are accompanied by two different kinds of traditional Québécois music. As elsewhere in the film, the music is extradiegetic. It is not directly related to the fictive space created on the screen, except at one moment in Louis' house. After all the relatives have arrived, greetings have been exchanged, and presents have been opened, the adults all begin a traditional Québécois dance. All of a sudden, this music that we have been listening to becomes appropriate for their dance. For sensitive spectators, this moment on the screen can be orgasmic.

This is the moment of synthesis, of fusion, that all Lefebvre's films are striving for. By bringing together for this Christmas celebration the sound and the image, Lefebvre creates a harmony between the traditional and the contemporary, the old and the new, the communal and the personal, the country and the city. Yet Lefebvre doesn't sentimentalize this moment. The very young children, dressed in their Christmas costumes, are not part of the dance. They are sitting in a corner mesmerized by television. This moment of fusion still contains elements that have not been absorbed.

"For two thousand years, Christmas has been a celebration of love," we heard Lefebvre's own voice saying through a television set at an earlier moment in this sequence. While not without its ironies, this comment relates to the two Christmases that we see on the screen. If the sequence with Louis' family might be described as a celebration of communal love, then the psychiatrist's sequence could be described as a celebration of erotic love. On Christmas Eve, we see him and his wife drinking wine and beginning to make love beside their Christmas tree, even though Pierrot, their young son, is crying for attention from his room upstairs.

If the young children are only partially a part of the celebrations in Louis' family's home, young Pierrot is almost totally excluded from his parents' Christmas. Earlier, we had seen him stripping the decorations off the tree and smashing them against the wall—his own small act of "vandalism" that registers his aggression. And on Christmas morning, with his newly received tricycle, he pushes over the entire tree.

This section of the film ends with a close-up of Louis, turning silently round and round within a white and black frame, as if in his clinic. Once again the sound is separated from the image. As he turns, we hear him explaining to Jean Pierre Lefebvre the different ways of dealing with aggression in the world today.

This long voice-over ends with another kind of fusion—a fusion implied between the fictive character of Louis and the actual character who is portraying him on the screen. Like the Tremblay characters in *Backyard Theatre*, Louis crosses over the line that divides reality from fiction:

> That play of mine, I wrote it for myself, to convey something important, like you're making your film. Instead of breaking windows, you make a film. As for me at that particular time, instead of breaking windows, I wrote the play because I was really fed up to the teeth!

The final section of this film is dated the 27th January. Louis has been released from the clinic and it is his seventeenth birthday. As Louis, his family, and two close friends, Louise and Bob, are sitting around a table, the camera slowly circles around behind them. This scene creates a feeling of enormous human warmth as the camera unites these people within the circular form of its own movement, the slow pace of which allows us to observe all the human gestures, the exchange of glances, the smiles, the somewhat saddened eyes. His father is proud of him for accepting his "punishment." As a reward, he offers Louis the keys to his car for a night out with his friends.

If this circular movement bound them together, the extended travelling shot of the three friends in the car separates them in subtle ways. While they are all sitting together in the front seat of the car, their eyes are all separate. Each of them is looking ahead, as if at where they are going. Yet there is also a sense that there is nowhere they can go. Whether "guilty" or not, all three young people have been subjected to the collective force of authoritarian reprisals. While there is still great warmth within this final scene, there is also a feeling of sadness, of aimlessness, of an uncertain future. Something in them has been crushed.

This feeling is intensified by the Paul Piché song that plays throughout this scene. "I'll never be eighteen, even if I live forever," the song explains. The life required by eighteen-year-olds is not the life possible in society today. Young people will always be pushed around. They will be told what to do. "And poor boy," as the song continues, "they'll say it's for your own good."

The "good" that we have witnessed in this film cannot help but have a special meaning for the Québécois. Since the humiliations inflicted upon Louis and his gang directly parallel those inflicted upon many Québécois a decade ago, *Avoir 16 ans* is emblematic of the political situation in Quebec today. At the same time, the systematized repressions, the categorization of human knowledge, and the impersonal futility of most of what is offered as secondary education throughout North America cannot help but make the film meaningful to all kinds of people. By creating a "tone poem to the prison we call adolescence," (as Jay Scott once put it[12]), Jean Pierre Lefebvre has universalized these experiences. Like all great art, *Avoir 16 ans*, while speaking directly from the specificities of its own time and culture, speaks to the world.

This is a chapter from *Jean Pierre Lefebvre* (Ottawa: Canadian Film Institute, 1981).

---

1 The film cost only $350,000.
2 The film received a good press both at Cannes and at the Festival international du film de la critique québécoise in Montréal, and there was prolonged applause from a full house at the Toronto festival screening in September 1980, where it was screened as part of the "Godard Phenomenon."
3 If funds allow it, Lefebvre hopes to shoot the third section of this trilogy in two or three years' time. It will be called *La mort du Père prodigue* and will again star Marcel Sabourin.
4 Remember the strong sense of self that characterized Patricia in *Patricia et Jean-Baptiste.*
5 These gradations of green are more noticeable on the 16mm print of this film, the stock of which often has a stronger tint of green.
6 From "Democratie" in *Les Illuminations.* See Arthur Rimbaud, *Oeuvres complètes* (Paris: Gallimard, 1972), pp. 153–154.
7 From "Un coeur sous une soutane," in *Oeuvres complètes,* op.cit., p. 195.
8 Jan Dawson, "Rimbaud est Mort," *Take One*, 5, No. 12, (Nov. 1977), p. 10.
9 Shot in cinemascope and colour, and originally planned to have stereophonic sound, the film cost $225,000. No stereo copy of this film, however, has ever been made.
10 From an unpublished copy of the script, lent to me by Lefebvre.
11 The first section of this film was titled "Polyvalence," which is close to "*polyvalente,*" the Québécois word for high school. There is nevertheless a nice irony in the fact that the word might imply a choice of values which is nowhere present in the film.
12 Jay Scott, "Quebec flavour suits European palates," *The Globe & Mail* (Toronto), May 23, 1979.

# IV

# *Film and the State: The National Film Board*

# *After Grierson: The National Film Board 1945 - 1953*

## BY PETER MORRIS

*Canadian culture in general is not so much fought for as it is found. This is especially true of Canadian cinema, whose history was virtually unknown when, in July, 1967, a fire resulted in the accidental destruction of what had been the largest single depository of archival films. For a moment, Canadian cinema seemed to be robbed forever of its past. Seventeen years later, however, that fire seems to have had the opposite effect. Not only have the national film archives been restored and expanded (as The National Film, Television and Sound Archives under the auspices of the Public Archives Canada) but the collections of films that exist throughout the country are, at last, receiving no small amount of scholarly attention.*

*Among the fruits of this new inquiry are discussions such as the following, in which Peter Morris, one of Canada's foremost film archivists and historians, examines a set of films that would in any culture be seen as central to the development of a feature film industry. Yet the proto-features made at the National Film Board in the immediate postwar period remain all but unknown to the majority of people concerned with contemporary Canadian cinema. This is unfortunate not merely because the films may be important as films but because, as Morris reports, more than a few of them are eminently watchable. Nor is their importance diminished by any imperfections they may have in the light of contemporary critical standards. If anything, the way in which these films come to terms with the Griersonian aesthetic provides a model for their descendants (who, consciously or unconsciously, are shaped by the same social realism). As Morris indicates, the manner in which the postwar* NFB *filmmakers wrestled with the Griersonian imperative went beyond the futile effort to establish a Canadian feature industry in the face of Hollywood resistance. There was, it seems, something like a group effort to establish a national style that could transcend a paucity of resources and monumental public apathy toward Canadian art of any kind. If nothing else, the* NFB *filmmakers described here provided a continuity that linked the most original aspects of Canadian production under Grierson—the "pastoral" films Morris describes—with the better known innovations of the Unit B and* cinéma direct *filmmakers to come. At their best, these films kept alive an international regard for Canadian cinema at a time when Canadians perceived their films as being little more than their government's sugar-coated public service announcements.*

Designed by John Grierson in 1939, fashioned by him during the war, the National Film Board grew from a modestly planned coordinating agency to one of the world's largest film studios, with a staff of 787 in 1945. Its achievements were remarkable: the release of over 500 films in five years; two propaganda series (*The World in Action* and *Canada Carries On*) released monthly to theatres in Canada and abroad; the establishment of non-theatrical distribution circuits that were international models; and, not least, the training of a group of young Canadian filmmakers. By 1945, when John Grierson resigned, the NFB could justifiably claim that Canada has "assumed a commanding position in the use of this great medium of human communication."[1]

But Grierson was not universally admired. Some perceived the NFB's films as being direct propaganda for the party in power, or as espousing left-wing (if not outright communist) views.[2] Even the federal government itself was, at times, distressed by the films' dabbling in foreign policy matters and the general internationalist stance of many of them.[3]

Any possible confrontation with Grierson himself was avoided when he resigned.[4] But the controversies and the ill feeling that had been generated during the war carried through the postwar years. Under film commissioner Ross McLean (acting until 1947, then fired in 1949), the NFB went through its most troubled period. The end of the war brought inevitable reductions in staff and budget.[5] And most of the experienced British and American filmmakers left with Grierson, leaving the young Canadians to develop their own programs. But it was the attacks on the NFB by individuals and groups outside it that initiated a crisis. There were accusations that the NFB was harbouring left-wing subversives, that it was wasteful, and that it was a monopoly which threatened the financial interests of commercial film producers.[6] These attacks climaxed in an article in the *Financial Post* in November 1949.[7] This article focussed the charges of the NFB's detractors and fueled a "red scare" scandal that led to the firing of Ross McLean, the appointment of Arthur Irwin as film commissioner, sweeping changes in the structure of the NFB, a new National Film Act, and the eventual return of the NFB to the politicians' good graces.[8]

Not far beneath the surface of these attacks were what one contemporary newspaper editorial bluntly characterized as "the most powerful movie interests in the world, located in Hollywood."[9] Those interests were suspicious of McLean's alleged interest in moving the NFB into feature films and television. McLean had also lobbied to decrease American domination of the Canadian film industry, and even proposed the imposition of a quota system based on the British or French models.[10] Hollywood's answer was the infamous Canadian Cooperation Project. This has been fully discussed elsewhere,[11] but it is worth noting that the lone Canadian official to raise his voice in protest was Ross McLean. One can only conclude that it is not coincidental that the orchestrated attacks on the NFB in general and on McLean in particular should have reached a peak at the same time. Nor was it coincidental that when Arthur Irwin took over as film commissioner those attacks quickly dissipated.

Arthur Irwin's primary concern seems to have been to steer the NFB away from political contention and to reorganize it on modern bureaucratic lines. Though he speaks in an interview of "restoring public confidence" in the Board,[12] it is clear that he is referring to the confidence of Ottawa politicians. (The "public" seems never to have lost confidence in the Board, as the supportive letters and briefs submitted to the Massey Commission give witness.)[13] Irwin was most pleased during his tenure that the Board's estimates were speedily passed in Parliament and that, by 1952, "there was absolutely no opposition to the Board at all."[14]

## THE FILMS

The dominant[15] approach during the war years was characteristically Griersonian: the exposition is essentially didactic, and relies principally on a voice-over narration to carry the weight of the argument. The films present a posture that is internationalist and socially aware, designed to inspire Canadians to participate fully in a global "war for men's minds." The approach has been neatly characterized as "totalitarian propaganda for the good"[16] and indeed many of the wartime films have a stridency that seems calculated more to "bludgeon the viewer into mute submission" than to stimulate reasoned reflection.[17]

Grierson also taught the young Canadians who joined the NFB that documentary, above all, must have a social purpose. There had been, before Grierson, no tradition of social documentary in Canada.[18] And if the filmmakers Grierson trained did not always adopt the Grierson style, they rarely forgot that documentary could not be separated from the community it served.

There was, under Grierson, some continuity of the "native style"[19] in Canadian documentary—though these films were invariably designed for non-theatrical release.[20] Less concerned with immediate social issues, they tend towards the observation of daily life or the exploration of the impact of our natural environment on Canadian culture and sensibility. Such films as Jane Marsh Beveridge's *Alexis Tremblay, Habitant* (1943), Budge Crawley's *Canadian Landscape* (1941), Graham McInnes' *West Wind* (1942) and James Beveridge and Michael Spencer's *Peace River* (1941) are best characterized by reference to Northrop Frye's "pastoral myth" with its "nostalgia for a world of peace and protection, with a spontaneous response to the nature around it."[21] They are clearly more identifiable with the evocative, observational approach to documentary of Robert Flaherty than with that of John Grierson—though, somewhat surprisingly, they tend to be more commentary-dependent than one would anticipate. Only in 1945 was this heavy reliance on an insistent narration abandoned. Such films as Gudrun Parker's *Listen to the Prairies* (1945) and *Children's Concert* (1950) and Pierre Petel's *Terre de Caïn/North Shore* (1948) point forward to an approach that was to become dominant in the fifties, tentatively in the *Faces of Canada* (1952-54) and *On the Spot* (1953-55) series,[22] and later in the remarkable work of Unit B that culminated in the *Candid Eye* series.

The postwar years inevitably brought changes in NFB production. The urgency of the war period dissipated and Canada slipped comfortably into an era of modest social reform under the paternal guidance of Mackenzie King's Liberal government. Consensus was the trademark: opposition tended to be viewed as radicalism and radicalism as one domestic manifestation of the communist conspiracy. Given the tenor of the times and, more particularly, the attacks on the Board under film commissioner Ross McLean, it is hardly surprising that the filmmakers tended to avoid any openly didactic or analytic approach to social issues. Certainly, the internationalist stance of the Grierson years disappeared.[23] Mackenzie King was more of an isolationist than an internationalist, and the Board's one major foray onto the international scene (*The People Between*, 1947, on the plight of refugees during the civil war in China) ran into problems with the department of external affairs.[24]

That the filmmakers tended to avoid contention under Ross McLean (and even more so under Arthur Irwin) is not to imply that social issues were not dealt with. Indeed, in the postwar years, the *range* of such issues was actually increased. There were films on drug addiction, mental health, women in the work force, trade unions, cooperatives, social workers and immigration—all more or less sensitive topics. Some of these films were designed specifically to illustrate Liberal government policies, but there were others initiated by the Board itself.

On the other hand, whole areas of social concern were ignored. There were, for example, no films on the congenital poor or the radically dispossessed, on corruption in politics or on the problems of Canada's native peoples. But such films would not have been made under Grierson either. More than anyone, Grierson was aware that production within a state-sponsored film studio was dependent on "the degree of sanction by the party in power."[25]

In the postwar films it is possible to discern three different methods of exposition. The classical documentary style (commentary-dependent with dynamically edited images of illustration), introduced under Grierson, of course continued. So, too, did the "native" observational tradition. But a third approach, different from the classical or observational, became dominant in the postwar years.[26] This approach straddles the ground between fiction and documentary, drawing on the syntax or conventions of both. The films are, evidently, scripted dramatizations involving performers (actors or non-actors) playing roles. Yet, just as clearly, they offer themselves for consideration in terms of what one can only call their documentary significance. They make the same claim to social truth or social reality as does the documentary, yet do so within a fictionalized format. Arguably, they are films whose antecedents can be found in earlier Canadian films, and that anticipate later Canadian documentary dramas.[27]

The use of dramatizations or reenactments was not at all unknown in documentary. Several British documentaries in the thirties and such earlier Canadian films as Dick Bird's *This Generation* (1934) and Stuart Legg's *The Case of Charlie Gordon* (1939) had made use of the technique. But, of the wartime Canadian films, only Julian Roffman's *13 Platoon* (1942) and Robert Edmond's *Coal Face, Canada* (1943) appear to anticipate the postwar approach, the former in its attempt to have real people "act" themselves within a fictional format, the latter in its attempt to use a fictional framework that would embrace the documentary significance of social truth.

The characteristics of the postwar films, and their application at that time, seem strongly rooted in their own period and appear to have their origin in an attempt not only to redefine documentary but to engage with issues of fiction filmmaking.

## STAGING THE REAL

Only two films of the period, *The Boy Who Stopped Niagara* and *L'homme aux oiseaux/The Bird Fancier*, might properly be considered true fiction films, in that they are primarily story films with no apparent claim to documentary significance. (One might also include Roger Blais' *Each Man's Son* and *L'avocat de la défense*—which dramatize extracts from novels of Hugh MacLennan and André Giroux respectively—were each not framed in the context of an educational discussion of their respective author's significance.) *The Boy Who Stopped Niagara* (1947) was written and directed by Leslie McFarlane and financed and released by the Rank Organization. It is a whimsical fantasy about a small boy who accidentally turns off hydro power across Ontario during a visit to Niagara Falls. Chaos results and the poor boy is pursued by vengeful citizens until it all turns out to be just a dream. Though elaborately staged (both in the studio and on location) and with a large cast (both professionals and non-professionals), it is not particularly memorable. Its significance in retrospect is more in terms of its standing as witness to the desire of some NFB filmmakers to broaden the role of the NFB into fiction films—a desire inevitably opposed by those "powerful interests" discussed earlier.

*L'homme aux oiseaux* (1952), directed by Bernard Devlin and Jean Palardy from an original script by novelist Roger Lemelin, is an anecdotal story about a Quebec City "character" who enjoys his freedom and prefers taking walks and watching birds to the routines of a daily job. After being fired, he explores other alternatives but rejects them all. As his wife frantically searches the city for him, he decides to run away to sea, but ends up working on the local ferry boat. It was apparently well received by audiences, and went on to win a Canadian Film Award. If one might now criticize its "folkloric," quaint, characters, at the time its freshness and appeal undoubtedly stemmed from its use of the Quebec accent and its lightness of touch—both then rare characteristics of NFB films.

There is another group of films that include dramatized sections or reenactments in the traditional manner. Jean Palardy's *Marée montante/The Rising Tide* (1949) is a typical example. This film on the cooperative movement in the Maritimes has a long dramatized section recreating the historical development of the movement in the twenties and thirties, but its opening and closing sequences are in the classic style of voice-over narration with illustrative images. There is in these sections (and in most of the classic style NFB documentaries of the period) a clutter of expository detail that seems to mitigate against viewer comprehension.

The social dramas—dramatizations to explore particular social issues or to convey information—work differently. Individualized characters act out the point to be made; a narrative structure ameliorates the didactic tone of the classical documentary. Though the films invariably make use, to greater or lesser extents, of a voice-over narrator (in the manner discussed below), the essential points are made through the *action* within the film; the narrators serve as summarizers, hosts or guides.

Of the social dramas the following may be taken as typical: Donald Mulholland's *File 1365: The Connors Case* (1947), Robert Anderson's several films in the *Mental Mechanisms* series, including *The Feeling of Rejection* (1947), *The Feeling of Hostility* (1948), *Over-dependency* (1949), and *Feelings of Depression* (1950), Julian Biggs' *The Son (1951),* and Bernard Devlin's *L'abatis/The Settler* (1953).[28]

*File 1365: The Connors Case* (which gained wide theatrical release) dramatizes a "typical" case for the RCMP: a man is killed, and through their nation-wide facilities the Mounties finally get their man. The film begins in a courtroom, moves back in time to show the origins of the crime (though the crime itself is not shown), and then focuses on the attempts first to trace, then to track down the murderer. Every scene was staged and acted with a narrator (John Drainie speaking in the royal "we" for the Mounties), providing a link between events.

The *Mental Mechanisms* films each dramatize the case history of an individual with a psychic problem that interferes with his or her social relations. Each narrative highlights crisis moments in that individual's life, with a narrator relating each event to another and explicating the meaning as the story progresses. Invariably, the focus of the individual's problem is shifted back onto that person's family. Some of the individuals depicted (as in *Over-dependency*) are easily recognizable as having a "problem." But others (as in *The Feeling of Hostility*) seem like well-adjusted people; only as the narrative progresses do we begin to discern the emotional and psychic problem and how it is affecting that person's life. Though the films have the overall impression of being a collection of vignettes of a person's life, these vignettes often make striking use of a complex association of sound and image. As Richard Griffith noted: "In them a door, a chair, a flower come to life: the noise of traffic or a poster outside a movie house pulse with meanings directly connected with the psychic experience of the individual under analysis. In this they resemble the old German 'instinct' films."[29] Several of the *Mental Mechanisms* films won awards, and all of them enjoyed a wide distribution and use for almost thirty years.

*The Son* is the most curious drama. It was ostensibly made because of the number of young people leaving the family farm.[30] That seems unlikely on the surface and, if true, the conclusion of the film can only be read as somewhat bizarre. It begins and ends in the context of a small town where (as one inhabitant in voice-over tells us), "everyone's got problems, but life goes on." Eli Mandel has noted that the small town is often evoked, nostalgically, as "a place of childhood."[31] And, indeed, the small town setting does provide a symbolic backdrop to the story of childhood that develops. The film then focuses on an obviously unhappy young man who is picking up supplies. Back at the farm he has a discussion with his father over a cow, a discussion in which there is evidently an undercurrent of buried aggression and tension. The young man (who turns out to be twenty-nine) wanders off into a field. In flashback, we see scenes of his childhood that represent a classic father-son psychic conflict. The father puts down the son, refuses to allow him pride in what he does, refuses to allow him to participate in the job of running the farm, and later uses him as cheap labour. The psychological conflict between father and son reaches its peak when the son announces he's had enough and wants to leave. But the psychic conflict (a classical "family romance" in Freud's terms) is given a bizarre resolution. The mother (virtually absent from the story) intervenes and suggests that the father legally sign over part of the property to the son. Quickly they go to a lawyer and the final scenes imply that happiness and harmony have been restored. A family conflict has effectively become an economic conflict, easily resolved by reference to the law.

*The Settler*, in retrospect, seems the strongest of all the social dramas. Using first person narration, it depicts the settlement of the Abitibi region of Quebec during the Depression, and eloquently conveys not only the backbreaking work and agony involved, but the paradox of attempting to "tame" the wilderness. It was planned initially by Bernard Devlin and Raymond Garceau as a feature-length film (based on Hervé Biron's *Nuages sur les brûlés*), but adequate funding was not available. (Devlin was later to make a feature length version for television under the title *Les brûlés/The Promised Land.*)

Though a range of styles is involved in these films, they do share several common characteristics. In a discussion of the *Mental Mechanisms* films, Richard Griffith pointed out some of these: "[They] have borrowed from all that has been learnt about the sound film and then have made a fresh start. Their vivid impact seems to stem most immediately from editing and, behind that, from writing so careful and foresighted as to leave no visual effect to chance. Yet they give no sense of having been staged. They use non-actors, their material is the ordinary routine of everyday life."[32]

This assessment could well be applied to all the social dramas. They have an elaborated visual style that clearly relies heavily on careful pre-scripting and pre-production. Their syntax derives from the then well-established Hollywood approach to narrative and involves both smooth shooting and editing in a manner that appears transparent and natural. Lighting is used to give depth to the image yet never draws attention to itself. (Occasionally even chiaroscuro lighting is used as in the contemporary film noir.) Editing creates a spatial and temporal unity in each sequence, yet never allows its seams to show. The stories themselves are redolent of film melodramas of the period: only "crisis points" in the story are depicted, so that attention cannot flag. (The *Mental Mechanisms* films are particular examples of this, since we are shown only "key" moments in, often, a whole psychic lifetime.)

Yet, for all this, they are nothing like Hollywood films—not even the short film dramas of the period, such as the *Crime Does Not Pay* series, which would appear to be the closest relative to *File 1365*. Griffith suggests "they give no sense of having been staged." But this assessment ignores the fact that they *were* staged. It might be better argued that they do not present themselves as *individualized* stories (as the classic fiction film does), but suggest that what is depicted is *generalizable*. The *Mental Mechanisms* films imply that it is not one individual problem we are seeing (as we are in Hitchcock's *Spellbound*, for example), but that such feelings are common and that their origin can be traced and treated. *File 1365* implies that it is not only depicting a unique story, but that all police work is reflected in it. (It is interesting to note that we are only shown the police point of view, in contrast to, say, the *Crime Does Not Pay* films.) Similar arguments can be applied to the other films: *Local 100* (this is how unions are formed), or even *The Son* (which, as argued above, would lead us to conclude that the problem of sons leaving the family farm stems from psychic repression and can be solved by recourse to economics and the law). Other social dramas such as *Drug Addict* or *The Settler* are already generalized in their structure and focus only minimally on individualized characters.

The classical documentary depicts or implies a generalized reality or social truth. The NFB's social dramas make the same appeal. But they draw also upon the documentary for their syntax; they derive their styles from assumptions as to how their images will be read by an audience. The characteristics that contribute to the connotation of "not having been staged" include the use of locations rather than studio sets, the acting styles, and the use of narration. Each of these elements, separately and in concert, helps carry the signification "this is real."

Though constructed studio sets were occasionally used, the films were shot mostly on location. This was, of course, a characteristic of documentary (though not of most fiction films at the time) and was also being applied contemporaneously by the Italian neo-realists and, to some extent, by British filmmakers in the Ealing Studios. There is no doubt that the use of locations (for example, the street scenes in *Drug Addict* or the cafe scene in *File 1365*, in which a busy Toronto street is visible through the window), help carry the signification of "reality." One might argue (as has been done in relation to neo-realism) that the preference for locations was one of necessity in that the NFB (like the Italians) did not have access to elaborate shooting stages. But the impulse, for the NFB filmmakers at least, seems to have come from documentary and the influence of Grierson. "The shinsham mechanics of the studio" and "acted stories against artificial backgrounds"[33] were anathema to Grierson, who preferred "the living scene and the living story."[34] Given this—and the postwar reaction to Hollywood's economic domination—it seems unlikely that Canadian filmmakers would have consciously adopted the Hollywood approach in any case.

The use of voice-over narration has its origins, too, in the classical documentary's use of a (usually male) voice-of-authority narrator to clarify the exposition and explain the theme. This convention of the classical, expository documentary was carried over into the social dramas—though, as noted in a British journal, Canadians "lost their terrible Transatlantic habit of making their commentators scream at the audience until it is bludgeoned into mute submission . . . and they write these same commentaries with a skill we rarely reach."[35] Occasionally the narrators of the social dramas are relatable to on-screen characters or events (as in *File 1365*, *The Settler*, *Local 100* and *The Son*). More commonly (as in the *Mental Mechanisms* films), the narrator retains his traditional stance of authority, clarifying and explaining points in the film.

Narration serves the practical purpose of bridging time and place and of describing off-screen events. More significantly, narrators reassure the viewer that the events on the screen are (as in a documentary) of more than individual significance.

The appeal to a generalizable reality is further reinforced by the almost invariable use of the "historic present" tense in the commentaries. The effect here is not only (as often argued) to accentuate the immediacy of the events, but also to deny the events any specificity of their own (as particular events in the past) and to imply that what is said is a general truth. An interesting exception to this is *The Settler*. Here, the use of the past tense reinforces the film's strength (and, arguably, weakens its generalizability as an issue of social concern), since we are made aware that the events happened "in history."

The acting in these social dramas is perhaps the oddest element. At first glance it seems merely appalling—inappropriately stiff and unnatural. The performers *were*, with a few exceptions, "non-actors" (real people playing themselves or non-professional actors playing roles). But this was also a mark of neo-realism and has always been considered one of its special strengths. One might assume that the filmmakers involved simply did not know how to direct actors. But, given that British and American critics of the time actually praised the "non-acting" in the NFB films, one is impelled to look for an alternative explanation.

It seems likely that the approach derives yet again from documentary syntax. In documentaries in the thirties when real people were allowed (rarely) to speak on the screen, they were invariably supplied with a script.[36] This was presumably done on the assumption that people unused to a camera would "freeze" as soon as it was turned on—an assumption difficult to credit in our era, when virtually anybody is happy to chat freely in front of a camera. The result, predictably, was a stiff and unnatural delivery which, in turn, came to connote a "real" person on screen as opposed to an actor, whose delivery would be "natural." In the NFB's social dramas the artificiality of the acting appears to be offered as yet another signification of "the real." In other words, the actors in the social dramas were not supposed to be read by the viewer as "actors" but as real characters plucked from life, as in a documentary. The viewer is invited to react with, "You can see he's a *real* policeman because he obviously can't act."

One further characteristic should be added: The images are presented to the viewer as though they were actuality, as though the events were not designed for the camera but vice-versa. They simulate the effect of actuality filming. The camera tends to remain at a diffident distance from the action; medium and long shots are common, facial close-ups relatively rare. Though editing is used to create spatial unity (as in the classical Hollywood manner), actions are presented as though recorded in real time. (A sense of duration has often been cited as one of the marks by which the "truthfulness/faithfulness" of an image can be judged.) Cross-cutting between parallel actions tends to be avoided. For example, in *File 1365* the events are followed only from the Mountie's viewpoint; we know nothing of the pursued except what the pursuer knows. This effect is so strong that when pursuer and pursued finally confront each other and classical cross-cutting is used, it is as though a note of artificiality were introduced.

The NFB's social dramas, then, seem to be attempts to stage a semblance of the real, to depict a social totality within a narrative framework. Their syntax derives from contemporary conventions of both documentary and fiction films. Their appeal is to a generalized reality.

The generalized reality offered was, of course, a rather particular one. In retrospect, its ideology is clearly characteristically postwar Canadian. Social change is possible and desirable but should be gradual. Everyone has a place in Canadian society and everyone should be in his/her place. Canada is a well-managed society and problems arise only when people do not trust the managers to manipulate the levers of the system on their behalf.[37]

The films deal with social issues (even contentious ones: *Drug Addict* had censorship difficulties in the United States because of its thesis that drug addiction was a medical problem, not a criminal one). But the treatment of those issues tends to merely displace the problem into other, safer areas. The *Mental Mechanisms* films remove the stigma of mental illness from the individual concerned (it's not his/her fault) and focus it on the family. But in doing so they merely displace the guilt from one individual to other individuals (it's the parents' fault) and fail to hint at the social root of those "feelings." *The Son* implies that deeply rooted psychic conflicts can be solved by recourse to economics and the law. *The Settler* makes no mention of why such an extraordinary resettlement policy was necessary.

One might note also the kinds of people presented in the films as "ordinary Canadians." These tend to be from the middle or lower middle classes: professionals (teachers, bank clerks, editors), skilled workers, or rural workers (who are associated with the prestige of the land). Unskilled industrial workers or the chronically unemployed had no place in NFB films. It is not hard to speculate on the origins of this. The filmmakers themselves were generally middle class intellectuals. Though they honestly wanted to depict "ordinary" Canadians and deal with issues of relevance to them, these "ordinary" people were those on their own social scale, or immediately beneath them.

But not all the films lack built-in criticisms of the system. *File 1365*, for all its evident paean of praise to the Mounties, contains odd anomalies: The accused is assumed to be guilty throughout, though no evidence is offered save his having been in the victim's car; a drawing at the end shows the Mounties rather viciously suppressing Indians; the plain clothes Mounties are suggestive of rather threatening SS men; a jackbooted Mountie strides down a deserted street. It is interesting to recall that this film was made at a time when NFB filmmakers were under investigation by the Mounties as potential subversives.

## ORIGINS OF THE APPROACH

Why would NFB filmmakers turn to social dramas in the postwar years? A simple cause and effect relationship is conceptually difficult to identify, since many variables were simultaneously interacting. The filmmakers operated within the smaller social framework of the NFB (with all that implies in terms of decision-making) and within both the larger social entity of the country and the international intellectual currents of their time. They were subject to influences, yet may have remained partially or wholly unaffected. The conceptual and practical difficulties involved in trying to trace the origins of a "style" are enormous. Yet, given this caveat, one can tentatively identify the following as key elements: the reaction to Grierson's approach to documentary during the war; the Canadian postwar interest in feature filmmaking and the negative impact of the Canadian Cooperation Project; the international postwar shift toward more "realism" in films, most particularly the British concern for the alliance of fiction and documentary, exemplified best in the films from Ealing Studios.

Grierson's influence on the young filmmakers' conception of their role was total: Film was most properly used as a tool of social communications. But on the form and shape of that "tool" there were differences—differences that began to surface mostly after Grierson's departure. As Roger Blais remarked in a recent interview, "When the master left we tried to cut the umbilical cord."[38] Credits began appearing on all films (something discouraged during Grierson's tenure), and more attention was paid to technical polish, to aesthetic priorities. Attempts were made to develop new approaches which, while still acknowledging Grierson's dictum that documentary was "the creative treatment of actuality," tried to broaden its base. It seems clear that the filmmakers were determined to prove that, though they could learn from "the Master," they were not mere slavish imitators. Reviewers of the time noted the changes and, as one of them acknowledged, though "still mostly anonymous," the achievements of the young Canadians "are already comparable with advanced, experienced, film work anywhere in the world."[39]

In these developments, Ross McLean played an important role. Though not as politically astute as Grierson, he seems to have been far more receptive to the notion of producing films that were not merely (or not only) educational and informational. He envisaged the Board, and Canadian film production generally, as "an expression of the Canadian ethos"[40] which, like painting and music, should contribute to Canadian culture. McLean was interested in moving the Board into fiction films and television, and he considered that the production of feature films in Canada was a viable option.[41] If that was not possible within the Board (or anywhere else in Canada as a result of the Canadian Cooperation Project), then the dramatic form might still be applied to shorter films that fell within the Board's mandate. McLean undoubtedly encouraged Don Mulholland and others to experiment with dramatizations of "real events."[42]

The possibility of feature film production was discussed within the Board and at least some filmmakers were interested in becoming involved in it—even though they knew this was likely to be impossible at the NFB itself.[43] It is interesting to speculate whether those filmmakers who made social dramas would have become active in feature film production had the Canadian Cooperation Project not stifled that option. Given the NFB style that evolved, it seems possible that the features they would have made would also have attempted to blend fiction and actuality.

This notion, indeed, was one of the international currents in postwar cinema. The impulse toward increased authenticity and realism (however problematic this might seem in retrospect) found expression in many countries, notably in Italy in neo-realism, and in Britain in both the application of a documentary syntax to feature length, scripted stories during the war and in the later films of Ealing Studios. The British experience seems most directly relevant to the NFB. British critics and such producers as Michael Balcon reasoned that British films ought to fuse documentary with narrative.[44] Documentary, it was claimed, necessarily had an impulse toward recording authentic life and reality, but, alone, it tended toward didacticism and lacked human appeal. But fusing it with a fictional narrative, and fiction's emphasis on individual values, could provide an empathetic link with reality. What was necessary was to "make the real world seem exciting."[45] The basic thrust was neatly summarized in 1946 by a British critic: "This new down-to-earth style [would rely] on a central narrative and a stressing of human values and relations rather than on a series of images for their own sakes related to each other by montage and cutting (the old fancy style of documentary)."[46]

The relevance of this to the NFB's social dramas is apparent. It is, however, unclear whether the Canadians were directly influenced by the British films and critical writings or whether they evolved their approach in parallel tandem. The Canadians did have access to British film magazines and almost certainly saw the British films. But the Canadian films, though similar in their syntax and strategies to the British films, are very different in effect.

As John Ellis has noted, " 'real people in real situations' is not simply proposing a certain kind of cinematic style, it is equally a social proposal."[47] Where the British films leaned toward what Balcon called "mild protest"[48] against the establishment, the Canadian films reflect a comfortable liberalism. No protest is implied, nor apparently necessary[49]; the guiding dictum need only be "peace, order and good government." But some of the "real people in real situations" who had no place on NFB screens speak eloquently by their absence.[50]

The ideas and arguments advanced here were developed during a seminar course (Film 422) on the postwar NFB at the Department of Film Studies, Queen's University. I am indebted to those students who participated and who contributed much towards my own understanding of the period. Some of the papers written for this course are specifically acknowledged below.

1 National Film Board, *Annual Report* (Ottawa: King's Printer, 1947).

2 C. Rodney James, *Film as a National Art: NFB of Canada and the Film Board Idea* (New York: Arno Press, 1977), pp. 126-34.

3 Piers Handling, "Censorship and Scares," *Cinema Canada*, No. 56 (June-July 1979), pp. 27-8, and reprinted in this volume.

4 Grierson's career outside Canada was by no means easy, especially following his implication in the Gouzenko spy scandal. See, especially, Kirwan Cox, "The Grierson Files," *Cinema Canada*, No. 56 (June-July 1979), pp. 16-24.

5 C.R. James, op.cit., p. 129.

6 Ibid., pp. 134-41; P. Handling, op.cit., pp. 29-30.

7 Kenneth Wilson, "Film Board Monopoly Facing Test?," *Financial Post*, Toronto, November 17, 1949.

8 C.R. James, op.cit., pp. 141-53; "A View from the Top: Interview with Arthur Irwin," *Cinema Canada*, No. 56 (June-July 1979), pp. 37-41; Basil Wright, "Documentary: Flesh, Fowl, or . . .?" *Sight and Sound*, 19 (March 1950), p. 43; Gerald Pratley, "Canada's National Film Board," *Quarterly of Film, Radio and Television*, 8, No. 1 (Fall 1953), pp. 20-3; Mark Henderson, Shelley Stuart, "The Origins and Motivations of the Commercial Film Industry Attacks on the National Film Board," unpublished paper submitted in Film 422, Department of Film Studies, Queen's University, 1979.

9 *Ottawa Citizen*, December 28, 1949.

10 P. Handling, op.cit., pp. 29-30.

11 Pierre Berton, *Hollywood's Canada: the Americanisation of Our National Image* (Toronto: McClelland and Stewart, 1975), pp. 167-91; Maynard Collins, "Co-operation, Hollywood, and Howe," *Cinema Canada*, No. 56 (June-July 1979), pp. 34-6.

12 "A View from the Top: Interview with Arthur Irwin," loc. cit., p.41.

13 C.R. James, op.cit., p. 153; G. Pratley, op.cit., pp. 20-1.

14 "A View from the Top: Interview with Arthur Irwin," loc. cit., p. 41.

15 By "dominant" I do not refer to those films that were necessarily the most dominant numerically, but to those films to which the studio paid the most attention (in terms of production and promotion), which were given the widest release, and to which the most critical attention was paid, in Canada and abroad.

16 Gary Evans, "The Politics of Propaganda," *Cinema Canada*, No. 56 (June-July 1979), pp. 12-15.

17 *Documentary Film News*, 7, No. 70 (November-December 1948), p. 119.

18 One important exception here would be the work of Evelyn Spice Cherry and Lawrence Cherry in the nineteen thirties on the Prairies.

19 Ernst Borneman, "Documentary Films: World War II," in Seth Feldman and Joyce Nelson (eds.), *Canadian Film Reader* (Toronto: Peter Martin Associates, 1977).

20 This does not necessarily imply that they had small audiences, since the non-theatrical circuits developed by Don Buchanan during the war were expressly designed to increase accessibility to NFB films and achieved remarkable successes. Unfortunately, budget cuts in the postwar years necessitated the abandonment of many of these circuits. See: C.A. Gray, *Movies for the People: The Story of the National Film Board's Unique Distribution System* (Montreal: National Film Board, 1973); Maryjane Martin, "The National Film Board and its Audience," unpublished paper submitted in Film 422, Department of Film Studies, Queen's University, 1979.

21 Northrop Frye, "Conclusion to *A Literary History of Canada*," reprinted in *The Bush Garden, Essays on the Canadian Imagination* (Toronto: House of Anansi, 1971), p. 245.

22 *On the Spot* was a remarkable attempt at "instant filmmaking" involving synchronous sound location shooting in a manner that clearly anticipates direct cinema. *Faces of Canada* also largely abandoned the omniscient narrator, allowing the characters to speak (in voice-over), either directly as in *Dick Hickey, Blacksmith*, or via an actor as in *Paul Tomkowitz: Street Railway*

*Switchman* and *The Charwoman* (which, astonishingly, uses a male voice for the central character).

23 G. Evans, op.cit., p. 15.

24 P. Handling, op.cit., pp. 28-9, C.R. James, op.cit., p.133.

25 Forsyth Hardy (ed.), *Grierson on Documentary* (London: Collins, 1946), p. 241. Grierson tries to distinguish between the "sanction" of the government and the "sanction" of Parliament and to argue for the *responsibilities* of government, but he is clearly pointing out that those who pay the bills inevitably set the standards. The documentarist can only hope that "inefficiency and frustration" don't result from a too partisan interference.

One important point to note here is that response to government policies need not necessarily, or not only, involve the transmission of direct orders from government to filmmakers. Within the NFB (or any other government institution), much depends on what those involved assume their political masters might want. This notion, described as "anticipatory policy reflex" by political scientists, is a most important one in terms of understanding the particular stance and tone of films produced within the NFB at any given time. See: Leslie Anderson, Michael Calich, Katy Hennessey, "The Relationship of NFB Production to Government Policies 1945-1953," unpublished paper submitted in Film 422, Department of Film Studies, Queen's University, 1979. The Board's failure to tackle controversial issues was noted at the time. See especially: Gerald Pratley, op.cit, p. 25.

26 See note 15, above, regarding the use of "dominant."

27 The most obvious examples here are several Canadian feature films of the sixties, though both intent and approach are significantly different. For a discussion of earlier films see: Peter Morris, *Embattled Shadows* (Montreal: McGill-Queen's University Press, 1978), pp. 240-241.

28 Other examples: Don Mulholland's *Accidents Don't Happen* series (1945-48); Robert Anderson's *Drug Addict* (1948), Gudrun Parker's *Opera School* (1951) and *A Musician in the Family* (1953), Bernard Devlin's *Local 100* (1950), and Morton Parker's *Labour in Canada* series. Stanley Jackson's *Shyness* (1953) is somewhat different, since it involves a personalized narration over scenes that are partly staged, partly actuality.

29 Paul Rotha, in collaboration with Sinclair Road and Richard Griffith, *Documentary Film* (London: Faber and Faber, 1952), p. 338.

30 C.R. James, op.cit., p. 168.

31 Quoted in Robert Fothergill, "A Place Like Home," in Seth Feldman and Joyce Nelson (eds.), op.cit., p. 356.

32 P. Rotha, op.cit., p. 338.

33 F. Hardy (ed.), op.cit., p. 80.

34 Ibid.

35 *Documentary Film News*, 7, No. 70 (November-December 1948), p. 119.

36 A Canadian example that might be cited is the committee meeting in Lawrence Cherry's *Soil for Tomorrow* (1945).

37 This argument applies, of course, to NFB films other than the social dramas. An analysis of individual films and their orientation is not included here but see Heather Moffat, "The *Mental Mechanisms* Series: It's Origins and Method of Production," unpublished paper submitted to Film 422, Department of Film Studies, Queen's University, 1979. See also: L. Anderson, M. Calich, K. Hennessey, op.cit.

38 Blais interviewed by Nick Gray and Elio Pennino, March 29, 1979.

39 P. Rotha, op.cit., p. 336. See also various reviews of NFB films in *Documentary Film News* and *The Monthly Film Bulletin*.

40 McLean interviewed by Nick Gray and Elio Pennino, March 28, 1979.

41 P. Handling, op.cit., p. 29. For a general overview of postwar Canadian interest in feature films see Anthony Dawson "Motion Picture Production in Canada," *Hollywood Quarterly*, 5, No. 1 (Fall 1950), pp. 83-99.

42 C.R. James, op.cit., p. 287. It might be noted that Grierson tended to disapprove of fiction films and at one time is reputed to have suggested that Canadians who wanted to make fiction films should go to New York.

43 Nick Gray, Elio Pennino, "What Features, What Films?," unpublished paper submitted to Film 422, Department of Film Studies, Queen's University, 1979.

44 See especially: John Ellis, "Made in Ealing," *Screen*, 16, No. 1 (Spring 1975), p. 78; John

Ellis, "Art, Culture and Quality–Terms for a Cinema in the Forties and Seventies," *Screen*, 19, No. 3 (Autumn 1978), p. 9.
45 Quoted in J. Ellis, "Made in Ealing," p. 108.
46 Quoted in J. Ellis, "Art, Culture, and Quality," p. 33.
47 J. Ellis, "Made in Ealing," p. 118.
48 Ibid. p. 119.
49 With the possible exception of the implicit (though not explicit) criticisms in *File 1365*.
50 It might be noted that the social drama approach continued in, notably, the *Perspectives* television series (1955-58). There are, though, significant differences in both syntax and ideology that deserve a separate analysis.

# *Censorship and Scares*

## BY PIERS HANDLING

*The latitude given any media agency by the government that funds it is perhaps a gift of questionable worth. At the very least, creative freedom is given by a government with a firm realization of the distinction between the permanence of film and the volatility of political consensus. The invitation to explore a nation and its people at public expense has the potential of being a trap for those brazen enough to accept the challenge.*

*In few instances have the dangers of public sponsorship of a creative institution been more apparent than in the forty-five year history of the federal government's relationship to the National Film Board, and in turn, the Board's relationship to its employees. As Piers Handling recounts in this study, the* NFB*'s first run-ins with the censor grew out of errors of enthusiasm. Hyping Mackenzie King to a sceptical public was in itself a thankless task. But to be the only wartime media producers denied the right to sell their own leader must have proven especially frustrating to the Board's fast-developing corps of young propagandists.*

*In the years immediately following the war it was inevitable that the Board's social democratic geopolitics would clash with the prevailing cold war mentality. Praise of our Soviet allies had been a bit too sincere; honest examinations of the situation in China a bit too honest. The result, as Handling contends, was the toll taken by the Red Scare, a toll that extended far beyond a bureaucratic reshuffling and the dismissal of three luckless Film Board workers. The Red Scare injected a certain fear into the manner in which the* NFB*'s hierarchy would oversee its mandated inquiry into all aspects of Canadian life. A political pragmatism that had once been dodged or manipulated was now internalized. As Handling demonstrates, that pragmatism led to a long series of disputes with the best and brightest of the Board's filmmakers. It was enough to drive out a generation of Québécois and to cast a shadow on any meaningful alliance between the Board and politically progressive Canadians. And, of course, it was counterproductive. Nothing the Board's censors wished to hide stayed hidden; if anything, the official repression lent new determination to the repressed.*

*If, in the last analysis, anyone has suffered from the censorship described here it has been those filmmakers who were not attacked either from inside or outside the Board. Rightfully or not, it is too easy to label the work of the noncontroversial workaday* NFB *directors as safe, in-house products. It is an image that extends to the Board per se. But it is also an image that may be beginning to change. If recent brushes with the Ontario Board of Censors (*Not a Love Story*), the American State Department (*If You Love This Planet, Acid From Heaven, Acid Rain*), the Toronto police (*Home Feeling*) and veteran's groups (*Billy Bishop Goes to War*) are any indications of a trend, then we could yet see the restoration of a lively, contentious* NFB. *But as Handling shows here, there is a lot of history that will have to be overcome.*

*Re the National Film Board's classic of inept, inaccurate and outrageously expensive filmmaking, No Act of God (*NFB *Rejects Pressure to Ban Anti-Atomic Film — Nov. 23).*

*My "demand" that it be withdrawn was not made on the grounds that it was biased and incorrect. The* NFB *has already acknowledged the first charge and can hardly deny the second in view of the evidence provided it . . . .*

*The grounds for my complaint were that as the custodian of film footage for Atomic Energy of Canada Ltd., the* NFB *had taken footage and maliciously misused it . . . .*

A.R. Burge
Director, Public Affairs
Atomic Energy of Canada Ltd., Ottawa

*N.M. Ediger (letter, Nov. 29) accuses the National Film Board of bias in producing and distributing No Act of God, and implies that tax money is going to present problems of nuclear power while none is going to present advantages. This is not so. The* NFB *distributes at least six films commissioned by Atomic Energy of Canada Ltd. (i.e., produced with taxpayer money) presenting nuclear power in a very favourable light. If Mr. Ediger is really concerned about equal representation on both sides of the nuclear question, he should be calling for more films on the problems of nuclear power . . . .*

*With this in mind, it is difficult to take Mr. Ediger's complaint about one-sided information seriously.*

Jan Marmorek
Energy Probe
Toronto

Both letters appeared in *The Globe and Mail* December 2, 1978.

The uproar over *No Act of God* is the most recent in a line of political controversies in which the Film Board has been submerged throughout its history. There are perhaps more illustrious predecessors which caused far more furore in their day. Denys Arcand's documentary on the textile industry in Quebec, *On est au coton*, was banned in 1971, ostensibly over its factual inaccuracies. But more to the point, its position had shocked the textiles lobby into insisting on its withdrawal. The ensuing publicity, apart from establishing Arcand's reputation, ended in the banning of the film. But numerous video "bootleg" copies were circulated throughout Quebec, and in fact, although under censure, it became one of the most widely seen Film Board films in the province. A year later Gilles Groulx's *24 heures ou plus* was similarly banned, although this time the Board's management had learned its lesson—it never allowed a composite print to be made, and stored the elements in different warehouses. This film called for the overthrow of the present government, a position that the film commissioner of the day, Sydney Newman, found indefensible, coming as it did from a government agency. There are other interesting episodes, one example being Mick Scott's *The Winner* (also known as *Albert, la grenouille*), made as part of a language training series which gleefully satirized the whole concept of bilingualism. Newman was enraged by it, and Scott describes it as a film "totally in bad taste and meant to be." It has never been seen outside the Film Board. Another example is Jacques Leduc's black and pessimistic *Cap d'espoir*—withheld by film commissioner Hugo McPherson in 1969—described by Leduc as "a film about the despair which floated in the air in Quebec a year before the October Crisis. It was about the muted violence that existed and about the monopoly over news held by Power Corp."[1] Arcand succinctly summarized his and Leduc's position: "The Film Board makes thousands of films to marized his and Leduc's position: "The Film Board makes thousands of films to say that all goes well in Canada, that the western wheat fields are very beautiful, that Glenn Gould plays the piano well and that Paul Anka is an extraordinary star. So I think it is just normal that there should now and then be a film which says that everything is rotten and that we live in a country that is corrupt from top to bottom."[2]

There are other more insidious, less transparent cases. Don Brittain and John Kemeny's *Bethune* was a courageous film, dealing with the famed surgeon, made in 1963 and 1964. The Department of External Affairs was cool to the idea, perhaps afraid of offending the Americans. The Board did not give the film its official sanction. External Affairs refused to carry prints in its embassies. In the mid-sixties, post-Cuba era, it was risqué to admit that there had been a Canadian communist. Robin Spry's *Action: The October Crisis of 1970* had its share of problems. The Board of Governors, amidst other objections, insisted that the final line of narration be dropped. Originally Spry's script stated that the 1970 crisis involved a painful loss of innocence for Canada; however the question still remains—will Quebec separate? The second half of this statement was taken out, placing the final emphasis on Canada, not Quebec.

In the late fifties, Groulx had made a film on a mining town which was overtly critical of the economic and social realities that dominated this particular community. The people in *Normétal* were shown to be slaves of the mine, dominated by an economic enterprise which essentially did not serve their best interests. Groulx's original cut of the film ran to forty minutes. But it encountered difficulties, running, as it did, counter to the prevailing economic philosophy of the day. Groulx cut the film to thirty minutes, but this was still not satisfactory. The board cut it to its present length of seventeen minutes; Groulx refused to attach his name to this version.

Ten years later Pierre Perrault presented the Board with *Un pays sans bon sens! ou Wake Up, Mes bons amis!!!* The message was simple: the people of Quebec will be spiritually lost if they do not find a country of their own. Sydney Newman originally allowed the film to be released with a restriction: It could be shown to audiences that specifically requested it, but not on television or in commercial theatres. This decision was eventually altered by Newman.

Perhaps half a dozen films are not enough to get upset over, but more examples exist. Although the films discussed were made, others were not, and others, moreover, were toned down by the filmmakers. Self-censorship is an indefinable process; cumulative experience teaches you where your borders are and how far you can go. To grapple with political censorship at the Film Board necessitates a look at its early history and the lessons it learned.

More than anyone else, John Grierson was responsible for the National Film Board—its structure, its purpose, its function. He wanted it to operate close to the politicians, to be, in effect, the voice of parliament. He saw a great role for film—as a tool for social change, as an educational instrument, as a weapon to spread the democratic word. Yet the financial wherewithall provided the key, since film was an extremely expensive medium. He had two choices: to look to the public or to the private sector for sponsorship. He chose the former, deciding that it would give him more freedom. But as someone spending the public's money, he was keenly sensitive to the responsibility inherent in that arrangement. When the National Film Board was created in 1939 (as a supervisory board, not a production agency as we now know it), it was to be comprised of a chairman, who was to be the Minister of Trade and Commerce, another member of the King's Privy Council for Canada, and six other members: three civil servants, and three others from outside the civil service. The potential for political interference was obvious, and through the years would become more complicated, particularly when Cabinet policy clashed with decisions of the Board. The chairman and one other were both Cabinet ministers, yet they could be outvoted by the Board on matters that contradicted government policy.

But Grierson considered it essential to operate a mere step away from the political forum. Only in this way could the Film Board represent the desire and dictums of *parliament*, which to him distilled the wishes of the country. The war simplified this relationship to a certain extent, because the will of the people was relatively clear and united as one force—to win the war. However there were problems, and they were uniformly of a political nature.

After accepting the job of film commissioner in October 1939, Grierson was faced with an unenviable task. He had to provide films for a country that lacked any real production industry. It's true that the already existing Government Motion Picture Bureau had a trained staff and equipment, but the Bureau was by this time a tired workhorse, and it lacked both inspiration and drive. Associated Screen News was a steady producer in Montreal, and Audio Pictures was operating out of Toronto. Leon Shelley had formed the Vancouver Motion Picture Company on the west coast, but all of these companies produced little more than a steady diet of newsreels and industrial films. Looking around, Grierson got in touch with Louis de B. Rochemont in an attempt to persuade his prestigious American *March of Time* unit to feature Canada in one of its monthly releases. Rochemont agreed, and a crew was sent to shoot scenes of Canada mobilizing for war. Grierson himself was due to leave for Australia in late January 1940, to complete a project that the outbreak of war had interrupted. A week before his departure, the premier of Ontario, Mitchell Hepburn, launched a bitter attack on Mackenzie King, and denounced the federal government for its failure to conduct Canada's war duties in the vigorous manner required. Parliament had been summoned for January 25, and on that day King asked for an immediate dissolution and an election on this issue. Grierson had left for warmer climes, leaving his assistant (and future film commissioner), Ross McLean to supervise the *March of Time* film entitled *Canada at War*. He had also suggested that the notorious Colonel Cooper, head of the powerful Canadian Motion Picture Distributor's Association, be appointed acting commissioner in his absence. Grierson obviously hoped to cement further relations with the dominant exhibition/distribution arm of the private sector through this move.

McLean, a staunch Liberal who had edited the publications of the National Liberal Federation in the 1935 election, helped steer the film to depict King in a favourable light. King had nervously appeared before the cameras to give a good account of himself, and recognized that the film's release at an opportune time would do him no harm. The film was due to appear on March 1, 1940, but J.J. Fitzgibbons, President of Famous Players, who controlled numerous Canadian theatres, warned Hepburn about the film's possible contents in a letter:

> I suggest that you see the March of Time issue to be released March 1st, entitled "Canada at War." While not planned, the subject matter will prove great political propaganda for the Federal Party.[3]

When Ross McLean went to an Ottawa theatre on March 1, after escorting prints of the film from New York, he found to his horror and amazement that the film was not being shown. Colonel Cooper was contacted, and he "seemed most anxious to shift the blame around and scouted any idea of politics entering into it, although jokingly saying that as a Tory he would be happier if the film held off for a month . . . ."[4]

Meanwhile the film was playing in the other provinces and was overtly used as political propaganda. King was furious with Hepburn, and felt that his election chances were being severely damaged in Ontario. King's administrative secretaries parried back and forth with Cooper and Hepburn, while de Rochemont was outraged that a *March of Time* film was used as a political football. But King was returned with a massive majority, and the storm was over.

The inference that the Film Board was just a mouthpiece for the political party in power was to dog it for years. Two and a half years later Hepburn banned another NFB film. *Inside Fighting Canada*, part of the *Canada Carries On* series, was a brief survey of Canada's contribution to the Allied war effort. Hepburn, although no longer premier of Ontario, was Provincial Treasurer, and the Ontario Censor Board was still within his jurisdiction. On Christmas Eve, 1942, Grierson discovered that Hepburn had delayed release of the film. This time Hepburn found inaccuracies in the commentary. There was a reference mentioning that the British Commonwealth Air Training Plan had graduated "hundreds of thousands of flyers." This was a gross inaccuracy. But the greatest exception was taken to a stirring passage near the film's finale:

> Behind the spires of parliament and the leadership of William Lyon Mackenzie King stands a people disciplined for war. Behind the new national management of price and wage controls, behind the efficiency of Government measures, stand the Canadian people themselves. A people who make a national policy of voluntary service.

As with *Canada at War*, the film had been released at a sensitive time. There had been labour strikes and threats of strikes, demands for the resignation of federal cabinet ministers, and a great deal of open criticism of the wartime administration. Under these pressures, the King government found it necessary to submit the question at issue to the Supreme Court of Canada by way of what is known as a stated case. Members of the Ontario Censor Board, who classified and censored all new releases, felt that:

> . . . the National Film Board acted in decidedly bad taste, at least, when it presented the film for censorship at the present time . . . It is impossible to suggest that the views of the government, as expressed by its spokesman for "Inside Fighting Canada" could influence members of the Supreme Court of Canada, but the Board must observe that unless the Court sees fit to unanimously and sweepingly support the Federal Government with its stated case, the opinion of the commentator becomes inaccurate beyond question.[5]

The Film Board seemed to be playing partisan politics again. Grierson's rationale for the inclusion of the King reference was succinct: "It would be strange to Canadians if in a survey of Britain's war effort special care were taken to omit the name of Mr. Churchill."[6] Under pressure, Hepburn and the Censor Board were forced to back away, and by New Year's Eve the film was surprisingly passed without cuts.

Meanwhile Grierson and Stuart Legg, who provided the creative thrust for many of the Board's films, were directing their attentions to the *World in Action* series, which had immense foreign distribution. The two of them were firmly committed to an internationally oriented postwar world, and, from the inception of this series, its films examined the social economic and political life of other countries. The philosophy was progressive and novel, largely directed toward potential problems of the postwar world, rather than toward the more immediate war aims of the Allies.

At first there seemed to be little danger in the NFB making films of this type, but criticism began in mid-1943 over *The Gates of Italy*. The film was attacked for being "soft" on fascism; one journalist headlined his article: "Will Someone Please Tell the NFB About Fascism."[7] Early in 1944, *Our Northern Neighbour* was held up by the Quebec Censor Board, because it was strongly pro-communist in its interpretation of Russian history. Questions were asked in the Commons:

> There has been a growing suspicion that the film board has become a propagandist for a type of socialist and foreign philosophy; heretofore it was merely an instrument of propaganda for the government . . . My objection is that we have a national instrument of government that is obviously putting out soviet propaganda. I feel strongly that it is not the duty of any vehicle of government to put out propaganda concerning any foreign country. The film board should be a Canadian film board and it should put out Canadian propaganda.[8]

However, Grierson and Legg were not to be halted in their vision of informing people about the future structure of the postwar world. The crisis came in January 1945. It involved another *World in Action* film, *Balkan Powder Keg*, and it was again the work of Legg. Historically the territory called the Balkans was political dynamite—Russia long regarding it as an important sphere of influence—and England was most sensitive to any Mediterranean threat. The film was critical of British policies, while concurrently Churchill and King were arguing over the possible use of Canadian troops in this area. To avoid further deterioration in relations between Britain and Canada, King asked that the film be withdrawn. It was pulled during its initial playdates. Grierson was upset by the censure, feeling that a matter of principle was involved. He told his board that the NFB should not become simply a spokesman for the official point of view. His maverick attitude had ironically seen him range across the entire spectrum while in Canada, being accused alternately as an apologist for King, and as a producer of left-wing propaganda.

Grierson was soon off to New York at war's end, but Canada and the spectre of communism were to follow him and seriously affect his career. Igor Gouzenko's defection in Ottawa would usher in the cold war period and implicate Grierson, and by association, the Film Board. Grierson appeared before the Royal Commission investigating Gouzenko's allegations twice, because a former secretary of his had ostensibly been part of the spy ring, and his name had been mentioned in notebooks uncovered by the RCMP. The entire affair was not kind to Grierson, and the "communist" tag was attached more frequently to the NFB as a result.

The Gouzenko affair seriously damaged the Board's reputation and no doubt left an indelible mark on the place, affecting decisions as to which films it felt it could, or could not, make. Certainly the scope of NFB films in the immediate postwar period reflects the first shifts. Legg and *World in Action* had looked at international problems and perspectives. It was natural that the people they trained should continue this work. At first they did, making films about the rehabilitation work of UNRRA (United Nations Relief and Rehabilitation Administration) and UNESCO in *Hungry Minds*, *Suffer Little Children* and *In the Wake of the Armies–UNRRA*, or the war crime trials in *Guilty Men*. Grant McLean was sent to China at the request of UNRRA to make *The People Between*. This type of activity abruptly ceased about 1947 and was never really to be revived until Brittain and Kemeny made *Bethune* in the early sixties. The Board began to retreat into itself to make films that either directly promulgated Liberal policy (particularly the sweeping social reforms following the war), or films that were standard scenics, or ethnographic films with no overt political overtones.

Furthermore, the opposition conservatives had, in the Film Board, a good device with which to attack the government. The Cabinet was suspicious of how many communists were actually at the Board. The opposition found time to question myriad details of the Film Board's operation—from taxicab accounts for Grierson and Legg, to the number of phones the Board had on its premises. Suddenly it came to light that the Film Board had sent an employee to China for a film. It was Grant McLean, nephew of the film commissioner, Ross McLean, and the film he came back with was to provide the next drama.

In February 1945, UNRRA requested that the Film Board record its work in certain parts of Europe and the Far East. Grant McLean was subsequently sent to China in 1946, where he shot footage of Mao Tse Tung and the communist forces in Yenan, as well as of the Nationalist leaders in Nanking, still embroiled in the civil war raging over the country. *The People Between* portrayed a population caught between these two ideologies. Upon completion of the film, Mike Pearson, at that time Secretary of State for External Affairs, requested that a screening be arranged for him. McLean described what happened in a recent interview:

> After the film had been shown, the lights came on, Pearson stood up and said some very nice things about the quality of the film. However he went on to say that the government couldn't allow its release because it indicated, naturally, that there were two governments in China, and he didn't think that Canada should recognize that. Pearson took the view that the Canadian government, I think at the behest of the American government, wouldn't even recognize that the communists existed. It was very unreal, but that was the position that Patrick Hurley and the China lobby was taking in Washington.[9]

*The People Between* was shelved for years, eventually getting occasional distribution to film societies and study groups. The next crisis would not be so easily dealt with. It was a crisis of major proportions which to some extent crystallized many of the previous problems.

The November 19, 1949, issue of *The Financial Post* had as its front-page headline: "Film Board Monopoly Facing Major Test?" The article included a long list of complaints about the Film Board, written from the perspective of the private sector, which had continually argued against the existence of the NFB. Furthermore it revealed that the Department of National Defence was no longer using the Film Board to work on "classified" films. Perhaps most damningly, it asked the question: "Is the Film Board a leftist propaganda machine?"

The walls quickly came tumbling in. Questions came thick and fast in parliament. Brooke Claxton, Minister of National Defence, and minister responsible for the NFB from October 1945 to February 1947, admitted that until the Film Board had had its employees screened for security, no classified material would be given to that organization.[10] In fact, the DND films were being given to Crawley and Associated Screen News. Many people felt that Claxton had become deeply suspicious of the NFB during the Gouzenko period, and that the suspicion had never left him. However, the significance of Claxton's statement took on a different dimension when it was revealed that in the case of the private firms, only those personnel directly connected with classified DND films had been screened, while in the case of the Board, every employee in the organization was to be checked out. Evidently, the government's concern with possible subversion within the NFB went beyond the question of DND films.

This period of the Board's history is one of its darkest. Suspicion and betrayal were rife. Through it all, while it is relatively easy to establish the salient facts, there is a much larger spectre continually in the background.

> It seems clear that the attack on the Board represents a concerted effort by a group of small Canadian film producers and laboratories to destroy the Board; and that behind this group stand the most powerful movie interests in the world, located in Hollywood.[11]

When Ross McLean succeeded Grierson as commissioner in 1945, he was faced with an awesome task. The transition from war to peace would determine the effectiveness of the NFB as an enduring agency. The growing pains were many—staff was reduced and budgets were cut. The Gouzenko affair had planted the fear of communism in people's minds. Furthermore, McLean moved the Board into areas where there were powerful and antagonistic interests at work. The small, but vocal, group of Canadian film-producing companies expected the Film Board to disappear after the war was won. When it didn't, they felt they were facing unfair competition. McLean was also keen on moving the Board into fiction films and television—veiled threats to the hegemony of Hollywood in the former instance, and its fear of the magic box in the latter. Furthermore, McLean had suggested that the Americans should begin to recognize a certain responsibility vis-à-vis Canada because of their domination of the market, and quotas were mentioned.[12] McLean had seen through the sham of the Canadian Cooperation Project, and was subsequently removed from any further involvement with the scheme.

The Canadian government had its own complaints. Louis St. Laurent had evidence that NFB employees were providing information to the opposition for use in preparing questions in the Commons. Jack Pickersgill, at that time parliamentary secretary to St. Laurent, felt that the Board needed to be disciplined.[13] In Quebec, Duplessis had ordered his censor board in 1946 to examine Film Board subjects for content sympathetic to communism, arguing that: "The National Film Board diffuses Communism and is showing films encouraging Federal centralization."[14] Three years later he stopped all distribution of NFB films in Quebec through one of his provincial agencies, the Service de ciné-photographie, because of the suspected leftist bias of the Board. The interests of the government, Hollywood, and Canada's private producers all coincided—the Board had to be brought down a peg or two, if not totally destroyed.

Ross McLean was the first to go. Conveniently, his term was due to expire in January 1950. It was not to be renewed, although McLean was not officially told this; he found out through the newspapers. His assistant commissioner, Ralph Foster, resigned immediately.

Meanwhile the Board's employees were going through the screening process. McLean had declared the Board a "vulnerable" agency in May 1949 at the behest of DND. Later that autumn the RCMP returned to McLean with a list of about thirty names. It was suggested that he might dismiss them because they were unreliable. McLean refused until clear evidence of disloyalty had been proved. In many cases he told the people involved and warned them that further measures might be in the air, and he might not be able to protect them. McLean was soon to leave the scene. His successor, Arthur Irwin, inherited the problem. Suffice it to say that it was admitted that three people had been fired. Others apparently had already been let go in mid-1949 according to Robert Winters, the minister responsible for the Board. The public sacrifice had been made. There was no outcry. Morale at the Film Board was rock-bottom. Evelyn Spice Cherry described it as a time "of tremendous fear. There were these subtle things going on. We weren't accused of anything, but it was suggested that some of us were enemies of our country."[15]

Friends became enemies, distrust was rampant. Some simply turned away from involving themselves in the crisis. Information was scanty as to what was happening. Irwin moved quickly into other areas. A management consultant company, Woods and Gordon, submitted their report early in 1950. Many of its recommendations were implemented by Irwin. They involved changes in administrative structure and finance. The Board was becoming more bureaucratized, more efficient. The civil servants could now begin to understand how the place functioned. Grierson's practice of employing everyone on three-month contracts was superceded by more permanent means of employment. But Woods and Gordon's report had another potential use, as Pickersgill explains:

> . . . there had been a security investigation of the employees of the Film Board, to which no publicity had been given because it was hoped the suspicions about a few employees would not be justified. Winters was the minister responsible for the Film Board, and when he wisely turned to St. Laurent for advice Norman Robertson and I were asked to assist him. In addition to the security investigation, we felt that there should be a review of the administration of the Board which might indicate that changes in personnel could be made without injury to individual reputations.[16]

A new Film Act was drafted and passed into law on June 30, 1950. The Chairman of the Board was now to be the film commissioner, and of eight other members, only three were to be public servants—there were to be no Cabinet ministers. The political and parliamentary contact that Grierson so valued was being dismantled. It had created too much controversy. Irwin began to investigate a new home for the Film Board. In Ottawa the Board was too close to the firing range. Montreal was chosen. This would have unforeseen results. The idea was relatively sound, but the eventual site chosen was disastrous. It was miles from the centre of town, and isolated from the creative core.

Late in 1950, Irwin wrote a letter to Vincent Massey, chairman of the Royal Commission on National Development of the Arts, Letters and Sciences. It explained the reason the Film Board was requesting more money from parliament:

> The principal increase is an item of $250,000 asked for the production of films to be used in the battle of ideas between the Communist and non-Communist world. The view was taken that the current conflict between the East and West was essentially a struggle of ideas, that the film medium was one of the most effective for expressing the ideas for which this country stood, and that this country was in a uniquely favourable position to operate in this field not being subject to the suspicion which is sometimes directed against our neighbour . . . .[17]

Window dressing? Perhaps. But it was a reflection of how far the Board had come in a couple of years. The program became known variously as the "Freedom" series, or "Freedom Speaks," and "Democracy at Work." Although it was felt that the whole concept was three or four years out of date, two people, Guy Glover and James Cowan, were sent to Europe to study distribution problems for the series. Various films were made, or co-opted into the program, but the scheme gradually died a quiet, innocuous death.

People left the Board, and new employees arrived to ultimately leave their stamp on the place. But as Evelyn Spice Cherry reflected:

> The whole nature of the Film Board changed. When one doesn't wish to fire people, you create conditions under which the worker, if he or she has any self-respect, is eventually forced to resign. And I'm sure this was a method that was used. There is a trend to seek a form of escapism from controversial subject matters and certainly it prevailed among us. And if it's carried very far you almost get into a condition of "nothingness." I really

do believe that when you're terribly preoccupied with what a camera can do to create a lot of very beautiful images, you end up with something that really hasn't much to say—you have reached a period of nothingness.[18]

An extreme view perhaps. After all, the artistic flowering of Unit B in films like *Paul Tomkowicz: Street Railway Switchman, Corral, City of Gold* and *Lonely Boy* was just around the corner. The Québécois filmmakers would make great strides in cinéma vérité and go on to challenge the status quo in the sixties. *Challenge for Change* would deal with many specific social, economic and political issues through its films. To a certain extent, it is amazing what can be made at the Board, the freedom that is allowed people. Leaving aside questions of objectivity and bias, one cannot, however, ignore a drift toward self-censorship. This is arguably the most dangerous kind, because it is extremely difficult to perceive and can invariably be rationalized away. Self-censorship in a publicly funded, government agency is unavoidable. But how far can one go before restraint is imposed? Where are the limits to freedom of expression, and who establishes and enforces these largely indefinable parameters? Is one actively encouraged to make films on the borderline, so to speak; or, alternatively, to tread a safer path, away from controversy? A few films have actively explored these limits. But the question remains: if a filmmaker explores the contradictions and mechanisms of his society, how far can he go with his criticism before he is censured? Especially if he is using the taxpayers' money for his purposes.

*Cinema Canada*, 56 (June-July 1979)

---

1 William Johnson, "Nothing's changed since Duplessis maker of banned film says," *The Globe and Mail*, December 27, 1972.
2 Ibid.
3 Ontario Archives, RG 3 Box 303. Letter from J. J. Fitzgibbons to Hon. M.F. Hepburn, February 17, 1940.
4 Public Archives Canada, MG 26 J4, Vol. 273. Memorandum from Walter Turnbull to WLM King, March 2, 1939.
5 Ontario Archives, RG 3 Box 218. Memo to O.J. Silverthorne.
6 Unidentified newspaper article.
7 *Canadian Film Weekly*, July 28, 1943, p. 1.
8 *Hansard*, March 30, 1944, p. 2017-18. Mr. Adamson.
9 Interview with Grant McLean for *Has Anybody Here Seen Canada?* February 24, 1978.
10 *Hansard*, November 18, 1949, p. 1976.
11 *Ottawa Evening Citizen*, February 4, 1950.
12 Public Archives Canada, RG 27, Vol. 852. Letter from Ross McLean to J.J. McCann, December 1, 1947.
13 Personal interview with J.W. Pickersgill, February 1978.
14 *Canadian Film Weekly*, April 10, 1946, p. 1.
15 Interview with Evelyn Spice Cherry for *Has Anybody Here Seen Canada?* December 19, 1977.
16 J.W. Pickersgill, *My Years with Louis St. Laurent*, (Toronto and Buffalo: University of Toronto Press, 1975), p. 146.
17 Public Archives Canada, RG 33/28 Vol. 55. Letter from W. Arthur Irwin to Honourable Vincent Massey, October 30, 1950.
18 Interview with Evelyn Spice Cherry for *Has Anybody Here Seen Canada?*

# *The Diary Films of Michael Rubbo*

## BY PIERS HANDLING

*If as suggested elsewhere in this volume (see "The Silent Subject in English Canadian Film") the history of Canadian documentary is characterized by the search for a non-imposed voice, then the work of Mike Rubbo must surely be regarded as central to that history. Rubbo not only embodies the tradition of rebellion against authoritarian documentary, but, in the personal intrusions discussed here by Piers Handling, he speaks back to the authoritarian voice with a strength that emanates from the film itself. In films like* Waiting for Fidel *and* I Hate to Lose *we see more than a self-reflexive inquiry into the making of a film about a particular subject. We see how the preconceived film is not made. Rubbo's films systematically work their way from a preconceived response to the subject through the frustrations generated by that preconception. The "diary" aspect of these works is perhaps more than a filmmaker's diary. Rather, it is the recording of a shared growth between filmmaker and audience when both must admit that they are no longer interested in ritualistically considering what they already know.*

*As Handling demonstrates, Rubbo's work documents the failure of any kind of certainty. A personal look at the Vietnam war,* Sad Song of Yellow Skin, *cannot be relied upon to stay either personal or political. The tragedy of Vietnam, it tells us, is that the well-defined line between the two no longer exists. In* Waiting for Fidel, *the protagonists' political outbursts are both heartfelt and ridiculous. Nothing happens in the film. Yet it is a hard-fought, deeply revealing* nothing, *entirely worthy of the source for its title.* Solzhenitsyn's Children *are all style and bravado; style and bravado become very important. That Daisy needs no help from a plastic surgeon (or anyone else) should make* The Story of a Facelift *a futile inquiry. Instead, it becomes an inquiry into the nature of "help," "appearances" and, perhaps, the superficiality of both. In his latest work on the famed author, Rubbo's exchanges with Margaret Atwood are mutual celebrations of their joint exclusion of finality. Rubbo joins forces with his subject to demonstrate the writer's secret as being the writer's privacy. In the end, we learn more about that privacy than we do about the clichés that might leave us with an illusory command of the subject at hand.*

*I just knew that any film that tended to show any sense of order or control about the situation would be false.*

Mike Rubbo talking about *Sad Song of Yellow Skin* in *Sightlines*, Fall 1975

Michael Rubbo is one of the most inventive and challenging filmmakers in the world, yet few Canadians have even heard of him. In one way this is surprising; even though he is a transplanted Australian, he has been working in this country at the National Film Board, a state organization with a national distribution system, since 1965. But Rubbo is far better known outside Canada, where his films win awards, receive festival screenings and appear on educational television. Television is the name of the game, but Rubbo has only been dealt the joker in the pack by the Canadian Broadcasting Corporation. Why, one might ask, do his films, made by the state film organization, not get shown by the state television network? Pierre Perrault, another renowned documentarian, has described Canada as "un pays sans bons sens"—a ridiculous kind of country—and nowhere is this more true than when it comes to questions of culture. Because Rubbo's films are so subjective (indeed, what isn't; Rubbo just chooses to foreground this notion), he has been denied access to the CBC, which "protects" us from this material under the guise and excuse of "objectivity," a misnomer if ever there was one. So, despite the fact that Rubbo is an award-winning filmmaker who has made highly topical films, the CBC has effectively "censored" him as a presence from our screens. This is unfortunate, for Rubbo's films are fascinating—personal and intimate in approach, often self-conscious in manner, but evidence of a probing and analytical mind.

If Donald Brittain's carefully assembled documentary artefacts epitomize the Film Board documentary, then Rubbo's films are a complete contrast. Brittain is the heir to the Griersonian legacy, while Rubbo is the troublesome second child who is a part of the family but has rebelled against it. His films operate within the tradition of the social documentary, but he has stood the form on its head. While Brittain and the NFB as an organization make films that order and control their material, Rubbo has continually been troubled by this concept, as the introductory quotation makes clear.

In another way it is astonishing that Rubbo has managed to carve out his own niche at the Film Board. Few of his films deal with Canada at all (although his global wanderings have been curbed of late), the settings being as exotically diverse as Vietnam, Indonesia, Cuba, Australia, France and Ghana. This could explain parts of Rubbo's singular style, and why he has evolved the way he has in terms of the aesthetic decisions he makes as a filmmaker. But how is Rubbo's style distinct and what does it mean?

Traditional documentary has adopted specific cinematic codes that we all take for granted. As a form it has also been perceived largely in terms of its information value. The way this information is being passed on to us has not really been questioned at all. If it's a documentary it must be "real," or more insidiously, it must contain "truth." Modern semiological criticism has dissected the traditional, narrative fiction film of Hollywood to reveal the illusionism and complicit ideology that lie at its core. As Bill Nichols has pointed out, the same forces are at work in the documentary film.[1] In fact the danger of illusionism is even greater, because most people unconsciously accept the assumption that documentary equals reality. Yet, as we know, film of any sort presents a highly selective reality. Ideology is inscribed into every image that we see, but for most of us this ideology remains invisible. It does not announce itself, so apparently it is not there. Contemporary criticism has alerted us to the complicit assumptions that underlie this passive acceptance of what we assume to be real or normal. As Robin Wood has noted, for Marxists this belief in the structures of realist cinema is the way that "bourgeois ideology reproduces itself and passes itself off as 'reality'; for the feminists it is the means whereby the patriarchal order is naturalized as universal and unchangeable; and for psychoanalytical theory realism is the means whereby an 'imaginary' sense of wholeness, transmitted through family structures is endlessly reiterated and reinforced."[2] Nichols has also observed that "documentaries always were forms of re-presentation, never clear windows onto 'reality'; the filmmaker was always a participant-witness and an active fabricator of meaning, a producer of cinematic discourse rather than a neutral or all-knowing reporter of the way things truly are."[3]

Despite critical concern with the question of cinematic illusionism, few have dealt with the documentary film as a form where this problem arises. One who has, Jean-Louis Comolli, writes:

> The basic deception of *direct cinema* is really its claim to transcribe truly the truth of life, to begin the position of witness in relation to that truth so that the film simply records events and objects mechanically. In reality, the very fact of filming is of course already a productive intervention which modifies and transforms the material recorded. From the moment the camera intervenes, a form of *manipulation* begins. And every operation . . . constitutes a manipulation of the film document. The filmmaker may well wish to respect that document, but he cannot avoid manufacturing it. It does not pre-exist reportage, it is its product.[4]

Questions of manipulation are endemic to the documentary, haunted as it is by ideological concerns: What is being repressed? What is being hidden—the structured absence or, to use Althusser's expression, "the internal shadows of exclusion"—and its contrary, what is being foregrounded? These structural concerns also extend to other formal properties of the documentary film: sound/image relationships and their implications. Most documentaries use direct as opposed to indirect address, the two basic modes defining whether or not the viewer is explicitly acknowledged as the subject to which the film is addressed. In other words, in direct address the narrator, off-screen or on-screen, directs his/her comments to the viewer, who is acknowledged either through the narration itself, or by the narrator talking directly to the camera. The majority of television documentaries (for example, *the fifth estate* or *60 Minutes*) use this mode of structuring their material. Indirect address (used by virtually all of narrative fiction film and most cinéma vérité) presents problems for a documentary filmmaker through its shapelessness or the accusations of manipulation that can be levelled against its practitioners.

> Historically, most documentaries have used the mode of direct address, and it is still preferred by television documentary, political films and most sponsored or commercial films. Indirect address seems to invite risks of incomprehensibility (the lack of a guiding hand) and, for political filmmakers, empiricism (a risk well confirmed by much cinéma vérité). Conversely, the adoption of direct address has run the perennial risk of dogmatism, while offering the advantage of analytical precision.[5]

The use of direct address suggests a number of things to the viewer. In its most obvious guise it represents the voice of authority, and through its organization of the material can suggest a comprehension of a situation that it doesn't really understand, or an order where none exists. It's as if it is telling us that this is the truth of the situation. It is no accident that television news is presented to us this way, combining both forms of direct address: on-screen (sync narrator) and off-screen (non-sync narrator). A certain order has to be imposed on the material for a number of reasons, but it doesn't allow for questioning or doubts. The use of direct address tends to enclose the film into a unified statement which often excludes the viewer from any kind of active participation as a producer of meaning. We are presented with a situation which is made sense of by the narrator/filmmaker. The manipulation of reality is then complete and subject to multiple distortions.

How then to avoid these formal and aesthetic problems? The method of indirect address is one alternative, and the cinéma vérité movement which employs this style did so in reaction to the overbearing commentaries used by Grierson and his followers. Social actors (*not* film actors) do not address the viewer as subject. This, however, raises other formal problems, as Nichols notes, because indirect address is also the principal mode of fictional narrative cinema. It only gives the illusion of removing the filmmaker from the action being filmed. Nichols identifies two other strategies that have come into contemporary usage: a form that incorporates direct address usually in the form of the interview, allowing people to tell their own stories; and an approach that sees the documentary beginning to recognize the complexity of certain epistemological and aesthetic assumptions. Nichols refers to these as "self-reflexive documentaries."[6] Mike Rubbo's films fall into this category; they attempt to deal with some of the serious formal problems of the documentary which I have briefly outlined. *Sad Song of Yellow Skin* (1970), *Persistent and Finagling* (1971), *The Man Who Can't Stop* (1973), *Waiting for Fidel* (1974), and *I am an Old Tree* (1975), as well as the later *I Hate to Lose* (1977), *Solzhenitsyn's Children . . . are making a lot of noise in Paris* (1978), *Yes or No, Jean-Guy Moreau* (1979), and *Daisy—The Story of a Facelift* (1983) all share similar structural strategies. Rubbo narrates all of them using non-sync direct address (off-screen narration), and he appears on the image-track as a social actor in all of them.

His narration is consciously the opposite of the serious, well-presented, impersonal, patriarchal voice that we have become so accustomed to after listening to the official voices of the NFB—Lorne Greene, Stanley Jackson and Don Brittain. Rubbo reads his narration in a slow and quiet manner, at times almost in a gentle monotone, occasionally even stumbling over words. There is a complete lack of insistency about what he says; and that, combined with his use of the first person, which projects his personal thoughts as to what is happening on the screen, results in an avoidance of any attempt to persuade. His voice is used as a bridging device, to recount stories that were not captured on film or to reveal his own thoughts concerning the pro-filmic event. The films become journalistic diaries, subjective reactions to generally totally unfamiliar situations. Initially *Sad Song of Yellow Skin* and *Wet Earth and Warm People* seem to lack any real focus as a result. In the first instance, Rubbo has been sent to Saigon. We are presented with a picture of the city and its people which seems removed from our expectations of Vietnam. We are shown no jet fighter strikes, helicopter attacks, or infantry patrols—the traditional images of war that have become so familiar to us through television coverage (just compare *Sad Song* to the CBC's *Mills of the Gods*). Instead the war intrudes and becomes visible in different ways. There are the children, often parentless, who steal to get by; the American journalists working for the independent wire company Dispatch; or the young Vietnamese soldier who is visiting his family under the watchful eye of an officer because he has already deserted once. *Wet Earth and Warm People* is pervaded by this same picaresque sense of a real inability to say much more about Indonesia than an ordinary tourist. Continually shown to be the centre of attention and curiosity, there is little chance for Rubbo and his film crew to capture the spontaneous.

Reinforcing the personal reflections that we hear on the sound-track is Rubbo's own presence in the films, always as a social actor. In this way there is a very important recognition of his participation and involvement in the action being filmed. Rubbo does not give us a detached, third-person account of what is happening. He foregrounds the first person, through both the image- and the sound-track. His presence and indeed his involvement in the pro-filmic event varies from film to film. Nevertheless his presence is never disguised, and in the more recent work he has imposed himself more forcefully into his films. Rubbo makes us continually aware that we are watching a film, a construct, and not some veiled attempt to appear as a window opening out on reality. If other documentary filmmakers leave no trace of their presence, Rubbo consciously leaves his fingerprints on his films. Furthermore, he uses this device to comment on his own actions within the film, which permits him to voice his doubts, fears and concerns. This allows Rubbo to view himself in a number of different ways, at times humourously—as an awkward participant in events—or ironically—as perhaps not belonging. His confusion is often revealed: After interviewing what seems like dozens of intellectuals from the French left in *Solzhenitsyn's Children*, he admits that their arguments all sound convincing, but that may be due to the fact that *he* doesn't strongly believe in anything. The outdoor screening of films in *Wet Earth and Warm People* provides further evidence of the complexity of thought and feeling that Rubbo can deal with by using this technique. The warmth, excitement and wonder of the film evening (for many it is the first time they have seen this incredible invention), with Rubbo delightfully addressing the villagers in Indonesian to hoots of laughter, is delicately replaced the next day by a sense of questioning when they pack up their projectors and generators before leaving. Rubbo's narration while they are doing this voices his own doubts about whether the whole thing was a good idea—introducing the technological complexity, of which he is a representative, to these people. His feelings of inadequacy, and perhaps guilt, are subtly reinforced by the inherent magic of the scene that immediately follows the film evening: natives dancing to their music in a forest intercut with the chopping of bamboo—images of natural rhythm and timeless rituals. There is a conscious dialectic at work in these scenes, "a cultural battle"[7] as Rubbo calls it, that is constructed for us out of a complex intricacy of film components.

This cultural battle is at the centre of *Waiting for Fidel*, where an unusual threesome visits Cuba with the ostensible purpose of interviewing Castro. Rubbo finds himself in the company of Newfoundland's fiery ex-premier Joey Smallwood, and Geoff Stirling, a millionaire who owns radio and television stations. The Castro interview never materializes, but Rubbo finds much of interest in Smallwood's and Stirling's reaction to the Cuban experiment as they tour the island visiting hospitals, universities and construction sites. Stirling is the continual sceptic, a product of the free-enterprise system that has given him his millions. Smallwood, with a history of socialist legislation behind him, acts as a foil to his business friend, responding with great interest to what he sees around him. And where is Rubbo in all this? He is certainly a presence, perhaps more restrained than he would like to be, unwilling to commit himself too strongly for fear that it will unbalance the film. However, in the marvellous confrontation scene where Stirling attempts to put an end to the film that Rubbo is making but shouldn't be, the filmmaking process is brought under fire and we are made aware of some of its economic contradictions. Accused of being wasteful and extravagant, Rubbo is confronted with the private enterprise mentality of western society. Stirling claims that he is paying for the film in the cameras, the tape for the sound recorders, the processing, and so on. The Castro interview is all that is required of Rubbo, so why is he wasting all his footage on what seems to be irrelevant?

Now the documentary process can place a "simple" set of demands on a filmmaker. For instance, one is sent to Vietnam or to Cuba, and is expected to bring back certain images. There are preconceptions as to what material should be brought back. This inevitably imposes subconscious restrictions on a filmmaker, who is expected to satisfy the sponsor, and ultimately the audience, which imposes similar expectations. Particular images assume a position of requirement. If these images are not included, there is a fear of turning people away to something more exciting or more familiar. But Rubbo's style is the complete contradiction of this, even to the point of suppressing purely aesthetic moments if they don't serve to advance the film. He is concerned precisely with that which is apparently not relevant. But not relevant to whom? This is another facet of the "cultural battle." So *Waiting for Fidel* becomes not the film that was expected, but something completely different. It arises out of situations, as opposed to trying to control or dominate them. This is true of all Rubbo's "diary" films. He finds what is there, not what he expects to see, and in fact the "irrelevant," as Stirling would describe it, is elevated to a position of central importance.

Earlier, I placed importance on the final effect of Rubbo's own voice on the sound-track, suggesting that it was substantially different from the anonymous "voice of authority" style that marks so many documentaries. Although Rubbo uses direct address, he manages to sidestep the pitfalls of this particular formal choice. While he creates meaning for the viewer, he also acknowledges us as the producers of meaning. This is inextricably tied to important thematic concerns that unite Rubbo's work. If the choice of certain modes of address indicates subtle filmmaker/audience relationships, it is also tied to an active/passive response to the material. This is linked to the reinforcement of invidious power structures; we as an audience either participate in the film and become producers of meaning, or we are spoken at and become consumers of meaning. This aesthetic is translated into practical terms within the films. Rubbo is intrigued with power and the social process, and how this power affects the individual in everyday, commonplace ways. In *Wet Earth and Warm People* we are drawn towards Hussein, the betcha, or bicycle-taxi, driver. The betcha's are being continually harassed by the police and the military in Jakarta. They cannot use certain roads at certain times, yet as Rubbo argues, the betcha is an ideal form of urban transport, quiet and pollution-free. In trying to get an answer to why these bicycles are disliked by the authorities, Rubbo is met with evasive replies. He eventually proposes that it is perhaps because the betcha is a symbol of the past, of something that Indonesia is now ashamed of in its attempt to move into the twentieth century. So to make his living, Hussein must take back roads to avoid police traps.

However, Rubbo doesn't stop here. We are shown how this touching inconvenience interrelates with the curious web of society that surrounds him. The chief of police who must enforce the law is dealt with as extensively as Hussein. He is seen as an intermediary who must enforce laws not of his making. Instead of being remote and officious, he is as human as Hussein—kind, gentle and amusing, with a paternal sense of care for people. In fact we feel a great deal of sympathy for him. The governor, Sadekin, is handled in a similar fashion. When we first see him, checking the identity papers of a nervous street vendor, he is presented as a traditional authority figure. But as we come to know Sadekin he becomes a benevolent type of father-figure, proudly showing Rubbo his successes in improving the slum conditions in Jakarta, while in the villages he is surrounded by adoring children.

But the suspicion that marks many of the contacts between the "two sides" in *Wet Earth and Warm People* is also a part of *Persistent and Finagling* and *The Man Who Can't Stop*. The women of STOP (Society to Overcome Pollution) have a series of frustrating meetings with people they think can help them in their crusade—university researchers at Université de Montréal, municipal civil servants, and the radio announcer, Blaker, whom they want to persuade to act as their host for the bus trip around Montreal—all representative of establishment patriarchal power structures, who are either uncooperative, or place a number of demands upon their participation. Similar situations are visible in *The Man Who Can't Stop* when Francis Sutton, a middle-aged Australian commercial advertiser, disgusted by the pollution of Sydney's beaches, tries to get people interested in an inland sewage system. The indifference or guarded hostility of their encounters is treated in both films as inevitable annoyance, to be expected because of what they are doing. But their frustrations are balanced by those occasions on which they receive support and encouragement—the student in *Persistent and Finagling* who researches pollution levels of various Montreal factories and is happily prepared to share his information, the environmental expert who urges them on in their efforts and the woman who recognizes Sutton and voices her admiration for him. If those people in power positions are anonymous, or at best detached, glimpses of touching humanity are evident around the fringes of all the films.

Standing in stark contrast to these skirmishes are the two Cuba films, and in particular *Waiting for Fidel.* There is no need to persuade or cajole power or people in authority in Cuba, and this is manifested in a variety of ways. The weekly political meetings of citizens provide a forum for dialogue and evidence of everyone's participation in the social and political process. Nevertheless Rubbo remains slightly sceptical of what he perceives to be an "organized" outlet of expression. But he is confronted with numerous examples of a benevolent allocation of a society's power through its institutions—its schools, universities and hospitals. Attitudes toward the insane and mentally ill, resulting in the successful rehabilitation of many patients, are viewed with admiration for the simplicity and humanity of approach. Similarly, the visit to the construction sites of a new city being built by those who will live in the apartments once they are finished is met with the same kind of fascination. Many of the workmen are fishermen by trade, untrained in construction work, but they have learned on the job. Throughout Cuba there is an overwhelming sense of purpose and unity about what is being accomplished with their friend Fidel—a harmony of a people with its leader, an example of power and its constituency working together.

One may ask at what cost this has been achieved. Has anything been lost? Rubbo's second Cuba film contains parts of the answer, even in its title, *I am an Old Tree*. This line is spoken by a middle-aged doctor who talks about the revolution and what it has meant to present-day Cuba. He notices the changes, and remarks that the younger generation is different, but unfortunately there are things in him that can't be changed; it's too late in his life, he is too set in his ways, he is an "old tree." Although conflict between the individual and society is evident in virtually all of Rubbo's other films, even the doctor's thoughts do not prevent this film from being surely the warmest and gentlest of the diary films. The cultural battle is absent in *I am an Old Tree*. But Rubbo too sadly fears that he is also an old tree, admitting in part that the struggle between the West and the emerging Third World will continue regardless of how sympathetic we might be to their experiments.

Rubbo has gravitated toward countries in a post-colonial phase of their history, countries that have been victims of nineteenth century imperialism—Vietnam/Indo-China, Indonesia, Cuba, to a lesser extent Australia, and more recently Quebec within Canada. Its importance is undeniable for Rubbo, and it would seem to be related to the cultural battle that he perceives around him. As white westerners we are continually portrayed as usurpers, as a culture that is disturbing the natural flow of life. The film screening, placed next to the forest imagery in *Wet Earth and Warm People*, is a prime example. In *Sad Song of Yellow Skin* one of the American Dispatch journalists tries to insert himself into Vietnamese life, but he is always aware of a gulf he cannot hope to bridge. Vietnamese knowledge of Americans is that they either kill or give. This places a series of demands on both cultures—the American is misunderstood by the Vietnamese, while the Vietnamese turn into perverse imitations of Americans, like Ui, the small boy who is a parody of a small-time gangster. Ui's pidgin English is a further example of the mutations that are taking place, and this notion is reinforced in *Wet Earth and Warm People* when we find out that Hussein is picking up English. As Rubbo notes, they shed one skin only to replace it with another. Legacies of their historical past are a further reminder of their colonial roots. In *Sad Song of Yellow Skin* Rubbo comes across an old cyclo-driver who fought for the French in the First World War, while in *Wet Earth and Warm People* Rubbo and the film crew travel around in an incongruous beaten-up Chevie, similar to the American cars of the fifties seen everywhere in the Cuba of *I Am an Old Tree*.

While Rubbo has great affection for these countries and their struggle for survival, he is sensitive enough to realize that he is inextricably a part of that colonizing force. This is one of the reasons he is so attracted to the different elements of magic in these cultures. The Coconut Monk walking the map of Vietnam from south to north as a symbol of eventual unity in *Sad Song of Yellow Skin*, the dancers in the forest, the puppeteers and the theatre group in *Wet Earth and Warm People*, all function as beautiful mysteries in the face of Rubbo's film technology. There is a strong element of symbolism in *The Man Who Can't Stop* and *Persistent and Finagling*, seen in the dumping of the water through the hoop into Sydney harbour and the bus tour of Montreal to point out the polluters. *Yes or No, Jean-Guy Moreau* is a further celebration of certain symbols that serve to unite a culture. Moreau's stage act, a play on a variety of Quebec stereotypes, allows the community to see parts of itself and this recognition is central to defining who one is.

While the rituals and symbols of these various cultures often serve to unite their communities in highly different ways, Rubbo, nevertheless, places great faith in individual action. The members of Dispatch that we see in *Sad Song of Yellow Skin* are visible proof that the renegades can be of major importance, largely because of their strongly developed sense of individual action. Partially responsible for breaking the story of the My Lai massacre, their apartness allows them to view situations from a different perspective. Yet their solitude is ironically a direct function of their commitment. Sadekin in *Wet Earth and Warm People*, Sutton in *The Man Who Can't Stop*, and the housewives of STOP in *Persistent and Finagling* are all individuals who are challenging the traditional system. Even the two Cuba films, which have the strongest sense of community action to them, are overshadowed by the continual presence of one man—Castro.

It has been said that every action is a political action regardless of whether it is meant to be or not. The absence of something says as much in different ways as its inclusion. While Rubbo would probably not consider himself a "political" filmmaker, his films are all concerned with the body politic, its basic relationships, and what this does to us all. In *Sad Song of Yellow Skin* this may be the questions that arise through Ui's contact with Americans; in *Persistent and Finagling* it could be how a group of concerned individuals is forced to overcome certain obstacles to voice their point; perhaps in *Wet Earth and Warm People* it is explored through the daily annoyances that Hussein has to deal with to earn a living. Human interchange is very fundamental and simple; its problems are universal. Rubbo has also found unique ways of dealing with his concerns—an attempt at involving us in cultures that are essentially foreign but which can be explored for their lessons. Aesthetically he is challenging the boundaries of the documentary in highly novel ways that relate to what he is trying to observe in the world around him. One can only hope that he does not pull back from the challenges that he has set for himself.

This is a revised version of an article which appeared in *Cinema Canada*, 41 (October 1977).

While this is not exactly where my original article ended (I had appended a section on *I Hate to Lose* after seeing a rough cut of the film), I would like to discuss the four subsequent diary films together, not because they form a distinctive thematic whole, but for certain changes within the Rubbo aesthetic. Indeed, with hindsight they may very well turn out to be transitional films, marking a certain fracture with the previous work. In my original piece I commented on Rubbo's fascination with political process: the way power is manifested and change is attempted. If these questions gradually asserted their priority over the years, from *Sad Song of Yellow Skin* to *Waiting for Fidel*, they are paramount in the recent work. *I Hate to Lose*, *Solzhenitsyn's Children* and *Yes or No, Jean-Guy Moreau* centre around political events or questions—the 1976 Quebec provincial election that saw the Parti Québécois assume power, the "crisis of the left" in France, and the 1980 Quebec referendum on sovereignty association, respectively. Only *Daisy—The Story of a Facelift* apparently resists this trend.

Elections or referendums form the background to the first three films, and Rubbo has shifted his ground to Canada and France, two highly developed, technologically advanced western countries. He is still intrigued by the way society is shaped through its political processes. With an uncanny sense of how this dialectic operates, *I Hate to Lose* documents the 1976 Quebec election by focusing on the predominantly anglophone riding of Westmount. Originally Rubbo wanted to deal with the candidacy of Nick Auf der Maur, leader of the Democratic Alliance, a left-wing group who were expected to do well in the election. But, as in his other films, the material begins to chart its own course, and Rubbo follows these threads as they develop. Just as Auf der Maur lacks a strong presence in the film, his opponents—especially George Springate, the incumbent Liberal, and the Union nationale representative, "Shorty" Fairhead—begin to attract Rubbo's attention. Furthermore, this is an indication of how successful a campaign they are running. While Auf der Maur is a rational, sympathetic but relatively unemotional man, Springate is the opposite, a tough, gutsy and robust professional who stumps his riding with increasing confidence.

*I Hate to Lose* is essentially a portrait of the English minority in Quebec, long accustomed to power, watching history pass it by without really being aware of the significance of the change that has been wrought. There is a form of the cultural battle at the heart of this film too, wrapped around the emergence of a Quebec nationalism after two centuries of colonial rule. The final section of the film, which covers election night, contains some of the finest work that Rubbo has done, matching in sheer complexity and sensitivity the movie night in *Wet Earth and Warm People*. From the moment the election results come in and it becomes increasingly obvious that Westmount will elect a Liberal (the traditional party of Quebec anglophones), Rubbo shows us a people that, like an island, is lost in an ocean that threatens to swamp it. Even though the Parti Québécois victory is happening all around them, it is something they cannot bring themselves to see. It is an event that is happening "out there somewhere." Television sets in the background reveal the extent of the PQ victory, but no one really watches them; their attention is concentrated on the immediate fate of their riding. The successful Liberal candidate's unforgiving and vindictive victory speech is intercut with Lévesque's highly emotional appearance in the Paul Sauvé arena, again shown only on television sets, as if one step removed from reality. Yet the English "reality," symbolized for generations by the name Westmount, is sad, confused and lost, detached from the society to which it belongs.

*Solzhenitsyn's Children* witnesses a more pervasive fragmentation: the disintegration of the French left and the disparate and conflicting ideologies that separate its intellectuals. It is Rubbo's most difficult, perhaps least satisfying, but most ambitious work to date. It shows Rubbo examining political ideas that inform all his other films. What has Vietnam meant to contemporary society? How has our striving for social, political and economic change affected us? Marxism, the predominant philosophic force of the twentieth century, is scrutinized. The Soviet Union, Czechoslovakia, China and Cuba are all discussed in the context of their political experiments. What has been lost, what has been gained? The predominant impression left by the film is that there is no magic solution, although Rubbo finds it hard to discard his own Cuban impressions.

But *Solzhenitsyn's Children* would appear to be a pivotal film, perhaps because of its ambition, perhaps because it is an exception. Dealing as it does at the level of ideas, it remains an abstract piece of work. If the women in *Persistent and Finagling*, Sutton in *The Man Who Can't Stop* or the politicians in *I Hate to Lose* are all involved in trying to change things, the intellectuals in the Paris film are only talking about change. They are less active than their equivalents in the earlier films. *Yes or No, Jean-Guy Moreau* grows out of this context. Moreau, a political satirist, is employed as a device to examine different perspectives on the Quebec referendum. Like Rubbo, Moreau is uncertain as to how he will vote, and uses his art as an excuse to delay his decision. So, while the 1976 election is seen through the eyes of politicians campaigning for votes, the referendum is approached through the eyes of an actor preparing a stage show in Toronto. This disjunction from reality is potentially alienating—something Moreau seems to become increasingly aware of—and in the course of his Toronto show we witness a transformation. If Moreau has been remarkably like a chameleon until this moment, here, in Toronto, fully made up to look like Lévesque, he moves unconsciously from political satire of the Quebec premier to a point where he "becomes" Lévesque, confusing his audience in the process. Asked by someone about this contradiction—whether the show is devoted to political satire or to politics—Moreau/Lévesque replies that the two sometimes intersect. At this point we feel that Moreau finally reaches his decision, so that he can finally say "yes" in the referendum.

If *I Hate to Lose* and *Solzhenitsyn's Children* dealt with their subjects through the prisms of communities and groups of people, *Yes or No, Jean-Guy Moreau* scrutinizes the individual, albeit it in a social context. This shift of perspective, which is visible to a certain extent in the earlier work, becomes even more noticeable in *Daisy—The Story of a Facelift*, a film about a middle-aged woman who decides she needs to change her appearance. If Moreau was a device to explore the referendum question, *Daisy* is used in a like fashion to examine our fascination with appearance and surface impressions. Daisy is a dyed-in-the-wool romantic who has gone through three marriages, and is as she puts it, "thinking of upgrading the product, externally at least." Terrified of growing older, she is obsessed with her appearance and looking attractive to men. Apparently the least political of Rubbo's films on the surface, it is in fact full of implication. Dealing as it does with the cinematic, and I would maintain very regressive, representation of a woman, it contains an unmistakeable subtext. Daisy completely defines herself and her worth through the eyes of the male. Even though she has a successful career, it is nevertheless not enough to fulfil her. She sees herself as object, the way men would see her—coyly posing for the male gaze by the side of a pool—and undergoes a brutalizing operation to please the imaginary male who is not in her life.

It is extremely useful and sobering to compare the representations of women and the attitudes toward society in *Persistent and Finagling* and *Daisy*. Images of women are central to both films: in the first it is housewives trying to become activists, and in the second it is a woman trying to control the aging process. Female stereotypes are also scrutinized: women as housewives in *Persistent and Finagling*, or as eternally young and attractive in *Daisy*. The women in both films are shown to be efficient, competent and organized, but most significantly they are trying to effect change. In *Persistent and Finagling* it is a group of women trying to bring the issue of pollution to people's attention. Socially aware, they are moving out into the world as a group, challenging the male world that surrounds and controls them at every step. On the other hand *Daisy* portrays a woman trying to change her looks. Absent is a sense of real community. The film registers a withdrawal, a looking inward, a self-absorption. If *Persistent and Finagling* deals with women trying to control not just their lives but also their environment, largely for their children, who figure so prominently in the film, *Daisy* portrays a woman (and a society) for whom these concerns are totally absent.

Rubbo's recent work also witnesses other important changes. While he has always been present in the diary films, the nature of that presence has changed. In the early work, right up to *I Hate to Lose*, that presence was never intrusive nor, apparently, manipulative. It was sympathetic, and as we see in *Waiting for Fidel*, restrained. However, it was always possible to locate Rubbo's viewpoint in relation to his material. His last three diary films, from *Solzhenitsyn's Children* on, all show Rubbo becoming more involved in the pro-filmic event and on the image-track. There is an acknowledgement of increasing manipulation by him of events. He instigates meetings and conversations. There has also been a move toward the employment of fictional strategies within the material—the donning of masks in *Solzhenitsyn's Children*, the roller-skating scene in *Yes or No, Jean-Guy Moreau*. *Daisy* moves even further in this direction with the careful structuring and shooting of certain scenes (Daisy meeting Peters in the doctor's office), the use of music to create mood and ambience (the Willie Nelson song), and the highly mediated use of editing at particular moments (when we think we are about to see Daisy's operation, Rubbo suggestively intercuts a facial massage into this section, a scene full of implication and meaning). Yet, as Rubbo imposes his presence more and more upon his material, ironically it becomes more difficult to ascertain where he stands in relation to it. Does *Daisy* contain an implicit criticism of our obsession with appearance, or is it simply dealing with one woman who has been made happier by undergoing the operation? Is it a regressive portrait of women, or is it a condemnation of society as a whole? Perhaps it is all these things—or none of them? There is a sense of suspended judgement to these films, as if Rubbo has shied away at the last moment from the full implications of his subjective treatment of the chosen material.

Where does this finally leave us with Rubbo? To my mind he is one of the most important documentary filmmakers in the world. His formal innovations and questionings, his intervention as a social actor on the image-track, and his acknowledgement of his role as instigator, creator and manipulator are central to the documentary debate, yet are questions being addressed by few filmmakers. If there is a radical element to Rubbo, it lies with this desire to question and perhaps rupture the illusionism at the core of documentary. (It is any wonder, then, that the CBC doesn't show his material? Their investment in maintaining the illusion of reality and the status quo that it serves is self-evident.) He is scarcely less important than others who have innovated in similarly novel ways.

Yet I find the recent work troubling and problematic. In his article on the NFB's Candid Eye movement of the late fifties,[8] Bruce Elder describes these films as being detached, non-involved and passive. Applying Frantz Fanon's analysis of colonial art,[9] Elder concludes that these anglophone films articulate their subject matter from an external point of view, a stage that is characterized by an ironic sort of humour. Committed to a national culture, they nevertheless view it from a detached, external and often amused point of view. This description is fitting when dealing with Rubbo's most recent work. As he admits in the film, one of the reasons for making *Yes or No, Jean-Guy Moreau* was to "selfishly find out if I had a place here," in Quebec. Perceiving himself as an outsider, as not belonging, he searches for something with which he can identify. But if Moreau discovers who he is in the course of mounting his Toronto show, Rubbo has no similar, privileged moment. *Daisy* also deals with a rootless character, a person who feels more at home in London, Vienna and Salzburg than where she is. As a displaced person, perhaps she is even Rubbo's alter ego.

1984

---

1 Bill Nichols, "Documentary Theory and Practice," *Screen*, 17, No. 4 (Winter 1976/77), and also "The Voice of Documentary," *Film Quarterly*, 36, No. 3 (Spring 1983).
2 Robin Wood, "Bertrand Tavernier: Realism Rehabilitated," *Canadian Forum*, 62, No. 724, (Dec-Jan. 1982-83), p. 47.
3 Nichols, "The Voice of Documentary," op.cit.
4 Jean-Louis Comolli, *Cahiers du cinéma*, 209, 211, quoted and translated in *Realism and the Cinema*, ed. Christopher Williams (London and Henley: Routledge & Kegan Paul, 1980): 226.
5 Nichols, "Documentary Theory and Practice," op.cit.
6 Nichols, "The Voice of the Documentary," op.cit.
7 Dave Jones, "The Man in the Picture," *Lumiere* (April 1973), p. 14.
8 Bruce Elder, "On the Candid-Eye Movement," *Canadian Film Reader*, ed. Seth Feldman and Joyce Nelson (Toronto: Peter Martin Associates, 1977), pp. 86-94.
9 Frantz Fanon, "On National Culture," *The Wretched of the Earth* (New York: Grove Press, 1968), especially p. 179. The three phases of colonial art are: 1) "the native intellectual gives proof that he has assimilated the culture of the occupying power." 2) "the native is disturbed; he decides to remember what he is . . . But since the native is not a part of his people, since he only has exterior relations with his people, he is content to recall their life only." 3) "in . . . the fighting phase, the native, after having tried to lose himself in the people and with the people, will on the contrary shake the people. Instead of according the people's lethargy an honoured place in his esteem, he turns himself into an awakener of the people."

# *The Search for Country: The Films of Derek May*

## BY PIERS HANDLING

*The lack of attention given the work of Derek May is in many ways illustrative of structural dilemmas endemic to the perception of Canadian cinema. Approached as an auteur, as he is here by Piers Handling, May displays all the characteristics of the complete filmmaker. His vision is his and his alone. His work is a response to his personal circumstances; it grows in complexity in time to the filmmaker's own growth in experience and understanding. May's work reflects his time and place. Even the critics cooperate; reaction to the films (or, at least, such reaction as there has been) is mixed according to one's sympathy with the auteur's world view.*

*What is problematic in the Canadian context is not so much May's work itself, but the placement of that work within the demands of his culture. All his films—from* Angel *to* Off the Wall *(the film that was to come out of the footage described by Handling toward the end of his article)—fall within a form that is perhaps unique to public sector filmmaking: what might be called "the institutionalized experimental film." This seems to exist at the National Film Board in a space between the technical innovations of public-spirited animation and generalized impatience with conventional forms of documentary presentation. Films like May's (and Rubbo's, and Duckworth's early work—as described elsewhere in this volume) appear to exist in reaction to the implied call for self-sacrifice that comes with the territory of civil service filmmaking. But can (or should) these demands ever be fully rejected, given the institutional restraints on the Board and the public expectations of its products? It is more likely that the answer to these demands will be framed in the language of the demands themselves, and that as a consequence "the institutionalized experimental film" will always speak with one eye looking over its shoulder at the gaugers of public responsibility. The pure, experimental filmmaker is expected to be completely self-indulgent; the documentarian may strive to erase any trace of himself or herself in pursuit of the subject. But to mix the two could be an invitation to the worst of both worlds: the obscurity of self-indulgence and the faceless pendantry of documentation.*

*And yet, does the theoretical weakness of a mixed genre necessarily negate the work of its practitioners? Is the difficulty in viewing May's work his problem or that of his Canadian audiences? Fidel Castro is supposed to have permitted his state-sponsored filmmakers "everything in the name of the Revolution, nothing against it." Perhaps part of the problem is that Canadian society does not have a revolution (or a single coherent ideology) against which to judge "everything." Handling's writing is, in its appreciation of May, a message written from the point of view of this as yet unattained critical confidence (and is perhaps an invitation to its attainment).*

Derek May has made only eight films since joining the National Film Board in 1965. One of them is feature-length, two run less than ten minutes; a modest output to be sure. Yet May's films are all highly individualistic. They challenge filmic convention, no compromise is apparent in any of them, and they are all indisputably and recognizably *his*. The personal stamp that marks his films suggests that they were made with complete independence. Yet this apparent freedom could perhaps account for the relatively small number of films that he has made. His work has been described as difficult and self-indulgent. Critical reaction has often been hostile. His first film was quite successful; his second was greeted with a review headlined "More National Film Board Junk."[1] Every innovative artist is bound to elicit contradictory reactions to his work. Any reaction is better than no reaction at all, however, and more often than not May's films have gone unnoticed, unreviewed and, more distressingly, unseen. Yet May's films reveal a filmmaker in search of a style appropriate to his subject matter, a style indigenous to this country and its people, attuned to their rhythms and their uncertainties, sensitive to the external and internal landscape. This style has gradually defined itself over the years. Indeed, the notion of definition is itself central to May's work, as the search for a form to contain his concerns has been closely tied to his own search for identity.

These concepts of definition and identity are perhaps more immediate for May than for other Canadian filmmakers. As an immigrant (he was born in England), married to Patricia Nolin, a Québécois film and television actress, he has been caught in a paradoxical situation, adapting to a new country that has suffered from its own identity crisis, while living in a province that over the past twenty years has defined itself in a very conscious way. The manner in which May has dealt with this complex reality is what makes his work so interesting. The confusions in the films are his confusions, very personally felt and presented. At times, his work has been autobiographical, combining elements of the self-portrait with the home movie. In some of the other films, he is not an immediately recognizable presence; the subjects exist outside himself and he merely brings his sensibility to bear on them. However, every film has been a witness to May's personal desire to perceive himself in relation to the world around him. His early films seem to ask the question, who am I, and how do I relate to the world? His last three films add a further dimension to this quest. They seem to ask, who are we, and what does our country mean to us?

May's work forms itself rather neatly into four distinct groups, and for the purposes of this essay I will approach the films in pairs: *Angel* (1966) and *Pandora* (1971), *Niagara Falls* (1967) and *McBus* (1969), *Sananguagat* (1974) and *Pictures From the 1930's* (1977), and *A Film for Max* (1971) and *Mother Tongue* (1979). Although these groupings are not chronological, they will help distinguish between what I perceive as the various stages of May's career.

## THE ABSTRACT FILMS

His two experimental, abstract films belie their length and apparent simplicity by distilling a number of May's concerns within their brief running times. His first film, *Angel*, depicts a playful encounter between a young woman and a man. Set to the wistful and vital music of Leonard Cohen, *Angel* uses a pair of angel's wings that the man wants to borrow from the woman as its narrative base. A brief, somewhat ephemeral relationship is struck between the two of them, and they eventually retire to his room after their outdoor merriment.

The three most interesting aspects of *Angel* are its pictorial imagery, the use of sound, and the structural strategies employed by May to reinforce the thematic content. Through the process of optical printing May eliminates all detail in his image, all contrast, any illusion of three dimensions, and finally the landscape itself. The two characters, devoid of visual detail and definition, wander through a stark black-and-white world, with only the occasional glimpse of trees or outlines of a door and a bed shown to suggest place. This elimination of the landscape suggests a denial, or perhaps an unfamiliarity, with the environment in which one is living. One cannot show "images" that have no meaning, or are "foreign" and therefore not understood. This notion of separation from one's surroundings is central to an understanding of May's films. His subsequent films chronicle a search to establish some knowledge of what it is that surrounds him, to define some constituent elements of his environment, and finally this leads him to examine where he is living.

Duality is implicit in *Angel* in a number of ways: man-woman, black-white, indoors-outdoors, and finally in the possession or absence of wings. This concept of duality is continually restated by May, and it is employed both thematically and stylistically, often suggesting polarization and oppositions, or implying separation, detachment, disharmony. This antithetical device is woven into the encounter portrayed in the film. Visually, we are removed from the two characters through extreme stylization. However the sound-track works in opposition to the image. It is intimate and personal, and communicates warmth and emotional contact. This disjunctive tone, with various elements working in opposition to one another, is common to much of May's work, and is used with great sophistication from film to film.

May's other visual abstraction, *Pandora*, is similar to *Angel* in many ways, although new elements have been introduced. The film is in colour and, while the image with no detail is still predominant, he introduces normal photographic shots into the film in three or four instances. Significantly, these are all of his wife. The dream-like quality of *Angel* is more apparent in *Pandora.* Here May plays a number of visual tricks on his audience, tricks meant to suggest that appearances are not in fact what they seem to be. A dog stands on what appears to be a hill, until an arm detaches itself from this "hill" to pick it up. The "hill" is, in reality, a reclining woman's body. One is left with the overriding impression in *Pandora* that in fact there is only *one* thing that May is certain exists. The only "thing" he shows us that approaches reality, as we know it in the true photographic sense, is his wife. The other images—a woman hanging washing out to dry, a woman playing with her child, the child playing with its toys—are located only in the mind of the filmmaker.

Neutral images are contextualized through *Pandora's* omnipresent sound-track. Sounds of ocean waves breaking against the shore in a dull continuous roar (at times almost like that of jet aircraft) add a feeling of struggle and tension to the film. This sense of conflict is apparent in some of the stark pictures and graphics employed. At one point two faces puffing coloured smoke at each other eventually obliterate the entire image, while in another moment clouds of smoke whirl and eddy like exploding bombs.

*Pandora* has a strong sense of uncertainty about it, implied by the visual jokes May plays on us. This uncertainty extends to the use of his wife in the film. The normal photographic shots of her are infrequent; they seem to interrupt the film. More often we see her in silhouette, like a phantom, unknowable, her body a part of the trickery that is employed; or she is shot with a video camera, making her image blurred, distorted, and imprecise. As in *Angel*, visual polarities abound. But there are also powerful arrangements of three objects in the frame in *Pandora*—

May and his wife had by this time had a child, yet he is shown almost entirely as a featureless shape that moves and crawls, but lacks an identity.

These abstract works are particularly important to our understanding of May's later films. They are evidence of May's maturing visual and aural experimentations. Both of them use sound and image in counterpoint, the dual nature of the medium seeming to have struck an artistic nerve that he would explore more fully. Both *Angel* and *Pandora* are uncertain films that veil contact with reality through their use of a high-contrast image. The search for definition is a powerful force in both films; it is also a subjective, interior search. The next step would see May looking outside himself at the external world, a world which had hitherto been denied real recognition in these abstract pieces.

## THE TOURIST FILMS

May's second and third films were more ambitious in scope, size and structure than the experimental works. They were live action films, strongly controlled and shaped by the filmmaker, having more traditional documentary elements to them. More importantly, both *Niagara Falls* and *McBus* contain the idea of tourism at the centre of their structural strategies. The choice of Niagara Falls as a location was not arbitrary. To a foreigner its name is synonymous with Canada in the same way that the Eiffel Tower is with France, or the Statue of Liberty with the United States. In this way Niagara Falls functions as a symbolic microcosm of Canada, revealing certain things about our country, our history, and perhaps even providing insight into our own self-image.

The idea of tourism is reinforced by the interviews in the film; the people interviewed are all involved in the phenomenon of Niagara Falls as a tourist centre—the tour guide, the Mayor who explains what honeymoon certificates signify, the policeman who recounts the exploit of a man going over the Falls in a rubber ball, and the hansom driver, who proudly remembers some of the famous people who have ridden in his buggy: Marilyn Monroe, Jean Peters, the Real McCoys and Joseph Cotten.

Parallel to these interviews is another story that May constructs: a search for an Indian girl, featuring the American actor, Michael J. Pollard, famous for his role in *Bonnie and Clyde*. The two levels or "stories" intersect in one important way. In the fictional portion Pollard is searching for the Indian girl, the Maid of the Mists, whose legend is also recounted in the tourist show which begins and ends the film. The dual structure, visible in *Angel* and *Pandora,* is evident in the structure of *Niagara Falls,* allowing May to juxtapose fiction and reality in continual balance. While the interviews with the good burghers of the city allow access to the clean and tidy picturesque surface reality of Niagara Falls, Pollard wanders through a much more disturbing landscape of seedy motels, run-down garages, abandoned lots and backstreet shops. The interviews are graced with a polite deference occasioned by these transitory meetings. However, Pollard's encounters are far more natural, and range from the good-natured lunch he enjoys with the grape-pickers, to the outright hostility with which the portrait artist greets his enquiries concerning the Indian maid.

*Niagara Falls* is a film constructed around these oppositions: between its "fiction" and its "reality"; between Pollard and the native inhabitants May interviews; between the city as a tourist centre and its decaying, backstreet environment; and between the myth of Indian legend and the reality of commercial exploitation. May shows that the legend of the Maid of the Mists, an indigenous, pure and lovely evocation of humanity and its relationship to nature, has become perverted by contemporary demands. To increase the humiliation, the Indians are little more than puppets in the enactment of the sacrifice of the Maid, which is merely a light entertainment provided for the tourists.

Central to *Niagara Falls* in Pollard's search for the Maid, implying a symbolic search for parts of our native history. May suggests that this history has been denied to us in its true context, that it has been subverted and subjected to distortion. Pollard, like May, is only a tourist in the film, although as an outsider he is perhaps more conscious of disrupting and disturbing the status quo. He is less inclined to accept societal norms, unlike those people interviewed, who are completely integrated into an environment that they accept without question: a society of exploitation (the tourist guide), of commercialism (the Mayor), of gimmicky stunts (the policeman's story), and of colonization (the hansom driver whose list of personalities includes only American movie stars). The rootlessness of this society is compounded by the choice of Pollard as the central character. Not only is he a tourist in the film, he is also a foreigner, an American, literally drifting through a world to which he is not connected. The addition of these various levels of alienation in *Niagara Falls* combines to create a disturbing ambience. May values only the indigenous, the Indians, who have all but "disappeared" from the visible landscape. Their native heritage has been totally distorted over the years. To emphasize this, May presents us with a group of Boy Scouts, who merrily sing gory songs about a mythical frontier past with a bland incomprehension of the implications of what they are singing.

*McBus* is an extension of the disturbing world shown in *Niagara Falls*, full of powerful, disjunctive images and sounds, lacking any real sense of narrative. Like its predecessor, *McBus* uses the idea of the tourist as its central visual symbol, this time following a bus tour of Montreal, led by a female, black tour guide. From the opening shot of *McBus*, a Scottish piper playing his pipes amidst a maze of concrete highway supports, we are subjected to a barrage of incongruous scenes. A man shouts indecipherably through a loudspeaker to the piper, the tour guide's talk is little more than a sonic jumble, a shot reverberates on the soundtrack, we hear parts of a movie plot involving a condemned man and a long-distance operator, a steel-drum band plays, and a black girl, wearing a tam, dances around a Scottish piper in a barren landscape. At times *McBus* has the sense, to use Godard's subtitle to *Weekend*, of being a film found on a scrap-heap. It is a work of fragmentation, of dislocated pictures and unconnected sounds. There is a quixotic feel to what is shown, as if May had selected images at random. Yet the choice of the black tour guide, and the other scenes with blacks in *McBus*, are too carefully selected to suggest that this is in fact the case. They, like Pollard and the Indian girl in *Niagara Falls*, are foreigners in the landscape of this film. Like May, they are either tourists or outsiders.

*McBus* contains an underlying edge of despair, revealing an almost desperate urge to communicate. People speak, but what they say is indecipherable. The piper plays his haunting refrain in an empty, unforgiving landscape of concrete, while being harassed by a trench-coated man, who shouts at him through a loudspeaker. There is a paranoia to their encounter, as if the man with the loudspeaker epitomized everything that wants to suppress the urge to make music. There is something furtive about the piper, as if he has been condemned to play to no one. Joined at the end by the tourists from the bus, the piper has finally connected with an audience and, as if defeated by this contact, the man in the trench-coat walks away, to the accompaniment of a rousing cheer from thousands of voices.

Pollard's search for the Indian girl in *Niagara Falls* finds its mirror in the piper's search for an audience in *McBus*. Both quests are apparently resolved by the end of each film—Pollard walks off with the Indian girl, and the piper is surrounded by people. Yet the frivolity of the ending in *Niagara Falls* runs counter to the tone of the rest of the film, and in *McBus*, although the piper has met his audience, their encounter is tentative. They surround him and do not react to his performance, unlike the black girl who joyfully dances around him earlier in the film. Significantly, the black tour guide, who has shepherded the tourists around Montreal, does not join them when they go out to meet the piper. She drives off in the bus alone, dancing to her calypso music.

*Niagara Falls* and *McBus* see May move beyond the carefully controlled artificiality of *Angel* and *Pandora* to grapple with the "real" world. If control is an integral element of the abstract films, the opposite is true of the two tourist films. They depict a chaotic world, full of turmoil, devoid of any harmony. After dealing with these two "glimpses of reality," it appears that May had found little of value. The intimate encounter of *Angel* does not have an equivalent in either *Niagara Falls* or *McBus* (although May tries to develop a relationship between his main characters in both films, and in *Niagara Falls* he even includes visual references which allude to *Angel*). Perhaps the warmth of *Angel* was only possible within the limited and finite world within which May chose to set this subject. The world of the tourist films is an alienating one. It has lost its soul, it provides no answers, offers no alternatives, has no compassion. If it is alienating, then alternatively, he is alienated from it. Yet within this absurdist world, some people are at least reaching out, trying to overcome the "cold" environment in which they live. This is the only optimism that he allows us.

*McBus* was followed by May's feature, *A Film for Max,* and *Pandora.* He then took a break from film, working in video for the NFB's Challenge for Change unit, and travelled and painted on a Canada Council grant. Aesthetically he had reached a turning point in his career, for *Pandora* was in many respects a return to the ground covered in his first film.

## THE ART FILMS

When May returned to film, new elements appeared in his work. The mannered obscurity and fragmentation of his earlier films disappeared. However the visual and aural experiments of that period obviously provided May with a rigorous preparation for the three films that constitute his most recent work. Two of these were sponsored films, and both of them dealt with aspects of Canadian art. The first, *Sananguagat: Inuit Masterworks of 1000 Years*, is a synthesis of all of May's previous work. Technically it contains the visual and aural components that he had worked so hard to refine. Structurally it continues the notion of duality. Thematically, the search for definition which had underscored his films has here come much closer to some sort of resolution.

*Sananguagat* is suffused by a feeling of peace and tranquility. It is May's most relaxed, most gentle film. Gone is the dissonant, electronic polyphony of *McBus.* In its place we find more natural sounds—Inuit chants and songs, running water. It is uncluttered, a film of silences. The concrete wilderness of *Niagara Falls* and *McBus* has been replaced by wild and beautiful northern landscapes. Pollard's search for our native past, implying the quest for an indigenous culture, has here been partially resolved through May's depiction of the Inuit's daily life. He has found a society in harmony with itself. Its art has grown out of its culture. Gone are the tension and stress of contemporary life which define *Niagara Falls* and *McBus.* The quest for identity and resolution has achieved a degree of certainty.

While the dual structure of *Niagara Falls* suggests conflict, that of *Sananguagat* is primarily, although not totally, harmonic. The inseparable connection between the soapstone carvings and Inuit life is demonstrated as May intercuts between the two. Arctic life unfolds in scenes of unobtrusive observation; the pace is languid. The artworks, shot in a studio set, are often presented dynamically, suggesting hidden power and mystery. At certain points the two intersect visually in subtle ways. An Inuit child shrugging in his jacket is placed next to a carving of an owl assuming a similar position, while in another shot a perfect mirror image of a beached iceberg covered with seagulls is used as a beautiful visual counterpoint to May's technique of shooting some of the artworks on mirror glass. There is great sophistication in the way May uses these images throughout *Sananguagat*. The carvings reflect Inuit life—hunters and the animals hunted, women and their babies, primitive gods. One comments on the other. While little tension is visible in the film, there is nevertheless a sense that Inuit life has undergone permanent change as it moves to adopt the accoutrements of the twentieth century. Now the Inuit hunt seals with rifles, not harpoons, from small motorboats, not kayaks, and they use snowmobiles, not dog teams, to travel overland. In one shot May superimposes a gun, a saw, and snow-goggles over shots of gulls gliding over the ocean, reinforcing the idea of an increasing reliance on the mechanical.

In one sense, then, May is showing us a portrait of a society that is dying. When his camera pans from the local graveyard to the village below, we are made to feel this genocide most eloquently. The jetsam of industrial civilization has been abandoned around the village, and the rusting snow-tractors and graders, a modern scrap-heap, comment on just how much life has altered. *Sananguagat* is full of powerful, tiny moments—a child discards a chocolate bar wrapper; a snowmobile traces its way through the tiny outpost as an Inuit woman enters the church in the background; a song is replaced on the sound-track by the motor of a boat as it moves off into the distance. The final shot of *Sananguagat*—water washing over an Inuit carving of a child's face—is complex in its implications, and perhaps expresses the ambivalence visible in the rest of the film. On the one hand it represents something that has been submerged, or washed over—a culture that has literally been drowned. On the other hand it is an image of purification, uniting the two elements so apparent in *Sananguagat*: stone and water, the carvings and the ocean.

Regardless of the understated conflicts suggested in the film, *Sananguagat* is a landmark in May's career. The early films point to an artist who is alienated from his society, uncertain of his place in this landscape. The films remain cerebral statements, no matter how personally felt the pain may be. *Sananguagat* is a celebration in a way that none of the preceding films (with the possible exception of *Angel*) ever was. There is a timelessness to the Inuit artifacts that defies the transitory sensibility of *Niagara Falls* and *McBus*. The film is also the first indication that May had found something to value.

*Pictures From the 1930's* extends many of the preoccupations visible in *Sananguagat*. If the latter provided May with access to a native sense of identity, then *Pictures From the 1930's* contains a closer, more discriminating portrait of other aspects of Canadian history. Like its predecessor, this film intercuts the paintings with scenes of daily life, in this case archival shots of the period. Furthermore, May adds narration to this film, which he reads, and this allows him to be a more forceful editorial presence in the material.

Early in *Pictures From the 1930's*, May includes an interview with a woman who talks about Lawren Harris' northern landscapes. The Depression was less a political and economic crisis for Harris than a crisis of the spirit, she says. His icy, angular, and symmetric landscapes reflected a wish to see that which was "uncontaminated." In relation to May's own *Sananguagat*, which dealt with much the same landscape, there is a sense that this comment could be attached to that film. Much of *Pictures*

*From the 1930's* is marked by a powerful feeling of escape and isolation, a desire to remain "uncontaminated." May's dual mode of structuring his material reinforces this response. Images of the Depression, the dust-bowls, and the empty, disillusioned faces of the unemployed are continually counterpointed with the paintings from the period. At certain times we feel a curious gap between the two, as if the painters had worked in isolation from events that were happening around them. Landscape paintings predominate, juxtaposed with the brutal realities of the Depression. While there is an emptiness and desolation about some of the paintings, conveying an impression of impending doom, none of them treats the social reality of the period. Their full, luxuriant and vibrant colours clash with the black-and-white archival shots, suggesting that the former are detached from the realities of the latter.

Some of the painters mention that they were aware of their isolation at the time. However May seems to tie this isolation to a basic incomprehension of external events. He deals with the group that formed around John Lyman—artists attempting to overcome their feelings of insularity—and then notes that "other people were getting together for different reasons." These "other people" that May is referring to include marchers in May Day parades, auto-workers striking in Oshawa in 1937, and Hitler and Mussolini meeting in Berlin. If their isolation was essentially personal and artistic, May implies that it was also a complacent political ignorance. He quotes Emily Carr's characterization of itinerant workers, who had fled from work camps and occupied the art gallery in Vancouver, as "those brutes, like a scourge of grasshoppers." The scorn with which May imparts this information implies a condemnation of the unforgiveable detachment from social events of the day. Other editorial interpretations, implicit in the narration and the ordering of his material, position May's attitude in an equally forceful manner.

Yet the paintings themselves are treated with the same reverential awe so visible in *Sananguagat,* as objects of beauty that will live beyond their creators and the circumstances under which they were created. They are never used as mere illustration. In effect they are the real subject of the film. All but two of them are shown in their entirety, bounded by a black border, and often framed by a pause of silence before and after their appearance. Both the art films, as has been suggested elsewhere,[2] deepen the silence around their material, a silence essential to what the artworks are saying about this country. This silence demands that we look at the paintings and respond to them.

This apparent contradiction—on the one hand being highly critical of the artists, while retaining great respect for their art—is not surprising when we consider the vital importance of the landscape for May. From his first film we witness a sensibility attempting to confront this phenomenon. Initially uncertain of what it is, he represses it. In *Pandora,* the landscape becomes his wife. He acknowledges the existence of the landscape in the tourist films, but is repelled by it. In *Sananguagat* he responds to its northern magnificence. The landscape art of the thirties must have had a similar fascination for him, as the artists struggled to portray their world in the same way that May aspired to portray his own.

If *Sananguagat* allowed May, for the first time, access to his adopted country, it also dealt with a peripheral lifestyle, and one that is constantly changing. Yet May consciously avoided dealing with the social, economic and political problems of the Inuit. Visually, they are alluded to in the film, but they are never confronted. In *Pictures From the 1930's* May does not avoid the issues raised by his material. The artist it seems has a responsibility to respond to his society and his environment, to its "contaminations." We sense more of a need to confront in this film, as the Russian expatriate Paraskeva Clark has done in her paintings. May seems to be saying that we must confront politically, as well as personally.

## THE AUTOBIOGRAPHICAL FILMS

Many of the tensions that form a part of May's work are treated in greater depth in his two autobiographical films. These also fall into the two periods of his career, if we treat *Pandora* as a turning point for him. *A Film for Max* contains the experimentation, and resulting confusion, of his first films. At times it is a painful experience to watch. Virtually plotless and non-narrative, it has the appearance of being little more than a patchwork of images, scenes and sounds, focusing largely on May and his wife, with the occasional friend making an appearance on the fringes.

*A Film for Max* is composed of three sections. The first third consists of scenes of May, his wife, and some friends, shot largely in black-and-white, although some colour material is present. This section is dissonant and fragmented, marked by periods of ennui. Shots of physical tenderness are punctuated with those of self-conscious observation. The second section, also largely photographed in black-and-white, centres on an argument between May and his wife. We are not shown the argument itself. Instead we are presented with two, separate, post-facto interviews. The two interviews mark a kind of fracture in the film. They represent one of the few instances when consistent thought is presented. May, very seriously, tries to express his feelings about his relationship with his wife. She talks about him, but feels awkward in the situation. "I can't help feeling that this is far too serious," she says. These interviews acknowledge the failure of verbal communication. Words seem to be ineffective; they solve nothing.

The final third of the film is a happy contrast to the first two sections. The intensity of verbal communication has disappeared. Set in the country, it is shot almost entirely in colour, adding an idyllic tone to some of the scenes. This section is also more relaxed, lighthearted and playful, an impression underlined by the music that is used. May and his wife are joined by their son, Max, who adds an unselfconscious naturalism to the film, a contrast to the weighty self-examination in which his parents have indulged. The film ends on a joyous shot of Max gleefully playing with the family dog in the water. It portrays communication of a different order—uninhibited and exuberant play.

Nevertheless, *A Film for Max* remains to some extent a closed and difficult piece, open to a multitude of interpretations. No doubt it is meant to be this way. To a large extent it is little more than a visual diary of images and sounds taken from May's life. There is no attempt at interpretation on the filmmaker's part, no desire to explain or elucidate in a traditional narrative way. This arbitrary quality in the film extends even to the choice of black-and-white, or colour, for certain scenes. However the final sections point us in a slightly different direction. Their child is viewed with wonder, bringing May and his wife together in a visual way as well. Furthermore, the country interlude has a tranquillity to it that looks forward to *Sananguagat*. The impressions of agony and gestation seen in the first part of the film are dispensed with. We are left with the shot of Max playing with the dog, or May, carrying Max on his shoulders, walking down a country road with his wife, singing nonsensical songs to the child.

Despite this, *A Film for Max* remains extremely disconcerting, not only because of the fragmentation of its form, but also in the absence of a strong, specific reality. May and his wife are not "situated" in a normal way. They simply exist without a past, in an undefined filmic "space." We have no idea where they work or what they do, and are only occasionally allowed access to their innermost thoughts. There is an "other world" sense to this film that leaves an audience puzzled and disoriented. With *A Film For Max*, May appears to be withdrawing into himself in an attempt to comprehend certain simple facts about his life. The turmoil of the film is evidently his own, and it only reaches some form of resolution in the final sequences. However, after the apparent despair of its first sections, it ends on a note of optimism, finding magic in the son.

Eight years later May directed his second autobiographical film, *Mother Tongue*, which is also his most recent production. Much had happened in this interval as we have seen—*Sananguagat* and *Pictures From the 1930's* had given May a stronger sense of his country, and of himself. These two films revealed a growing awareness not only of Canada, but also of the artist in his society. *Mother Tongue* extends this insight in a personal and contemporary way. While *A Film for Max* is constructed of little more than fragments of his personal life, unsituated and very private, *Mother Tongue* is a beautifully achieved and comprehensive artistic statement that places May, and his life, in a specific historical and political reality, that of present-day Quebec. The film is as personal as *A Film For Max*, but it contains concerns that resonate well beyond May.

As the title infers, *Mother Tongue* is a film about linguistic differences, more specifically the bilingual relationship of May and his wife, Patricia. By extension it is also a film about our own national dilemma. Needless to say, it is a film of oppositions—linguistic, political, racial and personal. Similar tensions had hitherto informed much of May's work, from the simple, stark polarities of *Angel*, to the more complex and incisive ironies of *Pictures From the 1930's*. With extraordinary perception May depicts the realities and problems of two people with different languages, coming from diverse cultural backgrounds. The linguistic fact pervades their entire life. He is unilingual, so their relationship is conducted almost entirely in English. At times she resents her fluency: "I'm tired of speaking English. My tongue hurts, my lips ache." Yet this linguistic selfishness on May's part is nothing more than a reflection of the society he lives in, an indication of Canada's historical reality. Through this personal scrutiny and inquiry, May alludes to the problems that we face as a country. If he, as someone who is involved in a relationship with a Québécoise, is, as she puts it, "postponing fluency until he will no longer have the choice," is there any hope for the rest of us?

Ironically, the marriage has acted as a kind of liberating device for Patricia, which she acknowledges when she says: "I'm attached to my roots because they free me from you; I'm attached to you because you free me from my roots." This antithesis is central to *Mother Tongue*. There is also a commonality of feelings and experiences throughout the film, reflected in the use of stills and other previously shot material. We are shown old photographs and home movies of Patricia as a child, her parent's wedding, and snapshots from her past. Similarly, May looks into his past and his heritage, including analogous moments—a picture of his parents on their wedding day, the London blitz. Yet, on a fundamental human level, this past does not necessarily separate them as their language does. On the contrary it speaks to universal and shared experiences. At one point home movie footage of her parent's wedding is followed by a photograph of Patricia in her wedding dress, which subsequently leads us back to the present when, in the next scene, we see Patricia talking to her mother on the phone. Instead of potential rupture in these successive moments, there is a continuity suggested by the ease with which generational and temporal lines are crossed.

Despite the common elements of their lives—children, weddings, etc.—there are moments when May and Patricia are isolated from each other, living a life that cannot be shared. At one point May, alone at home, watches Patricia's performance in the prestigious *Duplessis* television series. Detached from her reality, it becomes a secondhand experience for him. Significantly, at a reception held after this broadcast, May is not visually present to share her happiness; it becomes a moment that belongs to her.

True to the complex nature of the film, there is yet another kind of isolation depicted. There is a cocoon-like quality in *Mother Tongue*, which has something to do with the interior nature of the film. This hermetic feeling is accentuated when May intercuts languid, silent shots of a snowstorm into the film. Rather than opening the film out, these wintry shots seem to stifle the exterior world, adding a gentle, dream-like quality to it. The film only occasionally escapes from this seductive grasp when May, or his wife and children, venture outside to skate, or play street hockey. At different moments in the film Patricia speaks of escape—escaping from the film, escaping definition, escaping not being her own master. Yet within this desire to get away from it all, simply to watch the snowflakes fall, lies a personal political reality that is as enigmatic as it is individualistic. By tying this apparent apoliticism to Quebec's past, through the *Duplessis* material included, we cannot help but feel that May is confused by the contradictions that surround him. While Patricia confronts him, personally and politically, there is another part of her that is parochial and insular, that wants to detach itself and escape.

Despite the paradoxical nature of *Mother Tongue*, May does not try to hide behind the implications and complexities raised by his material. He does not want to mystify us; rather his guiding impulse is to attempt the definition and comprehension of another person and her culture. Patricia speaks directly to us in one scene because, as she says, "I want them to understand." This dialogue is built into the film. It is as much Patricia's film as it is May's, and we are keyed to this from the first moments when they introduce themselves on the soundtrack—he in English, she in French, their lines alternating with one another, inextricably linked together. Unlike *A Film For Max*, May is here more concerned with articulating his thoughts, thus allowing *Mother Tongue* a unity denied the former. If it is also his most circumspect work, it goes a long way toward resolving a number of the tensions found in his other films. Its strength and passion is transmitted from its sense of identity, an acknowledgement of who and what he is. Finally, in *Mother Tongue*, May seems to be saying that politics have a deeply personal base, that the needs of the individual are what motivate people. Patricia and he live a life that is full of "political" implications, that is composed of numerous decisions—conscious or unconscious, everyday and commonplace—that have subsequent ramifications which affect their ability to live a satisfied and equal life.

May's work is rich and complex when closely watched, only gradually revealing its secrets. This does not imply that the films are inaccessible, although many would argue this point. They are, however, demanding, and require our participation if they are to be fully understood. Perhaps this is not surprising when one considers that the notion of communication is a theme that May returns to with some regularity. *Angel* is a film where word and image are held in a continual balance, and much of the action on a dramatic level takes place through dialogue. *McBus* deals explicitly with somebody who is trying to establish contact with other people through his music. The same could be said of the two art films, which contain this idea within the very nature of the medium they have chosen to examine. The art in both of these films "speaks" to us in some way and what it "says" is pivotal to an understanding of the works. *A Film For Max* and *Mother Tongue* explore various facets of this theme, the former admitting that verbal communication is limiting and finite, the latter demanding that some form of dialogue take place.

May's films reveal a consistent aesthetic at work. From a position of total unfamiliarity with his new country, evident in *Angel*, he has struggled to give us not just a reflection of himself, but also of ourselves. Who are we and where do we live? his films seem to ask. *Niagara Falls* and *McBus* were painful steps along the way to a resolution of this question. The art of this country allowed May, himself a painter, access to the society in which he was living, and a deep appreciation for the landscape that is uniquely ours. *Sananguagat* and *Pictures From the 1930's* speak directly to our national experience in the same way that *Corral* and *City of Gold* did for an earlier generation. *Mother Tongue*, despite its deep, personal base, touches a responsive chord amongst us all.

May is now (Spring, 1981) working on a new film dealing with the art world of Toronto and the people who inhabit it. From the two or three assembled sequences I have seen, it is impossible to grasp what the final film will look like, but it is clear that he has lost none of his flair for visual experimentation. His innovative and challenging style has attracted its share of abuse, but also some richly deserved accolades. In a recent letter to *CineMag*, Peter Watkins, director of such internationally acclaimed films as *The War Game*, *Culloden*, and *Edvard Munch*, described *Mother Tongue* as "one of the most interesting and meaningful films that I have seen for a long time . . . ."[3] The term "interesting" is, as always, a critical understatement. But the search for meaning in the work of Derek May is a task that the responsible student of Canadian film can no longer afford to forego.

*Journal of Canadian Studies*, 16, No. 1 (Spring 1981)

---

1 Roy Shields, "More National Film Board Junk," *Toronto Daily Star*, May 2, 1968.
2 Dan Driscoll, "*Sananguagat—Inuit Masterworks*," *Pot Pourri*, November 1974, pp. 18-19.
3 Peter Watkins, "Maintaining Standards," *CineMag*, June 16, 1980, pp. 10, 17.

# *The Cinema, Memory and The Photographic Trace*

**BY PETER HARCOURT**

*The parameter of Martin Duckworth's career encircles most of the multidirectional thrusts undertaken by both the* NFB *and the Canadian film community as a whole during the last twenty years. Beginning as an assistant cameraman in 1963, Duckworth found himself involved in such productions as Don Owen's* The Ernie Game, *the infamous* Christopher's Movie Matinee *and Mike Rubbo's* Sad Song of Yellow Skin. *His directorial debut in 1970 extended these varied interests into films that ranged from the deeply personal works discussed here to the socially committed documentary experiments of the* Challenge for Change *program. Duckworth's best known recent work is* No More Hibakusha *(1983), an eye-level account of a mini-peace campaign waged by a small group of Hiroshima survivors.*

*In his discussions of* The Wish *and, to a lesser extent,* Accident, *Peter Harcourt finds in Duckworth's work questions central to the contemporary understanding of cinematic practice. That understanding, as R. Bruce Elder notes elsewhere in this volume ("Image: Representation and Object—The Photographic Image in Canadian Avant-Garde Film"), rests on a reevaluation of the nature and worth of the photographed entity. If, as Elder contends, this reevaluation is of special pertinence to Canadian cinema, then it becomes incumbent upon the critic to find and explore the consequences of new theoretical dimensions as s/he finds them in actual practice. Harcourt may go even further here. It may be possible to see in these moments of Duckworth's* oeuvre *a conscious elicitation of these questions. From the filmmaker's point of view,* The Wish *and* Accident *seem to act as a reflective hiatus, a pause during which the neophyte director and committed social documentarian searched his tools for their worth, and for the new directions in which they were to lead him. In the context of Canadian cinema as a whole, the films act as a reference to the theoretical issues cited by Elder. More importantly, the insight that Duckworth provides comes not from a peripheral figure, but rather from a major practitioner in a tradition of dependence upon photographed reality.*

For Martin Duckworth

*. . . when we are nostalgic, we take pictures.*

Susan Sontag[1]

*There is a delicate form of the empirical which identifies itself so intimately with its object that it thereby becomes theory.*

Goethe[2]

In 1970, working at the National Film Board, Martin Duckworth completed a short film that, on the level of intention, might have been just a home movie. On the level of achievement, however, *The Wish* is really something else. Through the intricacy of its structure, the circularity of its form, and the originality of its syntax, the film becomes a disquisition on time, on memory, and on the relationship of the past to the present, of continuity to rupture, of the personal to the historical, and of the morality of emotional involvement versus aesthetic detachment. The film invokes feelings both of desire and guilt, of presence and absence, of life and death. By intercutting direct cinema footage with stills from the past, the film achieves a dialectic between the sense of how-it-is-happening-now and of how-it-was-then.

> . . . art mediates between what is given and what is desired.
>
> Berger, p. 158

*The Wish* takes as its "given" a visit of Duckworth's own twin daughters, Sylvia and Marya, age about eight, to his parents' summer home in the Eastern Townships. Through its actuality footage, the film captures what appears to be a series of unrehearsed events: the girls play on the veranda, they help to clean the house, they go fishing with their grandfather, they all have a picnic lunch in a graveyard. On this level, *The Wish* is very much an observational film. However, whether by accident or design, Duckworth disturbs the apparent transparency of his own documentary practice by systematically employing a disruptive syntactical device: Whenever one of the twins breaks with the agreed fiction that she is not being filmed and looks at the camera (which is, of course, at her father), Duckworth freezes the frame and cuts away to a series of stills derived from the past. Observation of the living moment is thus disturbed by its contiguous relationship to that which is past. The living moment is suspended as memory intervenes. As Sontag has written about *Menschen am Sonntag*: "The photographs shock, in the flow of the movie—transmuting, in an instant, present into past, life into death" (p. 70). They also create desire for what is no longer there.

> It is the double-sided nature of the concept of representation—the fact that the *presence* of the original is suggested by an artistic representation even while its *absence* is demanded—that explains the peculiar course of desire a representational image—or any other form of representation—evokes. This desire projects itself toward the Other the image represents. Yet nothing can retain its Otherness when it is actually present; the desire is impossible to sate, because inherent in the very concept of Otherness is the idea of absence.[3]

Hence, a filmic record of reality is ideal for someone who wants less to analyze its meaning than to preserve its mystery. It is equally ideal for someone who wishes more to observe a series of events than (at any rate, at the moment of their occurrence) to get involved with them. "The person who intervenes cannot record; the person who is recording cannot intervene" (Sontag, p. 12). To film an unstaged event is to establish a distance from it—paradoxically with a medium that seems to bring us closer to the surfaces of reality than any other form of the representational arts. The technology of the medium is never totally absent from the viewer's consciousness. Only the most unsophisticated spectators would assume that this closeness to surfaces that we can experience with film eliminates the established distance from which the filmic act began.

In *The Wish*, we have both a narrative complexity and a theoretical one: The mother is wished for by the children and desired by the film. Has she gone away or is she dead? The verbal expression of the children's desire is too private to be more than whispered. It is virtually too private to be shared with the audience, with the intended recipients of the film. Furthermore, the moment of wishing that both opens and closes the film is itself idealized by the selective focus detectable within the image, by the sun on the water sparkling in the background and by the distance established in our minds through the knowledge that the lens is in its telephoto position and, finally, by the cutaway to Duckworth and his crew in the distance—a cutaway that we later realize is diegetically dislocated.

The film begins with its ending and ends with its beginning—but we cannot know that until we get to the end. The film ends with the twins' arrival, thus leaving us with the suggestion that the *real* experience of the visit is yet to take place. Hence the nostalgia, endemic to memory—indeed, to the very essence of photography—is challenged by this final sense we get that what we have witnessed is not what took place. We have watched a construct. Reality, in the brute sense, is yet to be undergone. And for all the detail of documentation, both filmic and photographic, that we have observed in the film, the absent one, the desired one—the wife and mother—is only present in the film in the form of a photographic trace, the presence of which confirms her absence and preserves her mystery.

> The sense of the unattainable that can be evoked by photographs feeds directly into the erotic feelings of those for whom desirability is enhanced by distance. The lover's photograph hidden in a married woman's wallet, the poster photograph of a rock star up over an adolescent's bed, the campaign-button image of a politician's face pinned on a voter's coat, the snapshots of a cabdriver's children clipped to the visor—all such talismatic uses of photography express a feeling both sentimental and implicitly magical: they are attempts to contact or lay claim to another reality (Sontag, p. 16).

Toward the end of *The Wish*, as the colour bleeds out from a freeze-frame to become a still of the two children and their grandparents standing by a tombstone, and after the final expression of the wish, once again whispered, when the colour bleeds in on a still to become the scene of the twins' arrival, the effect does seem "magical." This cinematic magic, however, has been designed to signal a key sequence within the film and is very much the result of the film's technical polish, of its emotional sensitivity, and of the authority of its form.

By way of a more detailed analysis, one might offer three structuring principles that inform *The Wish*:

1) First of all, there is the gaze—the gaze both of the twins as they look directly at us and of the photographs that these frozen moments in time introduce. Being lodged within a narrative, these family photographs are rescued from what Barthes has called "the vast disorder of objects."[4] While they are obviously "an emanation of the referent" (Barthes, p. 80), these photographs refer collectively to both a sense of the past and a sense of loss. "The realists do not take a photograph for a 'copy' of reality, but for an emanation of *past reality*: a *magic*, not an art" (Barthes, p. 88). The photographs are all self-conscious. They are all intensively *posed*, as if indeed to deliver up their "essence". For me, however, their collective *punctum* resides in the fact that they all involve holding.

Although severed from the present by their place in time past, the characters in these photographs are all joined together. A little girl (is she the grandmother?) stands on a smiling man's shoulders, while hints of country music are whispered in the background. Near the beginning of the film, we see a shot of the youthful Martin holding one of the twins; then another shot of a woman whom we cannot yet know is the mother holding the other twin; and then there is a four-shot of all of them, united now in the present moment within the frame as they used to be in the past in their life together. As in all the other photographs in the film, while holding one another the characters gaze out at us like some kind of plea, as if asking to be remembered, accepted, understood.

This touching motif is also strongly present within the actuality sections of the film, between the girls themselves and between the girls and their grandparents—but never, inevitably, between the girls and their parents. With their immediate past, the twins are apparently "out-of-touch."

2) There is an opposition between severance and suture that is also intimately structured into the form of the film. Throughout *The Wish*, there is a deliberate dislocation of space and time within the images and between the images and the sounds. This dislocation simultaneously parallels and kinaesthetically recreates the disjunctive, non-linear nature of memory and of dreams.

The second shot of the film provides a characteristic example. After the twins have been established with a wishbone making their wish, we cut away to a group-shot of Martin with his crew, as if presenting the point of view, as if shooting the opening shot. But this image cannot be sutured in the way it appears to be. It is "irrational" (in the sense that a drawing by Escher is irrational or that an equation in algebra can be described as irrational). It doesn't fully match.

To begin with, although the twins have been established together by the lake, the camera in tight close-up panning from one to another, thus "joining" them within the shot, one of the twins is also present in the group-shot of the crew. Furthermore, by the time we cut back to the twins and hear Martin questioning them about their wish, not only is the distance implied by the sound of his voice different from the distance implied by the long-shot of the crew, but the girls have changed their position within the frame. Though both the purpose and the context is different, this effect is analagous to that found by Bill Nichols in the central still from Godard/Gorin's *Letter to Jane*:

> The play between word and image remains a site for disintegration as well as integration, of non-cooperation as well as incorporation.[5]

There is something in these dislocations, in this "irrational" quality, even if just *sensed* on an initial viewing, that contributes to the anxiety of the film, to its sense of loss and its desire.

By the end of the film, while these disjunctions are resolved in terms of the narrative (the group-shot of the crew is placed within a sequence that shows the twins arriving during the penultimate scene of the film), the anxiety remains. Furthermore, the twins give voice to the film's controlling mystery. "We don't know yet," one of them replies when asked about their wish. "So far," says the other. Then the Kodak punchmarks flash through the image as it freezes on this note of non-resolution. The mystery is preserved.

3) While there are many other examples of disjunction and dislocation within *The Wish*—most obvious is the train journey *to* the cottage that appears in the middle of the film—the third structuring principle that I would like to discuss as central revolves around the motif of the palimpsest. This also evokes ideas of changes over time, always with the potential of a sense of something lost.

An actual palimpsest is present in the film in the form of an old French manual from 1850. It has been transformed into a cookbook. Similarly, in one scene we see the girls dressing up in old clothes and in another we see that someone is using the grandmother's old house in a new way. Artefacts from the past are utilized to bring about transformations. So Martin Duckworth has utilized his own past to bring about this film.

This transformational process is most intricately associated with the use of two stills. Let us call them the Tombstone still and the Arrival still. For it is not true (as I have implied) that all the stills in *The Wish* are derived from the past. Some of them are stolen from the actuality footage, their colour is erased, and they are introduced into the film's structure—once as a recapitulation (the crew-shot still), but generally as anticipations of moments yet to come.

Both the Tombstone still and the Arrival still appear several times in the course of the film; and like the cutaway to the crew at the opening of the film, their appearance can create anxiety because, if we are watching the film closely, we can recognize that they do not match the "real" stills that are derived from the past. These freeze-frame stills, on the contrary, anticipate the future—or at least a future moment in the narrative when their purpose will be resolved. Furthermore, this sense of anticipation which builds in the film also contributes, kinaesthetically, to the film's desire.

These two particular stills are crucial because they are used, finally, to frame a key moment in the film. This occurs at the end of the graveyard sequence, which is the last extended narrative sequence in the film.

The graveyard sequence is rich in the twin associations of death and life, contrasting as it does the immobility of the tombstones with the energy of the children; and like the still photographs, the tombstones also contain traces of the past, of the local family history. They refer to what is absent (and what is yet to come). Indeed, it is largely because the girls' wish is associated with this sequence that we might defensibly assume that their mother is dead.

"Will you come home?" or "Will you come home again?" This wish has twice been heard before in the film (if our ears are attentive and the acoustics favourable): once over an earlier shot of the Tombstone still and once again over a still of the mother. This time, it is slow in preparation. After their lunch, during which Marya had asked her question about dying and burying, the children have been playing about the graveyard, looking for signs of their grandparents' past. Marya discovers the Ball tombstone, which is the burial site of the grandmother's family. Sylvia runs off to fetch the grandparents, and then they all gather round it in contemplation of this collective trace of death. The action ceases, the image freezes, the colour bleeds out, and it becomes the Tombstone still that we have seen several times before; once again we hear one of the twins whisper: "Will you come home?" Then comes the four-shot that we have also already seen of the young Martin and his wife and family, and then we cut to the Arrival still (which also restates the "touching" motif) as the colour bleeds in and the arrival scene begins.

This bleeding of the colour—here very much like a palimpsest—out and in again, framing the final references to the past and the whispered hope for the future, recapitulates with enormous formal authority both the death/life oppositions that inform the film, and the statement of the children's wish and of the film's desire. Furthermore, this formal authority helps to create the extreme delight (indeed, *une jouissance*) that we can experience from an art work in which an aesthetic problem has been so innovatively resolved.

Arguably, it is also the formal authority of this film that helps to imply a loss beyond that of the actual mother. The film creates a sense of something missing. "No fish!" one of the twins exclaims when they return from trolling with their grandfather; and during a later moment when the grandfather goes out alone, all he brings back is "one medium perch." Next time, as he says, he hopes to bring back "something worthwhile." There is thus a generalized feeling of something-that-was-there-then that-is-not-here-now. These effects all reinforce the sense of loss and absence, and it is by these means that personal nostalgia can be elevated into art, that empirical film practice can transform itself into theory, and that—

indeed—traces of the physical can connote the metaphysical—that which lies beyond.

"These ghostly traces, photographs, supply the token presence of the dispersed relatives." (Sontag, p. 9). Will the mother return? The twins cannot know. But other questions are suggested by the film to which there are no easy answers. They too become part of its mystery, part of its generalized sense of *angst.*

While not wishing to get trapped in the intentional fallacy that would involve Martin Duckworth the man, I might nevertheless approach this matter another way by asking a highly speculative question: Why was this film made? Could we suggest hypothetically that, like most family photographs, the making of the film initially had something to do with the preservation of memory?

> Memory implies a certain act of redemption. What is remembered has been saved from nothingness. What is forgotten has been abandoned. (Berger, p. 54).

Kracauer also believed that, through its articulation of the natural, photography could "redeem" reality, that it could atone for past sins. Now it may be an extrapolation to speak about the feeling of guilt that one may derive from *The Wish* (i.e., the feeling may be my own); at the same time this feeling is reinforced by another "personal" film that Duckworth made at the Film Board in 1973.

Although less finely nuanced (I believe), *Accident* is structured in much the same way. While simulating a crash sequence for a film about flight that Duckworth was making with Pat Crawley, the plane actually crashed. The pilot was killed, and Pat Crawley, who was filming from inside the plane, was seriously injured. Crawley's footage of the crash survived, as did Duckworth's (of course), who was filming from the ground. While the flight film was cancelled, Duckworth went on to make *Accident,* which basically investigates Crawley's feelings during the crash, indeed the "vision" that he experienced during what he was sure would be the moment of his own death.

It would require another paper to investigate this film, but I mention it briefly simply to suggest certain parallels between *Accident* and *The Wish. Accident* also alternates black-and-white with colour sequences, and it also makes use of interpolated photographs. If the structure of each film implies a dialectic between how-it-is-happening-now and how-it-was-then (as I have said), one might also sense a more speculative tension at work in each film.

In *Accident,* Duckworth might have been in the plane. He might have been killed. In *The Wish,* the mother might not have left; and if the children's wish is to be honoured (it is honoured in the film with the force and delicacy of a prayer), she might come home. Thus there is in these films the additional dialectic between how-it-was-then and how-it-might-have-been. It is the possibility of perceiving in these films this more speculative tension that makes each film, whether in Kracauer's or in Berger's sense of the term, seem like an act of redemption. And where there is a need for redemption, there has always been a feeling of guilt.

This feeling, finally, is inescapable for all photography and all actuality footage that draws its raw material from actions of living concern. All images of real people are in one sense predatory. They can create simultaneously a feeling of extreme pleasure and moral unease. If all images are emanations from the referent, then in a certain sense something from the referent has been taken away. Even the extraordinary form of *The Wish,* a film which literally tells its story backwards, on reflection creates an aftertaste of personal manipulation. "Reality is summed up in an array of casual fragments—an endlessly alluring, poignantly reductive way of dealing with the world" (Sontag, p. 80). And later on Sontag suggests that "photography inevitably entails a certain patronizing of reality" (p. 80). Actual people and actual events have been utilized to create a cinematic reality in which, finally, they have no part.

While endemic to the photographic and documentary process, these moral considerations have little to do with *The Wish* as a film. With its fragmented form, its richness of connotation, the sense that it conveys of a past that can barely be heard (the hints of the gigue music) and of a future that can scarcely be hoped for, *The Wish* is finally a philosophical poem about the nature of time and memory which celebrates the precariousness of the living moment within an irrational world pervaded by loss and need. It is a unique achievement within the history of cinema. It ought to be better known.

*Ciné-Tracts*, 17 (Summer-Fall 1982)

---

1 Susan Sontag, *On Photography* (New York: A Delta Book, 1978). All further references are to this edition.

2 Quoted in John Berger, *About Looking* (New York: Pantheon Books, 1980). All further references are to this edition.

3 Bruce Elder, "Image: Representation and Object: The Photographic Image in Canadian Avant-Garde Film," reprinted in this volume.

4 Roland Barthes, *Camera Lucida: Reflections on Photography*, trans. by Richard Howard (New York: Hill & Wang, 1981), p. 6.

5 Bill Nichols, *Ideology and the Image* (Bloomington: Indiana University Press, 1981), p. 64.

# *Two Journeys: A Review of* Not a Love Story

## BY R. BRUCE ELDER

*To say that English Canadian cinema has yet to come to terms with adult sexuality is not so much to comment upon the films as it is to define them. Like the Yonge Street strip, sex in our cinema bristles with adolescent giggles and unsatisfied voyeurism. From Julie's virtually immaculate and narratively convenient pregnancy in* Nobody Waved Good-bye, *to the clumsy avoidance of the homosexual overtext of* The Wars, *the feature films of English Canada reflect a society as nervous about its denial of carnal sin as it once was about that sin itself. Experimental filmmakers such as Michael Snow, R. Bruce Elder and Al Razutis do far better. Their work, capable of either accepting (even laughing at) sexuality or studying its iconography, has met with wide interest abroad and near panic at home. All three have found themselves in court doing battle with the Ontario Censor Board.*

*Bonnie Sherr Klein and the National Film Board also had a run-in with the Ontario Censor over their film,* Not a Love Story. *For them, the confrontation has been a complete success, making the film one of the most popular productions in the Film Board's history.* Not a Love Story *also owes its appeal to its lure as a travelogue that descends into the world of hard core pornography, a world with which its repressed Canadian audiences have little contact. Like all travelogues, the film's penetration into the savage landscape is conducted in the name of civilized exploration. In this case, civilization is more specifically embodied in the Griersonian tradition of the social documentary filtered through the liberal feminism of the* NFB's *Women's Studio (Studio D).*

*But is the Griersonian documentary English Canada's best bet in coming to terms with cinematic pleasures of the flesh? Elder's contention here is that the documentary nature of* Not a Love Story *is far less interesting than the film's appeal to its audience's latent theological bias. Whether or not sin and redemption lie beneath a facade of enlightenment, Elder makes a strong case for the assertion that the cameras of* Not a Love Story *point both ways. By watching the film, we learn as much about what is expected of the contemporary Griersonian documentarians (and their audiences) as we do about the subject at hand.*

If Canadian documentary films have had a single, overriding characteristic, it would surely be that of using forms that tie knowledge to direct experience. The most common means of organizing such films has been to use what I refer to as "observational structures"—structures which lead the spectator through the development of some process—and the most common of these has been the chronicle of a filmmaker's "intellectual journey" into one domain or another. In order to ground the film's claim to being authoritative—to impart *knowledge* rather than mere *opinion*—and, furthermore, in order to encourage the spectator—who is always assumed by the makers of such films to lack any information whatsoever about the subject matter with which the film deals; to be, so to speak, a *tabula rasa*, a blank screen on which the film will inscribe its information—to identify with the filmmaker's quest for truth, the makers of these films set out on the journey devoid—or at least pretending to be devoid—of any preconceptions whatsoever. Furthermore, such films show that the filmmaker acquires understanding not through an intellectual act of synthesis, but rather exclusively through the agency of the experiences depicted in the film. Needless to say, the didactic program which motivates such filmmaking rests on the assumption that because film is a realistic medium, and so presents the filmmaker's experiences veridically, and because knowledge is produced exclusively by experience, the spectator will gain precisely the same knowledge that the filmmaker is depicted as acquiring.

While I find these beliefs not just wrongheaded but downright abhorrent, the frequency with which forms of film construction based upon them have been used at the National Film Board has virtually given them institutional sanction. It is hardly surprising, then, that the Film Board's recent production, *Not a Love Story*, has been written about as though it were exactly this sort of film. Indeed, its resemblance to this form of film is striking—so striking, I shall show, as to somewhat embarrass the film.

The impulse for making the film, we are told near its beginning, arose when Bonnie Klein, one of its co-makers, discovered that her eight-year-old daughter was exposed to magazines containing images of naked women at the local variety store. This discovery stimulated her desire to know what effects that exposure would have, particularly on her daughter's self-image. Consistent with the conventions of the form of construction we have been describing, we see Bonnie Klein, on-camera, searching out experiences and experts in order to find the answer to her question. Furthermore, as in so many films of that type, the beginning of the film presents two models for understanding the topic under inquiry—in this case, for understanding the functional effects of sexually explicit imagery. One model is articulated by Kate Millet and is based on the assumption that such art can be positively life affirming; the other is, I infer, represented by instantiation by the person of David S. Wells, the publisher of *Elite* magazine,[1] and is based on the assumption that such imagery invariably becomes negative, violent and pornographic. It appears at first that, as in most films of this sort, we will be asked to determine which model is more adequate—which, in this case, realistically expresses the more commonplace role of sexually explicit imagery.

Furthermore, as though to reinforce the impression that the film is unbiased, that its conclusions are conclusions that would be accepted by anyone with the requisite experience, whatever her class background and whatever beliefs she previously held about such issues as public nudity and the conversion of the personal body into a commodity—in short, whatever the condition and character of her subjectivity[2],—this film also depicts stripper Linda Lee Tracey's quest for understanding. This quest begins as the film opens in the relatively genteel nightclubs in which she performs (although, as the filmmakers so pointedly inform us, under the stage name "Fonda Peters"), and leads her into the world of violent, "hard-core" pornography. Predictably, the film concludes with Linda Lee Tracey's decision to stop performing as a stripper, because, the film's form leads us to infer, she has gained some insight into the social practices involved in the commodity-fetishization of the female body.

Many commentators on *Not A Love Story* have found themselves uneasy with the filmmakers' use of Linda Lee Tracey and have explained that this uneasiness results from watching the filmmakers manipulate an honest, working-class woman into feeling badly about the work she does. There is truth in these claims, but they do not go to the core of the problems either with the filmmakers' use of Tracey, or with the film's organizing principles. These, I believe, lie in the deceptiveness of *Not A Love Story*'s appearance. While it *seems* to be an empirical documentary, while it *seems* to begin free from preconceptions about "pornography," while it *seems* to be a chronicle of a search for information, it *actually* begins with a definite—if not fully worked out—theory of sexuality that converts Linda Lee Tracey's apparent quest for understanding into a mythically structured moral odyssey.

The theory of sexuality which informs *Not A Love Story* is adumbrated in its opening sections. Bonnie Klein explains her concern about her daughter's exposure to sexually explicit imagery with the comment, "Everything has a reaction." She elaborates by remarking that while *she* had avoided dealing with the pornographic imagery which surrounds us all by putting on blinkers, her "daughter would be affected" by such imagery. Somewhat later Kathleen Barry clarifies these comments when she states that the images one sees are "going to stay with you and be translated later into behaviour." She also proclaims that such imagery makes all women victims.

The notion which underpins such assertions is fundamentally anti-psychological. It is that once an image is registered in a person—installed, so to speak, in his or her mnemonic repository—it represents a permanent threat to him or her. This is because, according to this view, all behaviour is modelled on—indeed mimics—the behaviour represented in these mnemic traces, and these traces represent a permanent potential for the performance of the actions that they depict. These notions, encapsulate a very crude form of behaviourism, one that neglects all considerations of how imagery is processed internally: of the dynamics by which memory traces are returned to consciousness or are repressed; of how images are transformed when they reappear in consciousness; of the relation between mental imagery and the drives; and of the role imagery plays in directing behaviour and in mediating between the drives and behaviour in a way that sometimes renders it unnecessary for the drives to pass over into action. Could any clear-thinking person ever believe that by merely observing some piece of behaviour, a person—even a very young person—was forever threatened with the spectre of committing that behaviour himself?

That *Not A Love Story* is based on such an anti-psychological, "monkey-see/monkey-do," theory of learning is, after all, not really so surprising when it is recognized that what the film ultimately offers us is not a scientific theory of sexuality, but rather a theological view of the effects of the abuse of sexuality. The film describes the effects of sexually explicit imagery not in terms of the intra-psychic functions of mental representation, but rather in terms of its potential to corrupt the soul. The film is very clear about the nature of that corruption. At the very beginning of the film, feminist writer Susan Griffin asserts that pornography puts the heart in prison, puts the heart on its knees, renders the heart silent. One has only to substitute the term "soul" for the term "heart"—as the filmmakers ultimately do, by identifying a gentle form of eros with the highest form of human love—to produce the very traditional Christian view that sin is a form of bondage that renders one spiritually impotent and morally ineffective. Dr. Ed Donnerstein, a research psychologist, has constructed a film quoted in *Not A Love Story*—a film depicting a woman sucking on a gun inserted in her mouth as though performing fellatio on it, which many have taken to be yet another of the film's many examples of the unlovely pornography that is commonly available for sale—that he claims incorporates all the appeals of violent pornography known (his list is neither very long, nor very revealing). When he tells us that pornography desensitizes a person, he is uttering a similar view. When poet and idealogue Robin Morgan expounds the view that the recent "revolution" which has gained for us all a greater measure of sexual freedom has only served to "benumb sexuality" to "render it comatose," she, too, is expressing a similar view. When she goes on to say—referring explicitly to a fall from grace—that the effect of this is to isolate the individual, the sketch of the traditional view is nearly completed. The filmmakers are telling us that when the soul is weakened by corruption, it can no longer experience the best form of love offered by one's fellow man, that is to say, can no longer experience the Divine. All that remains to be added to the outline to produce a total picture of the traditional view is the idea that corruption leads to the death of the soul. This is done during a group interview with members of the San Francisco-based Men Against Male Violence collective, one of whom speaks of contemporary sexual conduct as having its roots in a death-oriented culture. (Another even hints at the traditional belief that the God of Love is the Ultimate Reality, and to lose contact with God is to experience the dissolution of things into unreality, when he proclaims that "Everything is images [sic]. Everything is unreal. We are a victim of a fantasy.") Indeed, the filmmakers seem to construe the violence so frequently contained in pornographic imagery in a manner similar to that in which Freud conceived of the aggressiveness characteristic of *thanatos*, as expressing hidden death wishes. If images of violence are as widespread as the film shows them to be, it is, the filmmakers suggest, because our society is hell-bent upon death. *Not A Love Story*, then, is not a love story because it is a death story; it is not about *eros*, but about *thanatos*. It is about the death of the soul.

What *Not A Love Story* offers us is a spiritual vision, and it does so to establish the grounds for the moral judgements the film so liberally makes. Eros, we are told, should abet the soul's efforts to participate in a spiritual community; it should gentle the soul, for only a gentle soul can respond with sensitivity to all dimensions of the Other. But the soul is all-too-easily overrun by the demands of the flesh, wherefrom a brutal *libido* arises—a libido that has been fused with aggressive drives—which coarsens a person, rendering him, by the very potency of his own self-serving drives, insensitive to the needs of others. Thus, the film suggests, any sexuality other than a gentle, tender "other-regarding" sexuality isolates a person by failing to provide the means for the ultimate communion between people. There is, of course, much to be said for the view that a tender sexuality has a divine aspect. This notwithstanding, one should not be misled into believing that it is the whole of the story about sexuality; even the most basic consideration of sexuality's functional aspects reveals the importance of a harder and tougher sexuality. After all, intercourse is not just caressing; the act by which we propagate the species involves, for the male, a thrust that must not be simply tender but must also be forceful to a degree—sometimes even forceful enough to thrust against his partner's pain. Men must find a way to reconcile the conflicting demands of forcefulness and tenderness, and all the simplistic rhetoric in the world based on an ideal of sexuality that sees it as nothing other than tenderness and denies the role of a measure of force in the male thrust doesn't help men one whit in the task of successfully reconciling these demands. Perhaps it is a (unconscious) consideration of their necessary biological tasks that have made so many males to whom I have spoken about the film so angry at the scene portraying the interview with the Men Against Male Violence collective. More than one has remarked that if being like the men portrayed here were the only alternative to a coarse "macho" sexuality, they'd be forced to choose the latter.

The filmmakers even put forward the quasi-mystical notion that because love is an inner movement of the soul, it cannot be seen. Marc Stevens, an actor in sex films, tells us that he often really loved the actresses with whom he performed but, he exclaims, pointing accusingly at the camera, "That never got it. The camera never got it." Though it goes unstated, the argument advanced here is a key to the film's program. The film begins by differentiating between two possible sorts of sexually explicit images—let us call them "erotic" and "pornographic"; the former are supposed to embody love, the latter not. Now, it is suggested that if the camera cannot capture love on film, there will be no instances of sexually explicit images of the first sort, for by definition, they embody love. All sexually explicit images therefore are pornographic. Since no sexually explicit images can embody love, all will embody its absence, its lack, its death—or even, as we so frequently see in pornographic images, love's being killed. When making up our minds about the effects of sexually explicit imagery, we needn't, then, consider the possibility that it might be positive, erotic, life-enhancing. We have to make up our minds knowing it can only be pornographic—negative, violent, and death-driven. This argument, that the quest for a genuinely erotic art is doomed to failure, seems simply to confirm the filmmakers in their own view, for we know from interviews that *Not A Love Story* began as a project to make a genuinely erotic women's film, a project which was abandoned as impossible to realize.

The theological conception of the effects of pornography which we have been describing transforms Linda Lee Tracey's odyssey from the voyage of discovery characteristic of the empirical documentary into a redemptive journey, for it culminates not with the intellect's discovery of a truth but with the soul's purification and salvation. She, like the viewers of the film who are expected to identify with her, is not supposed to be informed so much as transformed. This is why, unlike the characters in empirical documentaries, the characters in this film do not begin without preconceptions; the dramatic structure of this film demands that their lack be not the want of information, but rather of virtue.

As we now see, it is Linda Lee Tracey's journey, not Bonnie Klein's, that is the principal one. Bonnie Klein acts more as a guide, leading our seeker, unbeknownst to her, ever deeper into the circles of hell on her way towards salvation. This description of the film's structure as mythological is not overstatement, for the film is, in all its aspects, informed by the myth of the fall and the redemption. At the beginning, Linda Lee Tracey tells us that she attended a feminist discussion of pornography. She felt judged by the condescension of the participants when she told them she made her living by stripping. "The party line," she states (using that very term) implies that she is stupid for allowing herself to be so used. She wonders whether "the party line" is not the same as the line men take regarding women; according to both, women are stupid. In this way, we learn that Tracey is situated outside the community of believers. In the next scene we see her, nude, at the end of her performance, raise her hands and exclaim, "God bless the working women!" The irony involved in the use of the term "working women" to refer to a stripper, and its undeniable association with the even more disreputable trade of prostitution, along with the profanity of the context of its utterance, make the statement, within the context of the film's theological framework, at least impudent, if not actually blasphemous. We also hear her refer to the strip club as "a very honest arena." Her self-deception in this, as in her rejection of "the party line" and her conviction in the rightness of her behaviour, is proof that she is so mired in sin that she fails to recognize her wrongdoings.

In the following scenes, we hear that pornography is widely circulated, that the sales of some pornographic magazines outstrip that of *Time* and *Newsweek* combined; that it is a growing industry (in one year, the number of pornographic magazines imported into Canada rose from eight to thirty-two); that the imagery is becoming "rougher" all the time; and that there are four times as many sex shows in the United States as McDonald's Restaurants. We also witness a photo-session conducted by Suze Randall, where the female model has to do a painful mid-air spread (though hardly as painful as the feats performed everyday by gymnasts and ballet dancers, without evoking much consternation on the part of the spectators), and hear sex-show participant Patrice Lucas say that the pleasure taken by at least some of the spectators at her show is in seeing her downed, and that a few even call out—apparently to her great amazement—for her black (and so presumably well-hung) boyfriend to "hurt her." The cumulative effect of all the scenes is the impression of a fallen world.

This impression reaches a culmination in a scene at a New York "sex supermarket," which the film presents as an emporium of emptiness, loneliness, pain and suffering. The purpose of the scene is made pointedly explicit when Tracey, after watching a sado-masochist film, turns accusingly to the manager and says, "That hurts!" The next scene portrays her meeting with Bonnie Klein in a sex bookstore, sharing an embrace with her and confessing that she now wonders whether she will be able to return to Montreal unscathed. In sum, we are presented with an image of the pain and the tribulations that follow upon corruption.

Shortly thereafter, inside a theatre with the ironic—but no less significant for that—name of "The House of Ecstasy," we see men sitting in isolated booths watching a group of nude women cavorting about. In a series of emotionally affecting shots, the camera moves to the front of the peepholes through which they peer; as the viewing time they have purchased comes to an end, the shutters over the peephole windows slide down, as though shutting them totally in their isolated environment. The isolation of the men, their sequestration by the downward movement of the shutters, the music that despite its tawdriness is reminiscent of an Albinioni composition, all suggest that these men are damned to a Godforsaken loneliness. An extraordinary shot follows. The scenes just described have occurred in near obscurity; now the camera, as though fleeing from what it has just been witness to, enters a dark tunnel and ascends a set of stairs that lead from the darkness below to the intense light above. Need one point out that the geography of this episode is patterned on the cosmology of Augustinian Christianity?

If the previous scenes hinted at the presence of a mythology in the film, the next several scenes provide a final confirmation of its structuring function. Immediately after the House of Ecstasy scene, we see Linda Lee Tracey, her previous beliefs about pornography quite thoroughly shaken, standing in front of a burlesque house, reading aloud to passersby a poem she has written. It includes the lines "They come to worship women in their nakedness/Corporate men confess their piety/in a holiness they invent to fill some hole." An invented holiness (i.e., an unnatural and fictitious religion) involving the worship of naked goddesses is nothing other than paganism. This is the charge being made against devotees of pornography.

In the next scene, we hear author Susan Griffin remark that "pornography is the mirror opposite of religious worship" for it involves "the ritual of desecration of the women's body." This mirror opposite of true religion, whose rituals involve desecrating a female, could be none other than Satanism. The enthusiasts of pornography are no garden-variety pagan; in fact, they are nothing less than devil worshippers, and pornography is integral to the devilist rituals. One recalls here the comment by the members of the Men Against Male Violence group that "Everything is images. We're a victim of fantasy," for in the traditional view, Satan is the conjurer of illusions.

The next scene depicts the strength that belongs to a community of believers, as the San Francisco-based Women Against Violence in Pornography and Media demonstrate outside a Columbus Avenue sex show. These women stand up against the bouncers and bigots, no doubt because the truth unites them, and in unity there is strength. Soon after, a confused and distraught Bonnie Klein seeks out Kathleen Barry. The purpose of the visit is tantamount to confession. She admits to the sin of having lost hope and asks for Barry's advice. Barry suggests to her confider that the way to overcome hopelessness is to seek understanding, for one can never turn one's back on the world that surrounds one. The significance of the advice, in the context of the film's mythological structure, is that once one has entered the fallen world, one cannot regain faith through recovering one's innocence, but only through achieving understanding; once one has lost an intimate knowledge of the Divine, one can learn of its ways only through the use of reason. Soon after, we hear Robin Morgan tell us that grace is possible, that one must determine to love men furiously, even in the face of all their oppressiveness. What she suggests, then, is the Christian antimonian solution to overcoming the ills of society. The paralleling of her advice with Barry's reflects the Augustinian paralleling of the effect knowledge has on the intellect with the effect grace has on the will.

After a brief interpolation, which follows the structure of a Women Against Pornography slide show in tracing a filiation of imagery from advertisements on billboards (including those for Calvin Klein jeans, one depicting a male, the other—sexier—depicting a female), through softcore to hardcore images,[3] the mythological drama reaches its climax: Linda Lee Tracey submits to having her genitals photographed by Suze Randall. She feels degraded by the experience. "I hit rock bottom," she states later, in a poem about the occasion. "I became an object." She reaches the nadir of existence, and having reached that point is, like Saint Augustine, redeemed.

The nadir of existence, as the statement "I became an object" implies, is the loss of subjectivity, of *soul.* Lest we miss the point, Susan Griffin interprets the Linda Lee Tracey/Suze Randall photography session for us, in the following scene, when she shares with us what she refers to as a "mystical truth," that spirit and matter belong together, that spirit cannot be separated from matter. The final scene makes painfully obvious that we are being invited to conclude that Linda Lee Tracey has felt the spirit awaken within her. Redemption, then, according to the doctrine the filmmakers espouse, is the integration of the person, the making of the spirit and the flesh one: "*Sentire non est corporis sed anima per corpus,*" as the Bishop of Hippo wrote. Only the banality of the final image exceeds the commonness of this notion in theological circles.

*Not A Love Story* has been hailed as a work that is important because it raises pressing issues for discussion. The form of the film makes lies of these claims. The film does not raise issues for discussion; it seals them off from discussion, for the theological framework of its normative considerations of pornography puts its claims outside the bounds of empirical verification. A psychological inventory of the roles that imagery plays in mental life, of their functions in directing behaviour, is useful because it offers statements that can be proven false and rejected. The assertion that pornography is evil because it separates the body from the soul affords no such possibility; it can therefore only be accepted on faith. *Not A Love Story* is ultimately a theological/moral text masquerading as an empirical documentary. This sort of form is thoroughly objectionable.

This is not to petition some form of the positivist verificationist standard in order to dismiss the theological claims the film offers; I believe that the only language our culture offers us is a language unsuited for discussing theological concepts, and that this is at the root of the great failings of modernity. However, distinctions of type are often important, and to offer theological statements under the guise of empirical claims seems to me the most insidious confusion of categories imaginable.

*Journal of Canadian Studies*, 17, No. 4 (Winter 1982-83)

---

1 By way of an aside, it is interesting that the film has women *articulating* their viewpoints while men *embody* theirs, a reversal of the usual arrangement.
2 Thus, the role of the subject in producing knowledge is downgraded so that experience can be understood as the exclusive agent in its creation. This confirms the thesis that the film appears to be what I call an empirical documentary.
3 It was, by the way, in the Women Against Pornography slide show that the parodic *Hustler* magazine cover, designed in response to condemnation of the magazine from sections of the women's movement, showing a woman's leg sticking out of the top of a meat grinder and a bowl of ground beef underneath, made its appearance as an object of condemnation on the grounds that it revealed the hidden desires of pornographers.

# V

# *The Experimental Challenge*

# *Image: Representation and Object The Photographic Image in Canadian Avant-Garde Film*

## BY R. BRUCE ELDER

*Nowhere is the coherence of Canadian cinematic practice stated more forcefully and convincingly than in the recent writings of R. Bruce Elder. Elder begins with the often-stated observation that Canadian filmmakers typically concern themselves with documenting the realities around them. This seems obvious within the social realism of feature filmmaking, particularly in English Canada. It is manifested by the disproportionate amount of energy that goes into the formulation and consideration of documentary film. It may even be seen in the orientation of National Film Board animation toward social and moral issues. But what is perhaps less obvious, according to Elder, is the manner in which this concern with the proto-cinematic world has shaped the practice of Canadian avant-garde filmmaking. While international experimental film has long been seen as synonymous with formalist and, more generally, modernist impulses, Elder argues here that the Canadian avant-garde is markedly distinguished by "the assumption that film is a photographically based medium." Our avant-garde films concern themselves not with self-enclosing, exclusionary strategies. Rather they work as a detailed reconsideration of, or a window into, the essence of Canadian cinematic pursuit.*

*In support of this thesis, Elder considers the work of some of the more important members of the Canadian avant-garde (Elder's own work is examined elsewhere in this volume). Of the cases cited, perhaps the most intriguing is that of Michael Snow. To conveniently classify Snow's films within the genre of structural filmmaking (with its fundamentally modernist assumptions of the artist's role) has always appeared to short-change the wit that characterized those works. Seen here, Snow's playful rendering of the world around him is, at very least, repositioned so as to allow us to see the films as integrated wholes. This view leads to a reconsideration of Snow as a classic Canadian artist, whose orientation toward the world that actually exists in front of the camera places him in direct opposition to the concerns of American modernism.*

*What works in Elder's analysis of Michael Snow is equally valid in his discussions of Andrew Lugg, Chris Gallagher, Ellie Epp, David Rimmer and Al Razutis. Taken together, these critiques reject the standard apologies for the avant-garde cinema in order to assert the domestic relevance of what is already seen internationally as Canada's foremost contribution to contemporary cinematic discourse.*

The first Canadian avant-garde filmmakers were relative latecomers to the field. While artists in Germany and France have been making experimental films for more than half a century, and American artists for over forty years, Canadians have been making such films for just over a decade and a half. But if the history of avant-garde film in Canada is a short one, it is also a rich one, for Canadians were pioneers in the development of the post-modernist forms of cinema which dominated avant-garde film throughout the seventies, and throughout the decade Canadian film artists continued to make very significant contributions to the field of experimental filmmaking.

The decades between 1940 and 1960 were the decades of modernism, though for film the latter date should perhaps be extended to the mid to late sixties. In this period, there was much activity in experimental film in the United States; some would even argue that it was in this period that the American avant-garde produced its finest work.[1] Curiously, there was almost no experimental filmmaking being done in Canada at the time. However a Canadian, Michael Snow, was among the innovators—indeed was perhaps the key innovator—of postmodernist filmmaking, and several other Canadian film artists have made very distinguished contributions to that practice. What, then, are the reasons behind the special affinity Canadian artists obviously have for postmodern practices?

Writing in 1964 with a confidence arising from the authoritative position he held at the time, the American art critic Clement Greenberg asserted:

> By now it has been established, it would seem, that the irreducible essence of pictorial art consists in but two constitutive conventions or norms: flatness and the delimitation of flatness; and that the observance of merely these two norms is enough to create an object which can be experienced as a picture; thus a stretched or tacked-up canvas already exists as a picture—though not necessarily as a successful one.[2]

Yet at the very time Greenberg was writing, events were occurring that would cast doubt on the adequacy of his critical theories. In New York, Andy Warhol had already begun to exhibit his serigraphs based on popular photographic imagery. In Toronto Michael Snow (b. 1929) had abandoned purely abstract painting and was producing works which incorporated representational elements. And in London, Ontario, Jack Chambers (1931-1978) was making paintings that revelled in the glory of the fully detailed renderings that copying photographs made possible.

Clement Greenberg was the foremost exponent of the artistic theory known as modernism. Modernists claimed that progress in art occurred through the elimination from artistic media of everything that was accidental, so that only that which was essential would remain as the artist's material. Consequently, much of the experimentation that took place under the banner of modernism can be described simply and succinctly: Artists tried to make works that remained within the boundaries of the media in which they were realized—that is, to write novels or pieces of music that remained novels or pieces of music even though they lacked certain traits, such as narrative line or tonic centre, that are commonly believed to define these media.

Nearly two decades have elapsed since these efforts attracted the energies of our best artists. One can easily identify, in retrospect, certain of their exemplary products. In Malevich's white-on-white works, for example, the materials of painting are reduced to what seem to be the fewest conceivable elements that still admit the possibility of being ordered according to the syntax of painted forms. Among more recent works, one could cite the novels of Alain Robbe-Grillet, which narrate the stories of their stories being narrated. As stories about stories, they are works that reflect upon their nature, not upon Nature. They "present" the structure of their own internal relationship rather than represent the external world. And, at the very source of the tradition, there are the novels of Gustave Flaubert, particularly the project that in 1878 he announced he intended to undertake after finishing *Bouvard et Pécuchet*, a novel that would be about nothing.

Flaubert, unfortunately, was captured by Nothingness before he ever caught nothing in the net of his fiction. Had he lived to carry out his idea, the art of the past century would likely have been quite different. As it is, his proposal has taken on the status of a legend, for it defined the *telos* toward which the artistic currents of the century after his death were leading. In the last three decades, many have come to realize, as Flaubert indicated a hundred and more years ago, that the process of emptying an art form of all but its essential elements was destined to culminate in a work that was about nothing at all.

Modernism's attraction was widespread; indeed, among the arts, only photography seemed reluctant to submit to its appeal. Photography's resistance to being reformulated according to the modernist ideal is hardly surprising; just try and imagine what a photograph would look like once it reached Flaubert's ideal of being a work about nothing.[3] While no one has difficulty conceiving of a painting that represents nothing, to conceive of a similar photograph seems impossible. It would be no more than an empty piece of paper or an empty screen.

One important difference between photographic images and most other artistic images is that photographic images are indexical signs—that is, signifiers which are causally related to that which they signify (as the presence of smoke is related to the fire which it signifies). Because a photograph's existence is connected to that which it signifies, a photograph can only come into being in the presence of its referent. For this reason, a photographer never confronts the same absence of form that artists working in other media do. While a painter confronts an empty canvas, and a writer confronts the blank page, a photographer never confronts his raw materials in a completely formless state. His raw materials are the contents of his viewer: the stuff of the world, observed from a certain point of view and transformed by the optics of lenses. The materials have a form that depends jointly upon the order of things and the laws of geometric optics. This form is only *discovered* by the photographer; it is not *created* by him. Accordingly, it is present even before the photographer begins his work. That absence of form, that nothingness, which has haunted so many artists working in other media, has no part of the creative experience of the photographer.

Film, on the other hand, has not proven so resistant to modernist reformulation; indeed, some of the finest examples of modernist art are to be found in the cinema. The American avant-garde filmmakers Paul Sharits and Tony Conrad, the Japanese-American Taka Iimura, and the Austrian Peter Kubelka, have all devoted their very considerable talents to developing cinematic forms that are fully consistent with modernist ideals. While no one has yet found a way of making an interesting film that would consist of nothing but projected white light,[4] these filmmakers have come pretty close, for they have created rich works out of nothing but bursts of white or coloured light projected for various durations.

There exists no similar body of work in photography. The reason that filmmakers have been able to come so much closer than photographers to Flaubert's "zero-point" of artistic construction is that film possesses a property that photographs lack: It unfolds at a measured and regulated rate.[5] The works that I have just cited can all be understood as demonstrations of film as a medium of light and time whose greatest ability is the articulation of forms that provide a temporal structure for changes in light. If the film medium is not embarrassed by the elimination of referential forms, it is not because a reserve of features that withstand the elimination of reference is inherent in its photographic basis, but rather because film possesses properties in addition to those that derive from its photographic basis.

Turning to the Canadian avant-garde cinema, one notes the lack of any endeavours comparable to the American or Austrian works. The modernist movement in Canada produced no experimental cinema whatsoever.[6] The closest approximation one could find would be the works of Vincent Grenier and even these were produced only after the filmmaker had lived in the United States for several years. Nor have Grenier's works seemed very much a part of the Canadian "art scene," since several years before they were produced, the issues of modernist art had ceased to attract the attention of the leading innovators living in Canada.

Grenier's films typically employ forms which present the illusion of possessing processive and recessive areas. This illusory depth generally appears quite shallow and fragile. Moreover these visual forms appear for the most part to be non-representational,[7] though, in most of the films, a few brief passages disturb this appearance by revealing that these apparently abstract images are in fact direct recordings of real (even if constructed) objects.

Grenier's main concern is to illustrate how slight changes in the tonal relations in a form affect our impression of the relations between the volumes in that form. However the most intriguing aspect of Grenier's films is his treatment of the theoretical issues inherent in the use of representation. On the whole, Grenier's works display a proclivity towards abstraction. He tends to use representational images as cadence points—points at which visual tensions are temporarily resolved. This conveys Grenier's conviction that it is through recourse to abstraction that the tension necessary to a work of art is created. Indeed, one could say about such films as *X* (1976), and *While Revolved* (1976), that the aesthetic power of its imagery correlates directly with its degree of abstraction.

The use of abstraction was one of the most common means by which artists attempted to carry out the modernist program for the arts. But Grenier's films do not use abstract images exclusively; in most, representational images are used to counterbalance the "aestheticizing" effects of abstraction. In *World in Focus* (1976) however, he uses representation in a different and more theoretically interesting way.

A prevalent notion in modernist circles during the nineteen forties and fifties was that the incorporation of representational elements in a work of art degraded its ontological condition from that of an object to that of an image. Accordingly, early modernists eschewed representation almost entirely. In the early sixties, artists found a way to make representational works whose ontological status, in relation to the original, was not a debased or diminished one. Jasper Johns, in his *Targets* series (1955-61) and *American Map* series (1960-63, 1965-66), pioneered the use of images that "re-presented" other representational images. Such images avoid the problem of opening up the ontological gulf between an image and that which it depicts, since an image of an image has much the same status and can serve many of the same functions as the original image itself. The images of maps in Grenier's *World in Focus* are a case in point: An image of a map can serve the same functions as the original map does; in fact, it is a map. Thus in this film Grenier found a way of using representational images in a fashion completely consistent with the modernist program.

One of Michael Snow's favourite tactics accomplishes exactly the opposite of what Grenier achieved in *World in Focus*. He demonstrates how an image from one medium is transformed when it is incorporated in another medium. In *One Second in Montreal* (1969), for example, a series of still photographs are reproduced in a motion picture. Each is presented for a protracted duration, the exact length of which depends on its place in the order in which the photographs appear.

During the first half of the film each successive photograph appears for a slightly longer time than its predecessor did; during the second half, for a slightly shorter time.

A viewer reacts to these lengthy, motionless film images differently than he or she would to the equally protracted display of slides or still photographs. When watching them, one is acutely conscious of the length of time for which they are presented, in a way one would not be when looking at, say, the original still photographs themselves. The difference points up the fact that temporality is inscribed in a film image. Duration, Snow demonstrates, is one of the filmmakers' fundamental materials—even more fundamental (*pace* such theorists as Siegfried Kracauer and Slavko Vorkapick) than motion, a trait of the film duration makes possible. In a similar vein, *Side Seat Paintings Slides Sound Film* (1970) shows that a photograph of a slide produces different effects than does the slide itself, and that a slide of a painting produces different effects than does the painting itself.

Issues associated with photographic representation also have a central place in Andrew Lugg's films. His works fall into two series: performance pieces (including *Plough Skid Drag*, 1973, *Gemini Fire Extension*, 1972, and *Trace*, 1972) and films using imagery derived from postcards (*Postcards*, 1974, *Black Forest Trading Post*, 1976, *Front and Back*, 1972). The strongest of the performance pieces demonstrates how photographic imagery can be used to illustrate a concept, while the postcard films deal with the effects of introducing movement into photographic subjects that commonly appear on postcards. *Plough Skid Drag*, to take an example of the former type, has a tripartite structure. In each section of the film a performer is pulled around the periphery of a field. Because the camera was not set exactly in the centre of the field, the distance of the action from the camera varies, beginning at mid-distance, moving farther away from and then closer to the camera, and finally returning to mid-distance. In each section the body of the performer has been positioned differently—this becomes clear as the action draws closer to the camera, if it was not clear at the beginning—so as to illustrate one of the concepts referred to in the title. In the first section, for example, the performer lies face down with his legs outstretched so that his feet act as a plough-blade, while in the second he lies on his back, with his arms and legs raised to form the shape of a skid.

In Lugg's performance-related films, the performance mediates between the concept and the photographic representation; this is what the simple and overtly illustrational style of *Plough Skid Drag* points out. Thus Lugg makes evident the distance that separates photographic representation from illustration and images from words, for he shows us how concepts must be enacted in a performance in order to become amenable to being photographed.

Lugg's postcard films confront even more directly the issues associated with still photographic representation. In *Postcards*, for example, he rephotographed buildings or scenes depicted in postcards, placing a motion picture camera in the same location in which the still camera had been placed when the original postcard photograph was taken. As a result, the images in this film closely resemble that of the still photographs commonly found on postcards. In fact, some of the images in this film could, on their first appearance, be easily mistaken for reproductions of postcards, since initially many seem to include no movement. Eventually, however, a movement is discovered—often near an edge of the screen—or the stasis is interrupted as a car or a person passes through the screen.

The central concern of the film is to explore the effect of introducing movement into a static image. Lugg points out that the effect is profound, for the introduction of movement destroys the autotelicity characteristic of the still photograph. Generally still images present themselves as two-dimensional objects isolated from any context. (Hence the narration of this film, which describes, in the style of glosses found on the back of postcards, facts about the scene the postcard depicts, such as its location. To specify the location of these scenes seems somewhat incongruous, for the imagery seems unreal and isolated from the real world; moreover, images exist only on the screen, not somewhere out in "the world.") The introduction of movement into the imagery changes this, for it makes the imagery appear three dimensional rather than two dimensional and connects the space of the representation to the space beyond the edges of the frame. The fact that the movement often occurs at the frame edge reinforces this relation. Thus Lugg uses the addition of movement to postcard imagery to expose the conventions of that genre; he uses the cinema's capacity to represent movement in an argument to disprove claims about "the realism" of the photographic imagery. At the same time, though, the similarity between still photographic imagery and film imagery that he points out, implies a relation between the media of film and still photography, and so extends his argument for the photograph's lack of realism to the film medium itself.

*Black Forest Trading Post,* another of Lugg's postcard films, exposes the lack of veracity of the photographic and cinematographic image. The film consists of an image of a building—the Black Forest Trading Post of the film's title—placed in a number of backgrounds while the voice on the film's sound-track supposedly identifies the location of each building by naming first the building, then the background—saying, for example, "Black Forest Trading Post, Jasper, Alberta." At first, each image seems to represent a single space identified by the words. Eventually we realize, however, that each image contains a discontinuity, that the background and foreground are separate. Properly punctuated, a transcription of the sound-track would not read "Black Forest Trading Post, Jasper, Alberta," but rather "Black Forest Trading Post"/"Jasper, Alberta," enumerating each separate element in the mini-collage. In this work, then, Lugg exposes how the presumed realism of a photographic—or cinematographic—image affects our apprehension of a photograph, leading us to infer that images that are actually constructions are direct reflections of reality. This assumption even leads us to overlook slight perspectival or scalar anomalies between foreground and background in an image. Lugg's "collages" argue for a recognition of the photograph as a construction.

Works like those by Snow and Lugg raise an enormous theoretical challenge to the very basis of the modernist enterprise. Modernists had insisted on the idea that every art faces the imperative of not losing its identity when it assimilates impulses, forms or norms from the neighbouring arts. Decades before, when confronted with a similar claim promulgated by the Russian formalist theorists, the Czech aesthetician Jan Mukarovsky had noted that while this was true, the threat of any art losing its distinctiveness when incorporating aspects of another is not very great, since even when two arts use the same means, they produce different effects. The point made by Snow and Lugg in these works is very similar. Modernism had taken the purification of each medium as an urgent task and had attempted to find for each medium a form that would have a set of attributes entirely different from those of the forms constructed for other media. Lugg and Snow propose a more relaxed attitude. They suggest that the task of preserving mediumist purity is not quite so imposing as modernists took it to be. *One Second in Montreal*, for example, shows that when aspects of still photographs are incorporated in film—indeed, when still photographs are incorporated *holus bolus* in a film—they acquire the durative properties of a filmic image.

A film like Snow's *One Second in Montreal* (1969) provides a clue as to why Canadian avant-garde film is anti-modernist in conviction. Much Canadian film, both experimental and non-experimental, seems to rest on the assumption that film is a photographically based medium. For this reason, Canadian cinema in all its forms has been preoccupied with an endeavour we find reflected in *One Second in Montreal*: the analysis of the nature of photography, and in particular, the attempt to comprehend the paradoxes inherent in that medium. It is the very intractability of the photographic image with reference to conformity to modernist reformulation that explains the dearth of modernist works in the *corpus* of Canadian avant-garde works. Conversely, the affinity of photography to postmodern practices explains the predominance of postmodernist works within that *corpus*.

The reason for photography's affinity for postmodernism involves complex issues. For one thing, the change from modernist and postmodernist forms in the arts reflects a shift in conception and understanding of the source of creative order. Modernists generally held the view that the order that aesthetic objects possess is created in the mind of the artist, while postmodernists generally believe that it is discovered in the world of things. In other words, the modernist tradition considered the universals of artwork to be transcendental universals, while the postmodernist tradition considers them to be immanent universals.[8] Photography, needless to say, is disposed towards postmodernism.

One other point of contact between photography and postmodernism can be easily described: By and large, both are concerned with issues which arise from the use of representation, and especially with the values, both aesthetic and cognitive, of a representational image. Even the paradoxes to which postmodernist works return with such regularity are paradoxes inherent in the concept of representation. Modernism, it turned out, rested on a paradox. Modernism was art seeking to be itself, but in the process of seeking its own essence, it became something else—namely philosophy. In reaction to this paradoxical outcome, artists attempted to restore visual art to its "original activity"—the activity of representation.

But there are other paradoxical features of modernism. What these are can be clarified by considering two examples: Jack Chambers' *401 Towards London No. 7* (1968) and an individual image from a photographic series by Snow entitled *Plus Tard* (1977). The former is a painting done from a snapshot—a casually produced photograph of an everyday event. The latter *seems* to be a casually produced photograph of Tom Thomson's *The Jack Pine* (1916-17).[9] The Thomson painting, well-known to Canadians, is a pioneering work of "documentary landscape painting," which many critics believe to be the quintessential form of Canadian art.

One's responses to these works run an interesting course. When looking at either of these works, we imagine the image that the work represents—the photograph from which Chambers painted or the painting which Snow photographed. Representations like these, then, evoke a desire to see the original; yet we can imagine that if the original were to be presented, we would then want to see the scene that *it* represented. And again we can imagine that if we were to be shown *that* scene, the curiosity and fascination that had been aroused by the original work of art would still not be satisfied.

If the presentation of its original model cannot sate the curiosity aroused by the original, it would seem that this curiosity must be directed not toward that which the image represents but rather toward something intrinsic in the image itself. This was the conclusion drawn by modernist theorists. Accordingly, they expended much effort on the attempt to identify the properties intrinsic in a work of art that might elicit such interest and curiosity. Some argued that it was because artworks possessed "significant form" that they fascinated us. Others claimed that it was because the artwork bore evidence that a human personality had shaped it.

More recent artistic practices have tended to refute these claims. Neither Snow's "casual" photograph nor Chambers' painting derived from a casual photograph possesses what would canonically be considered a "significant form"; in fact, if either were considered in exclusively formal terms, it would be found lacking. Moreover, the meticulous objectivity of Chambers' reproduction of his source photograph is calculated precisely to exclude the formative—or, as he considers it, the deforming—role of the human personality.[10]

What underlies the effects we have described, according to postmodernists, is not something intrinsic in the work of art itself; it relates rather to something intrinsic in the phenomenon of representation.[11] Quite simply, postmodernists argue that the special interest elicited by a representational image results from the fact that it presents the appearance of an object other than itself. Although this claim sounds almost tautologically trivial, it asserts an absolutely fundamental proposition. I choose the word "appearance" with care, for it embodies an ambiguity essential to the phenomenon of representation. The word "appearance" can refer either to someone or something actually present (as when we talk of a celebrity's appearance at some gathering) or to an illusory presence (as when we speak of a mirage in a desert as giving only an appearance of being there).

The concept of representation is similarly double-sided. A representation is at once an actual object and an illusion, an image that seems to present an object that is not actually present.[12] A representational image, then, is a fascinating matrix of presence and absence. In fact, only when the absence of the represented object is acknowledged can representation actually occur. For example, a man who, while putting on a show for a group of friends, imitates the sound of a rooster, is making art, though admittedly art of a very low order. On the other hand, a man who has gone mad and starts making rooster-like sounds in the street, believing he has become a member of that species, is not making art at all, since he does not acknowledge that his sounds merely *represent* or imitate the sounds of a rooster, but thinks they actually *are* rooster's sounds.

It is the double-sided nature of the concept of representation—the fact that the *presence* of the original is suggested by an artistic representation even while its *absence* is demanded—that explains the peculiar desire a representational image—or any other form of representation—evokes. This desire projects itself toward the Other the image represents. Yet nothing can retain its Otherness when it is actually present;[13] the desire is impossible to sate, because inherent in the very concept of Otherness is the idea of absence.

Just as the relationship between pictorial space and the picture plane was the fundamental relationship in modernist painting, the relationship between presence and absence has been the determining factor in postmodernist art. This explains the particular interest which postmodernists have taken in photography. The relationship between presence and absence in a photograph is a particularly intense one, since a photograph offers an unusually forceful illusion of the "Other" which it represents. Indeed, it offers that illusion with such force that the Other's absence becomes something of a Presence. This paradox has been remarked upon by Roland Barthes, who spoke of photography's "real unreality"[14], and stated that in a photograph, one discovers a new category of space-time that involves "an illogical conjunction of the here-now and the there-then."[15]

Modernists had forsworn any truck with an artwork's "Other". They insisted that a work of art must have a solid being, that it must be wholly itself with no part constituted by something other than itself. This coincidence of a work with its own being was gauged in two distinct, though interrelated, ways. One gauge was the degree of referentiality of the work; "illusionistic" features were alleged to throw a work out of alignment with its being, since they forced the work to surrender aspects of its internal structure to that which it represented. Another gauge was the degree of its conformity to the medium in which it was realized; to be fully aligned with its being, a painting must be *wholly* a painting and must not possess features from some other medium of expression.

Modernism, in sum, was a centripedal doctrine. It turned the artwork in upon itself. Postmodernism, on the other hand, is a centrifugal doctrine. Its techniques are techniques of "decentring," of dispersal. Postmodernism has proposed, for example, the dissolution of notions of mediumistic purity and has advocated instead the construction of forms which use the attributes of one medium in works realized in a different medium.

Along with that of other artists formulating the art which is now commonly referred to as postmodern, Snow's work involves a repudiation of the ideals of "purity" and "essentiality," at least as the modernists had understood those ideals. In essence, Snow's strategies and forms are based on the principle of non-exclusion. He demanded to use both representation and abstraction; his works employ both "illusionistic" devices and devices which emphasize the objecthood of a work of art. Snow, it might be recalled, entitled one of his works, *Two Sides to Every Story*. The catholicity implied by the title is a key feature of his vision. While modernist art was based on principles whose effect was to exclude certain characteristics from the various forms of expression such as painting and sculpture, Snow has laboured to reinstate those features into each of the several media with which he has worked, using them to balance those features of which modernist art admits.

The temporal structures of Michael Snow's films are a case in point. Most of them have very simple shapes which extend over protracted durations. Snow pioneered the use of such forms; in fact when he first used them, they provoked something of an outrage since they were so unusual. In the early and mid-sixties, avant-garde cinema was dominated by forms that had been developed by the American filmmaker Stan Brakhage, whose films typically employ intense, expressionistic camera movements, frequent use of extremely close camera positions, rapid cutting between shots having contrasting attributes, and complex rhythmic structures created by the conjoint effects of cutting and camera movement. The style forged from these devices tends to rivet the spectator's attention to the screen; his works are so rapidly paced and have such intensity that one is required to give one's entire attention to the task of grasping what occurs in the very instant of its happening. Hence one's mental energies are devoted wholly to the perception of what is immediately present; there are none left over for the apperceptive acts of recollection or anticipation. The spectator of a Brakhage film is a fascinated spectator, absorbed completely in the given moment. He occupies a realm without any temporal extension, for in it, everything exists in a timeless presence.[16] Snow's films have very different temporal qualities. The temporal characteristics of his films are related to features of photography. They do not follow directly from photography's own temporal characteristics; indeed, Brakhage's timeless present has more in common with the instantaneous character of a photograph than do Snow's extended durations. The influence of photography on the temporal structures of Snow's films is mediated by the concept of representation.

The temporal forms of Brakhage's films employ tactics calculated to consolidate the viewer's experience, to assure that only that which is present in time is present to consciousness. And since, according to the phenomenalism his films are almost wholly given over to exploring, only that which is perceived exists, these temporal forms also assure that whatever is seen is totally revealed, that there is no "hidden other" outside the manifold of perception. Snow's temporal structures, on the other hand, like the phenomenon of representation itself, employ a strategy of dispersal. By using a form that unfolds over an extended period in a nearly predictable manner, Snow encourages the viewer of one of his films to recall the course the film followed to reach a certain point in its development and to speculate on its future course. Snow's temporality, then, embraces the past and future; it is not confined to the present alone. It leads one out of the present, away from what is actually given, toward that which is furnished only by reflexive acts of consciousness: away from presence toward absence.

Snow's decision to use such temporal constructions reflects the fact that he is as interested in apperception as in perception. Snow has adopted an anti-phenomenalist position, for the structures of his films, unlike Brakhage's, imply the existence of a thing, an "Other", that lies outside the manifold of perception—an Other which, in fact, has a dual existence, for it is both a mental image, furnished by an act of reflection, and the material object that underlies a perception. Like representational images, then, the structures of Snow's films present something that is both "real" and "unreal" (in the sense of being non-material).

The temporal forms of Snow's films are related to features that are specific to the form of representation found in a photograph. A photographic representation,[17] unlike the representations found in many other forms (painting, poetry, drawing, fictional writing), cannot depict objects or events which never actually existed. The distinction between those forms of representation that are constrained to represent actual existents and those which are not so constrained is an important one in mimetic theory. It was first introduced by Aristotle, who noted that the former sort of imitation stands to the latter as history stands to poetry. Aristotle's comment is apposite to characterizing the contrasting temporal structures of Brakhage's films and Snow's, for Brakhage's films really are poetic and Snow's really are historical. The temporality of Brakhage's cinema figures in his endeavour to fashion his films into a form of poetry. The fascinated absorption in the timeless present he seeks to induce, suggests his poetic commitment to the ecstasies of imaginative creation. Snow's films, on the other hand, use continuous periods of time so as to allow their viewer to scrutinize how experiences evolve. The study of how things evolve over time is one that can properly be termed historical; these historical concerns Aristotle would have considered appropriate to a medium which, being based on photography, can represent only actual existents.

If the extended durations of Snow's films make the viewer aware of the passage of time, another of their temporal qualities acts as a counterbalance to this. Many of Snow's films have diagrammatic shapes, the conical shape of *Wavelength* (1967), based on the gradual narrowing of the zoom, being the prime example. Such shapes allow one to grasp the film's lines of development as wholes—to apprehend them in what are, in effect, spatial rather than temporal terms. In sum, the use of such shapes acts to arrest the flow of time by transforming the films' lines of development into spatial forms, even while the use of extended duration makes one aware of the flow of time.[18]

Thus, while Brakhage had developed a cinema in which movement and repetition were used as they were in the writing of Gertrude Stein—to create the sense of a perpetually moving present—Snow has constructed structures which, while containing time, are themselves timeless and eternal. It seems obvious that the quasi-religious aspiration this reveals is one that is closely associated with photography. Unlike Brakhage's moving present, the timeless in Snow's work resists change; this is why he uses spatial forms to give it a figure. Even the tension between time and timelessness which Snow so often exploits is a tension which characterizes the photograph. A photograph, too, seems to depict the unfolding of an event in time even while it lifts those events outside time. So strongly do these conflicting qualities assert themselves, that each has provided the basis of a separate tradition of photography. One approach, as exemplified by the works of Robert Frank, exploits the photograph's ability to depict the speed of unfolding events; the other, represented by Weston, exploits the photograph's capacity to freeze a form and render it timeless. Snow's brilliant insight was to see how these competing qualities of a photographic temporality could be reconciled in a temporally extended form with a diagrammatic shape.

Snow's work involves still another type of dispersal. Snow allows his works to cross the boundaries which separate different media. As we have seen, he sometimes does this by reusing imagery created in one medium in works realized in a different medium, as when he reused still photographs in his film *One Second in Montreal*. But he also does this by incorporating features of one medium in forms constructed in another—for example by incorporating characteristics of sculpture in a film. A fine instance of this is ⟷ (1968-69), which was produced by stationing a camera in front of a classroom wall and first panning it back and forth, then tilting it up and down. Because the camera was not positioned equidistantly from the two ends of the wall, the pan contains a slight asymmetry; during the pan, the wall seems to swing one distance toward the camera, then a different distance away. As a result, the space in front of the wall seems to expand and contract while the wall itself undulates aperiodically toward and away from the image's picture plane. As the panning accelerates and decelerates, these spatial variations are reinforced; rapid panning streaks and blurs the image, flattening it further, while a more leisurely pace restores the illusion of deep space. Thus, ironically, a back and forth movement almost parallel to the picture plane results in an apparent movement toward and away from the picture surface.

As the title suggests, the film balances opposites: an optical space is balanced by a haptic space; self-referential constructs are balanced by "illusionistic" constructs; abstract passages are balanced by narrative episodes. The film, literally, oscillates between poles of cinematic construction. Its monomorphic shape, based on the variation of a single operation—the rate of the panning—was used to demonstrate that these poles are joined in a continuum of possibilities for film construction. This monomorphic form suggests that there must be something common to all these possibilities, since all can be realized by varying a single parameter; even the extreme ends of the continuum must partake in this common nature. These two poles of cinema construction cannot be the simple opposites (opposites which exclude every feature of their contraries) that modernists took them to be. In essence, the nearly monomorphic form of ⟷ acts to reconcile diversity by demonstrating that seemingly opposed forms of construction have something in common.

Chris Gallagher's *Atmosphere* (1975) uses camera movements which resemble those Snow used in ⟷. In *Atmosphere*, the camera pans, at various tempi, back and forth over a body of water. There is no apparent symmetry in the pans; they frequently travel different distances on their return swings than on their forward swings, and on a number of occasions the camera comes to a standstill and remains at rest for varying lengths of time.

Most people watching the film assume that a camera operator is in charge of the direction, the length and the pace of the pan and suspect that these parametric variations are governed by some system. The film encourages one to speculate about what that system might be. However, when the film ends with an image of a movie camera with a sail mounted behind it, the spectator realizes that these parametric variations were determined by changes in the direction and velocity of wind currents.

The final image in the film opens up a gap between the film's appearance and its reality—between what it *seems* to be, and what it *really* is. But what it appears to be—what it *imitates*—is not what films commonly imitate, namely an object or a scene from everyday life. What is imitates is a *film*, for it gives the impression of being a different sort of film than it really is. *Atmosphere*, then, is not just an imitation, but an imitation of an imitation.

*Atmosphere* is a meditation on photographic mimesis. A photograph, after all, like the camera movements in this film, is machine-made, not man-made. More interesting, though, is *Atmosphere's* demonstration of how our concept of representation turns on the notion of absence. The final image of the film simultaneously demonstrates that the film is an illusion (that it is not what it appears to be), and that there is no human agent responsible for the film's structure. It ties together the concepts of representation and absence, for it demonstrates that only when an absence is acknowledged does representation occur. The film's last image has one final significance. For most of the film's duration, the relationship between the camera movements and the landscape—that is, between the film's cinematic aspects and its photographic aspects—is inscrutable; one cannot discern why the camera moves over certain parts of the landscape when it does and at the speed that it does. The final image resolves this quandary by revealing that the camera movements were caused by wind—that is, by something integral to the landscape the film depicts. But at the same time as it brings the film's photographic and cinematic aspects together, the final image also reaffirms their separateness, for it points out that photography has limitations that film does not—limitations that result from the fact that a photograph can record only what is visible. Gallagher's choice of wind currents as the natural element that provides the structure of the film was a good one. The visible effects of wind are commonly used to suggest the unseen forces of nature. Hence, by developing a structure that depends upon wind currents, Gallagher reveals how the cinema can reveal the unseen forces of nature that a photograph can never depict. The form of this film, then, in which the relationship between the structural and the descriptive elements imitates the relation between observable and unobservable aspects of nature, resembles that matrix of presences and absence from which, as we have seen, postmodern art so frequently derives its structures.

Like ⟷, *Wavelength* (1967) demonstrates that pictorial conditions generally understood to be complete opposites (in the case of *Wavelength*, the conditions of primary importance are the spatial conditions of hapticity and opticity, though there are others) actually share a common nature, since both belong to a single continuum of pictorial form. And, as in ⟷, Snow establishes this by using a monomorphic form which is based on a single operation to unite the two conditions. In the case of *Wavelength*, it is a simple reduction of the camera's field of view that transforms the one condition into the other; as the zoom is extended farther and farther, the image appears flatter and flatter.

*Wavelength* begins with a wide-angle shot, taken by a camera set at one end of a loft and looking straight across it toward the interior surface of an outside wall of a building; in the wall there are four panels of windows which look out onto a street scene. During the film's forty-five minute running time, the zoom is adjusted intermittently, restricting, in uneven decrements, the camera's field of view. In the course of the film, four events involving people occur, as well as numerous changes in colour (some of which are very pronounced, others quite subtle), positive/negative reversals, and transitions from day to night and from night back to day. As the film progresses, the camera's field of view narrows down, centring on a number of images which are tacked on the central column of the wall on the opposite side of the room. The narrowing of the field of view continues until, at the conclusion of the film, the camera's field of view is contained within one of the photographs—a photograph of waves.

The conclusion of the film alludes to a paradox inherent in our conception of the frame. Generally, to frame a section of the world is to single it out for that special sort of attention that we give to an art object. The usual function of a frame, then, is to convert a section of the world into an art object. In the concluding portion of *Wavelength*, Snow demonstrates that a frame can serve the opposite function; by re-photographing a portion of the photograph, he creates the impression that what we see on the screen actually *is* what in fact it only represents.

Like Snow's films Ellie Epp's *Trapline* (1976) also takes framing as a central concern. *Trapline* is structured by a number of opposites: sound/image; on-screen space/off-screen space; action/reaction. All these oppositions devolve upon the fundamental opposition between presence and absence.

Throughout this film (in which the camera is focused on portions of the interior of a bathing house), the frame is *empty*, or at least devoid of character and action—of those very attributes which ordinarily hold one's attention within the boundaries of a film image. Because the space within the frame contains little to hold our interest, our thought is drawn to the source of the sounds which emanate from off-screen locations. By placing so much of the content of the film in the off-screen sound and by the use of prolonged shots, Epp suggests that absence which, we have seen, constitutes the very condition of photographic representation. She offers us an important insight: The frame, by its very nature, constructs a relation between presence and absence which is homologous to the relation between presence and absence in the imagery it contains.

Epp's strategy of emptying the frame of character and action raises a challenge to one of the most important conventions of the dominant cinema. Unless he or she desires to create suspense, the Hollywood type of filmmaker will choose to give that image which, at any particular moment in the story, presents the most important event or element in the dramatic action in sufficient detail to bring that element to the spectator's attention (for example, he or she will use a close-up if a detail of an action or response is the key element in the drama, or will use a two-shot if the interaction between two characters is the key to the ensuing dramatic action). This form of construction is based on a theory of visual pleasure which in turn rests on a theory of presence. Dating all the way back to Pudovkin's early work in film aesthetics and called the ideal-viewer theory, this theory of pleasure prescribes that the filmmaker, at any point in the development of a story, should always present that element in the dramatic action which an ideal viewer—a viewer with an ideal understanding of the dramatic development and with ideally developed human sympathies—would choose to look at. As the first section of Snow's *Presents* (1981) implies, this prescription turned the aesthetics of narrative cinema, like those of painting, toward an aesthetics of presence. Epp, on the other hand, by draining the image of any overtly presented narrative, reminds us that the photograph is based on absences—absences which the illusionistic cinema, *in order to be illusionistic*, must attempt to deny. If that absence were admitted to, the image's illusion of *being* the object that it actually merely *portrays* would be subverted.

Furthermore, the fact that the images Epp presents in *Trapline* give no privilege to important actions—indeed the film contains almost no action at all—while the sound track conveys the impression that significant actions do actually occur offscreen, implies the arbitrariness of the photographer's cut in space. Thus she shows that dominant cinema, by presenting important actions, overcomes the arbitrariness of the frame; this indeed is a basic principle of theatre or narrative.

Epp also assigns equal importance to all portions of the bathing-house, thus deemphasizing the conventional hierarchy of spatial significance. This is accomplished by having the off-screen sound come from undetermined directions, for this brings the whole of the off-screen space into play. In fact, the structure of *Trapline* draws a distinction between two types of off-screen space. The tight framing of the shots, their apparently nearly metonymic relations, their extended durations and the use of off-screen sounds which emanate from undetermined locations make us imagine an *undefined* off-screen space which we expect will soon be revealed to us. We anticipate that the camera will pan or zoom or that a new shot will occur which will place the current, tightly framed shot within a total context. As the film progresses, and no such camera movement or cut occurs, we realize that the total space will not be depicted. Consequently, we alter our expectation, anticipating that the space will be made concrete in another way—that shots will serially present an image of that total space. This space, while still imagined and not depicted, would nonetheless be a concrete space, not an indefinite space like that imagined early in the film.

The extended duration of the shots prolongs this period of waiting—the period in which we anticipate the conversion of the imagined, total space from an indefinite space to a concrete one. This very extension itself makes us aware of these two different forms of off-screen space, or at least conscious of the fact that we are awaiting the conversion of a spatial form possessing tension into one devoid of tension. Thus Epp conveys that off-screen space is a complex phenomenon which takes on different forms. At the end of the film we realize that the relationship between the various spatial fragments the film presents is inscrutable and that we remain unable to form a concrete image of the total space. The very act of denying us the power to form such an image makes us aware of the important role such images usually play in relaxing the tension created by the fragmentation of space.

Epp's *Trapline*, in its countering of the hierarchy of space, recalls some of Snow's films, especially *Presents* and *La Région Centrale* (1970). In both cases, this attack on hierarchical space is accomplished by Snow's unorthodox camera movements. The lateral or vertical camera movements that are the norm in orthodox filmmaking tend to privilege that sector of the off-screen space toward which the camera is moving—in other words, the space adjacent to the side of the screen on which the objects appear to be entering the frame. Snow's circular camera movements in *La Région Centrale* and the frequently twisting and whirling camera movements of *Presents* deny any privilege to any sector of off-screen space, since they assure that for the entire duration of any camera movement, there is no one edge of the frame at which objects will enter or leave the frame. Encouraging us to consider the entirety of off-screen space is part of Snow's purpose in *La Région Centrale*; that film uses the sphere as a model of unity and perfection. The lack of privilege accorded to any sector of off-screen space also emphasizes, in a fashion quite consistent with the nature of the photograph, the arbitrariness of the frame. Indeed, the vision of unity which *La Région Centrale* proposes amounts, essentially, to the view that all points—everywhere in space—have an equal and common nature, even if that equality is the equality of opposition. This proposition entails the claim that what is off-screen is equivalent to what is on-screen, and hence, the choice to depict any given segment of space at any given moment is quite arbitrary. One can, then, reasonably conclude that the vision of total equivalence that lies at the heart of *La Région Centrale* and *Presents* is based on an understanding of the frame that is rooted in the qualities of the photograph.

The camera movements found in *Presents* and *La Région Centrale* are implicated in the temporal structures of these films. In *La Région Centrale*, for example, the sphere implied by the camera movements exists as a complete entity for all time; however in the film, that sphere is analyzed and its various parts presented in succession. As a result, the extended temporal duration of the film is emphasized and set in opposition to the totalized, "all-at-once" temporality of the imagined sphere. Furthermore, because the camera movements are of uncertain vectorial attributes, the expected conversion of the indefinite, imagined off-screen space into a concrete, but still imagined, space never occurs. The tension created by our expectation of this conversion emphasizes the linear and successive properties of film's temporality and hints at the idea that the conversion would transform the film's temporality into one characterized by completeness and simultaneity.

Like Michael Snow, Jack Chambers is well-known as a painter. Many of his paintings depict features of the immediate situation in which he lived: his family, friends, places in the town where he lived, and the landscape of Southwestern Ontario near his native city. He was evidently deeply in love with his local environment and strongly committed to the ideal of depicting it.

This was not always so. In the late fifties he had left Canada, somewhat disgusted at what he perceived as its anti-artistic attitudes. He studied painting in Spain,[19] and painted there briefly after graduation. Before long, however, he felt the urge to return to his native country. He explained to an interviewer:

> The Castilian landscape was always something impenetrable for me. It was something I desired to become by entering but never could or did . . . There was an organism within an organism that appeared as landscape. But I knew I was not inside.[20]

The beauty of the experience of the unity of one's self with nature recurs throughout Chambers' writing and painting, and underpins his use of the photograph. Chambers is a Romantic artist; his commitment to making realistic paintings depicting scenes from his immediate surroundings relates to his Romantic ideals. These images have an ambiguous existence: since their contents are rendered with such meticulous objectivity, they seem to depict things in the material world; since at the same time they are rendered with great intimacy, they seem to represent Chambers' inner world. Their contents, then, appear to be both subjective and objective; in fact, they seem to exist at that point where self and world meet.

Chambers values photography highly because, for him, a photograph is a paradigm of this sort of amalgam of subjectivity and objectivity. A photograph is a product of a machine, since, in an important sense, the presence of a consciousness is only accidental to the making of a photograph, its nature being scientifically determined. Paradoxically, though, a photograph conveys, perhaps more forcefully than any other medium, the presence of a consciousness. A photograph always suggests a viewing subject; that is why "the look" of a photograph and "the eye" of the photographer have of late, become so celebrated. This paradox, that the more objective a description becomes, the more subjective it seems to be, underlies much of Chambers' work.

Canadian avant-garde filmmakers other than Jack Chambers have used the photograph's bond to the past to counterbalance the force with which a film image presents itself as belonging to the here and now. David Rimmer's films frequently make use of this sort of tension, usually by exploiting the contradictions which arise from the dual nature of a film's existence. A film, Rimmer points out, is both a material object—an object with an autonomous existence—and a representation—something whose existence is relative to that which it represents. Accordingly, Rimmer, in such films as *Seashore* (1971), *The Dance* (1970), *Surfacing on the Thames* (1970), and *Watching For the Queen* (1973), uses footage whose dated content invites nostalgic associations. At the same time, he reworks this material, building from it a structure which does not exploit these nostalgic associations, but rather depends on physical characteristics of the image—on its grain or the dirt particles that adhere to its surface, or on the motion that occurs between one frame and the next. As we have noted before, this tension between past and the present, between absence and presence, is characteristic of a photographic image.

Rimmer also shares with many other Canadian experimental filmmakers an interest in the nature of the frame. This interest is most clearly evident in his *Canadian Pacific* (1974) and *Canadian Pacific II* (1975), a dual projection film, shot from two slightly different points of view, of a railway yard and Vancouver harbour. Taped on the window near the corners of the screen are markers that signify the corners of the frame. By fastening tape on the window's surface to make us take notice of its presence, Rimmer hints at the camera (in Latin, "a room") and its lens. By shooting from two rooms on different stories in the same building—in other words, from slightly different vantage points—Rimmer demonstrates the interrelationship of framing and point of view. And by shooting in different weather conditions, on clear days and foggy days, Rimmer shows how the camera's rendering of depth is affected by changes in the aerial perspective, a spatial effect proper to photography. Rimmer thus relates several of a photograph's attributes to the nature of its frame.

The contrast between Rimmer's manner of reworking historical footage and that of Al Razutis is a measure of the distance separating Canadian avant-garde filmmaking from American. Razutis is American-born and moved to Canada only after completing his university education. His work is quite unlike anything in the Canadian avant-garde. Razutis shares with American pop artists an interest in visual forms which lie outside the acknowledged Fine Art tradition. Thus, while Rimmer, in *Surfacing on the Thames*, recreates the amber glow of a Turner canvas, Razutis, in *Message From Our Sponsor* (1979), reworks his footage—footage which like the imagery of American "pop" painting comes from Hollywood films and from advertising—to make it even more garish and more abrasive. Films like *93.8 KZ: Bridge At Electrical Storm* (1966-1973) and *Wild West Show* (1980) (even the title of the latter film reveals the "Americanness" of Razutis' films) work by arousing the viewer, by stimulating him or her to intense feelings. Razutis, one imagines, would find appealing Pater's theories that one measures the quality of life by the number and intensity of the sensations it contains. Needless to say, the nuances of temporal ambiguity which Rimmer works with are quite foreign to Razutis' films, which are designed to create their impact through their immediacy, vitality and vividness.

Another strategy of diversification has appeared in Canadian avant-garde films with considerable frequency; many film artists have worked with visual forms that incorporate printed words in the imagery. This form of construction is found in several of Joyce Wieland's films (*1933* (1967), *Reason Over Passion* (1965-9), *Solidarity* (1973), and *Pierre Vallières* [1972]); in several of Razutis' (*Sequels in Transfigured Time* (1976), *Cities of Eden*, and *Message From Our Sponsor*); in Patricia Gruben's *The Central Character* (1977); and in some of my own (*1857 (Fool's Gold)* (1981) and *Illuminated Texts* [1982]).

Perhaps this frequency is explained by the fact that this form of construction is a loaded strategy. For the past 150 years, visual artists have shown a considerable antipathy to literary forms of construction. One manifestation of this has been the proscription of illustration; an image, purists maintained, must never illustrate a text. As though to oppose these claims, the image-text relations in Razutis' the *Cities of Eden* and *Sequels in Transfigured Time* are illustrational, and those in Wieland's *Solidarity* and my *1857 (Fool's Gold)* possess at the very least certain attributes of that form of construction.

The tension created by conflict between the activities of reading and viewing (one of which occurs across successive moments in time, the other in a single moment) is another obvious reason for the use of forms which incorporate texts in images. Still another—and perhaps a more important—reason is based on the conflict between images which are actually presented and images which are presented only by the imagination. This sort of conflict takes place when the text describes something (a person or a location) that is not presented by the image. In such cases, the film spectator (or more accurately, spectator/reader) is asked to imagine one scene even while he or she looks at another. The contrast between the image actually presented and the image produced by the imagination emphasizes the "imaginariness" of the latter. As I noted in the discussion of framing, "the only-imagined" image (an image that is not actually presented but is only evoked by some form) is frequently called forth to act as a sign for what is absent. Thus, this form of construction conveys the notion that the relationship of a word to the image it evokes is the same as the relation of presence to absence in a photographic image. Sometimes, too, the image in such a construct will disprove or contradict what is asserted by the text it incorporates. This construction, too, is motivated by the attempt to deal with issues relating to the nature of photography, for it questions the often assumed veracity of the photographic image.

The writing of this article was funded by the Canada Council. It was originally prepared in 1982 for the catalogue of the OKanada Berlin exhibition.

---

1 See for example: Parker Tyler, *Underground Film; A Critical History* (New York: Grove Press Inc., 1969), pp. 177-184.

2 Clement Greenberg, "After Abstract Expressionism," *Art International*, 6 (October 1962), p. 30.

3 It was the great American avant-garde filmmaker, Hollis Frampton, who, citing how central Flaubert's project was to the modernist ambition, first indicated the incompatibility between Flaubert's project and the nature of photography. See Hollis Frampton, "Impromptus on Edward Weston," *October*, 5 (Summer 1978), p. 53.

4 Though the banal idea of exhibiting the light from the beam of an operating projector for a specified period of time and calling this occurrence a film was many times expressed in many countries and, of course, was often actually carried out.

5 In fact, one can easily make sense of the claim that the showing of a film is a type of performance, while similar claims in connection with a photograph seem pretty nearly, if not completely, nonsensical.

6 That is, "live-action" cinema. In animated film (which I consider a completely different medium, since its photographic properties are quite accidental to it, in the sense that any method of duplicating images for subsequent rapid projection would be suitable) we have the splendid work of Norman McLaren. I consider it a confirmation of my thesis that the only true modernist filmmaker that Canada has produced works in a medium that is not photographically based.

7 Actually, the images in Grenier's films only appear to be non-representational. While they seem to consist of purely abstract patterns, they are actually, as is generally revealed in the course of his films, direct recordings of actual constructs. These constructs themselves, however, are purely aesthetic, non-functional constructs. That this is so further complicates the theoretical issues in the relationship between representation and abstraction in Grenier's films.

8 On this matter see Charles Altieri, *Enlarging the Temple: New Directions In American Poetry in The Sixties* (Lewisburg: Bucknell University Press, 1979).

9 The appearance of being casually produced is created by its slightly soft focus and the blurring of the image caused by moving the camera—that is, by features of the sort which typically appear inadvertently when one makes a rapid snapshot of a work of art hanging in a gallery. The appearance is deceptive; Snow uses these apparently accidental features in a highly calculated fashion.

10 See Jack Chambers, "Perceptual Realism," *artscanada*, 26, No. 5 (1969), p. 8.
11 Or, more technically, the special effects of representation depend upon relational rather than absolute properties. The error that the modernists made was to assume that the special properties of representation must be absolute properties. It was this assumption that underlay their notions about the autonomy of the work of art.
12 The magical thinking characteristic of pre-artistic representation equated both forms of presence (i.e., the illusion represented was taken as having the same reality as the representing sign.) Artistic representation, as I argue immediately below, depends upon separating out these two forms of presence. To express the point more technically, I argue that artistic representation occurs only when a consciousness of the nature of symbolism replaces the effects of magical thinking in one's psychology.
13 Or is taken as being so, as in magical thinking.
14 Roland Barthes, "The Rhetoric of the Image," in *Image-Music-Text* by Roland Barthes, selected and translated by Stephen Heath (Glasgow: Fontana, 1977), p. 44.
15 Loc. cit.
16 As a result, the forms of Brakhage's films are related to collage. Like James Joyce, Brakhage is interested in depicting conscious processes, in which all noematic objects are equally present. The form both men developed for their endeavour was that of collage.
17 Or, in the case of photo-montages or photo-composites, the individual components of the image.
18 The former is a reflective, apperceptual form, the latter a perceptual form. This conflict between perceptual and apperceptual processes is one of the watermarks of Snow's work. It is, for example, basic to his famous installation in Toronto's Eaton Centre entitled *Flight Stop*.
19 Significantly, because he felt that there he could receive the best training in traditional disciplines of drawing and painting.
20 Ross C. Woodman, *Chambers* (Toronto: Coach House Press, 1967), p. 8.

# *Forms of Cinema, Models of Self: Jack Chambers'* The Hart of London

## BY R. BRUCE ELDER

*The Canada that is presented to us by most of Canadian cinema is an amorphous landscape filled with metaphoric locations that never quite seem to have a name. Cities become "soulless urban centres" or "anonymous hubs of activity." The countryside represents "pastoral idealism," "the retreat into a more innocent time" or "a cauldron of atavistic passions." Particularly striking scenery is particularly striking scenery per se—backdrop country. And the North is a tabula rasa hungering for human complications.*

*There are, of course, exceptions to these depictions of a homogenized geography. Chief among them is Jack Chambers'* The Hart of London. *London is London, Ontario. It is a place that is described to us in the film through exhaustive photographic evidence ranging from family album extracts to items from more than a decade of local television news. The hart referred to in the title is depicted in one of these items as a stray deer trapped in the city's laneways and eventually destroyed by the London police. The hart is also "the heart," the essence of this very specific locale. Nor is this simply a critical assumption. It is, instead, as expressed in the aesthetic proclamations of the filmmaker, a foregrounded assertion of what Chambers called a "wow moment." The images of the deer incident represent an instant when photographed reality and all of the meanings latent in those photographs (in this case, a strip of movie film) are one and the same.*

*Chambers' doctrine of Perceptual Realism and its expression in* The Hart of London *is discussed here by R. Bruce Elder as being of central importance to an understanding of the way in which Canadian filmmakers express a unique congruence with the world outside the cinema. As stated in the previous article ("Image: Representation and Object"), Elder's thesis centres this congruence around a contemplation of the nature of photography. For him, it is of particular importance to document the manner in which Chambers' evocation of place through photographic means works toward a broader creation of self. Although it appears here separated from Elder's larger discussion of the psychological nature of perception, this analysis of creativity is sufficient for a positing of the hart/heart as personal essence. But what makes the argument, and indeed Chambers' work, so crucial, is that this personal essence grows out of a photographic consideration of the world outside—the place that, in the Canadian context, has always proven as desirable as it is elusive.*

*The Hart of London* begins with a nearly pure field of white light accompanied by white noise on the sound-track. The image has several connotations: death, desolation, and above all that non-existence in which consciousness has its beginnings, that nothingness that is the ground of our being. It suggests, in a way quite familiar to those who know Chambers' work, that the beginning and end of our existence coincide—that our end is a return to our beginning.

The field of pure white light changes to an image of a white snow-covered field. A hart runs and leaps in the middle of the field, as though startled by something. This image, too, is richly laden with connotations. The hart is an animal of the forests and so evokes associations of unspoiled nature, of nature before civilization encroached upon it and corrupted it.

But this is a startled hart; it is feeling, not playing. The ominousness of the shots of the hart is reinforced by the alternation of normally exposed images with over-exposed images and fields of pure white light, inasmuch as shots of these latter two types have qualities in common with that annihilating nothingness we have just been considering. As yet we do not know what has startled the hart and why it is fleeing, but we soon learn, for we next see a gun being loaded. The gun is shown a number of times, first in over-exposed images, then in multiply exposed images; thus the line of regression from "normal" perception to "the wobbly image" to the negative hallucination is drawn.[1] The movement from normal to regressive and back to normal perception is repeated several times as the image of the gun alternates between normal and negative imagery which, overall, is very light-toned. By means of this alternation, the gun is associated with the negative hallucination.

The deer is shown leaping over a fence in a newsreel image that will be familiar to many viewers from Chambers' painting *The Hart of London* (1968). As in the painting, the deer is juxtaposed with a picture of a policeman carrying ropes, that is, with an image of the regulatory forces that ensnare and destroy playful innocence.

The film again changes to a field of white light, which once again suggests the negative hallucination and the idea of death. From this field of white emerge undefined, barely visible images of men walking on a city street carrying an ensnared deer. The focusing device on the lens is then racked over and we see a tree. Obviously this pull-focus is a device for making a transition from the idea of civilization to the idea of nature. But what is implied in this transition? One might be tempted to interpret it as expressing the familiar notion that our civilization is destroying nature. While this interpretation is given support by the fact that a deer—an animal that traditionally has served as a symbol of innocence—is used to represent nature, other attributes of this passage and of the film as a whole contradict it. For one thing, the film does not present nature as something that is wholly kind, gentle and innocent, for Chambers associates nature with the annihilating emptiness. Chambers' vision of the relation between civilization and nature is far more complex and far more disturbing than this interpretation would make it out to be. In *The Hart of London*, Chambers shows that while both civilization and nature have their innocent and gentle sides, each also has a violent and aggressive side that drives each to destroy the other.

Chambers here seems to be developing a tragic vision of the relation of civilization to nature akin to Martin Heidegger's vision of the relations of World to Earth. Heidegger, in "The Origin of the Work of Art,"[2] speaks of two fields of being, World and Earth. World comprises all conscious beings and all those beings which are manipulated by consciousness for its own purpose. Its will is to master and to control the Earth. It seeks to assimilate the earth by making the Earth knowable to consciousness. That which it cannot understand, it seeks to destroy.

Earth, on the other hand, is (or more precisely, is understood by World to be) the ensemble of material beings. It is driven by unconscious instinct. Like

World, it too is self-aggrandizing and wants to return the World to the state of Earth. Finally, it is inscrutable to World.

Not the least troubling aspect of this description of the relation of these two fields of Being is that the distinction between World and Earth is not a knife-cut distinction, as that between nature and civilization is generally understood to be; it does not neatly categorize every object that exists as belonging exclusively to one or the other of these two domains. In fact, everything that exists can be understood as belonging simultaneously to *both* domains, for everything that exists is made of material that comes from the Earth and operates according to the laws of nature (that is, Earthly laws), and yet at the same time has now fallen under the control of the World's impulses.

More startling still is the fact that though everything belongs simultaneously to both domains, the two domains can be seen to be inevitably at odds with one another. The conflict between them can be understood in two ways. One is that each is self-aggrandizing—World seeks to assimilate Earth and Earth seeks to assimilate World—and the other is that Earth is inscrutable to World and World attacks in order to destroy that which it cannot understand.

Like Heidegger, Chambers seems to have believed that civilization and nature are locked in a closed circle of struggle. (Perhaps Heidegger's terms World and Earth better reveal Chambers' beliefs about the distinction between the two domains, for Chambers too seems to believe that World incorporates aspects of Earth and that Earth incorporates aspects of World.) And like Heidegger, Chambers seems, at least at the time he made *The Hart of London*, to have believed that the struggle makes existence essentially tragic, since this essential tension unleashes destructive forces.

As consciousness starts from the void or blankness of this annihilating nothingness, so World evolves from Earth; civilization from nature. In a similar fashion, the film begins with snowy fields, then shows animals in the snowy fields, then animals on city streets, and finally developed cities. But even though civilization is shown as developing from nature, and consciousness is shown to have its origins in the blankness of unknowing, still it is suggested that World (i.e., civilization and reason), when far enough developed, tries to overcome Earth (i.e., to eliminate nature and unreason) and claim everything for itself. And so it is with life and death: The life force drives all beings toward immortality, and the death force strives to destroy all life. This is quite a different conception of the relation between life and death than the one Chambers held when he made *Circle*; he then saw life and death as holding each other in balance. At the time he made *The Hart of London*, his vision of the relation of the two was a much more disturbing one, for he came to believe that each is locked in a tragic struggle with the other.

The images of World (i.e., of civilization) that follow are a montage of faces, buildings, and "cityscapes" arranged in what Christian Metz would call a bracket syntagma, that is, achronological groupings of loosely associated images which follow one another in the manner in which a parenthetic interpolation follows on the main text. As the passage proceeds, the city appears more and more industrial, but also included in the passage are a large number of old school photographs, photographs of groups of people wearing outfits that identify them as dating from a few decades ago, and pictures of people standing in formal poses before the entranceways to some turn-of-the-century buildings, in the manner used in old photographs. Thus the passage takes on the features of a souvenir album. As the sequence proceeds, however, the montage becomes more rapid, and more and more of the images are in negative. The resemblance of the images to actual memory images becomes more striking, for the images cease to present themselves as the external representations of real events, as the contents of a souvenir album are, and seem more like the internal imagery of memory. Even the rapidity with which one image replaces another, and the indistinctness or indefiniteness of these images that results from their being in negative, seems calculated to convey the instability and uncertainty that so often characterizes memories, and to evoke that sense of loss which is so deeply involved in the process of remembering. The fact that some of these images, such as the images of the entrance to the Kellogg building, the Carling brewery truck and the McCormick biscuits factory, seem to belong to some indeterminately remote past, stresses the achronology of the passage, and so emphasizes its interior quality, at the same time as giving the imagery a very local character. In this way, Chambers provides a figure for the relation between consciousness and place. In fact, the alternation of negative and positive imagery, the recurrence of some images, the presence of flipped images and the use of rapid montage give this passage characteristics which resemble those of the process by which consciousness endeavours to form a stable image fixed in—or at least associated with—a time and space other than that of internal time and space consciousness, that is to say, a stable image. It therefore suggests the struggle of consciousness for a sense of place.

We realize by this point, too, that the film imagery is becoming more distinct and definite, and that it is becoming more three-dimensional. In fact, the rest of the film will follow along on this course of development, for the imagery will change from black-and-white to colour, will become more stable, more conventionally "realistic," and will take on greater depth. This general development is one from imagery with the qualities of less stable, early, internal imagery, to conventional imagery representing the world external to consciousness. It represents a move from within to without, or better, depicts the way in which the self finds a place in the real world. It shows how that imagery which is the ground of our being, and which at first seems to be purely internal, achieves a locus in the real world, thus bringing self and other into a fundamental ontological relationship.

Chambers' decision to have the opening passage begin with that primal "blankness" from which imagery emerges can certainly be taken as indicating his interest in the origins of consciousness and the foundations of identity. But the structure of the opening passage has other significances. It is largely composed from still- and moving-picture imagery of London, Ontario's, local history. Chambers uses this imagery to convey the idea that one's sense of identity is forged in a community and that one's self is inextricably bound up in that community; this explains the "extended family" album quality of the passage, for a family album also interrelates personal and family identities. The instability of this imagery, which, I have shown, is to be taken as representing the contents of consciousness, is used to demonstrate that only when internal imagery comes to be associated with a fixed time and space, only when it achieves a place, does it become stable. Finally, inasmuch as the wobbly image is a product of the drives, the structure of the opening passage indicates that the sense of personal identity which is forged on the site of the stable image regulates the derivatives of the instinctual drives. Thus Chambers associates the notion of community[3] and that of a regulatory order; *The Hart of London* then, is in part about the vicissitudes of the instincts within the regulatory order.

The film continues with a passage which conveys a sense of difficulty of "fixing" these conscious images, of making them stable. Several devices are used to convey this difficulty. Close-up images of what appears to be branches create a flat, rather Jackson Pollock-like construction. Because these images lack in "space," they also seem not to have a fixed "place" in the real world. Positive-to-negative and negative-to-positive reversals (for example, of factory buildings and street scenes) are used to create a literal lack of stability. Negative images (of buildings, cars, etc.) are used to produce flattened spatial fields. Images are flipped left to right so that the direction of the movement in the image alternates between movement from left to right and movement from right to left. Superimpositions are used to create multiple vanishing points within a single frame, a Cubist-like strategy which has the effect not only of reducing depth by multiplying vanishing points until none is especially effective, but also of suggesting, as the Cubists themselves realized, the synthetic nature of perception. Grid-like structures such as bridges, girders and buildings with square windows are used with a similar purpose, for they flatten the image by reducing it to simple geometric forms that lie flat on the picture surface. Moreover, most of the movements in most of these images occur in directions that parallel the surface of the picture plane, a feature which also helps to eliminate any impression of depth. But of all these devices, it is probably the use of bas-relief (as in the image of the horse and buggy, created by combining positive and negative versions of the same image slightly out of phase with each other, with the result that the product of the combination is an image composed of silver-white forms in shallow relief with jittering at the edges of the forms) that most resembles the wobbly image of anxious drive-perception, and most clearly reveals the purpose of all these devices.

One set of images which appears several times in this passage and is of special importance is that of men dragging corpses of wolves across snow fields. Some of these are images of a single man with a wolf, others are images of several men with wolves. They suggest the interlocking violence of humans and nature, for the wolf, a violent animal, represents nature's violence, while the fact of its being slaughtered represents the violent human reaction to the violence of nature.

Near the end of this section, there appears an image of a man in the middle of a snowy field holding a hose as though flooding a skating rink. The whiteness of the field and the freezing cold are obvious allusions to death. This shot anticipates other images of water that occur right at the end of the passage—images of flowing water that obviously signify dissolution and death (i.e., are analogues to the impulses motivating the negative hallucination)—for it is followed by a short passage which contains no distinct imagery whatsoever; following it is a shot, in clear focus, of maple keys.

The water image is a transitional device that carries us into a new section of the film. This sectionalization is marked by a change in the sound-track from intermittent bursts of white noise (which are a kind of aural equivalent of the negative hallucination) to the sound of flowing water. This latter sound, while somewhat more representational and less aggressive than white noise, still carries connotations of dissolution and death. And while one might be inclined to conjecture that the main shift of implication in this aural transition is a shift in the represented locus of the destructive drive from the internal realm to the external realm, this cannot really be so. Since Chambers seems to have believed, at least at the time he was making this film, that human violence interlocks with the violence of nature, and that each holds the other in a circle of mutual struggle (and much of the film's imagery embodies this belief), this aural transition can be interpreted only as a shift in attention from the internal to the external—from one part of the circle of violence to the other.

In this new section, shots or passages which signify life, birth, and the process of generation alternate with shots or passages which signify death and the process of dissolution. For example, images of maple keys are juxtaposed with images of a snowy field, as though to emphasize the deathly significance of these later images. Similarly, another passage begins out of focus with what to all appearances seems to be another "field of pure light" that, we have learned by now, signifies the negative hallucination. This field of pure light forms (through a pull-focus) into an image of a snow-covered field, in the middle of which is a mother holding her two sons. This shot itself, then, comprises symbols of both birth and death. Shortly thereafter, we are shown a mother carrying a baby out into the snow, in a shot that again relates the ideas of birth and death. This image is soon followed by a passage constituted of what seem to be overlaid images of branches; the sliding of images overtop one another, and the flat space that results, suggest the "wobbly image."

The appearance of "wobbly" perception at this point is most interesting. Because snow-covered fields are most frequently used in these passages to convey the idea of death and destruction, it might have seemed that Chambers believed that the forces of destruction belong to the world external to consciousness, and that the image of the mother and child standing in the middle of the snowy field was meant as an image of Cartesian dualism, as an image which portrays humans as weak and vulnerable beings in the middle of a hostile nature—were it not that is, for the presence of these wobbly images. Wobbly percepts are percepts affected by the drives, and the anxiety they register is anxiety about the drives themselves or, more precisely, about the drives *felt as attacks on the structures of the ego*. Given the context in which these wobbly percepts occur, we can safely infer that the drives whose effects are here registered by the "destabilizing" of perception are the aggressive drives. The "wobbly" image juxtaposed against the field of snow thus conveys the notion that humans answer external forces of aggression with their own aggressive drives. Here again, Chambers implies that humanity and nature are locked in mutual combat.

The section continues, alternating images which signify birth and growth with images which signify death and decay. Images of water are cut together with images of farmers ploughing fields, creating a conjunction which conveys the idea that water has fertilizing, life-sustaining powers. These images, which signify the life-sustaining forces, are followed by overexposed, intensely bright images which signify violence, aggression, destruction, and generally the negative drives which produce negative hallucination. In keeping with these connotations, the next images are of flooded areas and ruined houses rather than of farmers ploughing fields. The passage thus conveys the idea that water can be life-destroying as well as life-sustaining and, on a broader level, the idea that there is an intimate relationship between creation and destruction. In the next passages, shots of leaves and maple keys are superimposed over shots of the face of a person who appears to be lying quite still, as though dead. Here again, images of birth and death are associated with one another. We are then presented with several extreme close-up images of shoots on a hedge being cut down by a man wielding a pair of enormous shears.[4]

With the next image, a new section begins, which although marked off from the previous section by different visual qualities, nevertheless is thematically nearly identical to it. This passage begins with a close-up of one eye, then moves to a close-up of a hand searching out a medicine bottle. The deathly significance[5] of these images is emphasized by the next shot, a shot of a dripping tap, which condenses the idea of the corrosive effects of passing time and the idea of the dissolution of structure by water. This construction, inasmuch as it comments on the human condition, is a kind of intellectual montage; the next shots continue the pattern of the alternating syntagma which has provided the structure for this passage. They are shots of various parts of the body of a baby boy. We see first his hands in close-up, then extreme close-up shots of his entire body which, because they were taken with a moving camera, seem to represent the baby's own perception of parts of his body, for they are not in clear focus; the shots soon come to emphasize first his eyes, and later his teeth. These later images are used to suggest that even a seemingly innocent baby possesses aggressive instincts, and thus that innocence and aggression can be associated with one another. When, still later in the passage, images of the baby playing with his penis are linked with images of his teeth, the pattern of alternation of images of behaviour motivated by creative drives with images of behaviour motivated by destructive drives is continued.

A new section of the film begins when the image changes from black-and-white to colour. Like the previous one, this section is structured by the alternation of images of birth and images of death. In this passage, however, the images are more literal than those in previous passages, for they are images of the birth of a child and of the slaughter of a lamb. The lamb has obvious religious connotations, and the table on which it is slaughtered strongly resembles an altar. The scene is a transformation of the crucifixion scene, with the lamb representing Christ—*Agnus Dei*, the lamb of God that "taketh away the sins of the world." The Blood, whose redness, we surmise, the switch to colour was calculated to emphasize, is thus the blood of Christ that washes away our sins. This image is a complex one, for it brings together notions of sin, death, redemption, salvation and rebirth. Being a transformation of the crucifixion, it relates ideas of death and birth. At the end of the passage, shots of the newborn baby are juxtaposed with shots of a lamb embryo, presumably from the womb of the lamb we just saw slaughtered. This juxtaposition again relates ideas of birth and death and articulates the notion that there is a destructive force in things, a force that effectively slaughters innocents.

The next passage consists of red-tinted images of a bonfire in which Christmas trees are burned. The Christmas tree is a symbol of Christ's birth, the red bonfire, of death. This, then, is yet another image which fuses allusions to birth with allusions to death. The following passage consists of images which deal with such notions as separation and merging, individuality and loss of individuality, and death as dissolution of individuality. We see pictures of a mother teaching her son to swim (in this image, water is depicted as the universal solvent which dissolves all individuality, leaving only a common "soup"); a lamb embryo (the whole) being divided into parts; and a human embryo (the individual part) enveloped in the surrounding tissue (the whole). In all these cases, it is the newly born or the not-yet-born whose individuality and integrity are threatened. Here again, then, the ideas of birth and death are linked to one another. The pixillation effect used in this passage further emphasizes the dialectic of unity and division.

The passage continues with a soft-focus shot of light reflecting off water, that is, of short-lived dots of light dancing on an ever-changing, indeterminant ground. This is yet another variation on the theme of the dialectical unity of particularity and universality, and of death and life. This scene is followed by images of people near an ocean which, like the image of the children swimming, conveys the threat of the impending dissolution of individuality and particularity.

The fear of the loss of individuality with which these sections of film are concerned relates closely to the notions of identity with which the earlier sections of the film dealt. For one thing, the images of water are rather like the negative hallucination. Furthermore, one's sense of identity, we have shown, is forged on the site of the specific, concrete, definite image. These images of universality are all, to a greater or lesser degree, non-specific, abstract and indefinite. Thus, even in their formal characteristics, they represent the antithesis of a sense of identity. But the matter is not quite as simple as this. We have seen that Chambers believed that one's sense of identity develops in a community and in a place—in society and in nature. The use Chambers makes of "images of universality" in the last passages we have discussed implies that "the universal" has aspects other than its nurturing ones. The images reveal that at the same time that "the universal" helps forge "the individual," it threatens him/her with the dissolution of that individuality; thus the very agency that creates a person also threatens him/her with destruction.

The next section of the film presents additional examples of the duality within nature of nurturing and destructive forces. We see a man going for a brief swim in the icy cold water of a stream. Here, an activity that would normally be delightful and restorative has turned into a potentially lethal one. We then see men emerging from a hole, as though from a mineshaft which has collapsed. The implication that they very narrowly missed being destroyed is quite obvious, but the image also contains another less obvious implication: The way the men emerge from the underground cavern resembles the way a baby emerges from the birth canal. This passage also has a double connotation of birth and death. We then see shots of sailboats on a lake, some of which resemble scenes that appear in Chambers' well-known painting *Regatta No. 1* (1968), a painting which alludes to the story of a boy dying at a boating event. Hence this passage at least adumbrates the notion that an activity which is normally life-enhancing can also result in the destruction of a life.

This is followed by a passage in which images which show individual units being brought into a unified whole and images which show unified wholes being broken into individual units alternate with one another. We see people crossing a bridge, their individual footsteps "joining" to create a journey, and then railway watertowers being toppled over and destroyed. We see the image of a train, composed of a series of individual cars (in fact, this image suggests, at once, both integration and disintegration), and then a group of parachutists breaking up as the individuals plunge out of the plane one after the other. This section is followed by one that deals primarily with decay. We are shown fruit dying on a vine, and then scenes from some sort of recreational event, apparently at a nursing home or an asylum (some attendants are dressed as orderlies); rather sorry-looking old men stand in barrels and box one another until one tips over. With this scene the theme of balance—the balance of life and death, for in all these games the loser is knocked to the ground—is made explicit. This theme is articulated again in the next passage showing a wheelbarrow game in which participants end up getting dumped on the ground. The destructive potential inherent in that which ordinarily supports and nurtures life is again depicted in a scene of huge flowers in the shade of large umbrellas; when looking at these shots, we realize that while the sun once nourished these flowers, it now threatens to destroy them. In the next scene, some young children enter a room and kiss an old couple who sit in rocking chairs. While the vitality and "lovingness" of children is depicted in this scene, the overriding impression it produces is of the immobility of the old people; thus it suggests more the fate of youth than the continuity of the generations, even though the latter is also definitely implied by the scene. Next we see old people looking at old photographs, perhaps searching for lost friends. Chambers seems to be suggesting that the loss these people obviously feel is not counteracted by the ability of photographs, or memories, to preserve moments against time; a photograph can never secure a moment against loss, precisely because a representation can never really make what was past, present again.

The use of photographs in this sequence reveals something quite important both about the use of dated newsreel footage in this particular film, and more generally about Chambers' interest in creating images that derive from photographs, as nearly all his paintings after 1962 did. Part of Chambers' interest in the photograph is obviously that it acts as a sort of memory. A photograph is like a memory in two respects. Firstly, it is a "re-presentation" in the sense that it renews the past. In this regard, the photograph has the power to affect us with bygone things; it can disturb us in the same way that the thought of and the affects surrounding the "lost object" can disturb us. Chambers' paintings have consistently exploited the capacity of the photograph to inflict nostalgia on us. *Olga Visiting Graham* (1964), one of Chambers' earlier "realist" paintings, depicts his wife visiting a departed friend. The family scenes such as *Sunday Morning No. 2* (1970) and *Diego Sleeping No. 2* (1971) are simple scenes of passing childhood, depicting moments that are known to all parents, retrospectively, to be both very perfect and very short-lived. Even the later still life and nude pictures present objects and people whose beauty is bitterly transient. The dated quality of the found footage in *The Hart of London* evokes feelings of sadness similar to those we feel when we think of objects that we cherished or people whom we loved who have now gone. The faded, undetailed quality of much of the found footage only emphasizes the pastness, the "bygone-ness," of these lost objects, just as the indistinctness of memories—and the fundamental unrecoverability of their missing details—provides an index of the loss of the events and objects which are their source.

Secondly, like some memories, a photograph can present us with an illusion which so closely resembles our experience of actual objects that it very nearly overwhelms our recognition that it is an illusion, and convinces us, rather, that it has actually rendered the object it depicts eternal. There are two consequences to this. One is that memory, and consequently love, can very nearly render events and persons enduring and save them from destruction. This, I think, is the conviction behind Chambers' repeated insistence that perception, which begins in love, ends in a photograph. The second is a more bitter consequence, to wit, that the eternity which a photograph seems to achieve for its object is achieved only by turning the object into an illusion—into something unreal. A dialectic between eternity and unreality that lies at the very heart of the photograph is the reason why the photograph, as I put it earlier, "breaks so many promises." To render something permanent, a photograph must first render it unreal. Chambers seems to have been haunted by this dilemma, for it appears to have been the source of the realization that life-sustaining and life-denying forces—creative forces and destructive forces—are intimately interrelated even in artmaking. Like Michael Snow in *Presents*, he seems to have come to the saddening conclusion that a photograph is marked by both the presence and the absence of its model. When making *The Hart of London*, at least, Chambers seems to have been convinced that it is the illusory nature of the photograph that is its primary attribute; that a photograph—like a memory—triumphs over time only by rendering its model unreal. One is left only with ghostly traces of a bygone world—with "Flying Dutchmen," as Snow remarked in his conversation with me.[6]

The theme of the destruction of natural beauty that occurs when things of beauty are turned into art objects is reworked in the scenes of women picking flowers to wear as boutonnières. The following scenes, of birds "trapped" in their cages like the spirit in the flesh, like the "real" in the illusory, like the transient objects of nature in the eternal time of the photograph, offer additional articulations of the same concept. The fundamental destructiveness of human beings, nature, and the process of making art (and perhaps even of the process of forming memories) is suggested by the following images of corpses lying in rows.[7]

In the final passage, Chambers' two sons, John and Diego, approach some deer in what appears to be a zoo, seemingly wanting to pet them or to feed them. The sound-track presents Olga Chambers' voice, lowered to a chilling whisper, giving the boys instructions and repeating over and over again, "You've got to be very careful." In certain important respects, this scene is a reversal of the opening scenes in the film, for there the hart was the victim, and here it threatens to be the destroyer that kills innocent victims. The scene also clarifies the role of the hart in the film. This role, it turns out, depends upon the traditional symbolic value of the image of the hart. Like the eagle and the lion, the hart has traditionally been understood as an enemy of the serpent, and so has been associated with light and goodness. The slaughter of the hart depicted at the beginning of the film, therefore, represents the slaughter of innocence, while the menacing quality of the hart at the end of the film implies that even goodness has turned threatening and destructive. Moreover, the hart, because of the way its antlers are renewed, is also a traditional image of regeneration. The image of the slaughter of the hart is an image of destruction of the regenerative forces, that is to say, of the ultimate victory of destruction over regeneration; while the hart's menacing the children at the end of the film is another image of the potential lethality of the creative force, and of the manner in which creativity threatens to destroy innocence. Finally, because of the resemblance of its antlers to branches, the hart is linked with the Tree of Life. The killing of the hart is thus a symbol of the destruction of life, while the menacing hart is a symbol of life-sustaining forces turned aggressive and destructive.

I am, however, being imprecise, or rather, too simple, for there is a central ambiguity to this passage that I have ignored entirely. Olga Chambers may be taken not as cautioning her children about the hart's threats, but as exhorting them to take care for the hart. "You've got to be very careful" may also be taken as a moral statement, encouraging her children not to frighten the deer unnecessarily. References to the violence of humans and the violence of nature are thus condensed in this ambiguous exhortation.

*The Hart of London* is a film concerned with the activity of creation and with the process by which identity is constituted. It establishes that the means by which a person's identity is forged have their roots in imagery, in images of self, of nature and of community; or, more precisely, of self-and-community-and-nature, for it shows that self, community and nature are indissolubly linked. But it is, in addition, a film based on a profound understanding of the nature of types of mental imagery. The interest in memory of which the film gives evidence arises from Chambers' concern with the stable image upon which a stable sense of identity is grounded. These images, because of their stable, object-like characteristics, normally belong to—or at least are closely associated with—what the psychoanalyst Donald Winnicott referred to as the third space, a space which is neither external to consciousness nor internal to consciousness, and it is this that makes them valuable in the process of forging an identity which relates self to world within a stable matrix. However, we have seen in retrospect that as these images grow fainter and less distinct, the fact that they are internal to consciousness becomes increasingly evident, as does the fact that they are subject to the same vicissitudes as all internal objects. Above all, it becomes clear, as *The Hart of London* intimates, that they are as much prey to being eliminated in aggressive rage, to being done away with by the negative hallucination, as any other internal objects. The negative hallucination does away with the ground of one's identity, and is therefore felt to pose a threat to the very foundation of one's being. Nevertheless, in an almost paradoxical fashion, because these images are, under ordinary circumstances, believed to belong to "the third space," and because we normally deal with our destructive impulses by projection, the destructive forces involved in the negative hallucination, forces that are felt to threaten our very being, are attributed to the community and nature which surround and support us. This explains Chambers' notion that the violence of self, nature and community interlock, and why, in Chambers' work generally and especially in *The Hart of London*, images of community and nature have the dual characteristic of supporting our sense of identity as well as threatening it.

1984

This is an excerpt from an article comparing the conception of the self implied by Jack Chambers' *The Hart of London* and Michael Snow's *La région centrale*. A long introductory section outlining the theoretical underpinnings of this comparison has been omitted. The writing of this article was subsidized by a grant from the Visual Arts Critics Program of the Ontario Arts Council.

---

1 I use the term "wobbly image" to refer to mental representations yet unstabilized by language or destabilized by the impact of the drives, and the term "negative hallucination" to refer to that gap in consciousness which occurs in moments of rage as the aggressive drives do away with the image/object of their rage.

2 Martin Heidegger, "The Origin of the Work of Art," *Poetry, Language and Thought*, trans. Albert Hofstadter (New York: Harper and Row, 1971). My reading of the essay has been deeply influenced by Dennis Lee's *Savage Fields: An Essay in Literature and Cosmology* (Toronto: Anansi, 1977).

3 The contrast between the conceptions of self and of personal identity which Chambers proposes in the passage and those of Stan Brakhage, to whose work *The Hart of London* bears a strong resemblance, highlights these differences between the typical Canadian and American concepts of the self. Chambers, we have seen, believed that a sense of the self develops along with a sense of the community. Brakhage, on the other hand, believes that all social influence on consciousness represents a corruption of the basic, primal self, and that one discovers one's own identity by stripping away all the effects of the social and recovering one's own unique vision.

4 These images are obviously metaphoric; indeed, the obviousness of the fact that they are metaphors makes us aware that, unlike *Circle, The Hart of London* is a poetic film in much the same sense that Brakhage's films are poetic films: They are films whose imagery is highly condensed, highly metaphoric and highly charged.

5 *The Hart of London* was made shortly after Chambers learned he had leukemia. The man in this scene is likely Chambers himself.

6 "Michael Snow and Bruce Elder in Conversation," *Ciné-Tracts*, 17 (Summer/Fall 1982).

7 The period during which Chambers made *The Hart of London* was also the period of some of the most concentrated attacks by the United States on the Vietnamese people's liberation movement. The American assault on Vietnam was something that disturbed Chambers greatly. Thus Chambers was acutely aware at the time he was making this film of a struggle going on in his own body and in the outside world. The analogies between these personal and public events made Chambers horribly aware of the general destructiveness of the prevailing order. At the same time, Chambers, a devout Roman Catholic, was, like George Parkin Grant, horrified by the legitimization of abortion under Trudeau's new laws and the consequent dramatic increase in the number of abortions performed; so disturbed was Chambers by this phenomenon that he even prepared prints and posters to help support the "right to life" movements. Doubtless these activities were wrapped up with his view, expressed so powerfully in *The Hart of London*, that there is a frightful order of things that involves the slaughter of young innocents.

# *David Rimmer: A Critical Analysis*

## BY AL RAZUTIS

*The Canadian experimental film field is quickly becoming large enough to develop several schools. Added to the divisions between the National Film Board's pursuits (in both experimental documentary, drama and animation) are the distinct efforts of well-defined groups in Toronto and, to a lesser extent, Montreal. But as Al Razutis argues here in his examination of the work of David Rimmer, the largest chasm between sensibilities can be measured geographically. The split between central Canadian and west coast filmmakers is, as Razutis suggests, an outgrowth of the similar split south of the border. Historically, Vancouver experimental filmmakers were part of a "west coast network" with roots in California, while other Canadian avant-garde artists looked to New York and Europe. Razutis finds in Rimmer's rejection of "imported" iconography a recognition of an intrinsic regional style of experimental pursuit, and in so doing challenges the theory of a unified Canadian practice posited elsewhere in this volume by R. Bruce Elder ("Image: Representation and Object").*

*Rimmer's work is a particularly interesting battleground for a nationalist versus regional interpretation of experimental filmmaking sensibility. In a relatively small number of short studies, Rimmer has developed an international reputation for his precise manipulation of the minutia of motion. As exacting as Rimmer's mini-worlds are, they are never totally divorced from the vibrancy of their original subject matter. The people in* Watching for the Queen *remain people; if anything they become more alive through Rimmer's painstaking manipulation of the image.* Surfacing on the Thames *is not simply a formalist study. Rather, like any landscape, it proclaims its dependence upon the place that gave it birth. To this may be added the social landscape of* Real Italian Pizza, *a film which, like the people walking through it, strives to inhabit its chosen environment.*

*Given this aspect of his work, it is not surprising that Rimmer has moved in* Al Neil/A Portrait *and* Shades of Red *toward longer studies, whose singular pursuit of the subject lead to their consideration as documentary. In fact, whether it is Razutis or Elder who is finally writing from the correct side of the mountains, it must be acknowledged that Rimmer himself is formulating in his films yet another approach to the definition and limits of Canadian experimental practice.*

### CONTEXTS AND INFLUENCES

To appreciate the significance of David Rimmer's films, we should consider first the general context within which they were created. In the sixties an avant-garde movement sprang up throughout North America. The dominant features of this movement were multi-media experiments, a rejection of formal art history (notably Modernism), a rejection of intellectual art "establishments," and a focusing on experience and the ideology of intervention. Though it can be located historically (1963-1973), it is predominantly ahistorical in nature, owing more to the Surrealist and Dada traditions of severance, political action and provocation.

On a political front, the sixties featured open revolt against militarism, authority and the capitalist state; and on a social front, revolt against middle-class mores and conventions in the form of alternate dress-appearance and communal-family social interrelationships. Traditional religion and Western philosophy were displaced by Eastern cosmology, self-realization and consciousness-expansion (via drugs, diet and meditation). With the shattering of traditional institutional values came the emergence of individual forms of expression through the support of communal organizations. The sudden availability of portable media instruments (16mm cameras, video portapaks, music synthesizers) made expression possible on a non-institutional and non-corporate basis. Social acceptance of counter-cultural expression was evident, especially in major urban centres. A parallel network of "underground" institutions suddenly sprang up. Cinemas, cinémathèques, distribution co-operatives and publications helped the avant-garde to begin to consolidate its position. The nature of this consolidation bears some attention.

## THE WEST COAST NETWORK

Vancouver artists in the sixties suddenly were involved in a network of activity that encompassed Los Angeles, San Francisco, Portland, Seattle and Vancouver. The University of British Columbia imported American poets, artists and filmmakers for special exhibitions and events. These persons travelled up and down the coast with a sense of international camaraderie. Influences from New York and Europe were felt less often, and usually in the form of critical publications.

The developing forms of West Coast avant-garde films were influenced most notably by two American filmmakers: Stan Brakhage and Bruce Conner. Brakhage in his landmark book, *Metaphors on Vision*, which served as a complement to his already vast body of films, implanted a sense of personal discovery and authorship in the minds of younger filmmakers. He elevated the notion of personal or home film to artistic levels and, more importantly, drew attention to the fact that the fundamental unit of film construction was the *frame*, rather than the shot.

Conner, on the other hand, brought forth socio-political satire in the form of compilation or stock footage that was organized into discursive and structured forms. The basic unit of Conner's filmic constructions was the stock footage shot. These shots were arranged in such a manner (distinct from "pop art" serialization) so as to allow a deconstruction of that mythic realm which Western media had treated previously as sacrosanct truth. The viewer could now participate in the process of fabricating history and meaning.

David Rimmer's initial propensities toward independent views, self-expression and cross-disciplinary modes of investigation were supported by the prevailing conditions. His attitudes were not moulded by film schools, since few, if any, existed at the time. He was inspired by radical techniques and concepts. Brakhage and Conner were among these sources of inspiration. The availability of inexpensive production methods allowed him to engage immediately in filmic discovery and expression. A definition for the term "film art" had not been determined, and thus all work was "experimental" and legitimate.

Rimmer's methods of production were initially very "unprofessional" by CBC, National Film Board, and industry standards. His projector doubled as a projector and rewinder. His viewer was, in fact, a studio window. His optical printer was comprised of a rear-projection screen and camera.

There was also a community of individuals which provided support. Stan Fox, a producer at the CBC, who later became an educator, provided production costs for the films *Knowplace, Square Inch Field* and *Migration*. Another important factor was the Intermedia Artists' Co-operative, which was organized by Joe Kyle, Bud Doray and Bill Nemtin, and later administered by Werner Aellen. It provided space, facilities and equipment for a variety of media artists whose interactive contributions provided much creative energy.

It is evident that Rimmer was able to benefit from this supportive community during his formative years as a filmmaker. In addition, although the Canada Council had not yet established a film section in 1968, his application for monetary assistance in the invented category of "film as art" was accepted. This acceptance of Rimmer's work, as well as that of certain others, would benefit an entire generation of future filmmakers.

A critical context, however, was lacking in Vancouver in the sixties. Noncritical acceptance was largely the method of interaction between artist and institution or between artists themselves. It is interesting to note that Rimmer's residence in New York from 1970 to 1972 not only provided him with an overview of what was occurring throughout the avant-garde world, but also enabled him to gain a perspective on his own work, along with deserved critical acclaim.

## THE CONTEXT FOR ANALYSIS

The nature of Rimmer's films suggests that the best critical and analytical approach is structural analysis. I have already located his work (in its inception) in the "postmodernist" era of avant-garde expression. The tasks of this essay will be the analysis, criticism, and assessment of the work, with the intent of informing the reader as to the aesthetic and formal structural characteristics contained within it.

Much of the work is highly "cinema-specific"—that is, referential to the actual materials and properties of cinematic production, image-representation and viewing-perception. Much of the work, at first glance, is "minimalist" (i.e., the content is subsidiary to, and limited by, strict formal parameters), and "industrial-constructivist" (i.e., the content and form proceeds from the actual materials used in production). Both of the previous categories fall within the Modernist tradition, and are acknowledged because it is important to note that these films do not represent a total severance with art history. Rimmer's films do not lend themselves overtly to cine-linguistic (semiotic) analysis because of an inherent subordination of the visual sign to structure and materials.

Sound is usually a subordinate element in his films, and often nonexistent. With the exception of *Al Neil/A Portrait*, the visual components of his films were completed prior to the introduction of sound.

Rimmer approaches the art of filmmaking from a conceptual and problematic point of view, one that is usually located around a specific stock footage ("anonymous") shot or its equivalent—an anonymous point of view, setting or event. He then immerses himself in a process of aesthetic discovery by analyzing and modifying the given elements of this footage and their initial parameters. The locus of his specific film "narratives" usually centres around the retelling of the details of the *concept*, rather than a literary story line. To fully understand the nature of his "narrative exposition," we must come to terms with both problem-concept and cine-technology.

Ordinarily, film does not lend itself easily to analysis. The average viewer cannot stop it and review it time and again. The mere fact that projection formats feature an inexorable progression of images, always "forward" in time and without the opportunity for sampling, tends to divorce many analysts (and viewers) from its rich aesthetic potential. Rimmer's work is, however, made for analysis. Within the exposition of their narratives, the films contain reflexive and analytical components. In fact, this is part of their design. Their austere, minimal qualities draw attention to subtle aspects of filmic structure and aesthetics, without the melodramatic embellishments common in "mass entertainment" films. They are also the work of an *auteur* who, by design and necessity, has been the primary agent in all aspects of their creation.

The films that I found to be most intriguing are those that contain an element of poetic ambiguity or a nonliteral quality within the complex of their aesthetic. It would be tedious indeed to analyze simple didactic exposition of a linear nature. Conversely, it is rewarding to examine the depths of poetic content, image metaphor, and the very discursive nature of filmic design. The quality that differentiates Rimmer's work from much of what is called "structuralist-materialist cinema" (notably and loudly emanating from New York and London), and its tedious didacticism, is precisely the presence of metaphor and poetic content.

## THE BREAK WITH SYNAESTHESIA–EMERGENCE OF THE ART

Rimmer's work, grounded in the sixties, initially featured the influences of the synaesthetic audio-visual culture. Although the avant-garde had begun to offer "declarations of aesthetic import," notably through Brakhage's writings, Mekas' criticisms and Maya Deren's recovered writings, the formalization of aesthetic principles was yet to be seen.

Within this general backdrop, Rimmer produced *Square Inch Field* which, by his own observation, suffers from "pop mysticism" and a grounding in "imported"(Eastern) iconic-mystical systems. Yet *Square Inch Field* displays an intrinsic awareness of filmic rhythm and design. It also heralded the beginning of Rimmer's use of the frame as a building block in montage. Rimmer's work, however, took a new direction, representing a significant break with existing "pop norms" and synaesthesia, with the completion of *Migration* in 1969.

Rimmer describes *Migration* as "organic myth," and he recalls that shooting began with the central image of a dead deer on a beach. Subsequently, he worked on either side of that image (shooting and editing) toward a composition that predominantly featured visual rhythms. The visual rhythms to which he refers are the result of an integration of two interesting techniques—flash-frame montage and "writing" with the hand-held camera. The flash-frame montage punctuates the dominant rhythms as a percussive element. The *camera-stylo* "writing" is precise (almost calligraphic) and maps out the region of cinematic expression that is both impressionist and expressionist. The influence of Brakhage also is visible—especially Brakhage's *Sirius Remembered*—not only in the scratched-on titles, but also in the aggressive interaction between camera movement and subject matter.

In *Migration* there are but few moments of a contemplative nature. Naturalism is subordinated to a kinetic interaction with organic life processes and decay. The variety of camera movements and points of view is startling. Swish-pans, sudden tilts and snap-zooms, as well as interpretive "writing" devices create a participatory/interpretive texture. Mimetic images become part of the cinematic *kinesis*. Not only are contrasting motions juxtaposed, but also extreme points of view. The camera pans down a cliff-face to the clouds! Solar flares are juxtaposed with a bird in flight, and sunlight, as seen through trees, dissolves to sunlight reflected on water. The last example, that of relating opposite points of view, becomes the *modus operandi* in the film's construction. Thus, it is not surprising that temporal points of view in their opposite states, such as accelerated time or time-lapses being cut with "normal" or extended time, are equally present. The rhythmic and contrasting elements of the film, and their use in montage, are reminiscent not only of Brakhage, but also of Vertov. Rimmer's *camera-stylo* successfully liberates itself from the confines of the literary narrative. But liberation is relative. *Migration* still contains remnants of the "old world," and its break with pop-symbolism is not total. The symbolic "elements" of earth, air, fire and water certainly are present in both content and form, but this presence can best be read as *narrative loci* (i.e., the "threads of interaction").

The "organic myth" that Rimmer referred to is thus comprised of four mythic/elemental domains which feature four narratives. Yet some images of ambiguous symbolic value such as the thorns of a rose, a diving seal and birds in flight remain. Perhaps the resolution of the film's symbolic content is alluded to in the beginning and end. In the opening section, the familiar West Coast image of a seagull in flight (the "unconscious liberation" pop-symbol) is frozen, caught, and burned in the projection gate. This act, though symbolic in itself, focuses the viewer's attention on the plural characteristics of cinematic representation: image; symbol; projection; grain; focus and texture. We are encouraged to see beyond mere representation and experience to the materials of the cinematic enterprise. *Migration* is a form of iconoclastic "heresy," a violation of the rules and etiquette of cinema. But it is also a heresy with a purpose—growth and development of style. The burning of such a cliché image becomes an introduction to future *materialist* and conceptual concerns which dominate Rimmer's films for a large part of the seventies—a "migration" towards post-synaesthetic structural cinema.

*Variations on a Cellophane Wrapper* (1970) represents a further breakthrough in the development of experimental aesthetics. Its structure is disarmingly simple: proliferation-variation-abstraction. But Rimmer's method and form of exposition is rich and complex.

The film is based on an endless ("closed") loop of a black-and-white stock footage shot that features a woman stacking cellophane sheets in a factory. This loop is repeated, reversed from positive to negative to positive, and transformed via optical printing techniques. The *paradigm* or "category of choice" that Rimmer employs is limited by the range of optical and contact-printer possibilities inherent in both technology and design. There is more than one version of the initial "parent" stock shot. The initial variations include low-contrast positive and negative, and high-contrast positive and negative copies. The structural organization of these elements along the time track is of major importance. The closed loop (a complete cycle), when featured as a series of successive shots, forms an obvious pattern of repetition and proliferation. In 1969, Rimmer had experimented at The Edmonton Art Gallery with a simultaneous projection of four loops. These experiments suggested not only graphic variations, but also compositional variables in time—ones that featured "synchronicity" and "asynchronicity" between each loop element. This latter condition became one of the key features of *Variations*.

The film begins with the "normal" (low-contrast) image/loop repeating and setting up a rhythm. Within a short time, higher contrast copies are introduced, and these begin to alternate between positive and negative, normal and high contrast. The negative cycle of image-proliferation follows, proceeding from low- to high-contrast, and also features positive and negative alternations. Up to this point in the film, the structural qualities of proliferation and variation have been quite simple (I would term the beginning as being purely expository). The exposition is now followed by "complication," especially in terms of the variable components of graphic and temporal organization. Rimmer begins to superimpose positive and negative copies of the parent loop, slipping in and out of sync, to achieve partial and total solarization of the image. This phase of *Variations* also alternates high-contrast positive and negative images. At this point in the film, a notable change occurs. Positive and negative strobing is introduced, accompanied by step-printing of each frame to slow the action, as though to stimulate the optical retina of the viewer toward an intended goal of colour perception. Only subsequently is colour introduced in the film, proceeding from fragmentary moments to complete colour separations and overlays. The film's progression through complex variations to complication reaches a state of abstraction—a *dénouement* or climax in which the image is resolved as a *disintegrating* line drawing.

In *Variations*, the central image of the woman is always present, the rhythm is nearly constant (even though a slowing down of movement occurs); and the motion is always one of vertical "wash"; that is, the cellophane sheet is tossed upwards. *Variations* is a departure from the domain of synaesthetic light-show loop projections because of its structural organization and simplicity as well as its aesthetic assertions. Rimmer chose, as parent footage, a shot by an anonymous author from an equally anonymous point of view. He then contrasted this anonymity with overt manipulative techniques that display both investigation and aesthetic. He has succeeded in combining both *synchronicity* and *asynchronicity* as aesthetic functions in time. The sound, by Don Druick, serves chiefly as accompaniment, loosely following the previously determined design. The ambiguity of the content-message permits the viewer to experience and interpret the film in a variety of ways. Some viewers, as Rimmer has pointed out, see the film as a "spiritual" message, and some see it for its "political" or "feminist" content.

Whereas *Variations* featured the closed loop as a primary unit of construction, *Seashore* (1971) utilized an "open loop," where the completion of the action does not synchronize with the beginning. The maximal length of the loop was predetermined by the length of the original stock footage. Again, proliferation and variation are dominant features. However, the short, fragmented shots of Edwardian bathers are not generally tied end to end, but rather are punctuated with black leader. Rimmer's decision in this regard seems quite logical. If the primary building unit is "open" or incomplete, then the absence of image (black leader) becomes the necessary structural correlation.

Instead of building graphic variations (as in the previous film), Rimmer fragments the shots themselves, reverses screen direction, freezes on water marks, repeats loops and fragments within the shot, and superimposes asynchronous elements. Rather than proceeding toward "complication," he engages in *deconstruction*. He even extends his investigation into the process of mechanical or optical image reproduction. Intermittent registered motion, with each frame held still for projection, is contrasted with non-registered or streaked and blurred motion. The two levels of content operating in this film, cinematic representation and mechanical ordering of motion, never seem to totally fuse. In that sense, I think it is less successful than either *Variations* or *Surfacing on the Thames*. The structural integration of the bleached-out image of bathers and the black leader is also problematic. The black contrasts with the whiteness of the original shot, and rather than integrating with it, becomes a counterpoint. (I would think that clear leader would have been appropriate.) The visual pulsations, or raising and lowering of light levels, is referential to the pulsation of the waves breaking on the shore, yet its overall structural ties are not clearly delineated. However, in a gallery installation the structural characteristics of *Seashore* will be more referential to kinetic "painting in time."

*Surfacing on the Thames* shocked the avant-garde community. It was as if the structuralists had "missed the boat" prior to this film. *Surfacing* is an elegant, restrained essay on cine-narrative and exposition. The structure and form employed is once again disarmingly simple; "found footage" of anonymous origin and chronological narrative are used in a way that is both austere, mythic and minimal. The parent shot is *expanded* in length from five feet to approximately 250 feet. The film's narrative functions on three levels—spatial, temporal and contextual.

Spatially, a barge travels from right to left in a mist of grain and surface texture. Ostensibly, this action once took place on the Thames, perhaps in the thirties. More curiously, Rimmer's recording and rendering place this action in the realm of myth, rather than history. The "mythic" movement is precise, with each increment carefully measured. Temporally, each frame of the original shot is rendered as a brief *pause* between a continuing progression of dissolves. The dissolves are ninety-six-frame or four-second transitions between previous and latter frames. The sensation is one of clockwork motion, seen as both increment and process. It is a chronology of events, normally occurring in real time, but seen in this film from an intensely magnified perspective.

The film opens with white frames, referring to the screen, and a slow zoom out from the grain and image. The initial edge fogging announces "the beginning of the roll" and the "beginning of camera-image representation." The zoom back *locates* the Thames landscape as an object, situated almost like a painting on some gallery wall. It is notable that Rimmer used a wide-screen aspect ratio for this composition—one which is in keeping with landscapes. At this point, a series of ninety-six-frame dissolves commences, locating the image both in changing space-relationships and in a process of expanded time. The approximate age of the parent shot can be surmised by the predominance of surface texture such as grain, water marks, scratches and dust. The ageless qualities can be surmised by the fact that it is an object of contemplation and beauty. The time expansion that Rimmer utilizes can be seen in contrast to the incessant flicker of the projected image. In this sense, and it is crucial, the film is not equivalent to a series of dissolving slides. It is highly cinema-specific and cinema-chronological. While the locus of the film is parallel or has a narrative and chronology, the meaning of the film includes the "precious object" context of rendering or representation.

One question that often has been overlooked in various critical essays on *Surfacing on the Thames* is the question of what comprises the elements of its narrative. To even the most casual observer, the predominant event is the dissolve rather than the freeze-frame hold. With this consideration in mind, it is reasonable to propose that Rimmer has succeeded in constructing a narrative from a series of transitions. He has succeeded in challenging the accepted notion that the "shot" is the basis of any narrative. (Ten years later, we can see the commercial cinema equivalent to an aspect of this discovery embodied in the extended dissolves of *Apocalypse Now*). Rimmer also has succeeded in redefining the parameters of the cinematic landscape film. In 1968, he created a time-lapse cinema-landscape entitled *Landscape*. This film featured a compressed rendition, from dawn to dusk, of water, clouds and mountains, from a fixed camera point of view. In 1970, *Surfacing* presented the viewer with a completely unique view of what a cine-landscape could be.

As in all his films, *Surfacing* relates to earlier and later work. The zoom-out and zoom-in, which initiate and complete the film, are related to the opening and closing procedure used in *Migration*. The vertical displacements of image during dissolve, which reoccur several times, I find curiously inconsistent, if not disconcerting. They draw us out of the structural simplicity of the work and direct us to the filmmaker's technique. But these criticisms are minor. *Surfacing on the Thames* remains a bold, innovative and important film in both Rimmer's body of work and contemporary cinema-culture.

*Watching for the Queen* continued Rimmer's investigations of minimal narrative and the anonymous/autonomous shot. The results are quite interesting and innovative, and can be approached best from three main considerations.

The first is the original shot, a crowd of expectant, smiling faces, which features little camera motion. As in *Surfacing*, each frame is subject to time expansion. There is little indication at the onset as to what will constitute movement, and in what capacity. What is initiated (along with the familiar trademark of edge fogging announcing the "beginning of the roll") is a curious form of visual analysis, proceeding along the lines of *segmentation* and *collage*. Each change in perceptible movement, which corresponds to a change in the original frame, appears as a *spatial* rearrangement, segmented by a cut. In *Surfacing*, each frame is *joined* via a dissolve. In *Watching for the Queen*, each frame features a displacement. It appears as if the cinematic cut has found its graphic correlation.

Secondly, this "collage" changes in the process of projection according to defined time constructs which are based on arithmetic progressions. For example, the first frame of the original shot is frozen for 1,200 frames (approximately one minute), the next two for 600 frames, the next four for 300 frames, and so on. The result is a slowly accelerating montage and a concretization of the "real" event through time. It is as if a reinvention of the motion-picture domain of "reality" was being undertaken. The transformation of a "sea of anonymous faces" into a "narrative of personalities" becomes a distinct possibility as movement and reflexive action are consolidated. In a psychological sense, as we become more familiar with the details of the scene, our attention shifts to identifying reflex actions and changes in the crowd.

Thirdly, Rimmer creates a parallel narrative between specific people in the crowd. For example, the first stage of the narrative concerns identifying individuals in the crowd. This is accomplished by noting, or having our attention drawn to, the person who exhibits the greatest motion. As the freeze-frames lessen in duration, other degrees of more subtle movement engage our interest. The narrative elements that each character represents are parallel, because they are only connected by the theme of "watching for the Queen" (as we, in turn, are "watching for the characters"). Over several viewings, I arrived at the following ordering of the narrative "story": the crowd is composed of . . . a bald man smoking a cigarette . . . a man with a cap looking up . . . a man holding a pair of binoculars over his head . . . a man stretching to see over the crowd, and so on. It is curious indeed that I saw these characters in the present tense, rather than the past. I would attribute this last point to the fact that Rimmer requires the viewer to discover the narrative and participate in it through this discovery.

Pattern recognition, saccadic eye movement and feature rings are well known phenomena in the behavioural sciences. However, in *Watching for the Queen*, Rimmer has succeeded in employing these mechanisms in the *telling of a story*, by employing mathematical ordering in an aesthetic manner.

In contrast to *Watching for the Queen*, the short sketch entitled *The Dance* displays expansion of time by the use of an invisible cut. The parent footage featured a pair of dancers, seen from a fixed camera point of view, rapidly pirouetting across the foreground. Rimmer's use of the invisible cut proliferated this motion to the point of humorous exaggeration. The dancers become both spinning tops and an Astaire-Rogers duo performing feats beyond human endurance. The frenetic rhythm of the dancers, and its proliferation, becomes a distinct foreground effect in contrast to the background musicians. Although the use of the invisible cut historically belongs to the domain of *découpage classique* or

"Hollywood" action-cutting to condense the scene, Rimmer uses it for the purpose of *montage* or the "building of an idea." Once again, as in earlier films, the anonymous event is the cause for analysis and celebration; once again, the dance motif figures prominently. The presence of this film also supports the notion that Rimmer's filmmaking exhibits links to both sculptural and painterly concerns. Typically also, this film features formal opening and closing movements; in this case, curtains which open and close as an *auteurist* gesture.

*Fracture* presents the viewer with a narrative riddle, one which is related directly to the nature of parallel construction. The concept of parallel narrative is not new and has been often used in novels and in film. Both *The Great Train Robbery*, made by Porter in 1908, and many of Hitchcock's films illustrate the use of parallel narrative to build tension and suspense. In comparison, Rimmer's use of this technique is conceptual, minimal, and proceeds along the lines of *construction* rather than exposition. Two 8mm home-movie shots are used as "scenes" to comprise the basic elements of his parallel construction. These shots seem related, but they may have originated from two separate films. The extreme granularity of the shots suggests 8mm home-movie origin, and the viewer may assume that the people depicted are friends, relatives or the filmmaker's immediate family. This ambiguity prompts the viewer to examine possibilities rather than actualities. Rimmer's structuring of the implied narrative is strikingly reminiscent of the interpretive ambiguities found in Antonioni's *Blow Up*, in which the artist accidentally discovers, attempts to solve, and finally abandons the riddle.

The narrative construction (and I emphasize the latter word) of *Fracture* is comprised of eighteen shots. These shots are, in fact, optical renditions of two primary shots or scenes: the woman and child, and the male "intruder." Each shot is a partial segmentation and deconstruction of the parent scene, and they are presented as fragments which allude to the content of the whole. Shots 1 to 9, in chronological order, feature direct cross-cutting (a form of "parallel montage") between the woman and child scene and the "intruder." The woman looks toward the direction of the male and approaches the child in a protective manner. The intruder's hand, in an extreme close-up, opens the door and closes it. Shot 10 suddenly reveals to us the possibility that the action in shots 1 to 9 may have been in *reverse*. The implication is inescapable: Our assumptions regarding the meaning of the narrative may be completely wrong. Shot 11 seems to corroborate this; the woman now sits and reverses her previous actions. Shots 12 to 17, also presented in parallel montage, contrast the forward and backward actions of both persons, suggesting that the notion of "threat" is simply illusory and based on the manipulation of innocuous events. However, the final shot (18) repeats the earlier suggestion of "threat" and prompts a further reconsideration of the film's narrative.

Rimmer's *Fracture* successfully isolates and exploits basic cinematic codes and conventions, such as screen direction and open-frame composition, in the creation of an implied and poetic narrative. The use of optical step-printing allows the viewer to analyze the meaning of the actions. And since the actions proceed at a slower rate than the viewer's interpretation, Rimmer has structurally defined a process in which the "riddle" and "mystery" reside primarily in the viewer's mind. *Fracture* also is notable for its unique manner of ordering events non-chronologically and reversing them in time. Indeed, this is a unique combination of two categories of syntagmatic shot relationships—*bracket* and *parallel* syntagma, as described in *A Semiotics of the Cinema* by Christian Metz. The lack of "plot" resolution is not overly disconcerting, unless one is waiting for a "punchline." Obviously, these disconnected fragments or shots did not, in themselves, contain the resolution to the parallel narrative. But neither did *Blow Up* contain a full resolution of its narrative. The elegance and simplicity of *Fracture* is notable in that during the course of ten minutes we can observe both the deconstruction of parallel narrative and the mechanisms of the concepts behind it.

*Canadian Pacific* straddles the categories both of structural essay and interpretive documentary. This film is intrinsically related to Rimmer's earlier landscape films, *Landscape* and *Surfacing on the Thames*, by the presence of formal rules of framing, composition and temporal organization. It features, however, some interesting variations. In *Canadian Pacific*, the basic unit of construction is the shot as a scene, which is presented as a formal sample of a lengthy time-lapse. The camera point of view also is not neutral. It features the filmmaker's studio and personal point of view, which is specifically alluded to in the last shot. The composition contains a tension between "open form" (foreground action emanating from and proceeding to outside of the frame) and "closed form" (action contained by the frame, or framing devices such as mountains, shoreline, or even frames within frames). The use of chain-dissolves brings out similarities to *Surfacing*, but no clear chronology is established through either external or internal time referencing. *Canadian Pacific* (and its companion piece *Canadian Pacific II*) is best seen in its true context as a framed wall-installation piece. In this context, when previously on display at the Winnipeg Art Gallery during a *Winnipeg Perspective* exhibition, the two *Canadian Pacific* films were situated within window frames as part of a "domestic" environment.

## INTERPRETIVE DOCUMENTARIES

*Real Italian Pizza* initiated a long-term project in relation to Rimmer's evolving film style and conceptual concerns. Although this film is nearly ten years old, it displays a curious "totality," embracing both structural and documentary concerns.

*Real Italian Pizza* documents and interprets the social rituals of the transients and patrons of *Tom's Real Italian Pizza* shop in New York City. The film is episodic in construction and features a series of "movements" which are identifiable and demarcated by fade-ins and fade-outs or black frames. There is one camera point of view—Rimmer's fourth floor studio window. Several lens focal lengths are used to bring out the details of the setting. Similarly, several attitudes toward the ordering of time and "detailing" are evident. Actions within the frame feature both compression (pixillation) and expansion (step-printing or slow motion). The cinematography and editing are primarily comprised of a "sample and hold" quality. As interpretive documentary, *Pizza* samples and holds various characters, their gestures, the nature of their interactions, the changing seasons, and the arrival and departure of external social influences, such as the police and members of the fire department. There is both detachment (the action is left to unfold) and intervention (the action is interpreted). In the final exposition of the film's narrative, the original footage is segmented, analyzed and organized. The opening "movements" serve to establish episodes, proceeding from rendition of detail to wide-angle, integrating gestures. The lateral movement of passers-by is integrated into mass movements or parades—a condition that further underlines Rimmer's propensities toward dance and gesture. There is a variety of episodes that focus on black youths dancing, gesturing, panhandling or simply watching. There are episodes that feature the ritual of patrons entering and leaving. Winter rituals of human interaction are related to summer rituals. But this film is more than a sociological essay. It is interpretive, poetic and lyrical.

The structural locus for the film is determined by the paradigmatics of setting and time interval. By reducing these choices to a fixed point of view and a given period of time, Rimmer enables us to look at what is happening, and how it is rendered, with greater detail and insight. *Real Italian Pizza* established Rimmer's direction toward an evolving film style, one that includes the drama of social and human interaction.

*Al Neil/A Portrait* was created after a lapse of several years in filmmaking. Perhaps a period of integration and reflection had to elapse before Rimmer embarked on this significant change in direction.

Al Neil, the musician, poet, sculptor and "shaman," has been virtually an institution in West Coast art mythology. His work has spanned more years than most could accurately recall. He was considered an inspiration to many artists in the sixties, and he was featured in several avant-garde films including *How the West Was One* by Gary Lee-Nova. Whether he is a recluse, mystic or Dadaist is only of historical concern. The task facing Rimmer was the creation of a portrait of both an "institution" and a friend. This task has been carried out eminently.

*Al Neil/A Portrait* is more than a documentary profile of a man engaged in a life and death struggle with his genius and his obsessions. And while the narrative thread is centred around pathos, the film represents a coming to terms with what these generalizations really mean. During the course of the film, Al Neil is coming to terms with Rimmer the filmmaker; and Rimmer is coming to terms with Al Neil. The manner in which Rimmer chooses to address the viewer is both intimate and distanced. The episodic construction is one such "distancing" device. The long close-up shots are examples of intimacy and patience. The chiaroscuro of the profile shots, which render highlights against blackness, produce an emotional tone of almost medieval, gothic quality. Totemism, in both a West Coast and Al Neil context, is delivered in rapid montage sequences that feature hand-held tracking shots up equally totemistic doll assemblages. The film is notable for the absence of extraneous sound and visual elements. It retains a focus on the integrity of its narrative without embellishments.

*Al Neil/A Portrait* features the presence of two "narrators," Neil and Rimmer, who complement each other. Al Neil, as the narrator, or spinal column, which he describes in his work, is more than the source of music or verbal text. He is the "mythic location" for the film, identified by music, recollections, artifacts, gestures and presence. This mythic location, in the tradition of Alfred Jarry and Antonin Artaud, can be reached only through an understanding of its mosaic form, where each fragment does not constitute the whole. Rimmer, as narrator, not only presents the points of view, organizes the elements and interprets the results, but locates the events within their mythic domain.

It is evident immediately that Rimmer has relaxed many of his previously more formal structural concerns in the making of this film. There is less manipulation and overt structuring. His camera style is at times informal, at times conventional. Visual transitions usually rely on sound or text transitions, as in traditional sound-overlap cutting. There even are examples of images which function as direct support of verbal exposition, as in the exterior shots of Al Neil's house. This process of formal "relaxation" serves to provide greater emphasis on the subject rather than on technique.

There is one *expanded sequence*, among many, that merits specific analysis. In this sequence, Rimmer's genuine ability to structure film exposition and locate that "mythic" domain becomes evident. The sequence begins with a complex montage passage as a sub-sequence featuring superimposition of keyboard, sculpture, details in the room; and Al Neil reeling, intoxicated, away from the camera. The visual elements act as a complement to the staccato sounds of the piano. In contrast, Rimmer then presents us with a view of Al Neil's public performance, ending with applause. Then, via sound transition, he brings us back to one of the most personal episodes of the film, with Al Neil's recollections of family, relatives, and his mother's funeral. There is pathos and bitterness when he relates that "she'll die with her own love . . . they took the casket away . . . I hit my sister for two bucks . . . they continued their journey." It is like a journey down the River Styx, an "interview" on its ghostly barge. At this moment, there is a totality to the pathos—a totality that includes the many *personas* of Al Neil: the private, intoxicated and poetic man; the public performer and musician; and the family outcast. Rimmer's integration of these levels is masterful. Al Neil's poetry is compelling: "Masks leaving me . . . god among fools . . . ."

The film finishes with a public performance, employing conventional, reflexive techniques such as the presence of the filmmaker in a shot, title superimpositions and a freeze-frame shot as an ending. The irony is compelling and pronounced.

*Al Neil/A Portrait* is a monumental construction on many levels, and it tends to render some of the previous work as scale models or fragments in the pursuit of a life-long artistry in film. But whatever their scale, they are eminent works. One need only look at the scarcity of original film art to fully appreciate the place that these works occupy in our contemporary vista.

This article was originally written in November, 1980, and was published by The Vancouver Art Gallery on the occasion of an exhibition of David Rimmer's films, December 12, 1980 to January 11, 1981.

Some of my views have changed since this article was written. My thinking in regard to the sixties films is more adequately represented in the chapter ("Recovering Lost History") that I wrote for the Vancouver Art Gallery Retrospective Catalogue 1983, since it is there that the structuralist versus synaesthetic question (and the influences of multi-media) is acknowledged.

1984

# *The Films of R. Bruce Elder: The Evolving Vision*

## BY LIANNE M. McLARTY

*Near the end of R. Bruce Elder's* Illuminated Texts, *the computer previously identified as having controlled the optical printing and editing of that three-hour film begins to sing. The song it chooses, "Deutschland über alles," comes into a frightful congruence with the Holocaust imagery manipulated within the last hour. The net effect is that of a new and uninvited presence on the screen, the presence of a foregrounded apparatus unwilling to maintain the facade of anonymity. It is far more disturbing than if Elder had merely created a Frankenstein. Instead, the question posed is the degree to which the Frankenstein of mechanized perception has, through our passivity, created us.*

*As Lianne McLarty points out here, the ploy at the end of* Illuminated Texts *is typical of a definition of the artist's role that prevails throughout Elder's body of experimental films. In his* The Art of Worldly Wisdom, *that role is underlined as a deeply personal commitment when the illusory nature of perception is called upon to highlight the equally illusory nature of self. The signifiers of an autobiographical presence are deliberately flawed, until what remains is nothing but the audacity of their presumptuous signification. By the same token, the cinematic tempest brewed in* 1857 (Fool's Gold) *is a storm made of human constructs: texts written on the screen and read in voice-over, heavy reliance on optical printing, a counting of the film's very frames.*

*Elder's awareness of the highly defined yet arbitrary nature of his apparatus extends beyond the films discussed here. As seen in his writing elsewhere in this volume, this critical perspective grows out of an assertion of the centrality of that concern in all of Canadian cinematic practice. To Elder, the photograph, and its extension into cinema, do not provide evidence of the outside world so much as they provide evidence of an ongoing debate as to the characteristics of mechanical perception. As a Canadian filmmaker, Elder recognizes that his work will inevitably come from within this debate. As administrator, teacher and spokesperson Elder recognizes and sustains the priority of, to use McLarty's term, a "quest" for perceptual integrity.*

*Since western culture has seen consciousness as something which is other than Nature and that its mode is primarily one of self-reflection, that which characterizes consciousness is consciousness of consciousness. It is, in its very essence and being, self-reflective. That's how Western Man sees consciousness. He pictures consciousness as something alien from Nature. And one of the marks of that alienation is that, because it knows itself, it knows its destiny, and its destiny is a very solitary one.*

> *Any culture which is a self-reflective culture is one which is aware of the destiny of consciousness—that is to say aware of death—and a culture which lives with an awareness of death is a culture that's marked by a vision of consciousness as isolated, solitary, lonely and doomed.*[1]

In his early films, *Breath/Light/Birth* (1975), *She is Away* (1975), *Barbara is a Vision of Loveliness* (1976), *Look! We Have Come Through!* (1978), *Trace* (1980) and *Sweet Love Remembered* (1980), Bruce Elder created a world without context. These films seldom refer to any reality outside themselves; rather they present an enclosed, claustrophobic world that perhaps could best be described as a void. The space in which the figures move is undefined. This lack of a recognizable space or context suggests that the imagery of these films belongs to an interior world, to a "mind-space,"—that it embodies the artist's consciousness. It is as if the mind of the filmmaker has been transposed to the screen so that we, as spectators, can see his thoughts and visions before us. Given Elder's beliefs about the nature of consciousness, and the fact that his films are "consciousness on celluloid," it is not surprising that they stress this isolation.

Thus, in *Look! We Have Come Through!* a lone figure is situated within an entirely black, undefined space. When the film begins, the woman's form seems to be suspended in air. The lone figure moves against a dark and potentially threatening landscape. The distortion of the figure and of the space through which she moves further contributes to a sense of the ominous. Time, too, is distorted by repeating a single action over and over, so that it seems to continue heedless of naturalistic temporal reality. The world of this film is not ruled by conventional properties of time and space, and for this reason, it seems threatening and ominous to the viewer used to more traditional employments of time and space in cinema.

*Barbara is a Vision of Loveliness* shares stylistic properties with *Look! We Have Come Through!* Once again there is a highly distorted sketch of a female form which occupies an undefined, dark space. Again, the figure is alone, isolated from any context, though here her form is more severely fragmented than in *Look! We Have Come Through!* At one point, near the end of the film, a series of still images of the dancer flash on the screen, frame by frame. By this point, the figure has become quite abstracted and in the course of various transformations seems to split in two, the separate parts gravitating to opposite sides of the frame. Whatever attempt there has been to create unity and harmony here seems to fail. Reality seems to be irremediably fragmented, to be broken beyond repair.

In *Sweet Love Remembered*, two women are seen making love. The action, the women's lovemaking, is depicted positively; it is used to suggest the attempt of two beings to become one. Yet here again this sense of unity is ultimately undercut by Elder, who disrupts spatial continuity by editing together shots taken from different vantage points. The action is similarly fragmented: a shot of the two women lying side by side and then rolling apart on the bed is replaced by a shot of them standing; a caress is replaced by a different action recorded from a different angle; and so on.

Elder has said that he took as his inspiration for this work a quotation from Freud—"Eros nowhere makes its intention more clear than in the desire to make two things one"—and also one from Nietzsche—"What must these people have suffered to have become so beautiful?" Elder illustrates our desire to merge with one another, and our sense of separateness that gives rise to this desire. *Sweet Love Remembered* clearly speaks to this tension. The film begins with many close-up shots, taken mostly with a moving camera, of parts of the female body that are photographed in such a way as to lead the viewer to believe that a single woman is the subject of the piece. As the camera becomes somewhat more distant and larger portions of the body are shown for longer periods of time, it becomes obvious that there are two women. Retrospectively, then, we realize that the techniques of the film have been used to make two beings one. By the middle of the film that unity breaks apart. As though in response to that loss of unity, Elder attempts to recreate it "cinematically," by superimposing one body upon the other. Yet this attempt rings false, partly because it is too obviously cinematic—a product of technique—partly because the very structure of the film militates against the achieving of unity, for the actions it depicts are too fragmented by montage and the women's bodies too fragmented by the use of close-ups. Thus, the last portion of the film consists mainly of images of the women rolling apart, separating themselves from each other. At the end of the film, they are shown alone and isolated from one another.

Unlike the other films discussed which presented human figures in an indeterminate space, *She is Away* presents the viewer with a clearly defined space, but one in which no human figures exist. It is as if, at this stage in his filmmaking, Elder felt unable to unite the two, to reconcile the human form with his/her environment. The emptiness of the space depicted in the film is accentuated by the images of women seen in two paintings, because the presence of these representations makes the absence of actual women from the film all the more emphatic. Since these images represent lives frozen in the past, they suggest the absence of real lives in the present. This absence is also hinted at in the representational images which, one assumes, remind the filmmaker of the "she" of the title who is away; the sheets, the robe, the nightdress, Mozart and the paintings all seem to invoke her memory.

As with the other films discussed in this section, the sense of isolation evoked by this film reaches a point of claustrophobia. Although there is no dark void here, one still senses that the artist feels incapable of escaping the confines of the space which he inhabits. Near the middle of the film, there is a scene that is much longer than any other in the film, and is further privileged by the use of synchronized sound. The camera stares out through a balcony window overlooking a darkened street. This sequence is composed of three shots in all: the first includes a bar of the window frame, the second (in which the camera moves in a little closer) excludes this bar, and the third repeats the first shot. This seemingly minute detail has considerable significance. The second shot, because it is closer to the street, perhaps represents an attempt to reach outward from this space and to escape. It further suggests a sense of looking and waiting. The third, then, could represent a retreat, a moving back into the empty space, surrendering to it.

The final image of a tree is curious in this regard. Because it bears no immediately obvious connection to the other images in the film—it is the only image associated with Nature—it stands out, seems even a bit dreamlike, especially since it does not come from the physical space which Elder reveals to the viewer during the course of the film. Rather, it seems to stem from the filmmaker's unconscious. Perhaps it is used to suggest escape through dream, through a visionary sensibility.

While Elder's earlier films convey rather general notions of isolation, loneliness, loss and absence, the visions of the later, much more complex works are more concretely defined. These films are all informed by a prolonged illness Elder experienced in 1976 and 1977. This experience of suffering seems to have been the catalyst for the development of his vision. *The Art of Worldly Wisdom* (1979) depicts a quest for self-awareness, a quest which involves his attempt to situate both his public and private selves within a larger social context. What allows him to do this is the experience he shares with all beings—the experience of illness and suffering. *1857 (Fool's Gold)* (1981) explicates Elder's view of the artist's power more clearly as he attempts to illustrate the artist's ability to transcend reality. It is through the consciousness of the artist that the physical world is transformed and transcended. Indeed, it seems in this work, as in *The Art of Worldly Wisdom,* that it is torment and suffering which makes transcendence possible.[2] Elder's most recent film, *Illuminated Texts* (1983), also examines this idea; it also carries still further his attempt to reach outward to adopt a broader worldview. Since illness as a symbol of decay, corruption and suffering is a motif which links these three films, the meditation on illness offered in *The Art of Worldly Wisdom* is a good place to begin examining these films.

That film's credit sequence is a paradigm of the film as a whole. It begins with a series of drum beats. Soon the title of the film appears in block letters on a black screen. When the title appears, an inflated and pompous piece of orchestral music appears on the sound-track, humorously evoking the notion that the film will present an authoritative treatment of some subject matter that is of high seriousness. The opening credits, then, ironically suggest, using both visual and aural means, the pretence of order, control and logical progression.

This pretence is soon exposed for what it is. The drumbeats cease and the title is obscured by flashes of light; accompanying these persistent white flashes is the disturbing sound of a stereo needle repeatedly jumping the grooves of the record. This sound is replaced by carnival music, featuring the coarse and comic tones of a trombone, which seems to have been used for its conventional signification of the throwing off of order, of temporary anarchy. The entire sound-track then disintegrates into a complete cacophony of conflicting sounds: a singer singing the introduction to the choral passage of the fourth movement of Beethoven's Ninth Symphony; tunes emanating from a radio rapidly moving over stations; and a "live" female voice (actually that of Elder's wife, Kathy) singing, haltingly and under instruction, the popular song "What Have They Done to My Song?" Each sound in its turn evokes the sense of a loss of control, of the corruption of some originally "pure" sound.

The visuals which accompany this passage reflect the disorder one hears. The title reappears, sketchily scratched on the emulsion, and moves rapidly from side to side within the frame, creating a double-image effect. To add to this confusion, Elder mixes in a bongo drum, playing a fast, highly syncopated pattern which creates a state of excitation. Soon, though, the original credits reappear, this time accompanied by polyphonic choral music; then the screen suddenly goes black and the viewer is left in silent darkness.

The opening sequence has progressed from order to anarchy and back again. This indeed is the same progression followed by illness, by most works of art, and by the experience of transcendence. At one point later in the film Elder declares: "It is small wonder, then, that in disease, as the mortal part wastes and withers away, the spirit grows more sanguine with its lightening load." Just as the body racked with disease at first breaks down, so too does the credit sequence, and just as disease burns away impurities, lightening the spirit's load so it might reach a state of calm, so too does the credit sequence achieve a final tranquillity. Similarly, the film as a whole will follow the progression from order to dis-ease, to a "higher order," like that experienced when illness brings about a greater clarity of vision as it burns away the dross of superfluous self. The religious music heard in the film evokes this strengthening of the spirit which occurs as the suffering body withers away and the soul ascends to its highest Visionary potential.

The view that illness experienced and accepted can bring deeper perception is again articulated in the next sequence, which begins with a high-angle tracking shot of empty tombs, which takes up only the bottom right portion of the screen, the rest of which is black. On the sound-track one hears a mixture of wind and the well-known lyrics of Leonard Cohen (an artist who sensibilities Elder in some measure shares):

> I was handsome. I was strong.
> I knew the words of every song.
> Didn't my singing please you?
> No, the words you sang were wrong.

These lyrics, the wind and the images of tombs combine to produce a sensation of coldness, the tombs because they are an image of death, the wind because it is haunting, and Cohen's lyrics because they are melancholic. Furthermore, because in western culture one scans an image from left to right, by relegating the image to the bottom right corner of the screen, Elder leads the viewer's eye through total darkness to the image: this further strengthens the melancholic nature of the passage. As Cohen's lyrics and the image fade away, leaving only the sound of the relentless wind, a sense of ennui and tristesse remains.

The next image appears at centre screen. It is a brilliant blue image of water rippling softly, creating myriad shapes and shadows. This image is accompanied by natural sounds of birds chirping and of gently running water. In the preceding sequences the camera was searching, even relentless; here it is stationary and calm. Not only is this sequence more pleasant than the Cohen sequence, it is also decidedly more positive, because it evokes the harmony of nature. The narration too offers this positive view: "Sickness, too, individualizes a person, sets him apart from others even in his way of seeing."

The sequence of these two passages, then, follows the same natural progression that was followed by the credit sequence, the progression from disorder to order. This pattern of development is used to convey the idea that illness is not a final state but a transitional state, leading to further change. In this way, Elder reiterates the Romantic view that illness leads to a heightening of vision, to a greater apprehension and appreciation of the world that surrounds us, an appreciation expressed by his use of long takes of the rippling water, which acquires new colours, contours and clarity with each ripple. In this passage he allows us, as he so seldom does, to study the many manifestations of its texture, its shadow and light.

Later parts of this sequence continue to develop this idea. In this portion of the sequence, which is composed wholly of natural sounds and images, Elder presents the viewer with images of the natural world that suggest it is seen anew. Most of this imagery consists of close-ups. The camera tilts up from the water to reveal a snail magnified several times. This single image gives way to multiple images of the natural world as the screen becomes alive with colour and movement.

Still later in this section, Elder introduces images of European cities. In context, they seem to connote that which is foreign and unnatural. This sense of foreignness is underlined by the Dylan lyrics accompanying these scenes, which include the phrase "living in a foreign country." In all, the passage alludes to the notion of travel abroad, a notion Elder returns to later when he speaks of Keats, D.H. Lawrence, Chopin, and Robert Louis Stevenson, all of whom were artists who experienced serious illness, and all of whom were sent into exile by their quests for their art and their health:

> It (sickness) also makes one an exile, a wanderer in search of a healthy place. Sickness is an excellent reason for a life that is mainly travelling. It was sickness that sent Keats to Rome, Chopin to the Islands of the Mediterranean, Robert Louis Stevenson to the South Pacific and D. H. Lawrence around half the globe.

All these artist-travellers, it might be pointed out, espoused the Romantic view of art and suffering; indeed we insist on seeing Keats as the archetypal Romantic, wasted bodily by suffering but transcending his condition by writing sublime poetry.

The odyssey with which *The Art of Worldly Wisdom* is concerned is both actual and metaphorical; it is at once a journey out into the world and inward toward self-consciousness. The narration makes a statement about this latter journey:

> Disease was one of my better teachers . . . . Fever and illness, I have found, so jar the perceptual process that the world is seen anew . . . . Disease ennobles a person, etherealizes him . . . . The sadness that one feels in illness is a mark of refinement of sensibility . . . . In truth, a man in good health is rarely interesting. He lacks both the experience of the terrible which confers a density upon his ruminations and the imagination of disaster that allows him to see past the ordinary wretchedness of those boring people who have never suffered the calamities of illness and is oblivious to both himself and things around him. He becomes thing-like. Pain, like every other disequilibrating force arouses tension and conflict. It animates a person, gives him life. . . . So long as one does not brood over his ills, disease has singular powers of producing revelation.

The theme of self-discovery, of the development of sensibility, of learning that one is not thing-like, is central to *The Art of Worldly Wisdom.* As the product of a near-fatal illness, it involves considerable self-examination and self-scrutiny, and so includes several images of Elder himself. These images are of two sorts: of Elder as a public figure; and of Elder as a private person. Among images of the first sort are those that show him at work at his synthesizer composing the electronic music that accompanies his films, depicted on an advertising poster for a public appearance, and lecturing to a group of students. Among images of the latter sort are images of him examining his emaciated body in the mirror, and images of him masturbating.

These "images of self" share the frame with a wide assortment of other images, sometimes even with two or three other images at a time. These are street scenes, photographed in many European cities, shots of architecture old and new and of a variety of types of religious statuary, scenes from CBC television, of people in urban settings, at carnivals and even in nature. The precise motivation for each juxtaposition of image with image is difficult to discern, with the result that this multi-image format seems based simply on "the juxtaposition of incongruous elements," of which the narration makes mention. If the relationship between images is not readily discernable, it is not intended to be, for the viewer surmises that the appearance of incongruity, rather than of forthright clarity, is the very point of this form of construction. Even so, certain common oppositions are frequently evident in these juxtapositions. For example, different cultures are contrasted in the juxtaposition of a CBC religious program, "Hymn Sing," with European cathedrals; different times are contrasted in the aural juxtaposition of contemporaneous or near-contemporaneous songs by Dylan and The Beatles with "timeless" classical works. But the major effect of the juxtaposition of imagery in the multi-image format is to destroy the coordinates of physical time and space. This destruction of physical time and space, and its replacement with a new set of spatial and temporal relations constructed by (and in) the creative consciousness of the artist, illustrates the possibility of the imaginative transcendence of objective reality.

By juxtaposing his own image with those derived from his odyssey through Europe and into the external world at large, Elder implies that he is searching for a context for the self. At one point, he even shows himself looking at a slow motion image of himself. In this passage, he seems to stand outside himself, and even outside the world, attempting to find some place for himself in it. But to be searching for some place in the world implies that he is isolated from it. This sense of isolation is reinforced by the fact that while Elder shares the same frame as these scenes of the outside world, he does not share the same space with them. All such relationships are constructed and artificial.

There is, to be sure, a considerable pessimism expressed about the project of the work, the project of integration. But the credit sequence disintegrates and apparently fails. Furthermore, its mock-pompous nature expresses a mock-heroic attitude on Elder's part; the sequence involves more than a little self send-up. Elder keeps alluding to the idea of failure and of being a failure throughout the film. He seems at once, in the emphasis on the constructed, artificial character of the relationships of which the film is built, both to celebrate the power of creative control that, as an artist, he possesses, and to lament the extent that he exercises that control. The work is duplicitous, intentionally inauthentic. The narration begins with the statement, "This is a photograph of me"; Elder seems to introduce himself as the creator of this work. But in fact Elder himself is not represented in the photograph that accompanies this claim, nor is it his voice which we hear. This makes us call into question the authenticity of what we see and indeed the very notion of autobiographical authority. The narration makes a related point:

> . . . a photograph plays false with appearances. A photograph, after all, is a highly artificial construct, no more natural or true to the world than other visual arts of its time. It shares with them, in fact, a very specific set of conventions for the handling of pictorial problems which, though imperceptible to most people of the late nineteenth or early twentieth century, are nevertheless both well developed and highly arbitrary.

Neither a photograph, nor by obvious extension a film image, can be trusted to tell the truth, and the film itself, *The Art of Worldly Wisdom*, must be held suspect as neither art nor wisdom.

Even the form of the film seems to totter between order and disorder. There are many images on the screen at the same time (sometimes as many as four), and the sound-track is composed not only of the narration but also of music and sound effects: these latter types of sound frequently make the narration inaudible, with the effect that the film seems at times out of control. Elder has commented on the effect this apparent loss of control has on the audience. Most narrative cinema relies on the audience's illusory belief that they are in control of the events on the screen, that their expectations cause the film to answer their questions and meet their expectations; indeed the grandiosity implied by this is a major source of the satisfaction such films provide. A film like *The Art of Worldly Wisdom* not only denies this process but actively works against it. On this matter, Elder has commented:

> I believe that much of the dominant cinema tries to construct a viewer who feels that he or she is in control of the work . . . . I believe one feels threatened by the loss of control that he or she feels when watching some of my films.[3]

Thus *The Art of Worldly Wisdom* presents the viewers with a dense, complicated narration which demands complete attention in order to be comprehended. Yet the narration often cannot be heard because it is drowned out by the music or sound effects. Similarly, the frame is composed of several different and seemingly incongruous images, none of which the viewer can absorb, let alone relate to the others. Little wonder that the viewer feels he or she has lost control or even feels somewhat frightened.

In *The Art of Worldly Wisdom* Elder is never shown as a truly public figure who interacts with others. In the sequence with Elder teaching, he and the students are never shown in the same frame; it is as if even in his public persona, as a spokesman for his art, he speaks to no one. This sense of isolation is clearly illustrated in shots of Elder masturbating, for masturbation is a paradigm of an isolated act. He emphasizes the isolation using formal means, for he places the image of him performing this act at the bottom of the screen, and isolates it from surrounding images. Later, he is seen nude, filming himself in front of a mirror; above this image, in a separate part of the frame, are a series of close-up images of naked women. Placing the nude male and female figures in separate parts of the frame enhances the sense of isolation. Most tellingly, the film concludes with the relentless ringing of a telephone, a means for communicating, for establishing contact and connection. No one answers.

The questions posed in *The Art of Worldly Wisdom* are answered, albeit only partially, in *1857 (Fool's Gold)*. In describing the Romantic period, critic M. H. Abrams has drawn a distinction between two prevalent metaphors of mind:

> (There are) two common and antithetical metaphors of mind, one comparing the mind to a reflector of external objects, the other to a radiant projector which makes a contribution to the objects it perceives . . . The second typifies the prevailing romantic conception of the poetic mind.[4]

Like the Romantics, Elder, a Visionary, sees Art as a force which, informed by creative consciousness—the "radiant projector"—transforms the world, and in transforming transcends it. An examination of the film *1857 (Fool's Gold)* indicates how the artist achieves this transformation. In her discussion of the film, Carol Zucker observes:

> Elder has penetrated the natural appearance of things in order to present their "essence," or, as the vorticists would have it: Images are abstracted from (a) scene and act as equations or formulas for the emotions the artist derives from it.[5]

The film begins with a naturalistic representation; we see a gull, a sailboat and a bridge surrounded by trees. Using an optical printer, Elder then breaks these images apart; they become more coloured forms than representations of real objects. Thus, the film does not present the world "as it is," but the world as transformed by the creative imagination, a landscape that exists only in that imagination. If the film presents a journey, it is not an actual journey but an ascent of the imagination, a journey toward transcendence. Through the course of the film, the images become more and more distorted, and the viewer is transported farther and farther into the imaginative realm. S/he is bombarded with images which sometimes pulsate, a complex sound-track consisting of electronic music, electronically-processed percussive noise, thunder and crashing waves, and narration (drawn from Defoe's *Journal of the Plague Year*) which, because of the complexity of the sound-track, is often inaudible. The inaudibility of the narration, together with the difficulties involved in reading the Ezra Pound text while listening to this complex sound-track and watching the images, completely disorients the viewer.

As the film draws to a close, a woman's voice appears on the sound-track. It is soothing, calming; its liturgical quality suggests and perhaps induces a serene spiritual state. As the voice becomes more prominent, the sound of the storm subsides. At the same time, the images change from flashing and dark-hued to prolonged, slow-motion and white; the latter evoke a sense not just of relief, but even of restfulness. Elder has taken physical reality and distorted, extended and deepened it; in sum, by transforming it, he has transcended it. These transformations of the natural world demonstrate the artist's control over it.

The opening sequence of *Illuminated Texts* is yet a further demonstration of this control. Elder and his assistant, Anna Pasomow, act out the opening of Eugene Ionesco's *The Lesson*. The sequence begins in silence with Elder sitting on a chair; a grid is laid over this image. With a clap of his hands (which sounds like the clapboard used to commence filming), a passage from Mozart's *Clarinet Concerto* is introduced, and the grid (which suggests a planning stage) disappears. This suggests that it is only upon Elder's intervention that the film can commence. In this way, he demonstrates his complete control over both the action and the art form.

At a later point, Elder rises from his chair to answer the door. In doing so, he exits from the frame, and when he does so, the camera, which was previously steady, goes out of control, crashing into furniture and walls on its way. The implication of this is that it is Elder's presence which "stabilizes" the camera. When he is not present the creative act turns destructive.

The acting in this section of the film is deliberately stilted and unnatural. The characters read from a script, their eyes frequently meet the gaze of the camera, and they perform awkwardly. The unrealistic delivery undercuts the illusion of reality that conventional narrative and naturalistic acting contrive to establish. It points up the fact that the film is a construct only, a product of a creative mind, whose nature is determined by the artist. Further, the subject of the lesson is mathematics. Elder seems to be suggesting that the construction of a film is guided by rules as arbitrary as the axioms of mathematics.

Like the sound-tracks of *1857 (Fool's Gold)* and *The Art of Worldly Wisdom*, the sound of *Illuminated Texts* is a combination of varied and discordant sounds which often drown out the narration. Its complexity points up its constructed nature. Moreover, at its largest level, *Illuminated Texts* is divided into eight parts, of which half are "dramatic" sequences and half montage sequences. This structure makes the constructed quality of the film very obvious, as Elder is well aware, for in a proposal for his most recent film, *Lamentations*, which is currently in progress, he points out:

> I find particularly appealing the fact that this alternation between different forms of construction provides a means for stressing the constructed character of the work which does not rely on the now somewhat tired device of making reference to the process by which the work was constructed.[6]

In highlighting the fact that the film is a construct, the product of his mind, Elder is demanding that we recognize how completely he controls the nature of the work. This conscious sense of control, especially over nature—as seen in *1857 (Fools' Gold)*—relates Elder's later vision to that of the Romantics. It is *his* consciousness which interprets and even shapes the world, which acts as the "radiant projector."

In the middle section of *1857 (Fool's Gold)*, the barrage of images and sounds reaches apocalyptic proportions; the viewer feels that s/he lacks control over what is happening, that some catastrophic event is about to occur—or indeed is occurring—which cannot be affected by mere mortal hands. Against this is set the demonstration of artistic control that in the end reestablishes order. Nevertheless, the horror of the apocalypse is suggested. Like *1857 (Fool's Gold)*, *Illuminated Texts* makes use of the idea of the apocalypse, but redefines it and extends its ramifications. As mentioned above, *Illuminated Texts* is composed of both dramatic sequences and montage sequences. The dramatic sequences are composed of the following: the Ionesco play, *The Lesson*; a section dealing with Egerton Ryerson, the man after whom Ryerson Polytechnical Institute where Elder teaches is named; and a section in which Elder interviews a personal friend who is also an artist. The final dramatic sequence involves Elder's anguished response to a letter he received which accused him of breach of contract. Each of these dramatic sequences involves Elder himself, if only by implication. All of these sequences could be described as autobiographical to a certain extent; in fact, they all represent Elder's attempt to work through a problem in his professional life which appears to have been a source of great torment. The last of these dramatic sequences is composed of images of Elder suffering as a result of the Institute's accusations.

These personal sequences are juxtaposed with montage sequences which represent the "exterior" world—that is to say, the world which is not Elder's "personal world." Thus, like *The Art of Worldly Wisdom, Illuminated Texts* represents in part an attempt by the artist to reconcile his existence with the world around him, and more importantly, to understand his suffering in relation to a broader context. This is most evident in the relation between the scene depicting a tormented Elder, and the final montage sequence of the film, composed of images from Nazi concentration camps. The first montage sequence is composed primarily of rich, lush natural imagery. Over the course of the four montage passages, the imagery changes from depictions of a natural world, unsullied by human intervention, to imagery which depicts nature "corrupted" by human intervention to greater and greater degrees.

This progression suggests the Christian myth of the Fall, the expulsion from Paradise. Each successive montage sequence includes more and more images of the human destruction of nature, and human violence. There are, for example, images of boxers, and pornographic images of violence against women. Even the act of masturbation depicted in the final section of the film seems desperate and frantic. Elder takes us from images of a natural paradise to images of the personal, sexual and cultural violence which culminates in the ultimate violence expressed at the end of the film: the destruction, or attempted destruction, of an entire people—the Holocaust.

The poetic texts superimposed over the images make explicit reference to the Fall:

> Him the Almighty Power
> Hurl'd headlong flaming from th' ethereal sky
> With hideous ruin and combustion down
> To bottomless perdition, there to dwell
> In adamantine chains and penal fire
> Who durst defy the omnipotent to arms.
>
> (John Milton, *Paradise Lost*)

> This is not the greatest thing, though great, the hours
> of shivering, ache and burning, when we'd changed
> So far beyond our courage—altitudes
> Then falling, falling back.
>
> (Robert Lowell)

This notion of the Fall is, I think, meant metaphorically; it suggests a society plunging into an increasingly violent world. All in all, *Illuminated Texts* proposes a vision of apocalyptic doom. It offers its viewers a vision of global significance representing perhaps the threat of global annihilation. As Milton and Lowell used images of descent metaphorically, so too does Elder. Even the Holocaust becomes, in *Illuminated Texts,* a metaphor for the threat of a more immediate human disaster.

Elder is an artist working at a time when the threat of massive global destruction is immanent; his art is beginning to reflect that threat.

Elder's earlier vision, one of absence, loss and isolation, has been transformed into a more articulate attempt to reconcile himself with the world around him. Elder is developing as an artist who, while still concerned with questions of his role and the function of Art itself, is also concerned with an expression beyond the enclosed world of his art. Yet it is still an expression *through* his art. In *Illuminated Texts* the antithesis to destruction is creation, and specifically the creative imagination of the artist. Perhaps Elder is suggesting that Art is the way out or through this holocaust. However, an Art that possesses such an ability would have to be not an Art that is a mere diversion from the world around us, but rather an Art which is conscious of the culture from which it emerges.

1984

---

1 Bruce Elder, in an interview with the author, August, 1983.
2 In the interview with Bruce Elder he contradicted this notion of illness as a catalyst. Instead, he asserted that this suggestion, which does occur in the text, is meant ironically. Illness, he asserted, is merely dehumanizing; ". . . it's nothing more than degrading." While Elder may feel this way about his work, I believe there is certainly sufficient evidence to support the reading I have given the text.
3 Bruce Elder, in an interview with the author, August, 1983
4 M.H. Abrams, *The Mirror and The Lamp*, (New York: Oxford University Press, 1953), p. viii.
5 Carol Zucker, "Bruce Elder's *Fool's Gold*: The Experience of Meaning," *Ciné-Tracts*, 17, 1982, p. 49.
6 Bruce Elder, "A Proposal for *Lamentations*," 1983. (Text unpublished.)

# *About to Speak: The Woman's Voice in Patricia Gruben's* Sifted Evidence

BY KAY ARMATAGE

*As we have tried to indicate throughout this volume, the question of language and its repression is central to the consideration of cinema in Canada and Quebec. It separates the classical Griersonian documentary (with its imperial overtones) from a subsequent rebellion against that use of the spoken word. Language divides Canada's two cinemas. Similarities of language threaten anglophone Canadian cinema with assimilation into the American product. As argued in "The Silent Subject in English Canadian Film," the linguistic characteristics of English Canada may leave its films with nothing to say. Within Quebec, as the work of Pierre Perrault demonstrates, the insularity of language may cut both ways.*

*To these discussions, Kay Armatage contributes a consideration of the struggle for a feminist voice. Her choice of an exemplary text, Patricia Gruben's* Sifted Evidence, *allows Armatage to merge an evaluation of the traditional Canadian dilemmas in the use of language, with current feminist concerns. To this is added an understanding of what has come to be known as "neo-narrative" cinema. As a result, Armatage can define Gruben's film as a work made in response to a patriarchal formulation not only of language but of these structural questions of codification. Like Gruben and her protagonist, Maggie, Armatage looks for a rearrangement of perception that will enable the filmmaker, the spectator and the on-screen presence to rearrange the manner of their interaction. Her conclusion is that the removal of sexist bias from communication between all three parties is only now beginning to be possible. A common voice is only now "about to speak."*

*Well, the human voice is at once the clinker and the crunch. It lies, sings, floats, or emerges from a mouth from which it may or may not have originated. It speaks of things that may or may not—usually not—have originated in the mind behind the mouth in question. These three terms of possible dissociation—word, mouth, thought—suggest a fourth: the thought as a cultural given rising unbidden at a particular historical moment. And a fifth: the fourth in relation to each of the first three. Where and when is whose voice uttering whose thought through whose mouth and what for? Film is the place where the (extra)-ordinary (im)balances between culture and expression can be most visibly demonstrated and enacted.*[1]

Visual richness is a quality which we have learned to expect from Gruben's work. *The Central Character* (1977) evinces a heterogeneity of visual styles, through the use of printed text, still photographs, blueprints, superimposition, line drawings, stop printing, rotoscoping, and various levels of exposure or saturation of the image. *Low Visibility* (1984) returns to the use of maps (in the stunning image of the clairvoyant's hands tracing the lines of the map as if it were braille), as well as stop printing, rephotographing, shooting a television screen, simulation of a black-and-white surveillance video camera, the insertion of uncut rough footage from a documentary or news item, and an eccentric use of framing throughout, signifying limited or specific vision. In *Sifted Evidence* (1982), the visual discourse is equally complex, using a range of optical and cinematographic effects (front projection, travelling mattes, painted backdrops, dissolving pans, animation) to produce an almost garishly gorgeous image which operates a poetic and witty deconstruction of the cinematic illusion.

The three films also share a concern with language as a pivotal force in the construction of knowledge, character and meaning. The central character of *Low Visibility* appears to suffer from Korsakoff's syndrome, a form of aphasia which allows him to speak only in curses and expletives. Two psychiatric nurses assigned to his case communicate with him largely in jokes and surrealistic wordplay; the therapist quizzes him on the meaning of aphorisms; the clairvoyant tunes into the thoughts of other characters; and the documentary news host tries out a variety of descriptions and characterizations. In *The Central Character*, the auditory text operates a progressive disintegration of the woman as she recites grocery lists, struggles to voice her thoughts in the first person, careens wildly into scientific discourse, or voices instructions from an etiquette book. Much of this verbal text is processed to suggest that the voice comes from a radio or broken record, from under water, or as if it were an auditory hallucination. In its heterogeneity of play of the verbal signifier and in its position as Gruben's first long film featuring a female central character, *Sifted Evidence* provides a particularly rich text for discussion of a question which has in recent literature proven fruitful for opening up structures connected to feminist concerns in cinema: language and the voice in relation to the development of a feminine discourse.

Woman's relation to language has been a central concern for feminists in the past decade, especially the post-Lacanian psychoanalysts such as Michelle Montrelay, Luce Irigaray, and Hélène Cixous, and for poststructuralist semioticians like Julia Kristeva. Jacques Lacan suggests that the feminine is absent from language—that she falls like a shadow across language—because the entry into verbal language and symbolic systems comes at the Oedipal moment of separation from the mother, and because language itself is governed by and structured around the law of the father, the patriarchal order. In Lacan's theory, woman is characterized by and in that order as lack, as other, in her central relation to the Imaginary and the unconscious. Cixous, Irigaray and Montrelay have used Lacanian theory productively to speculate on the possibility of an alternative, feminine discourse which would operate as an interrogation of patriarchal discourse, by silence on the one hand or by practising a language that is "wild, on the body, unauthorized."[2] Such an *écriture féminine* would be characterized by ambiguity, multiplicity, wordplay, enigma, disguise; it would be metaphoric, interrogative, incomplete. In this sense *Sifted Evidence* suggests a feminine specificity: the voice-over narration describes a multi-faceted process of discovery, interrogation, quest.

The emphasis on the voice as the appropriate vehicle for feminine discourse—what Marie-Claire Ropars-Wuilleumier describes in *India Song* as an attempt to construct an *écriture* of the voice[3]—is theorized by Mary Ann Doane from Lacan's invocatory drive. The conventional uses of the voice in cinema—direct dialogue, voice-off and voice-over—all appeal to the spectator's desire to hear, the pleasure of hearing arising from memories of the first experience of the voice, the mother's voice.[4] Lacan—and Doane and others—situate these traces of archaic drives in infantile experience, although their origins may reside even in the womb, where hearing is the first working sense. In any case, the mother's voice is the major component of the "sonorous envelope" which surrounds the infant and which produces the first—imaginary—image of corporal unity.[5] The imaginary fusion of mother and child is ruptured by the intervention of the father's voice, which becomes the agent of separation, and thus constitutes the mother's voice as the irretrievably lost object of desire. The voice is thus the interface of the imaginary and the symbolic.[6]

Such a crucial status for the voice can be seen in the most important work by feminist filmmakers such as Marguerite Duras, Yvonne Rainer, Bette Gordon, Laura Mulvey, Sally Potter and Patricia Gruben. All of them have used strategies in which the separation of the voice from the image is central. Against the theorization of the look in cinema as phallic support of voyeurism and fetishism, the voice appears to lend itself readily as an alternative to the image, whereby the woman can "make herself heard." For Duras, for example, it was necessary, in her view, to establish a separation between the "film of voices" and the "film of images."[7]

Thus in discussions of a feminine specificity in cinema, emphasis is often placed on the use of the voice. Stephen Heath has concisely summarized the statements of Cixous, Montrelay, and Irigaray in relation to the voice/look, and it seems useful to quote his summary here:

> Hélène Cixous writes "all the feminine texts that I have read are very close to the *voice*, are very close to the flesh of the language." A closeness to the voice is seen as a trace of the intensity of the attachment to the mother: "To write in the feminine is to put over what is cut off by the symbolic, the voice of the mother, it is to put over what is most archaic" (Cixous), and Michelle Montrelay writes of a closeness in the voice to words "as in the first moments of life when they extended the body of the mother and simultaneously circumscribed the place of suspension of her desire" and for Irène Diamantis "something of the circuit of drive of the voice erogenises the feminine"—Lacan's invocatory "grain of the voice" (Barthes).
>
> The emphasis is on the voice as against the look: in women's texts, writes Montrelay, "no contour is traced on which the eye could rest." The look is a distance, an absence of grain. Luce Irigaray: "Investment in the look is not privileged in women as in men. More than the other senses, the eye objectifies and masters . . . The moment the look dominates, the body loses in materiality."[8]

Gruben's *Sifted Evidence* achieves such a separation of the voice and look through the predominant use of the female voice-over as an organizing principle of cinematic discourse.

*Sifted Evidence* begins with a printed text on the screen. A slide show (including maps) follows, accompanied by a voice-over narration in slow, well-modulated, pedagogical tones. As the last slide clicks off and the blank white "screen" remains, the camera pans to connect the female narrator's voice visually to a character speaking directly and personally to the film audience.

The adventure/memory begins, and the narrator's first person speech changes to third person as another female voice (that of the filmmaker) takes over to describe and comment on the action of the characters depicted in the image. Dialogue between the central male and female characters is consistently rendered in the third-person voice-over ("she said . . . and he replied"), sometimes surprisingly almost "synching up" with the moving lips on the screen. One climactic scene is rendered in direct sound with synch dialogue, with the male and female actors speaking in their own voices. The female narrator returns immediately, however, with her complex discourse, which shifts variously through a range of modes of address. The voice-over may assume the mode of authorial directive, as in "Maggi . . . look to your left. The bus is coming,"[9] to which the actress in the image responds appropriately. It may interrogate or analyze the image itself, as in "We might expect him here to be pointing at the sky . . . . How did they get from one point to the next? . . . Where did she get that bathing suit?" Or it may directly address the film audience, as in "Now you can see as well as she can that the sun is sinking."

Besides the complexity of the uses of voice and address at the level of narration and dialogue, language itself is at issue throughout as an element of the diegesis. The central character is visiting a foreign country and doesn't speak the language, and that is one of the most important factors in the development of the narrative. The issue of language enters also to further complicate the sound-track. Taped Spanish lessons (another—a third—female voice) are heard, and the everyday tourist phrases ("May I have the bill, please?"; "Quiero una habitacion para una persona") are used sometimes contrapuntally and sometimes diegetically. Such phrases may insert themselves into the dialogue, again almost "synching up" with the moving lips of the characters, or they may foreshadow or comment ironically upon the dilemma. Meanwhile, the troubled central character dreams in a third language (German) learned from her father, and snatches of a Rilke poem are quoted by the narrator.

This complex interplay of verbal, linguistic, and cinematic relationships can been seen as a strategy for challenging the conventional structures of narrative cinema and the patriarchal traditions in which that cinema is embedded. The emphasis on the female voice and its status as voice-over narration crystallizes that strategy. In the earliest moments of the film, the first sonorous tactics for challenging a patriarchal discourse and for decentring or confounding the spectator/subject arise. The first voice enters as a conventional voice-over accompaniment to the visual slide show. It has often been stated that the disembodied voice-over—the documentary voice-over which is situated outside of the diegetic space—has an authority, a knowledge, an ability to produce "truth" and to interpret the image which comes precisely from its radical otherness, the impossibility of yoking the voice to a space or body.[10] In the history of the documentary, the voice-over has usually been male, speaking in the masculine discourse of the neutral, knowledgeable, generalizing, authoritative third person. In *Sifted Evidence*, a female voice assumes this discourse, mocking its patronizing and simplifying generalizations. "For a few people," the voice begins, "the centre of this vast globe is a certain tiny village near the Mexican Gulf Coast, once known as Tlatilco . . . But to reach that spot, we must proceed from where we are at the moment."

This gentle challenge to the conventional documentary voice-over, a convention especially well-known in Canada through the films of the National Film Board, is almost immediately superseded by a shift to the first person: "Once I arrived, my whole trip seemed to organize itself around visits to the ruins. I was interested in the female divinities of ancient Mexico." This first-person narration gradually slides toward the more traditional use of the female off-camera voice, the convention often referred to as the voice-off.[11] In both enunciation and énoncé, the female voice-off commonly confirms woman's traditional role. It is used either for interior monologue—the subjective, reflective voice from the space allowed for woman in the patriarchy, the mysterious, interior, pre-rational space which links woman inextricably with the unconscious or "the half-life of the imaginary"[12]—

or it is used to introduce flashbacks, memories, or fantasies. Such uses of the voice-off affirm the homogeneity and dominance of the diegetic space, for the voice-off conventionally affirms the character's presence "just over there," "just beyond the frameline," and suggests that re-framing can return the character easily to "the destiny of the body."[13] Thus traditional uses of the female voice-off conform to the usual image/sound relationship of patriarchal cinematic discourse, in which the absence of woman confirms the male as the subject of the discourse, the maker of meaning.

Gruben immediately ruptures this movement just as the speaker introduces the conventional ingredients of the dominant cinema: "Adventure, mystery, and romantic love." The voice changes; a new voice enters, the voice of the filmmaker. It reasserts itself as voice-over, speaks in the third person, and produces a discourse which is complex and various in its approach to the analysis of the male/female relationships and to the woman's quest for her own origins (the ancient female divinities). Both are thwarted at every turn by her relation to language, a language in which she finds herself a stranger, both misunderstood and uncomprehending, and a victim of her exclusion from language.

There is one scene in the film which stands in marked contrast to this pattern of separation of voice from image. In the drama, the single scene of direct sound with synchronized dialogue is of course that scene in which sexual difference and desire are forcibly articulated: the scene in the hotel room in which the male protagonist says "You're breaking the rules, Babe," and uses violence and masculine force in the service of reasserting the sexual hierarchy. The scene adopts the strategies of the conventional dramatic film and achieves their traditional ends. Doane states:

> The aural illusion of position constructed by the approximation of sound perspective and by techniques which spatialize the voice and endow it with "presence" guarantees the singularity and stability of a point of audition, thus holding at bay the potential trauma of dispersal, dismemberment, difference. The subordination of the voice to the screen as the site of the spectacle's unfolding makes vision and hearing work together in manufacturing the "hallucination" of a fully sensory world.[14]

Not only does the hotel room scene re-posit the conventional unified spectator, but it argues once again the relation of woman to the fully illusioned, hierarchically integrated cinematic world. It effects the return of the woman as helpless object of desire, characterized by and victim of her lack.

The scene provides the turning point of the drama. It is the low point for the hopelessly passive and apparently incompetent female protagonist, awash in the anguish of her ambivalent desires. And it is the point at which the efficacy of the formal strategies of voice/image which characterize the rest of the film becomes most clear. As the scene ends, the synchronized sound-track fades out and the voice-over of the filmmaker returns to intervene in the woman's dilemma: "Just stop it, stop it and go!" And go she does, wresting herself at last from the domination of the male protagonist and from the hierarchical imperative of romantic love. The separation of voice from image (punctuated at this point on the visual track by an abstract optical effect which returns the image to zero) has indeed provided an alternative to the conventional relations of woman to the spectator's look, to narrative, to patriarchal discourse, and to patriarchal sexual relations.

But if an alternative has been suggested, there has been no solution to the dilemma. The central character continues to dream in her father's language (German), and even as she flees the man in the hotel room to resume her quest for the female divinities, apparently finding at last the archaeological site where the ambiguous little fertility figures were first discovered, the final stanza of Rilke's "Second Duino Elegy" (quoted in German on the sound-track) assures her that "our heart transcends us still/As it did in ancient times."

In *The Central Character*, a tape recorder dug up from the earth (like the mysterious shapes which the woman uncovers in the quarry in *Sifted Evidence*) repeats like a stuck record, "I would like to say that I would like to say that I would like to say . . . " The mechanical repetition suggests the locking of woman's desire into an endless circular intonation, signalling only itself—desire frozen and contained in its own impossibility, with no object, no content, no words.[15]

*Sifted Evidence* likewise posits no haven for women in a discourse of feminine specificity. The last shot of the film (behind the credits) circles back to the beginning, with a slow pan around the room of the woman who "stands for" the filmmaker, the room where the mementoes "of voluntary bondage: a bus ticket, a statuette, and a handful of faded flowers" were first displayed. This repetition underlines the dilemma. The "evidence sifted" has provided no answers to her quest. As if to assert the impossibility of resolution or escape into a finally activated alternative discourse, the woman is suspended in a freeze-frame just as she turns to the camera and opens her mouth. She is frozen in silence—about to speak.

1984

This is a revised and expanded version of an article which first appeared in *Canadian Film Studies*, 1, No. 1 (June 1984).

---

1 Yvonne Rainer, "Beginning With Some Advertisements For Criticisms Of Myself, Or Drawing The Dog You May Want To Use to Bite Me With, And Then Going On To Other Matters," *Mellenium Film Journal*, No. 6 (Spring 1980), 6.
2 Stephen Heath, "Difference," *Screen*, 19, No. 3, p. 83.
3 Marie-Claire Ropars-Wuilleumier, "The Disembodied Voice: *India Song*," *Yale French Studies*, No. 60 (1980), p. 243.
4 Mary Ann Doane, "The Voice in the Cinema: The Articulation of Body and Space," *Yale French Studies*, No. 60 (1980), p. 43.
5 Ibid., p. 44.
6 Ibid., p. 45.
7 Ropars-Wuilleumier, loc. cit., p. 25.
8 Heath, loc. cit., pp. 83-84.
9 All quotations from the films are taken from the scripts, provided by the filmmaker.
10 Pascal Bonitzer, "Les silences de la voix," *Cahiers du Cinéma*, 256 (Fév.-Mars 1975).
11 Doane, loc. cit., p. 42.
12 Laura Mulvey, "Visual Pleasure and Narrative Cinema," *Women & the Cinema*, ed. K. Kay and G. Peary (New York: Dutton, 1977), p. 413.
13 Doane, loc. cit., p. 41.
14 Ibid., p. 45.
15 Brenda Longfellow, "Failing Subjectivity or the Case of the Missing Character," unpublished paper, 1983.

# INDEX